HOSPITAL

Also by Julie Salamon

Man, Woman, Birth,

Death, Infinity,

Plus Red Tape,

Bad Behavior,

HOSPITAL

Money, God,

and Diversity

on Steroids

JULIE SALAMON

The Penguin Press
New York
2008

THE PENGUIN PRESS
Published by the Penguin Group
Penguin Group (USA) Inc., 375 Hudson Street, New York, New York 10014,
U.S.A. • Penguin Group (Canada), 90 Eglinton Avenue East, Suite 700, Toronto,
Ontario, Canada M4P 2Y3 (a division of Pearson Penguin Canada Inc.) •
Penguin Books Ltd, 80 Strand, London WC2R 0RL, England • Penguin
Ireland, 25 St. Stephen's Green, Dublin 2, Ireland (a division of Penguin
Books Ltd) • Penguin Books Australia Ltd, 250 Camberwell Road, Camberwell,
Victoria 3124, Australia (a division of Pearson Australia Group Pty Ltd) •
Penguin Books India Pvt Ltd, 11 Community Centre, Panchsheel Park,
New Delhi–110 017, India • Penguin Group (NZ), 67 Apollo Drive, Rosedale,
North Shore 0632, New Zealand (a division of Pearson New Zealand Ltd) •
Penguin Books (South Africa) (Pty) Ltd, 24 Sturdee Avenue, Rosebank,
Johannesburg 2196, South Africa

Penguin Books Ltd, Registered Offices:
80 Strand, London WC2R 0RL, England

First published in 2008 by The Penguin Press,
a member of Penguin Group (USA) Inc.

Library of Congress Cataloging-in-Publication Data
Salamon, Julie.
Hospital : man, woman, birth, death, infinity, plus red tape, bad behavior, money,
God, and diversity on steroids / by Julie Salamon.
p. ; cm.
Includes bibliographical references and index.
ISBN-13: 978-1-59420-171-4
1. Maimonides Medical Center—History.   2. Hospitals—New York
(State)—New York—History.
[DNLM: 1. Maimonides Medical Center.   2. Hospitals, Urban—New York
City—Personal Narratives.   3. Cultural Diversity—New York City—Personal
Narratives. WX 28 AN7 M223S 2008]   I. Title.
RA982. N5M357 2008
362.1109747'23—dc22
2007045629
Printed in the United States of America
1   3   5   7   9   10   8   6   4   2

DESIGNED BY MICHELLE MCMILLIAN

In memory of my father,
Dr. Alexander Salamon

May I never see in the patient anything but a fellow creature in pain. . . . Oh, God, Thou has appointed me to watch over the life and health of Thy creatures; here am I ready for my vocation, and now I turn unto my calling.

—*from the Oath of Maimonides*

"In short, a man comes into this hospital in perfect health," says the doctor played by George C. Scott in disbelief, on hearing about a patient's progress through the system. "In the space of one week, we chop out one kidney, damage another, reduce him to coma, and damn near kill him."

—*from* The Hospital, *a film by Paddy Chayevsky*

Contents

Cast of Characters

EXECUTIVE SUITE

Stanley Brezenoff . . . . former president and chief executive officer

Pamela Brier . . . . president and chief executive officer

Dr. David Cohen . . . . vice president, medicine/senior vice president, clinical integration

Lillian Fraidkin . . . . senior vice president, clinical services/chief of staff

Dr. Samuel Kopel . . . . medical director

Mark McDougle . . . . chief operating officer, executive vice president

Robert Naldi . . . . chief financial officer

Sheila Namm . . . . vice president, professional affairs

Sondra Olendorf . . . . senior vice president, nursing and hospital operations

Martin Payson . . . . chairman of the board

CANCER CENTER

Dr. Alan Astrow . . . . associate director, medical oncology

Bill Camilleri . . . . vice president

Dr. Jay Cooper . . . . director, cancer center/chair, radiation oncology

Dr. Bernadine Donahue . . . . . . associate director, radiation oncology

Dr. Yiwu Huang . . . . medical oncologist

Nella Khenkin . . . . social worker

Dr. Sushma Nakka . . . . oncology fellow
Dr. Beth Popp . . . . pain-management specialist
Dr. Petra Rietschel . . . . medical oncologist
Dr. Philip Rubin . . . . medical oncologist
Dr. Kathir Suppiah . . . . oncology fellow
Dr. Jason Tache . . . . oncology fellow
Dr. Mendel Warshawsky . . . . oncology fellow

DOCTORS, NURSES, STAFF

Jo Ann Baldwin . . . . assistant vice president, community outreach
Marcel Biberfeld . . . . vice president, psychiatry and community services
Ann Marie Ceriale . . . . nursing manager, ER
Lilia Colon . . . . labor-management developer
Dr. Joseph Cunningham . . . . chair, department of surgery/ senior vice president, strategic initiatives
Dr. Steven Davidson . . . . chair, emergency medicine
Clarence Davis . . . . director, safety
Dr. David Feldman . . . . vice president, perioperative services
Maria Ferlita . . . . vice president, finance
Dr. David Gregorius . . . . ER resident
Douglas Jablon . . . . vice president, patient relations/special assistant to the president
Dr. Israel Jacobowitz . . . . cardiac surgeon
Chris Kam . . . . social worker
Kathryn Kaplan . . . . chief learning officer
Lisa Keen . . . . social worker
Eileen Keilitz . . . . nurse
Carol Kidney . . . . director of nursing, women's services
Dr. David Kho . . . . radiology resident
Dr. Steven Konstadt . . . . chair, anesthesiology
Dr. Stephen Lahey . . . . chief, cardiothoracic surgery
Dr. Richard Lazzaro . . . . surgeon
Dr. Bing Lu . . . . medical director, Maimonides clinic, Chinatown

Pamela Mestel . . . . director of nursing, perioperative services

Dr. Howard Minkoff . . . . chair, obstetrics and gynecology

Margie Morales . . . . environmental worker

Dr. Carl Ramsay . . . . medical director, emergency medicine

Madeline Rivera . . . . associate vice president, case management

Dr. Jacob Shani . . . . chief of Cardiac Institute

Dr. Allan Strongwater . . . . former chair, orthopedics

Dr. Regina Tarkovsky . . . . hospitalist

Dr. Gregory Todd . . . . hospitalist

Janice Yang . . . . director of outreach to Asian community

COMMUNITY

Marie and Tina . . . . patient and her sister

Dr. Michael Bashevkin . . . . oncologist, former partner of Samuel Kopel

Michael Bloomberg . . . . mayor of New York City

Asghar Choudhri . . . . unofficial mayor of Little Pakistan, Brooklyn

Daniel Dube . . . . grandson of Newman Dube, hospital founder

Bernie Gips . . . . Borough Park Hatzolah coordinator

Ms. Hernandez . . . . patient

Dov Hikind . . . . New York State assemblyman

Marty Markowitz . . . . Brooklyn borough president

Miriam Lubling . . . . founder, Rivkah Laufer Guardians of the
                                          Sick, major source of patient referrals

Elliot "Lazer" Rosman . . . . Borough Park Hatzolah coordinator

Hafiz Mohammad Sabir . . . . imam, Makki Mosque

Aaron Twerski . . . . board of trustees, Maimonides

Mr. Zen . . . . patient

Prologue

This story began with a telephone call. Jo Ann Baldwin, a fast-talking, funny, Italian-American woman with a strong Brooklyn accent, had reached me through my publisher. Between the rush of words and wisecracks, I discerned that she had read my book about charity and philanthropy based on the teachings of the medieval Jewish philosopher and physician Maimonides. The pitch was this: She was an administrator at a hospital called Maimonides, she was certain we had a karmic connection, and she wanted to meet.

While I'd visited hospitals often enough for the usual reasons, and had even been a candy striper in high school, I had no special interest in them, had never written about them, and didn't even watch medical dramas on TV. I left medicine to the professionals in my family, of whom there have been many: my father, sister, stepbrother, and brother-in-law. On the phone, Baldwin wasn't very clear about what she wanted, but she was amusing and unrelenting. We agreed to meet.

Over cappuccino in Greenwich Village, she told me about Maimonides Medical Center (originally Israel-Zion Hospital) in Borough Park, Brooklyn, which had been opened a century earlier to serve local residents. For decades the mandate had remained the same: to take care of the community, which meant the Orthodox (and, increasingly, Hasidic) Jews who dominated the neighborhood.

As in urban areas all over America, Brooklyn's neighborhoods were constantly changing, as immigrants prospered and their children—the second generation—left, making room for new groups arriving from other countries. The area around Maimonides was no exception. While Jews still made up a substantial minority of the hospital's local patient demographic, the rising majority derived from every kind of ethnicity and hailed from all over the world. New Chinese immigrants represented the fastest-growing population in the vicinity. Meanwhile, the hospital's kosher kitchen was run by Patrick Lamont, born in Jamaica, and sixty-seven different languages, more or less, were spoken in the hospital.

Baldwin talked about the hospital's determination to understand its patients' languages and beliefs—an attitude, if not a practice, that had become more commonplace in many medical institutions. She ticked off a list of homey examples: For one thing, it had taken the hospital staff a while to figure out that the white blankets in the emergency rooms were keeping Chinese patients away. White, they eventually learned, is the mark of death in Chinese culture. Soon enough, new beige blankets were ordered for the entire hospital. They had learned the hard way (from the patients who had fled, never to return) that among many groups there was still a taboo against uttering the word "cancer," never mind acknowledging the disease. They'd also had to learn how to deal with patients like the pregnant woman, shrouded head to toe by a chador, who, when she unwrapped herself for examination, shocked the doctor by showing him that she was covered with chicken pox.

Baldwin painted a vivid picture of a big, bustling institution that was representative in many ways of any major medical center. Thanks to advances in science and technology, many illnesses that once required hospitalization no longer did, meaning that the inpatient population tended to be sicker and older, more difficult to treat. The emergency room was crowded with uninsured patients who couldn't afford anything else.

With 705 patient beds, Maimonides was a big hospital, among the largest 5 percent of the country's 4,936 hospitals. Its patients were primarily middle class but spanned the spectrum, with a sizable contingent of poor and elderly people who qualified for Medicare and Medicaid.

In 2003 the hospital admitted 38,667 patients, 127,319 people were treated in its outpatient clinics, and 81,190 passed through the ER. These patients generated $626 million in revenues; the hospital paid $618 million in expenses, including $17.7 million in malpractice insurance.

Four hundred and sixty new doctors trained there each year. Each week the kosher/Chinese/Italian/Caribbean kitchen used 2,000 pounds of chicken, 5,400 pints of milk, and 30 gallons of Jell-O. In 2003, 6,230 babies were born at Maimonides, more than in any other hospital in the state of New York. There were 1,075 deaths; 35 of those were stillborn babies.

What did it take to run a factory like this—and did it feel like a factory?

By the beginning of the twenty-first century, the practice of medicine had become industrialized and often seemed impersonal. What was the role of the hospital in a technocratic world where information and options were abundant while common sense and tenderness were scarce? What were the financial, ethical, scientific, sociological, personal, and cultural matters that determined what kind of care people received? What did it mean to care anyway?

As Baldwin talked about the social forces converging on the hospital in Brooklyn, I found myself mesmerized, though she never got around to telling me what, exactly, she wanted. When our meeting concluded, interesting as it was, I figured that was that. Still, every so often I would find myself mentally replaying that conversation, which felt unfinished.

A few months later, I received an intriguing invitation from a hematology oncologist at St. Vincent's Hospital in Manhattan, Dr. Alan Astrow. He, too, had read the Maimonides book, and he was inviting me to a series of lectures he'd organized, looking at how doctors do and do not deal with the spiritual concerns of very sick patients. I gathered that he wasn't advocating so-called alternative medicine or spiritual healing but was trying to understand how physicians, nurses, and other caregivers might help patients connect hope and reconciliation, deal with fear and despair—in other words, how to treat that part of the human entity not taught in anatomy class. I declined Astrow's invitation because I had something else to do that evening. He persisted, and I succumbed, unable to resist his gentle, insistent sincerity.

The speakers—a Jew and a Catholic—had nothing startling to say, but I was impressed by the heartfelt reaction they stirred in the 150 or so doctors, nurses, and social workers in the audience, who had stayed after hours on a freezing winter night to participate.

Mainly I liked Dr. Astrow. He handled the proceedings smoothly and intelligently, but at fifty still seemed like a gawky adolescent who hadn't quite adjusted to his growth. His shy smile and mournful blue eyes conveyed warmth and worry. A few days later, I received a thank-you letter, in which he wrote about his attempts to find a balance between his desire to be there for his patients, his need to set limits on emotional entanglement with them, and his professional ambition. I could see he was searching for something.

My encounter with Astrow led me to reread *Cancer Ward,* the great novel by Aleksandr Solzhenitsyn, and to a passage that I couldn't stop thinking about. "Sometimes I feel quite distinctly that what is inside me is not all of me," says one patient to another. "There's something else, sublime, quite indestructible, some tiny fragment of the universal spirit. Don't you feel that?"

A couple of months later, I received an e-mail from a friend who had been diagnosed with ovarian cancer two years earlier. The prognosis was neither dire nor completely reassuring, but a year after massive surgery and chemo-therapy she was reporting a healthy exam. She said she was feeling optimistic and energetic, but also sad, because the doctor she loved was leaving St. Vincent's for a new cancer center that was being opened in Brooklyn, at a place called Maimonides. Her doctor was Alan Astrow. In her e-mail she wrote:

> Astrow is a smart and caring doctor—how many others take their patients' phone number home with them so they can call at 10 Friday night to check up on them?!?!?

I decided these three events were related—*bashert,* Yiddish for "karmic connection," or, as the Chinese say, *min zhong zhu ding,* "life is predestined." The next day I sent an e-mail to Jo Ann Baldwin, a year after we met, as though no time had passed.

> Made one of those weird small world connections this morning I thought you would appreciate:
>
> Link one: My friend Lila, who has just been through a terrible bout with cancer, wrote a wonderful progress report, making special note of her amazing doctor, Alan Astrow.
>
> Link two: A few months ago, said Alan Astrow (unbeknownst to Lila) had invited me to a series of lectures he'd arranged on spirituality and medi-

cine. I went to one in December and was bowled over by what a brilliant, caring person he is. He invited me because he'd read *Rambam's Ladder* [my book about Maimonides, the philosopher, also known as Rambam].

Link three: Lila's note informed me that Dr. Astrow is moving to Maimonides Hospital in Brooklyn!

Link four: There you are!!!

Soon afterward I boarded the D train and headed across the river for Brooklyn.

Walking into the waiting room at Maimonides for the first time rekindled my first impression of New York when I was a newcomer, just out of college, feeling that same paradoxical rush of being overwhelmed and utterly engaged by the motley chaos, the interplay of harshness and sentimentality, the magnitude and intimacy of human convergence. In the small rural village in southern Ohio where I spent my first eighteen years, my family had been *the* diversity; being the Other was part of our job as the only Jews in a fundamentalist Christian farming community.

The Hasids who seemed to treat Maimonides as their home were alien to me, but also familiar, part of my background as a descendant of Eastern European Jews. Just as recognizable were the many people—patients and caregivers—speaking broken English in many accents. My parents, too, were immigrants—Hungarian speakers from Czechoslovakia—and my family had intimate connections with medical issues. My father had been a patient as well as a physician; he died of lung cancer when I was still a teenager. There was another connection. Borough Park was said to have the largest remnant of Holocaust survivors outside Israel; though my parents settled in Appalachia, they, too, had survived the death camps.

My father had been able relocate in an unlikely spot because he offered a necessary ingredient: He could tend to the sick. In return, this small, rural village provided him a haven and a source of meaning after he had lost so much. Was that formulation lost to history? Judging from the foreign names of the doctors who have replaced him, I didn't think so. But it was a different world.

Between 1970 and 1998, the foreign-born population in the United

States increased from 9.6 million to 24.4 million (according to official tallies, a low estimate). In 2004 the foreign-born population numbered 34.2 million, or 12 percent of the total U.S. population, approaching the 14 percent who moved here during the last big immigrant wave a century earlier. The attacks on the World Trade Center in 2001 exploded any residual sentimentality for the American melting pot. Now the mass movement of newcomers fueled larger apprehensions. The war on terror morphed into the war in Iraq, and large divisions loomed everywhere: Muslim versus Christian and Jew, Muslim versus Muslim versus Hindu, modernity versus fundamentalism, consumerism versus environmentalism, us versus them, us versus us.

It took just a few visits to see that Maimonides was an epicenter of these social forces, a petri dish of the post-9/11 world. What is alien and what is common? The question of community identity and responsibility was under constant discussion and examination. Ten years earlier the hospital had been in trouble because of a fractious board and an administration that wasn't responding to the community—make that communities—but specifically not to the local Orthodox, the original constituents. The board enlisted a politically connected outsider—Stanley Brezenoff, former deputy mayor under Ed Koch—to run the place, and he hired Pamela Brier, then the executive director at Bellevue Hospital Center in Manhattan, the oldest public hospital in the United States, most famous for its psychiatric ward. Within five years Maimonides was on the front page of the *Wall Street Journal,* featured in a laudatory article about a turnaround involving a bureaucratic overhaul and a new way of dealing with a population that demanded both kosher and Chinese food. Five years after that, the hospital was running in the black and in the middle of a major expansion—including building a bigger emergency room—that would improve the physical plant but not increase the number of inpatient beds. A comprehensive cancer center was about to open. These were ambitious plans when so many hospitals, including sophisticated teaching hospitals, had been struggling financially.

The hospital prided itself on the well-regarded doctors who had chosen Maimonides as the place to perform sophisticated technical procedures that required special skill and expensive equipment—and earned one Maimonides surgeon more than $3 million a year. But like any institution that is part of a particular place, Maimonides was also peculiar. It was a community hospital that employed many relatives—even generations of families—resulting in relationships that intertwined in ways that were healthy and ways that were not. It was a place in flux.

For every comforting parable about cross-cultural coexistence, there was an angry diatribe about rudeness and misunderstanding. In 1995, consultants hired by the hospital issued a report that declared "the level of rude behavior at MMC is astonishing." The report portrayed a "dirty environment" filled with angry patients, hostile nurses, and uncaring physicians. The prevailing mood, the consultants concluded, was "a culture of nastiness." How the hospital had been changing—and continued struggling to change—had become embedded in its lore. Many of the new administrators and medical practitioners felt that part of their mission was to civilize Brooklyn—a mandate that didn't sit well with the Brooklynites, another cultural clash.

At Maimonides nothing was simple. Half the staff couldn't even pronounce the hospital's name:

My-Mom-i-dees.

My Noni-dees.

Ma-Mo-nie-dees.

Maimonides ("my-MON-i-dese") Medical Center, I would soon learn, was the exact opposite of buttoned up. "There's an openness here, a willingness to allow people to express themselves, and it is not limited to the titled positions here in the hospital," said Carol Kidney, the nursing director for women's services, including obstetrics, an Irish immigrant who had worked there for twenty years. "Everybody believes they can and should speak up. That's a positive thing. You're going to pull out the best ideas, you're going to have innovation, you're going to have creativity, you're going to have good problem-solving skills."

Then, with characteristic Maimonides bluntness, she added, "If you open the venue for conversation and encourage the exchange of ideas, there's an opportunity for miscommunication. When you throw multiple cultures into the pot, there's plenty of opportunity for misunderstanding."

It was that lack of inhibition that led Pamela Brier, the hospital's president, and Martin Payson, the chairman of the board, to eventually agree to my impudent request: I wanted to spend a year at the hospital, without a minder, using the opening of the cancer center as a focus.

Later, Brier confided that she had always wanted to write a book about life in a hospital but never got beyond sixty or seventy pages of a journal she'd once kept. Payson never divulged exactly why he opened the door. Brooklyn born and bred, son of a father who bought and sold string and a public-service-minded mother who was an air warden during World War II, Payson rose to the vice chairmanship of Time Warner and then was squeezed out of the company after a bitter corporate battle. Upon leaving the corporate world, still in his fifties, he directed his energy to hiking the Himalayas, cross-country biking, and good works. Still, he had spent more than twenty-two years in the entertainment world, and his take on the hospital world reflected his time there. He told me, "When I first got here ten years ago, I realized hospitals have a lot in common with the movie business. You've got your talent, entrepreneurs, ambition, ego stroking, the business versus the creative part. The big difference is that in the hospital you don't get second takes. Movies are make-believe. This is real life."

Maybe it was his showbiz inclination to want publicity or the adventurer's spirit in him, but eventually Marty Payson—and Brier—convinced the other hospital administrators to sort out issues of patient privacy and to let me see Maimonides "warts and all" (Payson's words).

What Payson meant when he spoke of "real life" at Maimonides, I would learn, was action no less vivid than that in movies and TV shows, but more diffuse and often less obvious. There were, as would be expected, poignant, terrible, disturbing, and uplifting medical stories, and there were also bitter internal feuds, warm personal connections, comedy, egotism, greed, love, and loss. There were rabbinic edicts to contend with, as well as imams and herbalists and local politicians. Profound ethical issues gave juice to the proceedings, though most of the drama was humdrum but urgent, revolving around mundane work matters, like systems foul-ups that kept blood-test results from being delivered on time, anal-compulsive bosses, careless record keepers, shortages of everything except forms to fill out, an ever-changing regulatory requirement, recalcitrant and greedy insurance-reimbursement systems, and the surprising difficulty of figuring out how to keep rooms clean and get doctors to wash their hands.

Politicians have long made unkept promises about reforming a health-care system that has devolved into an unfathomably complex maze of overlapping bureaucratic fiefdoms. I began to see the hospital as a place of repairing and damaging, birthing and dying—and red tape and budgets and stress—but also a community struggling with the thorny social forces changing the world around it. As I filled reams of paper with my hand-scrawled daily logs, and boxfuls of taped interviews, I discovered the very human quality that remains the keystone of what can seem like a giant, impersonal enterprise.

Over the course of a year, I would become privy to many conversations and miscommunications, as well as the thoughts, interactions, successes, and failings of a remarkable confluence of compassionate and contentious people. They were ambitious, shortsighted, altruistic, selfish, foolhardy, and wise. They tried to respect themselves and their patients, a task that often appeared far more difficult than diagnosing illness or performing complex medical procedures or speaking one another's languages. They tried to remember—against the odds posed by a greedy and corrupted health-care system and by institutional and human frailty—that healing was the heart of the matter.

One

Occam Lied

*Occam's razor (sometimes spelled **Ockham's razor**) is a principle attributed to the 14th-century English logician and Franciscan friar William of Ockham. The principle states that the explanation of any phenomenon should make as few assumptions as possible, eliminating those that make no difference in the observable predictions of the explanatory hypothesis or theory. The principle is often expressed in Latin as the lex par-*simoniae *("law of parsimony" or "law of succinctness"):* Entia non sunt multiplicanda praeter necessitatem, *which translates to "Entities should not be multiplied beyond necessity."*

This is often paraphrased as "All things being equal, the simplest solution tends to be the best."

—FROM WIKIPEDIA, THE FREE ENCYCLOPEDIA

NEW SUCK REPORT, VOLUME 1, ISSUES: LOTS
JULY, 2005

Dudes

Greetings from the Big Apple, or as I shall henceforth refer to it as . . . . New Suck! . . . I actually am winning the War on Cockroach Terror, but it is a non-stop battle, so keep me in your prayers. So things here in The Brooklyn are not what I thought they would be. I only thought it would blow slightly, but alas, it blows severely. Anyone who said that New Suck is the greatest city on the planet obviously never lived in San Diego. or Boulder. or Denver. or the North Pole. Or even Grand Island, Nebraska. Yes, i would rather live in G.I. Nebraska than here. Sure there is lots to do. if you like doing them in a giant hot smelly city at the same time as a gillion other people, and paying up the wazoo to do them. . . .

I'll give you the goods now: I live in a place in The Brooklyn called Boro Park, which is the highest concentration of Orthodox Jewish people in the world, bordered by Sunset Park and the most diverse zip code in the United States. Our hospital has translators for 67 different languages, if that tells you anything about the population here. And the people here are also very sick. Not like "Dude that run was sick!", but more like "dude that old man is sick as hell, I'm pretty sure he's gonna die in 5 minutes!"

So it will be good to train here I guess. If you can get the translator down to the ER fast enough to figure out what the heck is going on, you can actually save lots of lives here. sweet.

And my favorite part about New York is . . . i forgot. was there one? I'm delirious now. I am working all night shifts with one day shift this week, so my schedule is all jacked up. . . .

In summary, New Suck is fairly sucky, hence the name. . . .

ok i gotta study or sleep or something now.

Love, davey

"Fishing kills me exactly as it keeps me alive." The Old Man and the Sea

. . . .

NEW SUCK REPORT, VOLUME 1, ISSUE 2:
DAVEY'S DAY OFF

Alright, so I got a day off and the most logical thing to do here in New Suck would be . . . go surfing, duh.
First problem—I live nowhere near the beach
Second problem—I do not have a car

But once I got to the subway stop, all i had to do was

1. Take the D Train all the way into Manhattan (8 stops)
2. Switch to the A- Train, and take it BACK into Brooklyn, through Queens, past JFK, to the stop before the beach (17 stops)
3. Switch to the S Line (which i had never been on, nor heard of until today), and one stop later you arrive at 90th Street and Rockaway Beach

4. Barely 2 hours out of Brooklyn and I am in the water and riding my first ever wave in the balmy Atlantic Ocean. And the waves did get bigger, and more fun! Interestingly, I noted that I caught significantly more waves (like a dozen) today than I did 3 weeks ago in Malibu . . . . . funny huh? So a great day off, I must say. . . .

Love, Davey

"Fishing kills me exactly as it keeps me alive." The Old Man and the Sea

. . . .

NEW SUCK REPORT VOLUME 1, ISSUE 3:
DAVE'S DAY OFF PART DEUX

Kids,

After working the night shift (7pm till 7:30am) I went home and slept for about 3 hours then got up to go to the beach again. . . . I know, this seems crazy, but apparently there was a hurricane named Irene not long ago, and her aftermath was sending larger-than-usual swells to parts along the East Coast. So, armed with my new friend Chris from San Diego (and his Jeep . . . . YES! no more surfboard on the subway) we headed off to the same beach where a child was sucked out to sea and drowned the day before . . . . and also near the same beach that one of my kid patients had been swimming at with his infectious diarrhea from South America the day before . . . wonderful. Ah, New York. Anyhow, I won't bore you with the details, other than Irene was AWESOME. Much better than the previous week's adventure. It was not like surfing a hurricane like in the movies, but it was big enough to scare me on occasion, and big enough to have some very excitingly gnarley and fast rides! . . .

What else. hmm. I have been doing great in the Peds ER, so that is good. I even got the Saved-the-Day Hero award (mythical) two nights IN A ROW, One for eyeballing a kid in the waiting room and deciding she looked a little sick to be waiting for another hour, so checked her out in the wait room and decided she was bleeding in her head, so got the CT scan and the Neurosurgeon involved quickly enough to save the little girl's brain . . . so that was cool. And the other one was just being in the right place at the right time, noticing a drunk psychiatric patient on a gurney in a hallway who was sawing through his leather restraints with a knife. I learned that I get yelled at if i try to wrestle a knife away from a crazy drunk guy. i guess "that is what security is for" i am told. the same security that let the guy INTO the ER with a knife. outstanding. New York. so that was kind of exciting. a bunch of people that night were like "you saved the day man, i totally respect you now". what the hell does that mean? did i garner no respect previously? I guess i am skinny with long hair and look like i'm 21, so nobody is quite sure that i am a doctor or something.

ok. i gotta go to bed.

Love, davey

p.s. Danielle, I don't hate New York completely, for the record. It just sucks completely. for the record. But I think this opinion has a lot to do with the suckiness of my occupation, and my long long hours. davey tired.

"Fishing kills me exactly as it keeps me alive." The Old Man and the Sea

David (aka Davey) Gregorius, first-year resident in emergency medicine, had bumbled into an agreement to spend three years of his life at Maimonides Medical Center because of his infatuation with a beautiful, long-legged blonde, who also happened to be brilliant, kind, and humble. He met Jennifer Pfeifer when he was a medical student at the Midwestern University–Arizona College of Osteopathic Medicine, near Phoenix, on his way to a rotation at a hospital in Sacramento. Pfeifer was at UCLA working on a Ph.D. in developmental psychology; one of her classmates, a boyhood friend of Gregorius's, introduced them. They fell in love. Gregorius was back at school in Arizona when Pfeifer told him she had been thinking about doing postdoctoral work at Columbia or New York University. So after Gregorius had already sent out twenty-five applications to hospital residency programs, she said to him, "Why don't you send a couple to New York?"

Later he remembered picking Mount Sinai because one of his teachers in medical school had gone there. As he recalled, "The other one was obviously

Maimonides, but I really don't remember picking it," he said. "I thought I put Methodist. I thought I put some kind of M. But the whole application process is clicking on computers, you know? Click, click. When I got the e-mail back inviting me for an interview to Maimonides Medical Center in Brooklyn, whatever, I went WHAT? But I still went. I thought, I've never been to New York, I'll check it out."

He traveled on the overnight flight from Phoenix, landing bleary-eyed in New York on a cold Sunday morning in December. He spent the day in Manhattan, staying with a friend on the Upper West Side. She showed him Times Square, Central Park, the usual tourist stuff. On Monday morning he took the subway to Borough Park, crossing the East River, away from the Manhattan skyline toward Brooklyn, once described by another transplanted midwesterner, Ian Frazier, as having "the undefined, hard-to-remember shape of a stain"—in other words, a place you wanted to be from, not head toward. In recent years, however, the real-estate craze in Manhattan had given the borough new definition, no longer stain but hot spot for the disenfranchised young people who couldn't afford the East Village or Lower East Side and for cramped, growing families looking for bigger spaces, more sky, yards.

Gregorius, born in Missouri but raised in Nebraska—fifth generation at least—had a vague TV- and movie-inspired notion of Brooklyn "as a knife and guns place." When he disembarked from the D train, he was relieved to find himself in a safe-looking (only slightly shabby) neighborhood, with rows of two- and three-story houses and little stores—newsstands, flower shops, delis, bakeries, and shoe-repair places—some of them displaying signs with Hebrew lettering.

On the short walk from the elevated subway tracks to the hospital, he passed worried-looking bearded men dressed in long black coats and large black hats and young women wearing matronly clothes and herding large groups of children. There were black people whose words floated by with a Caribbean lilt and Pakistanis with bright scarves sticking out from under winter coats. He didn't pay much attention; he was mentally preparing for his interview with John Marshall, the residency program director.

They hit it off. Marshall was balding but youthful, a calm man with dark, penetrating eyes, who seemed intellectual yet also knew how to have fun. He was thirty-seven, from Detroit, had been in the air force, and was a passionate downhill skier. What a coincidence! Gregorius had fantasized about becoming a fighter pilot but quit the Naval Academy at Annapolis when he was told his less-than-perfect eyesight nixed that ambition. He transferred to the University of Colorado at Boulder and reverted to his back-burner dream, being a doctor (like his dad). And yes, he would figure out how to combine work with pleasure. Maybe a job in an emergency room in the Colorado mountains, maybe two or three shifts a week. Make that an emergency room in Vail, add ski patrol a couple of days, leaving time for fishing twice a week.

The hospital in Borough Park did not fit Davey's blithe vision of work hard, play hard. His memories of his first foray into the Maimonides emergency room were vague: It was crowded. Really crowded. Stretchers with patients were lined up two and three deep, with the lucky ones semisecluded behind curtains that barely closed. He noticed but didn't fully comprehend that the melting-pot mayhem—Hasids, Chinese, Pakistanis, Haitians, Russians, Bulgarians—did not seem to include anybody like him, a tall, skinny, curly-haired, dark-eyed, non-Jewish, non-Muslim, non-Asian, non-African, non-Italian white surfer-ski boy from the Midwest. The visual overload was matched by the audio: Tower of Babel at top volume, accompanied by the constant beeping of monitors, pagers, telephones. The usual ER smells of antiseptic and bodily stink, but also strange spicy odors he couldn't place.

Had he landed in the Third World, or a developing nation, whatever the correct terminology of the moment was? Before he could panic, he came across evidence that he was indeed firmly situated in the First World, twenty-first century: Maimonides had HealthmaticsED, a very cool, very tomorrow computer system that, among other things, allowed doctors and nurses to track a patient in real time. The computer monitors were stationed like beacons of sanity throughout the room. For Gregorius they made the chaos seem almost comprehensible.

On the screen the mass of humanity was personalized—somewhat—by identifiable characteristics, but also depersonalized, transformed into useful bits of information. That large gray-blond uncomprehending woman staring into the noisy glare with frightened eyes became *Yevnosky, Irina, 41; F; vaginal bleeding; 11 minutes with nurse, 4 hours waiting for bed.* The husky kid wearing a Yankees T-shirt, off in the corner talking to a young woman, was *Diaz, 18;*

M; difficulty breathing; 14 minutes with doctor. The old man in a cubicle was Wang, L., 83; M; pain in abdomen; 15 hours, 9 minutes waiting for bed.

None of the emergency rooms he'd worked in—Sacramento, Phoenix, and certainly not Nogales, Arizona, a border-town hospital with ten ER beds—had such a sophisticated setup. Maimonides had been named one of the nation's one hundred "Most Wired" hospitals and one of the nation's twenty-five "Most Wireless," by *Hospitals & Health Networks,* a journal of the American Hospital Association (AHA).

Overcrowding had become commonplace in American emergency rooms, which had, for people without medical insurance, become the doctor's office. In June 2006, almost a year after Gregorius began his residency, the Institute of Medicine of the National Academies would publish a report that warned, "A national crisis in emergency care has been brewing and is now beginning to come into full view." The emergency department at Maimonides, which would process more than 84,000 patients in Gregorius's first year, was not the busiest ER in the country or in New York City. But it was arguably the most intense. Using a formula that measured not only numbers of patients but the square footage available in which to squeeze them, Steven Davidson, the department chairman, a crusty type who admitted he got along better with numbers than with people, once measured the concentration of humanity in terms of patients per square foot per year. Then he compared the density to other hospitals of comparable size. By this measure, Maimonides was packing in six patients per square foot per year; the average at other hospitals seeing comparable numbers of patients was two or three. The next-worst he could find logged a mere four and a half.

Surely this was the perfect fix for the adrenaline junkies who chose emergency medicine as their specialty. But even thrill seekers need a rest, and at Maimonides the flow of need was relentless. "Years ago you came home from one day when you are crowded like this and nobody died and you felt great because you'd reached up and found the capacity to deal with it," Davidson told a visitor one afternoon around a quarter to five, grinning a little crazily through his short, graying beard as he took in the scene. Actually, he was yelling, and pressing against the back of a resident to avoid being swiped by a gurney holding a young woman who had come in unconscious, just out of detox.

He continued trying to tell his story through the din. "But it happened once that month," he shouted. "The rest of the time you sat in the lounge and chatted with the nurses. One day in thirty, it happened, and you felt like a hero. But when it's one day a week, two days a week, or more, it grinds people down."

Gregorius was one of 450 applicants for the nine first-year positions in the three-year emergency-department residency at Maimonides; as Gregorius knew all too well, the computer click made it easy to apply. Marshall, the program director, interviewed 120 of the applicants, the ones who had decent medical-school records and good letters of recommendation, preferably from someone he knew. How did he decide which of those had the stamina to endure the Maimonides ER? On the medical side, he was looking for people who could handle the particular pressures of emergency-room medicine. As he explained it, in the quiet of his office, "In internal medicine you play the game to win, to get the right diagnosis, to figure it out. In emergency medicine you play the game of medicine not to lose. You want to make sure somebody doesn't have the things that are going to kill them. So if I exclude the fifteen things that are going to kill this patient, . . . I don't care if I don't know exactly why they have it so long as it doesn't kill them. I'm looking for applicants who are able to think that way, who have proven they are comfortable with a degree of uncertainty in not finding exactly the right answer."

He elaborated. "They need to be able to multitask. In most medicine you proceed diagnostically and then therapeutically. In emergency medicine you have to proceed diagnostically and therapeutically at the same time. You have patients coming to you with acute pain; they're sick, and we start treatment not knowing what we're treating. We'll give you an aspirin because we think this may be your heart before I figure out whether it really is your heart. You have to be able to do that with multiple patients at the same time. You need to be able to maintain situational awareness."

Those were standard emergency-doc requirements. But "situational awareness" at Maimonides took an extra-special something. Maimonides—representing Brooklyn, early twenty-first century—was an epicenter of the cultural forces that had been rocking and roiling the American experiment for a generation. The ideal of assimilation, finding your inner WASP, had given way to the glorious mosaic. Assimilation was out; the hyphenated American was in. Culture became multicultural. Then, September 11, 2001, the World Trade Center felled by Islamic terrorists, and suddenly the mosaic—or pieces of it—became suspect. The hospital, by necessity and tradition, remained a demilitarized zone, where patients dragged in not just their wounds, fevers, and malfunctions but their accents and customs, their immigration and insurance problems, their feelings about being outsiders. Hope and heartache in sixty-seven languages. Sick and scared, they yearned for kindness and prayed for competence from the doctors, nurses, floor cleaners, lab technicians, paper pushers, and social workers, who had their own troubles and were often newcomers themselves. This jarring symphony of strangers, an ongoing work in progress, was created out of exigency, in moments of greatest stress with an overwhelming crush of expectations, needs, and bureaucracy. At Maimonides, cross-cultural forces made for one big surf tide.

Was Gregorius right for the task? He didn't think so. After the interview, realizing he had six hours to kill before his flight left, he said to himself, "I'm never going to be in New York again, let's go!" He pulled a pair of tennis shoes out of his suitcase and then, still wearing his interview suit, went on a frantic tour—to the Guggenheim, to Ground Zero—pulling along his suitcase. "I'll never be back," he remembered thinking.

"David's nickname during the interview process was Deer in the Headlights," Marshall recalled. "He's so open, so impressionable, so wow!"

That openness—and the enthusiastic letters of recommendation Gregorius brought with him—made Marshall think the Deer in the Headlights would do just fine. He was wrong only once every couple of years. One of his residents had washed out because, as Marshall put it, "the multitasking thing didn't sink in." Another left the program because his wife had severe postpartum depression, so first he took a leave of absence, and then he left altogether.

Marshall was from Detroit and might have gone into the auto industry like his grandfather, father, and brother. But he was drawn to the mix of a different life. His wife was Iranian, an artist, and he had majored in anthropology and writing as an undergraduate at the University of Michigan. The air force paid for his medical-school education, which he repaid by spending four years of his life in San Antonio, Texas, at the Wilford Hall Medical Center, the air force's main teaching hospital—interrupted by a six-month stint in the Middle East, with stops in Afghanistan, Uzbekistan, Turkey. Not by choice: Three weeks after the September 11 attacks in New York, the base doctors got a phone call asking for a couple of volunteers. A few of them flipped coins to see who the lucky ones would be. Marshall lost the toss, which landed him in an army field hospital in Afghanistan, where his job was to stabilize the wounded brought in by helicopter so they could be put on a plane to Turkey or Germany.

For a fairly young man, he had seen a lot. Before he came to Maimonides, between medical school in Hawaii and residency in Denver and moonlighting, he had treated patients in fourteen ERs. At Wilford Hall in San Antonio, the military hospital took care of 250,000 retirees in the area who had access to the system, also lots of geriatric patients and children. The trauma center brought in Spanish-speaking patients from San Antonio, more Mexicans than Texans. In Denver he figured that Spanish was the first language of 20 percent of his patients. In Hawaii he treated Chinese, Vietnamese, Portuguese, and Samoan people. But nothing in his experience matched the cultural cocktail he found in Brooklyn. Maimonides served up diversity on steroids.

Marshall had specific ideas about what kind of person would be, as he put it, "comfortable in a polyethnic urban setting." It didn't matter to him whether the candidate had ever experienced a mishmash like that before. He was looking for a certain receptivity. "You get a sense from the thoughtfulness with which they answer a question, the openness they have to the questions, whether they are open to the experience, to listen to what people are saying instead of hearing what they expect to hear based on their closed-society cultural experience." He saw those qualities in Gregorius.

Marshall asked his residents if they had learned Occam's razor: *Given the choice between multiple explanations for any given phenomenon, the simplest explanation is almost always right.*

Forget that, he told them. At Maimonides, he said, the simplicity principle doesn't apply. To underscore the point, he intended to give his residents T-shirts that declared OCCAM LIED.

"Our patients never have one problem," he explained. "They almost always have a heart attack compounded by a urinary infection compounded by muscle breakdown. . . . There's never one clear explanation for the pathological phenomenon we see in a lot of our patients."

The reason? Maimonides patients tended to be exceptionally old, or exceptionally foreign. So fewer ankle sprains, broken arms, colds and flus. More belly pain, chest pain, strokes, heart attacks, sepsis. More weird symptoms and inexplicable infections. More off-the-boat things. "The pathology is great!" Marshall said.

Also, Friar William of Occam clearly had never had to contend with Hatzolah (from the Hebrew for word for "rescue" or "saving," in the sense of saving someone's soul). Hatzolah was the volunteer emergency medical service run by Orthodox Jews, and another undeniably complicating fact of life in the Maimonides ER. In the mid-1990s, the hospital was avoided by the local Orthodox community because local leaders felt that their needs were not being met. New management came, which actively courted the religious community—especially the leaders of Hatzolah, who decided which hospitals got their business. The plan worked. So by the time Gregorius arrived for his interview, Hatzolah was a major supplier of emergency patients, and Hatzolah patients tended to be religious Jews. (Orthodox Jews—people identifying themselves on patient surveys as keeping kosher—made up 20 to 25 percent of the inpatient population.) Hatzolah brought in as many patients as New York City's official EMS, 400 to 500 patients a month. Significantly, the Hatzolah patients were older and sicker; about 55 percent of them ended up getting admitted versus 30 percent of the regular EMS patients. Admissions were how the hospital made money, and Maimonides prided itself on staying on the plus side of the ledger, a rarity in the not-for-profit hospital world.

The Hatzolah men (there were no women) were tough—and tender, too, but the doctors and nurses had to contend with the toughness. The Orthodox ambulance-squad members were not content to drop their patients off. They hovered, ready to nudge, cajole, argue, and demand if they felt their charges were not being attended to quickly enough or with enough diligence. "It's really like having unionized patients," said Marshall. "Those patients, because they're part of the union, can demand certain things of the administration, though there's not a specific contract. The union can strongarm the hospital. Hatzolah can say we're not bringing patients to the hospital, and then the hospital starts losing money—it's happened before. So they can demand things for their constituency."

The Hatzolah men could be a nuisance, but they cared about the sick people they brought into the ER, and they had clout, so you had to learn to deal with them. The hospital was multicultural but kosher, and its mission statement made clear that the Orthodox had special status: *"We welcome patients of all faiths, and at the same time remain uniquely committed to serving the special healthcare needs of the Orthodox Jewish community, whose religious and cultural traditions help guide the provision of Maimonides' services."*

Dr. Carl Ramsay, the emergency department's medical director, a weathered beanpole who wore his graying hair pulled back in a ponytail, just sighed when he was asked about Hatzolah. "It's the good and it's the bad," he said. "This is an academic community hospital with a very interested community that wants to make their place better. That's what I keep telling myself, because if you don't say that you might as well walk out. That's how I always look at it. Plus, there's the whole Buddhist thing. They're my teachers."

He sighed again. "Teaching me patience."

Ramsay was a particular ER type, the swashbuckling hippie. He described his parents as *"Grapes of Wrath* folks," Okies who moved to California, where Ramsay was raised. He trained in public hospitals in New York and then ran clinics in Grenada, in a part of the country even the Peace Corps forgot about. After that he secluded himself and his family in the middle of nowhere Oregon for thirteen years, running a free clinic for people without insurance, then returned to New York. He'd been brought to Maimonides a year earlier to help unstick a stuck system, including unclogging the route from the emergency room into hospital beds.

Not the least of his problems were the sixty-seven languages that, out of practicality and social pressure as much as altruism, had become part of the hospital's identity and pride. "We do a great job making sure we have the right interpreters downstairs, but it is incredibly challenging," he said. "It is great training for your young residents to understand that when you walk up to a person from another country who speaks another language, that is a risk. Period. Period. It's as much of a risk factor as diabetes or anything else, because you can make a mistake on them."

He elaborated: "If you had an internal point system to admit the patient, you should add twenty-five percent of risk on that just to make sure you're not blowing something. It's the old children's game when you whisper in people's ears. Having an interpreter doesn't mean you are getting the right information. Immediately it should raise the red flag."

Ramsay met briefly with Carolyn and Chuck (Dr. Charles) Gregorius when they came to visit their son the first time. They liked Ramsay, but the emergency room itself made them feel, as Carolyn politely put it, "disheartened." Actually, she said, "I was quite upset by the conditions, the nuttiness." Before Davey went to Maimonides, his parents had never been to New York. "We're west people," Chuck explained. "We go west and into the mountains."

On the Internet, Carolyn had found a hotel that was about four blocks away from the hospital. When they got out of the taxi, they felt surrounded by Hasidic Jewish people. "They're lovely people when they talk to you—you couldn't ask for anything better," said Chuck. "But because of their dress and everything, that was the first time in my life I ever felt like a sore thumb."

Carolyn added, "We were the only people who look like this." Meaning like they'd stepped out of the pages of a Lands' End catalog, ready for a game of tennis or a neighborly backyard barbecue.

Chuck was an anesthesiologist at Bryan LGH Medical Center in Lincoln, Nebraska, a large modern hospital that had just undergone a $114 million renovation. He felt sucker-punched by the breathtaking volume he saw in the Maimonides ER. "The emergency room we have back in Lincoln is about twice as big as the hospital here in terms of space, and it sees perhaps twenty-seven, twenty-eight thousand visits a year," he said during a visit to see his son. "The one here with half the space sees eighty to ninety thousand. And they're *sick*. You don't see coughs and colds and runny noses."

What amazed him more than the volume was the patient mix. "I work in a hospital where we see Vietnamese, occasional Russians, Hispanics of course, Ethiopians and Sudanese," he said. "It's a problem for us dealing with four or five languages on a fairly common basis, but to deal with *that* many, that truly boggles my mind. How they can deliver health care under those conditions."

Yet he had checked and was relieved to find that Maimonides had received good and even some excellent evaluations from outside observers, including the Joint Commission on Accreditation of Hospitals, the industry's self-regulatory body, and an award for "clinical excellence" from Health-Grades, one of several private companies that profit from supplying insurers and the hospital industry with data.

Carolyn, too, tried to see the bright side. "I have an analogy," she said. "We're from the Vietnam era, so many of our friends went through the military to pay for med school. The ones who said they had the best training are the ones who ended up in the field in Vietnam. They had nothing, no support; they just had to figure it out. This isn't nearly as harsh, but in some ways it is comparable."

Her husband chimed in. "One day we were here and had just returned from dinner, around eight in the evening. David said, 'You want to see the ER?' I'd heard about these big ERs, big rooms with cubicles separated only by curtains, and he'd told me they'd be stacked as many as two or three and maybe five in each cubicle. You imagine that in your mind, but you're not prepared for it. You walk in, and it was exactly as he had said. It was so busy that night both the residency program director and the emergency medical director [Marshall and Ramsay] were staffing, and David introduced us.

"I was about five occupied gurneys away from a wall where I saw an Ambu bag [a lightweight, self-inflating disposable resuscitator], and I said, 'What would you do if you needed that Ambu bag to get to a patient on the other side of the room?' Dr. Ramsay said, 'I'd crawl over those five patients.' That just boggled my mind in the year 2006."

Chuck said he wasn't worried about his son. "David is ten times the student I ever was," he said proudly. "He really likes to learn. And the cultural diversity he is experiencing and the sheer volume—there probably isn't anything he's going to see for the rest of his life that he doesn't see here."

Carolyn nodded but looked worried. "I hope he comes out without an ulcer," she said.

Two

Pooh-Bah

n June 2003, Stanley Brezenoff, the president and chief executive officer of Maimonides Medical Center, announced that he was leaving the hospital. The news didn't come as a surprise to the administrators who ran the place. Many of them regarded Brezenoff as a larger-than-life figure who was destined for greater things. Brezenoff was an imposing man, maybe not larger than life but certainly big—tall, broad and confident, a Brooklyn boy who had successfully crossed the river to the big league of Manhattan. He'd been a deputy mayor under Ed Koch and the head of the Port Authority. Brezenoff was a galvanizer, shrewd and quick, adept at getting people to do what he wanted them to do while allowing them to think it was their idea.

Still, when the news of his impending departure came, neither the board nor the administrative staff expressed alarm. The hospital was prospering, and Pamela Brier had been chief operating officer, a capable number two, from almost the beginning of Brezenoff's tenure. It was understood that she would eventually take charge.

They were considered to be a well-oiled team—he was the master planner, she was a meticulous detail person. She may not have been as politic as he, but she relished political maneuvering and liked being in charge. By the time Brezenoff told her he was leaving to run Continuum Health Partners, a giant consortium of five major New York City hospitals, she was ready to be the boss.

Brier elicited a more complex set of reactions than did Brezenoff. He could be gruff, even fearsome, and his brilliance was intimidating, but he was

thought to be straightforward and easy to read. Brier was harder to catego-
rize. Few would deny that she was smart and capable, but she was also eccentric and unpredictable.

Brezenoff was scheduled to begin his new job in July. Brier had been
working nonstop in preparation. Her husband, Peter Aschkenasy, whom she
had married six years earlier, had also been on a work jag. A restaurateur who
dabbled in Democratic politics, Aschkenasy owned Concert Foods, which
ran the food and drink concessions for Central Park's Delacorte Theater and
Summerstage, and he had just opened the park's Sheep Meadow Café. Summer was Aschkenasy's peak season, as he coped with the crowds drawn to the
park by free Shakespeare and numerous concerts.

This power couple could barely remember the last time they had been to
their country house in Columbia County, a few hours' drive north of the
city. Late Wednesday evening, July 2, Aschkenasy called Brier and convinced
her they should take advantage of the extended holiday weekend. He was a
little weary, but they decided it would be worth the tiring drive that night for
the luxury of sleeping in the next morning.

At 2:00 A.M. they were just a couple of miles from their destination when
Brier noticed that Aschkenasy looked really exhausted. She remembered asking him if he wanted to stop and rest, though they were almost home.

When Steven Brier, Pam Brier's first husband, looked at the photographs their
daughter, Jenny, took of the car after the accident, for insurance inquiries, he
said to her and her partner, Kat, "It is a fucking miracle they're alive."

He had been asleep in his country house on Long Island when Jenny
called and asked him to drive upstate to meet her at Albany Medical Center.
She told him that her mother and Peter had been in a disastrous accident and
their survival was uncertain.

Their Audi station wagon had hit a two-hundred-year-old oak tree with
enough force to push the engine back into the passenger seat. The car's air
bags had inflated, protecting Pam and Peter from the waist up; from the
waist down, they were two sacks of broken bones. As if to underscore the fine
line between disaster and miracle, misfortune and luck, health and infirmity,

the dog riding in the backseat—a good-natured Chesapeake Bay retriever named Charlie—suffered no physical harm. (But it would turn out to be a bad day for Charlie, too. He was a big dog, and after the accident his owners would be too frail to care for him. They gave him away.)

People who saw newspaper photographs of the car marveled that anyone had walked out alive. No one did walk out. The couple had to be extricated from the wreckage by the Jaws of Life, a hydraulic cutting tool developed for auto racing that could slice metal without rocking the crushed vehicle and harming those trapped inside.

Their memories were fragmented. "I remember the accident, asking Pam if she was all right, someone coming down the road going, 'Oh my God, oh my God, let me get you help,'" Aschkenasy would recall. "I remember the fire department showing up and cutting me out of the car. I remember . . . being loaded onto the helicopter, the helicopter taking off, and thinking, 'God, it's freezing,' and then I remember nothing for two months."

His injuries were devastating; the prognosis was uncertain. When Lillian Fraidkin, the chief of staff at Maimonides, saw him at the hospital in Albany, she had to look away. "The man was so bruised, so bloated, so . . . It wasn't his face," she said. "Oh, I tell you, he was not Peter. He was just blown up—you could not identify him. If that man was in a morgue and they asked me was that Peter . . . I don't know."

Fraidkin could not talk about that moment without becoming teary-eyed, uncharacteristically losing her cool. "I was a basket case," she said. "Pam looked like a little doll. She at least was recognizable. Still bruised, bruises on her face. She had a collapsed lung. It was an absolute mess. I was a basket case. I was just standing there, holding her hand and talking to her."

After that, Fraidkin anointed herself Brier's health-care advocate. "She's very dear to me, even when she's driving me friggin' crazy," Fraidkin confessed one day. "She comes into my office and starts moving all my stuff. She kills my plants. She tells me, 'Get rid of that painting, it's hideous!' but I can tell her, 'Pam, go do something presidential and stop meddling in my things.' And she does."

Brier remembered little from the immediate aftermath, though she had been reminded, on prompting from Jenny, that on seeing her daughter she first asked for her pocketbook and how Charlie the dog was doing. She began issuing commands for her hospital, for Maimonides. Only later did she ask about her husband.

The injuries were horrific. Aschkenasy was on life support for several days. When he and Brier recounted what he had broken, it began to seem easier to itemize what *hadn't* been injured. The breakage included both hips, an elbow, his left leg, collarbone, ribs. His left ankle was shattered, a lung collapsed. One doctor said that twenty-eight bones had been broken. More gruesome was the loss of skin and flesh from his legs; his right ankle, foot, and lower leg had been almost stripped of tissue. The damage was so significant that the doctors came very close to amputating the leg.

Brier's injuries were not as devastating, but only by comparison. Hers were merely terrible. Her right leg was broken in two places; the lower part was nearly severed. She broke her hip in two places, had a collapsed lung and broken ribs. Like her husband, she lost significant stretches of skin and flesh on both legs and on her right hand and wrist.

Jenny Brier found it difficult to talk about the accident, even years afterward. At least for the moment, and possibly forever, the power balance had shifted. As the child of two working parents, Jenny had always been encouraged to be self-sufficient, but her mother had always loomed large (contrary to appearances). Theirs was a storytelling family, and on one of Jenny's birthdays she heard another emblematic tale: of how, as Pam was going into labor with Jenny, she finished typing a grant application for a child-care center, ate a piece of pound cake that her mother, about to become Jenny's grandmother, had made for her, because Pam wanted to appear appreciative, and dropped off the grant application on the way to the hospital.

Now Pam Brier was immobilized, and her only child had to run the show. Jenny Brier literally held her mother's well-being in her hands, in the form of a health-care proxy. Peter's belonged to his son, Paul.

New York is one of many states that allow people to appoint a family member or close friend to make health-care decisions for them if they can no longer make such decisions for themselves. As a hospital president, Brier knew, such consent could be vital when doctors dealt with patients on the verge of death. But, like most people, even those in their fifties, she and Aschkenasy had not gotten around to a formal discussion of the health-care proxy with their children. At some point, however, they had mentioned to Jenny and Paul that they would be in charge of their parents' health, envisioning some distant moment. The car crash had sped up the timetable, dropping Jenny and her stepbrother into a dreaded narrative, the pivotal juncture in a child's life that too often takes place exactly this way—in a crisis.

The accident was a defining moment for the Brier and Aschkenasy families, but it also carried profound institutional significance. Two months earlier the hospital had had the equivalent of two chiefs; Brezenoff was still there, and Brier was preparing to take over. Now, two weeks after Brier's official promotion to president and Brezenoff's departure, Maimonides had no one at the top. For Marty Payson, the board chairman, the accident provided the kind of fraught situation that had been his specialty when he was general counsel at Warner Communications and then vice chairman at Time Warner after the merger. He was a natural troubleshooter: mild-mannered, imperturbable, perceptive, and deeply loyal. He set out for Albany.

The chairman was part of a platoon of people from Maimonides who made the 150-mile drive upstate. Joseph Cunningham arrived first—with Lili Fraidkin, who insisted on going with him. Brier could drive her crazy, but Fraidkin couldn't bear the thought of her dying.

Dr. Joseph N. Cunningham Jr. was head of strategic initiatives, chair of surgery, and a significant force in the hospital. He was also chief of cardiothoracic surgery. Twenty-one years earlier, in 1982, he had left a promising career at New York University Hospital to go to Brooklyn, where he helped bring national prominence to the Maimonides cardiac surgery department. He remained striking at sixty-three, tall and still sexy, though his frame was slightly stooped and his shock of hair was gray and white. Smooth and courtly, he had star power, though he was in danger of self-parody, wearing cowboy boots to surgery and—senior citizenship be damned!—still generating rumors because he liked the company of attractive nurses.

In Brooklyn he was a novelty, with his accent doused in the syrup of his southern boyhood and his apparent identification with the Swamp Fox, Brigadier General Francis Marion, the daring Revolutionary War commander. The connection? Cunningham grew up in Marion, Alabama, and admired rugged men. A print of Ernest Hemingway hung on his wall, standing beside a boat called the *Swamp Fox*. Cunningham, too, liked to deep-sea fish in dangerous waters and named all his boats *Swamp Fox*. Even the mugs in his office carried the "Swamp Fox" logo.

In Steve Brier's recollection, though, it was Douglas Jablon who dominated. Jablon was conspicuous wherever he was: six feet two inches tall and broad, a yarmulke always perched on his head, looking like an Orthodox fullback who had softened into middle age. He always dressed the same way, ready for a funeral, in a black suit and white shirt. His official title was "special assistant to the president," but Steve Brier called him the "Mitzvah Man" (*mitzvah* means "good deed" in Hebrew). Jablon ran the patient-representative department at the hospital, meaning he took care of the VIPs—the Very Important Patients—a category that for Jablon encompassed anyone who asked him for help. Jablon managed to be simultaneously unflappable and on the verge of hysterics. He was in Albany because he loved (and feared) Brier and because his job—he would say—was to handle *tsuris* ("troubles"). If the situation in Albany didn't represent *tsuris,* what did?

Sondra Olendorf, head of nursing and hospital operations, went to the upstate hospital and so did a contingent of physicians besides Cunningham, including the chairs of plastic surgery, obstetrics, and orthopedics. Some were there to oversee the medical care; others went simply to provide support. Brier's assistant, Annette Cruz, accompanied a Hatzolah ambulance driver when it came time to bring Brier home; Aschkenasy would again be airlifted by helicopter, to New York University Medical Center.

Thinking about who could manage Maimonides right then, Payson turned to Fraidkin, hospital chief of staff, a nurse by training who had become personal manager for the hospital's physicians and who had been a favorite of Brezenoff. Fraidkin had been at Maimonides for more than twenty years and had everyone's respect. (No one would dare to disrespect her; Fraidkin knew where all the bodies were buried.) Still fabulous at sixty-something, she was known for her ability to get things done, her toughness, her streetwise swagger, her love of riding Harley-Davidsons in leather chaps, her cadre of loyal physicians.

Fraidkin had been shaking things up at Maimonides from the moment she got there. She found conditions at the Brooklyn hospital to be about a decade behind the Manhattan hospitals; she had previously worked at Beth Israel. To convince the board that the staff had no idea how to deal with an emergency cardiac arrest, she started doing mock codes, filming the physicians' and nurses' responses. She had put a dummy equipped to simulate human response in a room, called a Code-3, and videotaped the reaction of the medical staff.

She took the evidence to the department chairs and said, "Your physicians are killing our patients." Within a few months of arriving at Maimonides, Fraidkin had forced mandatory CPR courses on doctors and nurses, reorganized the operating-room schedule so half of them were no longer sitting idle during lunch break, and made sure the surgeons, nurses, and anesthesiologists got to the OR on time. They couldn't lie to her. She was at the hospital by 6:30 A.M., her presence marked by her silver Infiniti sports car, always parked in the same space. By 6:35 it wasn't unusual to find a physician in her office, wheedling and cajoling. Cunningham dryly referred to her as their "mommy."

Fraidkin, born Lilia Maria Escobar, was of Puerto Rican descent, having become Jewish and a Fraidkin via a marriage that ended after twenty-five years. (She said she stopped using Lilia because "gringos" always mispronounced it.) She wore three-inch heels and short skirts that emphasized her famous (at Maimonides) legs. She was loyal to her physicians and, as she put it, had no trouble boxing their ears when she thought it was necessary.

Brezenoff recognized Fraidkin's talents; when he and Brier took charge, Fraidkin became chief of staff. She was also given the task of outreach, beginning in Bay Ridge, an Italian and Irish enclave that viewed Maimonides as "the Jewish hospital." Fraidkin joined organizations, went to community meetings, ate unidentifiable food at banquets, and froze to death watching endless parades with local politicians.

When she discovered that nearby Lutheran Hospital, a major competitor, won Italian patients not just by attending the Ragamuffin Parade—an annual costume parade for kids in Bay Ridge—but by entering a float, she went to Brezenoff. "I want a Maimonides float. I want it to be the *Wizard of Oz*."

"I'll pay for it if you'll be the witch," he replied. Thus began a tradition: Fraidkin as bad guy. The Wicked Witch of the West one year, Cruella de Vil the next. It was a role she relished. More than once, Brier told Fraidkin she was scared of her. Everyone knew that it was not wise to cross Lili.

Payson also relied on Joe Cunningham, Dr. Cowboy Boots, the Hemingway man. In recent years new nonsurgical procedures had taken the shine off cardiac surgery, and this, along with personal problems, had in turn taken their toll on Cunningham. But he remained a powerful force, not least because he had won Payson's loyalty.

Cunningham and Fraidkin were old friends; they had arrived at the hospital around the same time, in the early eighties. They had both thrived under Brezenoff's leadership. Brier and Cunningham, on the other hand, were not natural allies. He found her quirkiness irritating and thought she was a snob. Now, Stanley Brezenoff, he would say, Stanley had a "presidential air," whereas he described Brier as a "micromanager." Brezenoff was someone he could relate to—and Brezenoff admired him as well. They recognized in each other a particular catalytic force; they were alpha males. As for Brier, her feelings were complicated: appreciating Cunningham's history with the hospital, cognizant of the loyalty Payson felt was owed him, but wary of the old-boy network he represented. Now she would have to add gratitude to an already thick gumbo of feeling.

In Albany, however, she was a patient, not a hospital administrator, and Cunningham was by her side. Whether he was there as a friend or to take charge of the hospital that had become part of his identity would later be a matter of speculation. But what Brier subsequently remembered from the painkiller fog that sheltered her the first days in the intensive care unit was a critical conversation with Cunningham. She asked him whether her husband was going to live (the answer was yes) and whether he was going to walk again (the answer was maybe, probably). From then on, no matter what her frustrations with Cunningham, she would remember that he had provided comfort for her, in the way she needed, at a crucial time.

Brier refused to be treated as an invalid. For the first several weeks after the accident, Hatzolah medics took her to work and back home by ambulance because she couldn't get in and out of a car. For months she needed a wheelchair but insisted on having the Hatzolah driver park around the corner from the entrance so she would not have to be pushed through the front door. She would rather limp in on her own.

The effects of the accident would linger.

Two years later, when I was trying to convince the hospital's management to let me hang around, I met with Brier several times. The second of those early conversations took place in a hospital room at Maimonides. The patient was Brier, recovering from yet another round of surgery, this one a knee operation to repair damage from accident aftershocks. Her blond hair was carefully combed (she made weekly visits to the Tribeca branch of Privé, the Beverly Hills salon), the nails on her delicate hands were well manicured. She wore an Issey Miyake jacket over a pair of sweatpants. Despite the attempt at gloss, she seemed tiny and frail—a first impression she soon dispelled by issuing a series of quick orders to Lili Fraidkin, who had delivered me to the room.

I had already heard about Brier's idiosyncrasies. People remarked that Brezenoff's meetings were electric; Brier's were often chaotic. She would get up while someone was talking, walk to a cabinet, pull out a bag of popcorn, and pour it into bowls. Her gaze was always wandering, landing on curtains that were crooked, which would compel her to leave her chair to adjust them. "She cannot sit still for a full meeting," Fraidkin had told me. "At first when she gets up and straightens out the window shades we went, 'Oh, my God! This lady's nuts!' We just couldn't believe it."

As Brier talked to me from her hospital bed, it was obvious she recognized and enjoyed her own foibles. "I was in the hospital for back surgery and was doing rounds just for exercise," she told me. "Peter was with me. It's boring to go to the same floors, so we went to pediatrics. I was in my nightgown and came across a family there, really obnoxious, and the nurse very politely asking them to leave—I thought very politely, and the family was being very disrespectful. I went up to them and said, 'Excuse me.' And this person totally blew me off! And I said, 'Excuse me, I am the executive vice president of this hospital,' and Peter was saying, 'Not now, Pam,' but I ignored him and said to this family, 'You've been most impolite here, and I would like to see you listen to this nurse, and I would like you to go. Go now!' And they did."

She grinned as she remembered the spectacle. "I don't know what I thought, wearing my bathrobe, that I could draw myself up like a pooh-bah!"

Pooh-Bah. The character from *The Mikado* also known as Lord-High-Everything-Else. I would come to see this as vintage Brier, relishing the incongruous, invoking the light comic opera of Gilbert and Sullivan in Borough Park, the Orthodox Jewish heartland. Yet it was also no joke. She wanted to be a pooh-bah, defined by Webster's as "an official or leader who maintains full control."

Less than six weeks later, I saw her in full pooh-bah mode, at the official opening of the Maimonides Cancer Center, the same cancer center that had drawn Alan Astrow—and then me—to Brooklyn, Borough Park.

The opening was the kind of event that Brier approved of: a tasteful gathering attended by important people paying attention. A white party tent had been set up in the parking lot adjacent to the brand-new building—so new, in fact, that the first floor was still under construction.

For the opening she again wore clothes from her favorite designer, Issey Miyake, this time a yellow-gold jacket, worn over an orange Miyake dress. But she was quite different than she'd been the last time I'd seen her, when she appeared to be helpless, the way patients tend to appear, even those who are hospital presidents. Now she was wispy but authoritative, apparently comfortable in her role as chief executive of a large, complex institution. She surveyed the crowd of three hundred well-dressed people crammed together on folding chairs. One group had the side curls and beards required by Orthodox Judaism; nearby sat a Pakistani imam accompanied by a small entourage; a few seats away she could see the leader of the local Caribbean community and a Roman Catholic monsignor. Young men and women wearing doctors' jackets shivered in the unseasonably sharp wind. The sky above the tent was alternately cloudy and sunny.

Mayor Michael Bloomberg sat on a makeshift stage, wedged between a Brooklyn selectman and Martin Payson, the chairman of Maimonides. Bloomberg looked tired. He was running for reelection and would stay at the Maimonides opening for forty-five minutes. Before the mayor left, he listened politely to a series of speeches, glanced once at his PalmPilot, and gamely exchanged whispered jokes with Marty Markowitz, the exuberant borough president, who frequently and publicly expressed his desire to have Brooklyn secede from the City of New York. It was Markowitz who was responsible for the amusing highway signs about to appear on the Manhattan-bound side of the Williamsburg Bridge: LEAVING BROOKLYN—OY VEY.

Walking to the microphone with a hesitant, awkward gait, Brier presided over the proceedings with her official blend of hominess and hauteur. She spoke warmly of the public and private partnership that had allowed for the creation of the center but couldn't resist interrupting herself to scold a local politician who showed up late. Her patrician diction could have an imperious overtone, most pronounced when she thought people weren't behaving as she thought they should. "I know the mayor has to leave before the program is over to celebrate Cinco de Mayo in another part of the city," she said, peering at the crowd through narrow, black-rimmed glasses. "Not through lack of interest, I'm sure."

As she talked, she glanced for reassurance at a robust-looking man situated near the back of the tent, sitting in a wheelchair with a woman's Prada bag on his lap. He smiled and nodded. That was Peter Aschkenasy, her husband. He remained an amiable man—even though he would never regain full physical functioning after the accident—the kind who didn't mind holding his wife's pocketbook while she presided over important public business.

Brier acknowledged the $5 million that New York City had contributed to the center and then announced how the hospital was going to show its gratitude. "We are partners in a special effort to eliminate colon cancer in our borough," she said. "We are going to have free colon-cancer screening regardless of someone's ability to pay. And if someone has cancer, we can't say we won't treat you if you don't have money. So we promise to treat any citizen of Brooklyn who has colon cancer regardless of their ability to pay."

She was rewarded for this nod to community responsibility with applause. She did not discuss the distasteful aspects of this gesture of noblesse oblige. How would the hospital convince people to take advantage of the freebie, especially once they understood this wasn't simple, like getting a flu shot, but a time-consuming procedure that required a nasty prep.

"Thorough cleansing of the bowel is necessary before a colonoscopy," explained the National Digestive Diseases Information Clearinghouse (part of the National Institutes of Health) on its Web site, "You will likely be asked to take a laxative the night before the procedure. In some cases you may be asked to give yourself an enema." The helpful guide failed to mention that the "laxative" meant drinking a gallon of a foul-tasting liquid designed to induce massive diarrhea, but it continued, "The doctor will then insert a long, flexible, lighted tube into your rectum and slowly guide it into your colon."

Even for free it wasn't going to be an easy sell.

A good percentage of Brier's own senior staff hadn't had colonoscopies, which annoyed her. Okay, maybe you could excuse Robert Naldi, the chief financial officer, fifty-four years old, not a medical man. But the scofflaws also included Samuel Kopel, the hospital's medical director and an oncologist. He was almost sixty years old—a decade past the recommended age for a first-time colonoscopy—and still eluding the scope.

Pragmatism as well as altruism had led to the conclusion that Maimonides should open a cancer center. Cancer was a growth industry; the National Cancer Institute reported in 2005 that cancer treatment in the United States accounted for an estimated $72.1 billion in 2004, just under 5 percent of total U.S. spending for medical treatment, and an increase of 75 percent from 1995. The institute predicted that cancer costs would grow at a faster rate than overall medical expenditures.

In the health-care business, however, large investments were often made on predictions that turned out to be wrong. A few years earlier, Maimonides had spent more than $1 million each on two robots that could do complex surgery. The robots generated far more press than patients, and their costs weren't expected to be amortized anytime soon, probably never.

The cancer center required a much larger investment, about $12 million to build plus an additional $40 million commitment on a twenty-year lease. While Brier talked earnestly about the 2.5 million people in the borough of Brooklyn who didn't have a comprehensive cancer center, she knew that the numbers that really mattered were the people who lived in the zip codes surrounding the hospital. These weren't the hipsters of Williamsburg, the artists and musicians who could no longer afford the East Village, nor were they the aspiring burghers of Brooklyn Heights and Park Slope. Maimonides tended to treat new immigrants and the working middle class—except when they had cancer. The finance people had conducted a study and found that only 26 percent of the people in the surrounding area came to Maimonides doctors when they had cancer. Where did they go? Most of them went across the bridge to Manhattan.

The statistics were worse, from a financial viewpoint, when you broke them down. "As many as fifty percent of people who get cancer diagnosis in Brooklyn receive some part of treatment in Manhattan—and those tend to be the people with private insurance," said Kopel, the medical director. "If you're a woman in Park Slope or Brooklyn Heights and find a lump on your breast, chances are you're going to Manhattan for treatment. If you live somewhere else in Brooklyn and are from Bangladesh, you're more likely to come to us."

Like the Brooklyn clerk played by John Travolta in *Saturday Night Fever,* the hospital administrators understood that they were perceived as something less because they sat on the wrong side of the East River. Proving that the care at Maimonides was as good as that of the Manhattan hospitals was an institutional obsession. It wasn't unusual for people to cross the bridge for radiation treatments and chemotherapy but then end up in the Maimonides emergency room when it was time to die. The cancer center was created to convince enough people—especially those with good insurance—to stay in Brooklyn for treatment as well as death, and to trust that for most types of cancer Maimonides could offer results comparable to Memorial Sloan-Kettering or Columbia Presbyterian, leading lights in the field. None of the administrators at Maimonides believed they could keep everyone close to home, but they figured they could do better than 26 percent. They didn't need 75 percent for the finances to make sense, only 45 percent.

The cancer-center strategy was as much a dream as a plan, but that was enough. No one understood better than Brier that plans were mutable and that change could be slow and maddening or quick and catastrophic. She was almost sixty years old and had been maneuvering through the hospital world for twenty-five of those years. Compromise was part of the terrain. She also knew from personal experience that one misstep—in an operating room or in life—could destroy confidence and threaten everything she cared about in an instant.

More than almost anything, Brier believed in the rules of propriety. She tried to charm the Orthodox Hatzolah wives with her designer clothes, which she made sure were cut modestly, and with her willingness to come to their numerous luncheons honoring somebody or other. She accepted home-baked cheesecakes with lavish thanks (and then deposited the cakes on the snack table outside the ladies' room on the executive floor). She believed that hostility and rudeness among the doctors and staff would translate into diminished care for patients. More than once I would hear her say, "I don't care what they think so long as they behave properly. That's the *least* they can do."

Brier's preoccupation with process was another thing that drove Fraidkin crazy. "Stanley was a doer," Fraidkin said longingly of Brezenoff. "I've gone to all the retreats, sitting there for two days and dying because we're not moving, we're just sitting and coming up with the big vision. I can do that also. Do I like it? No. Get it out, spit it out, it doesn't take you two days to see where we have to go. But you do it, you put up with it."

In the middle of a meeting, Brier would pull her cell phone out of her pocketbook and make a call; a few minutes later, her assistant would appear with a freshly made cappuccino. During a telephone call with a fellow hospital president, she might make a truly odd pronouncement, like, "I want you to know I'm considered one of the great constipation experts in the borough of Brooklyn." When Brier got the point of a presentation—and her mind worked fast—she might cut the speaker off abruptly. On occasion she would realize a few minutes later what she had done and would apologize, in front of the group. Her manner could be taken as refreshing or annoying, amusing or distracting—and sometimes as cruel. Yet most people seemed to believe that her skills outweighed her oddities.

"Stanley was a brilliant administrator," Aaron Twerski told me. He was dean of the Hofstra law school, a prominent torts scholar, and a Maimonides board member. His poetic features—haunted dark eyes, long gray beard— seemed like a living rendition of Rembrandt's *Portrait of an Old Jew.*

Twerski continued, "He was a brilliant politician. She is not the consummate politician that Stanley was, but Pam has the courage of her convictions. Pam knows how to fire people.

He seemed to like the sound of this. "Pam knows how to fire," he repeated. "Pam is a better firer than Stan was."

On the other hand, she saw herself—and she was far from alone in her assessment—as a nurturer and friend of the underdog, a broad category that included anyone who might be despairing. She embraced the unions that represented the vast majority of Maimonides' 5,700 employees, and she was vehement in her support of the hospital's nurses. At Maimonides, as at Bellevue, she was known for walking the halls, stopping to chat with nurses, asking an aide why she wasn't wearing her name tag, picking up gum wrappers off the floor. When I visited her first husband, Steven Brier, at his office at the City University of New York, where he was an associate provost, he reminisced about one of the first stories he heard about his ex-wife, told by one of her aunts.

"When she was five years old and about to begin kindergarten, Pam urged her mother to go early," he said. "It occurred to her the parents of the kids would be coming to the school and they wouldn't know each other, and she thought it was important she be there to introduce the parents to one another. As I like to say about that story, the personality was formed early."

Pamela Sara Engel grew up in Los Angeles and was educated at UC Berkeley during the free-speech movement of the 1960s. Her political consciousness was awakened even as she followed the old-fashioned tradition of bagging a husband before she graduated. When they married, she was twenty-one and Steven Brier was twenty years old. Her father was a peripatetic businessman who left her and her mother when Pam was thirteen; his father was a fur worker and a union man. When they married, Steven Brier recalled his father telling him, "'Stevie, you're about to make the same mistake I did. You're about to marry a petit bourgeois.' I told this to Pam, and her response was, 'Not so petit!' She was insulted by the 'petit'!"

Brier had gone east in her twenties because Steven got a job in New York. It was a difficult move, but she survived and eventually rose through the city's public-health system, the New York City Health and Hospitals Corporation (HHC), to become a powerful bureaucrat, worthy of gossip and speculation. Brezenoff had been her mentor.

Her aspirations were large, but not grandiose. She had no illusions that she had the answer to the problems of health care in the United States. When I asked her for a solution, she gave me a withering look. "Well, if I knew that, I guess I'd be a candidate for the Nobel Prize, wouldn't I?"

When Brier had her first face-to-face encounter with Maimonides, she was almost fifty years old, divorced from Steve Brier, her husband of twenty-six years, and dating the man who would become her second husband. Her only child was grown.

"I'll never forget the first time I saw Maimonides," she told me. "It was a March day. I had just accepted the job. Peter took me for a tour of Borough

Park and the hospital. We drove around Tenth Avenue, and my heart sank because it looked so unattractive on this very cold March day. No flowers, no trees, no nothing. And there used to be another overpass, which we finally took down, which was so ugly it just took your breath away."

One day I imagined what it must have been like for her when she first confronted the hospital's ungainly physical plant and the unusual surrounding neighborhood. I was approaching the main entrance at Tenth Avenue and Forty-eighth Street and had to circumvent a crowd of chattering elementary-school boys as they gathered on the sidewalk. At first glance they looked like any group of little boys, but then I noticed their side curls blowing in the breeze. The children attended Yeshiva Kehilath Yakov Pupa, the Jewish school housed in an old brick building across the street; the Maimonides boardroom on the top floor of the five-story administration building had a view of the school's rooftop playground. A tall, skinny Hasid in a black coat and big hat—style, Poland circa 1850—walked alongside the little boys as they formed a line, each placing one hand on the shoulder of the boy in front of him. As they began to march down the street—make way for *Yiddishe* ducklings—the lone adult appeared to be clutching the side of his head. Closer inspection revealed a cell phone in his grasp. Maybe the coming of the Messiah would be heralded by a text message.

The main campus stood about one mile northeast of the cancer center, but in Brooklyn a twenty-minute walk can feel like a trek across a cultural continental divide. A block from the cancer center on Eighth Avenue was a world of Chinese street vendors selling steaming noodles from carts, the noodles doused liberally with fragrant sauces poured from unlabeled bottles— a dollar a serving. Women and men selling piles of bok choy could gather a crowd, and it was common on sunny days to see skinny old ladies shading themselves under open umbrellas. This was no tourist Chinatown, but a crowded neighborhood shopping strip, where almost all traces of the Scandinavian residents of a generation earlier had been replaced by Chinese shops and stands selling fruit and fish, bubble tea and sweet buns, bargain cosmetics and herbal cures.

The cancer center had been carved out of 6300 Eighth Avenue, previously a long, almost-windowless two-story building on the periphery of Chinatown, just across the street from an auto-body shop (Bay Ridge Body

Shop/Service and Parts Department). Before the renovation, which required a massive excavation of the parking lot for the underground radiation vault, the building had a hunkered-down look, appropriate to its original incarnation as a Citibank check-processing center. In 1995, Citibank sold this drab relic of brutalist architecture to the Health Insurance Plan of New York (HIP), another faceless enterprise. The transformation wasn't complete, but at least now there were some inviting windows, and the inside—at least the parts that had been renovated—was airy and serene, in accordance with the recommendations of a feng shui consultant.

The hospital itself, however, where David Gregorius would begin his life as a physician, had an aesthetic that seemed mired in the middle of the twentieth century. While the Maimonides Web site featured a sleek glass structure, this was merely a virtual rendering of the new wing that was being built across from the emergency room on Fort Hamilton Parkway. At the time of the cancer center's opening, the actual "building" was a mass of girders and heavy equipment, mud and cement. When Pam Brier had been hired a decade earlier, the new wing didn't exist even in theory. Like many hospitals built in urban areas with limited land, the hospital was a jumble of buildings and architectural styles, add-ons and renovations, with the two main buildings connected by an overpass. Many department chiefs and administrators worked out of the two-story brick row houses—inexplicably referred to as "brownstones"—that lined the streets surrounding the hospital.

When Brier first confronted her dowdy new workplace, she recalled an earlier first, her first day as a hospital administrator, at Jacobi Medical Center, a public hospital in the Bronx. She had had knots in her stomach when she walked through the door and realized she knew nothing about running a hospital. She knew about health-care policy, finance, and government oversight from the decade she'd spent at HHC. But she'd never been a field commander, never directly in the line of fire.

She decided to treat her willingness to admit ignorance as strength. "The first thing I did when I got to Jacobi was walk around and shake hands with every person who was there, and the second thing was take almost every single doctor out to lunch or dinner with a paper and pencil and take notes," she said. "When I got to Jacobi, I felt like I was playing dress-up, very scary, very sobering. I made them put a sign up that showed the way to the director's office. The secretary didn't want to. She said, 'They'll come and bother us.' I said, 'That's all right.'"

Some found her methods disarming; others were dismissive. Steve Davidson, the ER chairman at Maimonides, had been hired shortly before Brier was. In advance of meeting his new boss, he called a physician friend who had worked with her at Jacobi for an assessment. "He said send her pretty flowers every month and send her a nice silk scarf twice a year," said Davidson. "Neither of which I've done since I got here."

Allan Strongwater, former chief of orthopedics for a decade, left Maimonides for the NYU Hospital for Joint Diseases in Manhattan a few months after the cancer center opened, after many disagreements with Brier over how his department should be run and over fees. "She would like her hospital to be the model for public health," he said. "Look at her history. That's where she grew up." The dispute, he said, was personal. "Most of the people in hospital administration, including Pam, want to deliver good-quality care and be in the black. The difference is, Stanley [Brezenoff] once told me he didn't want to be in the front of the crowd or in the back of the crowd—he wanted to be in the middle. He didn't want to be visible. Whereas Pam, it's all about Pam."

After Jacobi, Brier was put in charge of Bellevue—unwieldy, impossible Bellevue—the city's own Bedlam, best known for its infamous psychiatric ward. "They'd had ten directors in ten years, and I can assure you they were not glad to see me," Brier said. "Just the scale of it and the pitch of it make you feel like an ant." Jacobi felt bucolic next to Bellevue. "There were these huge plants in the back of the lobby, and they were dead, listing to one side. I thought, Oh, my God, what have I done. What are people going to think? You can't keep the plants alive, what are they going to do to the patients?" She bought new plants, listened to complaints, and ten months into her tenure was featured in an approving article in the *New York Times* that declared, "She has proved to be a rarity in New York City's municipal hospital system: an administrator who earns praise from such historical antagonists as the unions, medical schools and the city administration."

She stayed three years—record-making for a Bellevue administrator—but was ready to leave when Brezenoff asked her to come with him to Maimonides Medical Center as his number two.

"My friends said, 'You're going where to do what?'" she recalled. "'You're

going to be the number-two person where?'" Tired of city politics and assured
that she would be Brezenoff's likely successor, she went. The doubling of her
salary eased the transition. Within a decade at Maimonides, her annual income
had reached $850,000, including bonuses, a heady amount for a former public
servant, whose conscience was salved by telling herself it wasn't *that* much compared to the $2.5 million Memorial Sloan-Kettering paid its chief executive or
the $1.5 million that Montefiore in the Bronx paid her counterpart there.

What she found in Brooklyn was not the exhilarating chaos of Bellevue, the
rush reminiscent of the sixties, the feeling she was helping society's outcasts,
doing God-or-whoever's work. Instead she walked into a grim, unfriendly
atmosphere where things were done the way they had always been done, where
insularity ruled, and where a whole new set of politics had to be mastered,
including that of a strong Hasidic community with its own idea of what God's
work meant. The head nurse had an M.B.A. and dressed the part. She didn't
know what to make of Brier, who wore designer clothes but sometimes used a
shopping bag as a briefcase and liked to drop into the emergency room for surprise visits at midnight. The hospital board's members were fighting among
themselves, and there was hostility between the core Orthodox Jewish constituency and the nurses, many of whom were Caribbean and African-
American. Shortly after Brezenoff and Brier arrived, the nurses went on strike.

"It made Bellevue seem friendly, which, believe me, Bellevue wasn't," she
said. "In your brighter moments, you could say there are so many things to
work on, and in your dark moments . . . oh, dear." Brier fired the head nurse
and another senior nurse because she felt they weren't doing their jobs.
Brezenoff protested, not on the merits but because he believed that loyalty
counted for something, and then let Brier have her way.

"I think appearance is very tricky with my mother," Jenny Brier once
said. "Some people look at her and think she's a twig. But she's a big trunk in
a twig's body."

At the cancer center opening, many politicians offered speeches and boiler-
plate congratulations. The affair took a distinctly human turn when
Steven H. Cymbrowitz, a New York State assemblyman, approached the
microphone.

A boxy man with thin hair that was greased and combed back, he was well cast as a local pol. His voice sounded uncertain, but his message was strong as he brought home why it was important to have a multidisciplinary, one-stop-shopping approach to patient management. He spoke of his wife, Lena, a Democratic state assemblywoman, who had been diagnosed with stage-four colon cancer a few years before by a doctor at Maimonides but then was treated at New York University Hospital. He described the arduous experience of Brooklyn cancer patients who are treated in Manhattan and who keep their records in their cars as they move from office to office, doctor to doctor. Cymbrowitz told of the night when there wasn't room at NYU for a CAT scan and of his agony as he watched his wife being wheeled across Thirty-fourth Street in a gurney, while he stopped traffic. After she died, at the age of forty-three, Cymbrowitz was elected to her seat in the assembly and helped obtain the city's $5 million contribution to the cancer center. "To make sure there was something to come out of Lena's passing," as he put it.

He had another personal tie to the hospital, which he didn't discuss. Two months earlier he had gone to the front door to pick up the newspaper and found he couldn't reach the knob. When the ambulance brought him to Maimonides, he was paralyzed and couldn't speak. The hospital's neurologists dissolved the clot in his brain in time, leaving only a slight weakness in his left hand as a souvenir of the frightening episode.

As he stood before the crowd at the cancer center's opening, Cymbrowitz was struck simultaneously by three emotions—the sadness he always felt when he spoke of his wife's death, his loyalty to the doctors who had saved his life, and anger at Pam Brier. She had called him earlier and had the nerve to tell him not to mention Lena. "We'll have a naming ceremony," she told him. "This isn't the place."

It made Cymbrowitz furious just to think about it. After all the work he had done to put together the government money, Brier was trying to change the rules as he perceived them. He didn't think he was unreasonable. Taking Lena's name off the building—that he could understand; the hospital wanted it to be the Maimonides Cancer Center. He agreed to settle on a bust of Lena in the lobby, which would be called the Lena Cymbrowitz Pavilion. Now he was worried that even that might go. He had heard that Brier had been trying to raise private money for the cancer center; the hospital had no endowment like the big academic hospitals. Was the honor just going to go to the highest bidder? "With Stanley this wouldn't have happened," he remembered thinking. "Stanley didn't let anything fall through the cracks."

Whatever else people may have thought about Pam Brier, she possessed remarkable physical courage that commanded special respect in a hospital. Her most recent surgery—a knee replacement—had taken place a month before the opening. The trunk in the twig's body seemed to be made of iron.

But the last twenty months had caused her to doubt her abilities. An essential insecurity underlay the bravado, the royal gestures, the wackiness. Could she carry on what she and Brezenoff had started? So much to do, to fix, to build, to prove.

The cancer center's opening felt like a turning point. For the first time since the accident, she thought maybe she could keep pace with her ambitions. "Following Stanley was one of the worst things I ever did," she said once. "Truly revolting. He's the most brilliant public servant I've ever watched."

Then she gave a sharp crazy laugh, as if she realized the absurdity of . . . maybe everything. "That was my biggest worry," she said, and then laughed again. "Hah! Could I live up to Stanley!"

Three

_____

Insults and Injuries

Douglas Jablon, vice president, patient relations—the Mitzvah Man—said that gossip was the hospital's most vicious enemy. "That's why God gave you teeth," he said, "the cage to hold in the serpent tongue."

Political intrigue and turf wars were not unique to Maimonides; struggles for space, equipment, staff, and money are part of hospital life. "It's big business," said Allan Strongwater, former chair of orthopedics. "Big business with HMOs, big business with insurance companies, big business with the government—big big business. So even though you and I are colleagues as physicians, you are cutting into my market share. Naturally I think I'm doing a better job and should be paid more. If I send a patient to a doctor for a second opinion and he says, 'It's not that difficult, anyone could do that,' you as a patient don't know. There is this underlying competition for patients and that's why you get these battles."

Steven Konstadt, the chair of anesthesiology, who had been recruited from Mount Sinai a year earlier, paraphrased Oscar Wilde: "The joke at Sinai was, you can always tell your friends because they stab you in the front."

At Maimonides, however, feuds had become part of the personality, the hospital's yin and yang, nurtured in a familial atmosphere that promoted the idea of unconditional love and tolerance and acceptance, then erupted in fury when conditions, standards, and limits were imposed. Birthdays were celebrated and hurts were sustained with equal tenderness. When a surgeon was diagnosed with leukemia and left abruptly for home without telling anyone, everyone knew anyway by the end of the day. Within twenty-four hours, the physician's assistants in his department had offered to give him their sick time for the year. But when they called Lili Fraidkin to make the offer, she told them the offer was unnecessary; the senior staff had already donated enough sick-leave time to cover a year's pay, enough time for the doctor to finish his treatment.

Just as kindness was dispensed without hesitation, so were complaints and disappointments aired—with the expectation that someone would listen. Injuries weren't required to instigate insult.

"We are like a family," said Carol Kidney, nursing director of obstetrics, in her robust Irish brogue. "Johnny broke the window and everyone knows it and ten years later they remember that Johnny broke *two* windows. Everything that happens here becomes the talk of the community. We're integral to the community. It's like a small town in Ireland. It's like living in a frontier town a hundred years ago."

Mark McDougle, who came to the hospital to be Brier's number two, the chief operating officer, less than two years earlier, had been taken aback by this aspect of the Maimonides gestalt. "My issue with all this, I don't know if it's right or not, too much is taken as personal," he told me. "I guess being a midwesterner, it's easy for me to say that. Too much is taken as personal."

"It's like the Cymbrowitz thing," he said. "I can give you his side and I can give you Pam's side. Steve—his wife died of cancer. That's a personal thing. I think he had a notion of what we were going to name and how we were going to do it, a thought that was different from Pam's. So you had this misunderstanding. There was a misunderstanding, he should let it go."

Feuds were literally built into the foundation: The hospital's two main buildings—the Abraham Gellman Wing and the Benjamin and Betty Eisenstadt Memorial Pavilion, connected by an overpass over Tenth Avenue—were reminders of a bitter family quarrel. The benefactor, Benjamin Eisenstadt, made a fortune through his invention of sugar packets and of the artificial sweetener Sweet'N Low; Gellman was named for Betty Eisenstadt's beloved brother Abraham, a trauma surgeon who enlisted in the army during World War II and died in combat at the age of twenty-eight. His picture, showing a full-faced young man in uniform, smiling with his mouth closed, was displayed along with his Purple Heart in a display case in the lobby, with an inscription that began: "He gave his life so others might live." The memorial represented Benjamin Eisenstadt's legacy of philanthropy and family feeling—but not all his feelings about family. The business that made the hospital pavilions possible was also the subject of a blood feud that lasted forty years; Eisenstadt disinherited one of his daughters. (His grandson Rich Cohen recounted the tale in sad, often hilarious detail in *Sweet and Low,* published in the spring of 2006.)

Even Maimonides himself (Rabbi Moses ben Maimon, aka Rambam), the revered philosopher and physician for whom the hospital was named, had been attacked as an instigator and fomenter, for having the nerve to inject Aristotelian reason and logic into religious discussion. Abraham Heschel, in his classic biography, describes the hostile reaction provoked by the Rambam's teachings: "Just as quickly as reports of Maimonides' renown spread through the world, seeds of suspicion and misunderstanding also sprouted," wrote Heschel. "His opponents used their imaginations to spawn all kinds of reasons for rejecting and condemning" Maimonides' interpretation of Jewish law.

Stephen J. Lahey, another new chief, had been recruited from UMass Memorial Health Care, a large nonprofit healthcare system in central and western Massachusetts, and the University of Massachusetts Medical School. Boston bred, formerly a professor at Harvard Medical School, he had a noticeable Boston accent and an office full of Red Sox memorabilia. He was part of a delicate transition, replacing Cunningham as the head of cardiothoracic surgery while the hospital nudged the older doctor into a senior-statesman role, head of strategic planning. (Cunningham remained chief of surgery.) Lahey's mandate from Brier was to improve not just medical practice but behavior among the physicians. "The intensity of the emotions was way more than I thought it would be," he told me. "I'm dealing with the toughest thing in the world. Not changing atrial fibrillation but changing the way people think. That's a zillion times harder to do. To change a procedure I can issue an edict. But I want them to look at these changes as change in the way we think. We're going to think logically and collaboratively and that's not the way health care works in Brooklyn. It's rough-and-tumble. There are some pretty tough hombres here."

It didn't take long for me to hear about the two biggest fights in the hospital, both of them involving major players. One long-standing battle involved none other than Joe Cunningham, venerable chair of surgery, and his former medical partner, Israel Jacobowitz. Everyone referred to Jacobowitz as Izzy but Lili Fraidkin told me to be sure to call him Israel. He didn't like Izzy. The other feud—Kopel v. Bashevkin—was the one to watch, I was told, because it was already affecting the start-up of the new cancer center. I would quickly learn how.

In mid-September, Alan Astrow, who had unwittingly lured me to Maimonides, and who by then had been the chief of hematologic oncology for six months, invited me to the first of what he hoped would be weekly interdisciplinary meetings. In this team approach, doctors from different disciplines considered whether the cancer under scrutiny would be best treated through surgery, chemotherapy, radiation, or some combination. The practice was not new to Astrow; he had begun attending discussions like this as a resident at Boston City Hospital, now merged into Boston Medical Center, more than twenty years earlier. But this was the first such gathering at the Maimonides Cancer Center, which was still under construction four months after the official opening.

The radiation-oncology floor in the basement had been open since May, though not many patients seemed to have noticed. The office spaces were sleek but not cold—wooden furniture, earth tones, and fish tanks. The hospital had invested $5 million in a linear accelerator for radiation therapy and the subterranean fortress needed to house it—a room that was surrounded by several-foot-thick concrete walls covered by several hundred thousand pounds of lead, plus plastic impregnated with boron to absorb radiation. Yet, despite the absence of windows, the feng shui consultants and architects had dispelled any sensation of being in a bunker. It was a pleasant place to face the prospect of life and death.

The small conference room quickly became crowded with about twenty representatives from the departments of hematology and radiology, a surgeon, and several young doctors enrolled in the hematologic-oncology fellowship program. They discussed a variety of cases: two patients with leukemia, one a forty-three-year-old man from Turkey and the other a twenty-five-year-old from Mexico. There was a forty-two-year-old African American woman with a brain tumor causing excruciating headaches, and a forty-year-old white man with lung cancer. Bernadine Donahue, the brilliant radiation oncologist recruited from New York University Hospital, a dark-haired woman in her forties, with milky skin and a soothing, husky voice, rattled off several studies in response to each case. Matching wits with Donahue, study for study, was Yiwu Huang, a hematologic oncologist who looked like a schoolboy and spoke English with a heavy Chinese accent. Huang, who had trained at Robert Wood Johnson, carried a library of medical information in a small portable hard drive that had become like an extra limb on his thin frame. Amit Schwartz, a self-assured young neurosurgeon, explained with exaggerated patience how he would approach the case. The oncology fellows, whose medical training represented India, Pakistan, South Africa, Russia, the Caribbean—and yes, the United States—were quizzed by the experienced doctors.

I sat next to Samuel Kopel, the medical director, whom I had met briefly but hadn't yet seen in action. Kopel was also a hematologic oncologist; he and his former partners had run the hospital's faculty practice for many years. He seemed to be enjoying the colloquy, offering examples from his long history with patients, interjecting proverbs in fluent Italian. He was a formidable figure—balding, lean, and tall. His precise diction implied authority; his intense alertness indicated wariness. I would learn that both the slightly stilted manner of speaking and watchfulness were residues of his ruptured childhood. Born somewhere in Europe (he didn't know the place) in 1946 (there was no record of his birth), he lived with his family in a refugee camp in Germany until he was eleven years old. I had first seen him at the cancer center's opening, where Brier had singled him out as the person responsible for its creation. I wondered why he hadn't been invited to sit onstage. My interest deepened when I overheard someone whispering that Kopel's wife was quite sick—an advanced case of ovarian cancer.

When the discussion was over, I looked for Astrow. I found him deep in conversation with a gray-bearded middle-aged man wearing a yarmulke who had sat quietly during the conference. I overheard the words "Talmud" and "anger." Astrow spoke in a conciliatory manner, but the man he was talking to seemed too distressed to listen.

That was my introduction to Michael Bashevkin, Kopel's former medical partner, protégé, and friend—more than a friend, close enough to have once bought Kopel a piano, a gift that seemed both intimate and extravagant. Bashevkin's current partners included two other Kopel protégés, including a cousin of his and a friend who was close enough to sign the *ketubah,* the Jewish marriage contract, of Kopel's daughter when she got married.

Kopel and Bashevkin ignored each other during the conference, as usual. Bashevkin and the two others had split up with Kopel five years earlier but had continued to share the same office space for two years. They tried to avoid each other in the corridors. But the corridors were narrow.

The Bashevkin-Kopel fight never fully made sense to me, no matter how many people I asked about it, including the participants. Recollections were clouded by self-interest and the passage of time.

"Let me put it to you this way," said Sharon Kopel, Sam Kopel's wife, so weakened by cancer when we talked that she could barely sit up, but still able to muster lively indignation. "People who were supposed to be honorable weren't."

"It was personal," said Michael Bashevkin. "It didn't have to do with our greed. We felt we were treated like chattel."

"It was absolutely money," said Sam Kopel. "Yes! Oh yes. I don't think it, they said it."

"Bashevkin is a stubborn man," said Stanley Brezenoff, who tried to broker a peace and managed to make it worse. "He's not a bad guy but he's a stubborn man. And Sam [Kopel] is a stubborn man."

By the time I talked to Brezenoff, those negotiations were part of a vague memory for him. He was at a bigger place with bigger problems, and besides, he was a master deflector. "Honestly," he said, "all the cancer center at Maimonides needs is a surgical star or two, and that changes everything. Patients come to the surgeons. Remember, you don't need everyone, just a certain percentage to make it viable."

By then he was ensconced at Continuum headquarters on the nineteenth floor of a high-rise building on the West Side of Manhattan, with grand views of the working piers on the Hudson River.

He smiled slightly as he talked about the quarrels at Maimonides. "I spent a lot of time on that feud," he said when I asked him about Bashevkin and Kopel, but then he quickly demurred. "I can't remember all the details of it."

It *was* generally agreed that the fight involved neither charlatans nor thieves, but rather respected oncologists considered to be good and caring doctors and decent men, whose bad behavior was hot-linked to self-righteousness and pigheadedness—to being human—not chicanery.

This quarrel between former partners, between a mentor and his students, between cousins and friends, was petty perhaps, but it was no minor rift. Kopel, as medical director and driving force behind the cancer center, represented the institution. The Bashevkin group's hematologic-oncology practice covered a substantial portion of Maimonides cancer patients. The hospital relied on private practitioners like Bashevkin and his partners to keep the beds full.

The breakup began when Maimonides, at Kopel's urging, began seriously exploring the possibility of building a cancer center. By that time, in the late 1990s, Kopel had become medical director but was still in partnership with Bashevkin.

Dr. Bernard Salick had become interested, and that was significant. Salick, an entrepreneurial physician who grew up on the Lower East Side of Manhattan, had moved to California and opened a national chain of cancer clinics, including the one at St. Vincent's, Alan Astrow's former hospital in Manhattan. All Bashevkin recalled of the Salick episode, however, was "a very insulting meeting" with Brezenoff at which he and the other partners—besides Kopel—were asked to articulate their terms to participate. They asked the hospital president for an amount of money he dismissed—in a letter—as "totally outrageous." Bashevkin said he was offended by Brezenoff's response and, even more, by how it was delivered.

Kopel, on the other hand, felt his former partners were greedy.

The Salick talks fell apart. "Bernie would show up and be dazzling and very Bernie-like and talk about how he was a street kid from New York and Stanley's soul mate and a few other things, but we couldn't figure out how to do a deal that left us with a modicum of something and not turn it all over to them," Pam Brier recalled. "So we moved on."

But Kopel, Bashevkin, and their other partners were not able to move on. Their split was final, and it would have ongoing repercussions for the hospital.

How specifically? Kopel had helped to convince Jay Cooper, a renowned radiation therapist, to come to Brooklyn after Cooper's twenty-seven-year career at New York University ended on a sour note. Cooper brought along a team—including Bernadine Donahue—with strong credentials and reputations. In addition, there was the $5 million price tag for the linear accelerator

and its accommodations. The expenditure was rationalized by the understanding that radiation would be the economic engine of the cancer center;
reimbursements for radiation therapy were far more lucrative than those for
chemotherapy. But without patients, there would be no reimbursements,
and radiation cases came through referrals.

Referrals came from other doctors—primary care physicians, oncologists,
or surgeons. Patients never knew whether referrals were based on an assessment of competence and results, or on relationships. Cooperation among
clinicians, I was learning, was a deceptively simple concept. Hospitals were
interlocking systems. Just as medications produced harmful side effects as
well as cures, notions of progress resulted in distrust and anger as well as a
sense of hope. Insurance companies paid for procedures, not bedside manner, but when it came time for one doctor to refer to another, personality
often mattered as much as (and often more than) ability.

After the new cancer center opened, the Bashevkin group referred only a
handful of patients to the radiation group. And it hurt. Business was slow.

Bill Camilleri, who had been hired by Brezenoff to build the cancer
center—six weeks before Brezenoff announced he was leaving—described
the Bashevkin-Kopel battle like this: "It's a great cultural feud," he said. "In
my inappropriate way I compare it to why there will never be peace in the
Middle East. To work with doctors who walk around believing that if one of
them gets struck by lightning it's the other one's fault, it's shocking."

Not so shocking, considering Camilleri had his own private, internal
feud simmering with Pam Brier. She hadn't been consulted when Brezenoff
hired him, and Camilleri believed she simply did not like him. He thought
she was high-handed and egocentric. He couldn't get over the fact she had
chosen May 4 as the day for the cancer center's opening, and had locked in
the mayor and other politicians, knowing that Jay Cooper, the director of the
center, had a conference in Barcelona the day before and would have to
scramble to get back in time.

Even worse, in Camilleri's view, Brier had never recognized the coup he
had pulled off just getting the place built. When he'd arrived in March 2003,
the hospital had a vague agreement with Health Insurance Plan of New York
(HIP), the occupants of the Chinatown building that would become the
cancer center. There was no written plan, no lease, no drawings—and a

structure that would have to be completely overhauled. By being a bulldog in negotiations with the landlord, with contractors, with everyone, Camilleri reached the deadline. The new cancer center was ready in less than two years.

The achievement was all the more heroic—or foolhardy—considering his health. He had been a "blue baby," born with tetralogy of Fallot, a congenital, life-threatening heart defect. His parents were told he would live a year, but he tricked the odds and survived. At twelve he had open-heart surgery; in 1969, as a teenager, he had a pacemaker implanted in his chest. Short, bearded, and chubby, always panting a bit, he seemed bent on defying his heart's weakness; he kept jars of M&M's, pistachios, and Pepperidge Farm Goldfish cheddar crackers on his desk, and he worked from early morning until late at night.

Now that the center was built, Camilleri's job was to create a serene, efficient, and friendly atmosphere that would help take the edge off cancer, not the deadliest but perhaps the most dreaded diagnosis. He knew what it meant to be deathly ill. He believed he was running the most important program in the hospital, and yet he had never had a one-to-one meeting with the president. That rankled.

Sondra Olendorf, the head of nursing and hospital operations, remembered being surprised when she first met Camilleri. "Stan met him—no one else had—and hired him on the spot," she said. "He didn't match anyone's physical view of what we thought the administrator of the cancer center would be. It's horrible to say, but true. I think Stan was compelled by what Bill had overcome in life. Bill wasn't expected to live after a year of his birth. When Stan heard that story and saw what this guy had done, clawing and kicking and fighting his way through life and love and work, he figured this was a guy who would claw his way to success here."

When Daniel Sulmasy heard about the political situation at Maimonides, he understood why the hospital administration would be interested in hiring his friend Alan Astrow to become chief of hematologic oncology at the new cancer center there. "He's a calming influence," he told me. "I couldn't imagine Alan screaming or stamping his feet in a temper tantrum or throwing over an IV pole in a fit of anger at a nurse—that's not his style. He can listen to people attentively, make a reasonable judgment, let people think their case has been heard."

There had been full disclosure; in an early interview, the chair of medicine had told Astrow about the Bashevkin-Kopel feud, and how it might affect the cancer center. Hiring Astrow made sense for Maimonides but, Sulmasy wondered, did the move make sense for his friend? Astrow had a thriving practice at St. Vincent's in Manhattan and a warm feeling for the Catholic hospital where he had spent most of his career. When the morning recitation of the Lord's Prayer came crackling over the loudspeaker, Astrow actually listened, taking the Christian prayer ("*Forgive us our sins as we forgive those who sin against us*") as a daily reminder to be humble. Life was comfortable. He had the freedom to organize his conferences on spirituality and healing and to teach. He had enjoyable and satisfying relationships with his group of nurses and physicians' assistants. On nice days he rode his bicycle from his apartment on the Upper West Side, down the bike bath along the Hudson River, and over to St. Vincent's, which was surrounded by streets full of interesting restaurants conducive to long discussions and debate.

I saw what he was giving up when I visited Sulmasy in the old wing of St. Vincent's; the old-fashioned main hall had the hushed feeling of a monastery. Astrow had told me he wasn't that worried about losing the amenities. It was the loss of a whole history of relations. "Suppose I'd forgotten to call a doctor I'd done a consult for," he said. "At St. Vincent's, I had a whole history of giving good service, a wellspring of goodwill I'd built up over twenty years. If you've done things for people you know and like they'll cut you some slack. If you lose your temper or don't say the right thing, they'll know it wasn't quite you. At a new place, everyone is sizing you up."

Sulmasy told me his concerns for Astrow had to do with the job itself. Sulmasy was a clean-cut, handsome man who appreciated fine food and appeared to choose his wardrobe carefully. But he was consumed by higher callings. He was a Franciscan friar and chair of the bioethics committee at St. Vincent's, and he couldn't understand why a thoughtful, sensitive person like Astrow would want to become an administrator in any hospital. "One of the problems of being a leader of a section or a department in medicine these days, so much of it is running a business," he told me. "It's about cash flow, marketing to communities, coming up with gimmicks to get patients in. It almost sickens me in terms of what medicine should be about, part of that medical-industrial complex. I have no interest. I was worried in some ways about Alan pursuing that."

Sulmasy was a seeker. He had trained as a physician at Weill Medical College of Cornell University, done a fellowship in internal medicine at Johns Hopkins Hospital, and then completed a Ph.D. in philosophy at Georgetown. He thought of Astrow as a companion intellectual and a genuine healer. On the day Sulmasy arrived at St. Vincent's, seven years earlier, in 1998, Astrow was conducting a symposium called "Spirituality, Religious Wisdom, and the Care of the Patient," where scholars from different religions spoke to physicians, nurses, and social workers about the role of religion in medical treatment, particularly with very sick people. Astrow had invited Sulmasy, and though he wasn't able to attend, Sulmasy was impressed by Astrow's intention.

"He was thinking about getting scholars talking to doctors and nurses about the role of religion in the care of patients beyond simply complaining this person's religious beliefs won't let me transfuse them, or this person's religious beliefs lead them to denial, or complaining that religious beliefs won't let us get the DNR [do not resuscitate] order we want," said Sulmasy. "He wanted doctors to take religion more seriously, to acknowledge that the fear of dying is not new, and these traditions have dealt with them for centuries and still might have something to say."

Sulmasy and Astrow decided to continue the discussions and obtained funding for them from the John Templeton Foundation, which had been founded by John Marks Templeton, a Wall Street financier from Tennessee, who became a naturalized British citizen and was knighted by Queen Elizabeth II for his philanthropy. The foundation, based in West Conshohocken, Pennsylvania, was giving away about $40 million a year to projects concerned with exploring the benefits of cooperation between science and religion. In the late 1990s, Templeton had been giving medical schools grants to begin courses on the subject of spirituality and medicine. With the grant, Astrow and Sulmasy put together an all-day colloquium that drew five hundred participants. A few months later, with another foundation grant, they began a year's worth of monthly discussions, including the session I attended at New York–Presbyterian Hospital, which they videotaped and hoped to distribute to medical schools.

Sulmasy explained what attracted him. "Part of this groundswell of interest in spirituality comes from a sense of alienation that is not just experienced by the patient anymore. The past few decades, patients have been saying, 'I feel I'm just a machine, a widget on the assembly line.' But lots of doctors are now beginning to experience that, because of the medical-industrial complex that treats doctors as another widget. It's all interchangeable parts, and the chief virtue becomes efficiency rather than caring, compassion. Lots of physicians are feeling a sense of emptiness, alienation: 'Is this why I went into this? Is this what it's all about? If we're addicted to technology, is this the way out? Is there more to this than just thinking about how many colons I can put a scope up per day and how many polyps I can remove and how fast I can be and how few complications I can get?'"

He continued. "People have speculated that the Baby Boomers just don't want to accept the fact that people are going to die, and technology can't give us the solution. It's everybody's obsession. Of course, physicians can't be exonerated from this. We've been telling people we're going to win the war on cancer for decades, since [Lyndon] Johnson, and now they're playing the tape back: 'Why are we losing this war after spending so many billions on it?' It's hard, when they are playing back what we told them, to say we aren't to blame for patients' misconceptions."

Astrow thrived on this kind of debate, and he was aware of the pitfalls of becoming an administrator. But he had been determined to try it, and if the job at Maimonides hadn't come through, he would have gone somewhere else.

The stakes for him were high. He was fifty years old, with two young children, one in middle school and one in elementary school. He was tossing aside a secure job for an uncertain future at a hospital in Brooklyn in a brand-new enterprise that could fail. As a cancer doctor in New York, he was always acutely aware of status. Memorial Sloan-Kettering was the behemoth that always had to be dealt with. His own mother had lung cancer and chose to be treated by an oncologist at Sloan, even though Astrow had recommended NYU, where everyone knew him.

Nice he may have been, but not naïve. He knew that taking over the department of hematologic oncology at Maimonides would be much more than a simple matter of exchanging crosses on the walls for mezuzahs on the doorposts. He would be stepping into a charged situation—the feud. But, even without that, Astrow was aware that bringing in outsiders automatically set up a kind of class struggle within the discipline. He understood firsthand what it is like to be the old guard in a situation like this. A decade earlier St. Vincent's had contracted with Salick Health Care—which had been franchising for-profit, state-of-the-art cancer centers around the country. Salick invested millions in equipment and architectural niceties, and it was clear management felt that marquee-name doctors were needed to complete the picture of superior medical care.

Astrow realized he would never run a division at St. Vincent's, no matter how capable he was, no matter how much he was loved by his patients, no matter how much he was respected by his peers and superiors. He'd been there almost nineteen years, ever since he completed his training. "If you're in a place your entire career, you're seen a certain way," he said. "I'm a different person than I was eighteen-plus years ago. I was immature. People who have known me all along tend to see me that way. To do something different, you have to leave, so people can see you in a different way."

He realized it might not seem logical, his wanting to leave. Not only was he comfortable at St. Vincent's, he hated change. "I drive my wife crazy," he warned me when we first talked about letting me shadow him. "I like doing the same things all the time."

Yet his résumé revealed ambition: Yale University for his undergraduate and medical degrees, residency and fellowships at Boston City Hospital and NYU Medical Center, organizer of symposia, pursuer of grants, and contributor to academic journals. "I've felt very capable of organizing things, running things, motivating people to do good work, recruiting people, building a good program, and the only way you can do that is if you are the leader of the division. And it wasn't going to happen for me at St. Vincent's."

The first few months at Maimonides were very hard for him. No one told him exactly what he was supposed to be doing. Despite the fanfare of the cancer center opening, the floor where the heme-onc (hematologic oncology) group would be practicing wasn't ready. Astrow and his colleagues were stuck in the old building—in the old Kopel-Bashevkin practice space—until the end of September. Camilleri had just fired the billing person, a holdover from the old group practice, which infuriated Kopel. The lab was still under construction so patients had to wait longer for test results. The bright young woman he and Camilleri had hired to manage the department had arrived over the summer and immediately alienated almost the entire support staff by letting the nurses and technicians know she thought they were incompetent. At the same time, he was trying to ingratiate himself with the hospital administration and other doctors by showing his face at meetings at the hospital and at charity functions in the community.

He was always tired.

Jay Cooper, the radiation oncologist who was director of the center, kept himself aloof, disconnected from the daily operations and not showing much interest in doing public relations or worrying about his colleagues' anxieties. Meeting him reminded me of something Howard Minkoff, chief of obstetrics, told me he learned in medical school:

"We got assigned to a patient who was dying. Part of the course, you had to be in the room when they were told, up to the day they died," Minkoff said. "They asked, 'What does death mean to you?' The humanities people would say, 'Death is the loss of everything all at once. It's like losing a family member.' The science major would say, 'Death is the cessation of all spontaneous electrical activity.' So some people come to medicine because they use science to get to people, and some people come to medicine and use people to get to science."

Cooper seemed to belong to the latter camp. He told me he chose cancer as a specialty because the minute he saw a tumor under a microscope—experimenting on the thymus of a mouse while at New York University's medical school—he knew that whatever he did in medicine was going to have something to do with tumors. He was a monologist, the kind of person who would say, "Don't get me talking about photography," when what he meant was, "Let me tell you about photography" as long as you'd listen, then do the same for computers and the difference between CAT scans, MRIs, and PET scans, as well as the Tao of tumors.

"We live in a sea of radiation," he told me enthusiastically when we first met. "When you walk in the street, you get radiated with cosmic rays. When you fly in an airplane, you get more radiation. You have a granite countertop? That's mildly radioactive. We live in it, we've adapted to it through evolution. It's merely a question of dose. If you give any living thing a dose, you can kill it with radiation. The other half of the equation is that if you give enough dose to any normal tissue, you'll kill that as well. So if you had some magic way of differentiating normal tissue from neoplastic tissue and keeping it out of normal tissue, you could cure every cancer."

That, of course, hadn't yet happened, but technology had refined radiation treatment dramatically. Cooper had convinced Maimonides to purchase two linear accelerators, one equipped to do intensity modulated radiation therapy (IMRT); the other could offer basic radiation therapy. IMRT machines can alter the shape of beams to conform to the shape of certain tumors, making the radiation more effective. IMRT therapy also happened to have a reimbursement rate that was at least three times higher than that of regular radiation therapy. However, the IMRT function had been idle because another hospital had reported an irregularity in a machine made by the same manufacturer; until Cooper had tested and retested the IMRT, he wasn't going to use it.

He claimed not to be worried that the patients weren't lining up at the door for the sophisticated radiation therapy that was available. He believed in the *Field of Dreams* business model: Build it and they will come. "The way to do it is through education of doctors, and the way you do that is provide a level of care for the patients they're not used to," he said. "That's beyond what they could have gotten in Brooklyn up until now. We've seen already the patients we've treated have gone back to their communities and said to their physicians, 'Wow, you can't believe how well I was treated.' I think to some degree it's important we go back to the idea that quality is our most important product." The implication that the cancer center operated at a different—higher—level than the rest of the hospital wasn't lost on his colleagues.

"Sometimes it makes me crazy," said Sam Kopel, a major Cooper supporter. "It's hard for Jay, with all his accolades, to get himself to go to some Brooklyn doctor's office and say, 'Hi, I'm Jay Cooper. I'd like to help you.' Alan Astrow wants to. It doesn't come naturally to him because he's shy, but he'll grit his teeth and do it, and I'm proud of him for that. Jay is an intellectual elitist and it's got to be exactly right, exactly coherent, and he will be glad to explain it to you ad nauseam. I do think he recognizes that's exactly the wrong approach when you want to go to people to get them to refer to you.

You've got to be humble; you've got to be friendly. Jay can do that but he can't overlook anything."

Kopel had been instrumental in bringing Cooper in as a consultant when the hospital was still hoping to recruit a surgical star—as Brezenoff had wanted—to be director. But when the surgeon that Cunningham had been pursuing decided not to come, Cooper was the obvious choice. His medical and academic credentials—significant publication, membership on national committees—were impeccable, and his punctiliousness was invaluable in a branch of medicine that required the use of toxic drugs and dangerous machines. And he was available. Still, Brier told me she had been uncertain about making Cooper the head of the center and almost let him go before he stepped into the position. Leadership required more than mere brilliance, and she was concerned that Cooper would become "too mired in the details." Her feelings were a carryover perhaps from their old association, when Cooper ran radiation at NYU and Brier was president of Bellevue. The two hospitals—one private, one public—shared residents and supervisory medical staff, but Bellevue, refuge of the have-nots, was the poor relation, like the sister who didn't marry money.

Cooper almost dropped out because of Brier's reluctance to give him what he wanted. He was insisting that radiation oncology should be a separate department, as it was in most medical centers. Brier wasn't keen to establish another department, afraid of offending other physicians in the hospital. On the Friday before July Fourth weekend, a year after Brier's accident, they had a testy meeting. "I very clearly told her that was her decision, but unless it was a department and I was assured it was going to be a department, I wasn't coming, and she understood I was serious," said Cooper. He was even more upset when she told him that Brezenoff couldn't remember making such a promise and that nothing was in writing.

Kopel bumped into Cooper as he left the president's office. "He had a very dark look on his face," Kopel told me. "I asked him what happened. He said that he was on the verge of kissing this entire project good-bye."

Kopel stayed on the executive floor that afternoon, waiting to catch Brier before she left for the weekend. "I was quite beside myself," he said. "I told her that she might have just extinguished the only legitimate star in our firmament. She didn't quite see it that way but promised to think it over. Luckily for us, by the beginning of the next week, to her credit, she called Jay to apologize."

After that, Brier made a point of being respectful to Cooper, and he reciprocated. He did not like being reminded of that heated moment. "That story gets repeated and repeated and repeated," he told me tensely. "It wasn't as if Pam and I were yelling at each other or disagreed with each other. It was Pam telling me her understanding of what had happened. My making very clear to her my understanding of what had happened."

Back in the nineties, when the cancer center was a notion not a plan, both Brezenoff and Kopel had thought the perfect person to be director of the cancer center would be Estee Altman. Altman, a pharmacist by training, ran Infusion Options, a for-profit subsidiary of the same holding company that owned the hospital. Infusion Options provided intravenous therapies—antibiotics, nutrition, chemotherapy, pain management, fluid, and catheter care—for patients at home, as well as nursing care and equipment. Infusion Options also mixed the chemotherapy drugs at the cancer center.

Altman, who was a friend of both Bashevkin and Kopel, had both business acumen and diplomatic skills. She also happened to be a beautiful woman—the hospital's Jewish Grace Kelly, someone called her—not because she was a blond movie star–turned-princess but because she was slender, beautiful, regal, and touched by tragedy. Altman's parents were Holocaust survivors. On the day I talked to her in her small crowded office near the cancer center, a delivery of flowers came for her, an anonymous gift welcoming her back from a trip. She accepted them with gracious delight but also gave the impression that flowers came her way often.

Brezenoff told me Altman would be the best person to help me sort out the Bashevkin-Kopel feud. When I asked her about it, she looked pained. "I would hate to say it was about money," she said. "It's really not about money, though you could say it was all about money. But it wasn't."

She spoke of the two doctors as men who were passionate about their profession and purpose but who were different types. "Dr. Bashevkin is emotional about every one of his patients. Dr. Kopel is very scientific about what needs to be done. What does the data support, what does research support and that's what the patient will have. Dr. Bashevkin combines emotion, heart, soul—his entire being. Dr. Kopel is very brilliant but very rational, scientifically makes the decisions about what needs to be done. Never underserve. Never. Standard of care is always made, state of the art. But you have to know Dr. Bashevkin to understand the difference. I run a home infusion company. If ever I take care of a Dr. Bashevkin patient, he [Bashevkin] will show up at the door to do the delivery, he will come here to pick up the supplies, because he is planning on putting in the intravenous line and being the nurse."

Altman had a slight Israeli accent, which gave the suffering in her voice a special authenticity. How could these men not be convinced by her? I thought. They must be really, deeply angry.

"He doesn't stand on protocol," she continued, about Bashevkin. "He doesn't care what other patients receive or what the system normally does. He wants to do what he thinks is right. He will pick up the solutions, run to the patient's home, he'll be there, he'll call. Dr. Kopel knows there is a system out there. We have twenty-four-hour on-call service, nurses, respiratory therapists; he realizes existing systems are there to provide the care to his patients. He's not wrong. State-of-the-art standard of care is met this way in this country."

Yet when Altman described how Kopel tended to both her parents, both of whom died of cancer, she focused on his attentiveness. "He was very supportive," she said. "He did everything; from house calls to everything he would never admit to doing, he did. I am indebted to him. He is really one of a kind. When he believes in something, he does not care for personal gain. Finances to him are not important. But in the real world finances are important to a lot of people."

Her dark eyes glistened; maybe it was my imagination, but I thought I saw a tear.

"Sam views the world as right and wrong," she said, shaking her head. "He's definitely a right-and-wrong kind of person. He had strong convictions and he's very selfless when he believes in something. If you told him this cancer institute will only be successful if he does not draw a dollar from it and use all his savings, he would say, 'No problem!' He is selfless and very much a moral crusader. He will do what's right. People like that, there aren't too many of, and that's the issue here. It doesn't make the other people bad.

They have a lot of financial burdens, they have more children, Orthodox people do; they have large families. They were unbelievable doctors, they still are. Dr. Bashevkin is selfless but is in no position to work for little. He has quite a few children. His partner Dr. Liebowitz has been married twice, with children, responsibilities. These are real-life situations. You can't just do one thing without doing the other. Everybody could be happy. But the criteria would have to be established before you embark on a new program. That's where it came apart."

She sighed. "Sam believed what they were doing was something very important, very great, very necessary, and he had ethics on his side. Justice was on his side, and in his mind that's what counts, that's the way he operates. What's right! But I live in the business world and what's right can only go that far. You've got to work with people. And compromise and negotiations—or all of us would be out of business if we only dealt with what we believe is right."

Why had they come to medicine? Bashevkin grew up in a small town in Massachusetts, via a typically convoluted sort of Jewish-immigrant story: A grandfather who came to the United States for pleasure, started a junk business in Sioux City, Iowa, stopped in the Berkshires to say hello to family, and met a cousin who became Bashevkin's grandmother. They stayed in the small New England town of North Adams, where the grandfather sold coal and grain for chickens. Then people stopped using coal and raising chickens so the business became the wholesale grocery that financed a medical education: feed man to physician in two generations.

Bashevkin's interest in medicine may have begun with his asthmatic mother; he remembered being impressed with how immediately she improved when the doctor gave her a shot of adrenaline. In high school he worked as a nurse's aide at the local hospital. "You have no idea how good that was in terms of understanding the idea of how that job should be done," he told me. "Back then they had the real New England battle-ax nurses. I used to have to wash patients and make their beds, and I still remember Mrs. So-and-So would come to my patient, stick her nose in the patient's armpit, and say, 'You call that clean?' "

"She'd come, you had to get the patient out of bed, and if he wasn't, she'd ask, 'Why isn't the patient out of bed?' Now if I want to get the patient out of bed in the hospital, I put in an order, it doesn't happen, I ask, it may or may not happen, finally I yell and scream, it happens."

He had been raised with an allegiance to his religion—his mother kept a kosher home—and he felt compelled to study further and attended yeshiva, then New York University's medical school. He always had an impulse to do good, but he was not inclined to practice medicine as social policy. He simply wanted to be a good doctor for his community, which he chose to define largely as Orthodox Jews like him.

Kopel represented a different set of ambitions. He was a justice seeker and a mischief maker, a competitive man of many parts. When he and I talked the day after the interdisciplinary meeting, and I told him I'd spent the rest of that day watching Astrow with patients, Kopel wanted to know how many patients Astrow had seen. When I said about a dozen, Kopel brightened. "You should follow me around," he said. "I see about thirty in a day. I'm like a ballerina."

We had many conversations in his two offices, both small, one in the cancer center and the other at the main hospital, a mile away, on the second floor of the Eisenstadt building, where the top administrators were clustered, and where Kopel often held wine tastings on Friday afternoons. Both offices contained a large collection of CDs, mostly opera; family photographs; and memorabilia that reminded Kopel of Great Barrington, where he and his wife had a summer house—close to Tanglewood and music.

Like Bashevkin, he had also studied in a yeshiva; Sharon—his wife, his college sweetheart, his first real girlfriend—taught science in a Jewish school for girls. But he declared himself a happy pork eater. He had almost flunked out of Brooklyn College, he said, because he spent so much time demonstrating against the Vietnam War and listening to Dylan and the Beatles and smoking dope. But he parted company with his fellow radicals in 1967 after the Six-Day War, when the left denounced Israel. He married Sharon, and their only daughter was born in Bologna, during Kopel's medical-school years in Italy, a happy period that left him and his wife with a fondness for all things Italian.

Unlike Bashevkin, who could comfortably talk about family roots, who could locate his place on a page in American history, Kopel had an autobiography full of missing chapters. Though his passport said he was born in Mława, Poland, when he asked, his father told him, "You were born in bed, now shut up." Relatives said he was born in Russia. His mother said only that she carried him on foot from somewhere in the east to Germany, where they stayed with relatives while his father recuperated from amputations (one foot and part of another) and tuberculosis. The family reunited in a DP (displaced persons) camp, an hour south of Munich, with a picturesque name, Föhrenwald, "fir tree forest," and a clear view of the Alps, which lay to the south. Föhrenwald was the last of the DP camps to be shut down after World War II, in February 1957. The Kopel family was there until the end. Their United States visa had been delayed, Kopel believed, because his father was an amputee.

Toward patients he was brisk and straightforward, and could seem unemotional (though he kept his home telephone number listed so they could reach him). He saved tears and sighs for opera, safe entry into his well-protected heart. Just as vividly as he remembered his first infatuation with Sharon, he could place his initiation into Verdi.

Kopel lit up when I asked him about opera. "As a kid I would watch the *Ed Sullivan Show* and someone like Mario Lanza would come on and I'd go, 'My God!'" he told me. "Something about full-throat opera singing struck me. But at college I was about Dylan and the Beatles and the Band. That's what I would listen to while smoking dope. Opera started, I can actually place it: I was a resident at Brooklyn Jewish. I was driving down Flatbush Avenue, the radio tuned to WQXR, and Beverly Sills comes on singing '*Sempre libera*' from *La Traviata* and it was so great I had to pull over."

As he talked, I stared at a photograph on his wall, of a younger him, not that much different, a little more hair, smoother skin, leaning conspiratorially toward an attractive brunette—Sharon, his wife, smiling, confident—on his fortieth birthday. Was he telling her a secret? I asked him. That's what it looked like. "No," he said, "I was about to kiss her." That Sharon was full-faced, rosy, a little fleshy; not like the thin, gray, sick woman who showed up at the hospital periodically for chemo treatments. The eyes were the same, though. Sly, provocative.

"You know she's a striver, that she's good, that she is doomed by illness," Kopel was saying. He was talking about Violetta, the main character in *Traviata*. "In the first minutes of the overture. Those high violins, those dissonant notes, go home and listen to it. That is a musical depiction of tuberculosis, of disease. It's perfect."

His initial interest in starting a cancer center, in the early 1990s, was purely professional, a desire to implement at Maimonides the idea of multidisciplinary cancer care that had emerged in the 1980s. An ambitious surgeon named Rene Khafif recognized the financial potential, and he and Kopel drew up a business plan just as Brezenoff came in. The potential may have been there, but the new president said no, unable to justify making an investment that would take years to recoup at a time the hospital was in financial trouble. By then, Kopel was medical director, part of the administration, and he took Brezenoff's side. Khafif left Maimonides and sent Kopel a letter, accusing Kopel of not fighting for something that would provide better patient care.

That goad alone would have been enough to trigger Kopel's competitive instincts. But additional, painful incentive came later that year. In August 1996, Sharon felt a lump in her breast. A biopsy was pronounced negative—the wrong diagnosis, it turned out, a too-common oversight with youngish women with dense breasts. But a second biopsy was deemed suspicious; she had an extensive lumpectomy and then radiation.

Even with Kopel, the medical director, pulling strings it took six weeks of utter frustration to get Sharon's treatment organized. He didn't need *La Traviata* to touch his emotions then, from this new vantage point on the other side of cancer treatment. Watching the psychological toll on his wife, he said, he now saw the radiation therapy room as a "disgusting little hellhole." He became determined to resurrect the cancer center dream. Finally, when the hospital reached financial stability, Brezenoff agreed, though he would leave Maimonides and Brier would become president before construction began.

On the very day the groundbreaking took place, on September 26, 2003, Sharon Kopel received a new—more ominous—diagnosis. Kopel knew she might not live through the time the construction would take. But she was very much alive, though she had been too sick the day of the official opening in May to leave the house. Sharon was tough, and told Sam she planned to

be there for the next dedication, of the Lena Cymbrowitz Pavilion, scheduled
for the end of September 2005—and she was.

After I had been hanging around Maimonides for several weeks, I bumped
into Astrow near the front entrance of the hospital. By then I recognized the
expression on his face, just as I had become accustomed to noticing the difficulty he had keeping his shoelaces tied. He looked worried. As the usual
Maimonides mix of rebbes, women wrapped in *hijab,* and various others
walked by, I said, as a joke: "You must feel like a stranger in a strange land."

Astrow snapped. "Don't call me Moses."

I was startled by his vehement, almost angry, response, because he rarely
showed anger. When I first met him, he told me, "I'm almost pathologically
concerned about saying things that will be hurtful to other people." It hadn't
taken me long to discover why his patients loved him: That compulsive worrying was an admirable trait in the person in charge of your destiny. He had
empathy to spare. By then I had watched him reveal the most hurtful facts to
terminally ill patients, but in a manner that mitigated the harm as much as
humanly possible. He practiced what he preached: "Medicine should not be
caveat emptor. You should be watching out for the patient."

When I invoked "stranger in a strange land," I had been referring to the
science fiction novel with that title by Robert Heinlein. Astrow went straight
to the source, Exodus 2:22. This biblical passage takes place after Zipporah,
the wife of Moses, gives birth to their son, whom Moses names Gershom,
derived from the Hebrew verb *garash,* "to drive out," referring to the Israelites'
exile in Egypt. Moses explains, "I have been a stranger in a foreign land."

Later, during another, calmer conversation, I asked Astrow why he'd
reacted so strongly.

"Moses in the Torah, he had a direct relationship to God," he said. "He's
seen as the person who's supposed to solve every problem and ends up being
lonely and isolated. I'm not God, I don't have a direct relationship to God,
and I don't want to end up lonely and isolated. That's one reason."

The other reason was my fault. I had told him that Pam Brier had heard him
speak at a cancer center gathering and said she thought he was "luminous."

What I thought would be reassuring turned out to be fuel for more worry.

"I got in a lot of trouble, I think, at St. Vincent's for being seen as this spiritual ethical person," he explained. "If you're seen as a little too interested in religion and spirituality and ethics, you're seen as a nice boy and not a particularly effective person, and if you have a real problem, you go to someone who is a tough person interested in power. This nice one is seen as just interested in ethical issues, who nicely just puts a window dressing on everything, but that's not the person you go to if you really have a problem. I think I got into problems in that way at St. Vincent's and was underestimated as a result. I think I really have to watch that."

I said, "I don't think she meant it that way."

He replied, "It's like being seen as a nice Jewish boy."

"God forbid," I said.

"It's problematic," he explained. "If you're seen as being too nice, you cannot accomplish very much. You can't be too nice. You can be honest and principled and respectful of other people, but that doesn't mean you can't make a decision and tell people when they aren't doing their jobs and be effective. That's your job."

World-class worrier that he was, he couldn't finish the conversation without completing his thought. "Seeing yourself in terms of Moses is also being totally grandiose, isn't it?" he said. "I was talking to my wife about this. If you really want to do anything, if you want to accomplish anything, you have to be slightly grandiose. If you're writing this book, you must have some grandiosity behind it, large ambitions—you probably have large ambitions for every book. However you fantasize, it never turns out quite the way you fantasize. You haven't really transformed the universe. But that's what keeps you going. When people point out your grandiosity, you can feel a little bit foolish about it."

He laughed. "That's the Jewish religion! Our hero is Moses, who has a direct relationship to God, and we're supposed to look up to Moses and aspire to that somehow, but then Moses is praised for being very humble. He speaks directly to God, but he's the everyday Joe; he's very humble. Well, I'm not Moses."

Then he smiled and said slyly, "Of course my father's name was Martin, and his name in Hebrew was Moses—*Moshe*."

It was the kind of discussion people had at Maimonides—at least those who thought about such things—the hospital named for the man who was, for Jews, the other Moses. "From Moses to Moses," the rabbis said, tracing the line from the receiver of the law to the codifier. But the biblical Moses—the dashing man of action who defied Pharoah—was the primo Jewish leading man, not the bookworm Moses—Moses ben Maimon, Maimonides, the medieval philosopher and physician. Moses the Egyptian slayer may not have been Hollywoodized as many times as Jesus, but he was indisputably an icon, both religious and pop. *The Ten Commandments* had remained a perennial favorite for half a century, televised each year around Passover and Easter. The story had legs. Who doesn't know some version of it? Moses led his people out of bondage and became spokesman for God. What a hero! All the more compelling because he was flawed—human—subject to miscalculations in carrying out divine will, his honorable intentions frustrated by ego and impatience. In the end he was ordered by God to pass the torch, before his journey was completed, to his successor, Joshua.

Speculating about Moses in the context of the hospital and the cancer center, it wasn't Alan Astrow who brought to mind the uprooted child who became a dogged, uncompromising warrior, the man who led the people to the Promised Land but then was forbidden to enter. Maybe the more fitting surrogate was the behind-the-scenes man, Sam Kopel—the medical director who had willed the cancer center into being but whose feud with Bashevkin was damaging the new enterprise. "I feel I have a life sentence here at Maimonides," Kopel once told me. "I love it and hate it." No matter how much he achieved, he remained the displaced person, the immigrant boy who spent most of his life feeling rootless, stateless, not belonging anywhere.

Four

Safety Nets

September 2005
Daily Log—J.S.

Picked up my ID at Maimonides a week after Hurricane Katrina knocked the stuffing out of New Orleans. Charity Hospital, the city's big public hospital, refuge of the poorest people, was shut down. As I rode the D train across the Williamsburg Bridge and squinted at the early-morning sun coming in through the window, I experienced one of those weird movie moments, a dissolve, Manhattan skyline beyond the East River fading into gruesome television images: bloated corpses floating in dirty water, dazed people climbing on buses bound for safety or maybe exile, blundering president, sickening mold, weeping mayor, clueless head of Federal Emergency Mismanagement. Major systems breakdown, assuming—big assumption—that the systems were ever in place. Barbara Bush, presidential mom and former first lady, was quoted all over the place saying people forced to leave their homes, possibly forever, won't really mind, because they are so poor anyway. Later Googled and found replay on Internet of Marketplace *[the public radio show].*

Here are the exact words of the mother-in-chief:

What I'm hearing, which is sort of scary, is they all want to stay in Texas. Everybody is so overwhelmed by the hospitality.

And so many of the people in the arena here, you know, were underprivileged anyway, so this . . . this [she chuckles slightly] is working very well for them.

What's the word they use in Borough Park? Shanda? *That's it. Shame.*

. . .

There are many ways to be dispossessed—hurricanes, wars, poverty—and of course disease, the great disrupter, mercurial and unsparing as weather. In modern society we rely on complex systems to protect us when the winds sweep in, when planes attack, when we can't pay the rent, when we fall ill. At Maimonides the desire to take responsibility was great, to provide a safety net for people who were sick, but the system was overloaded. Sometimes people fell through the holes, despite the best of intentions.

Dr. Gregory Todd and a patient called Mr. Zen arrived on Gellman 7, a general-medicine floor, within a week of each other, in August 2005, a week or two before the levees broke in New Orleans. Although Todd was the older of the two, his arrival marked a new beginning, while Zen was at the beginning of the end.

Zen was one of Todd's first patients after he became a member of the hospital's in-house staff of salaried physicians, called "hospitalists," who treat patients only while they are in the hospital. This type of medical practice had grown significantly in the past decade, as insurance paperwork and malpractice costs have made private practice less and less appealing for primary-care doctors. Also, the hospital job required a more limited commitment: regular hours and patients whose demands would become someone else's problem once they were discharged.

Todd had grown up in Henderson, Kentucky, a small city on the Ohio River, onetime home of John James Audubon, the wildlife artist. Todd became a lawyer and came to New York to work in securities law, for an investment banking firm. At the age of forty, he decided to become a physician. By the time he completed his training at Maimonides, and then was hired as full-time faculty and met Zen, Todd was forty-nine years old. Along the way he had become a Buddhist. Zen was an atheist, but he indulged his doctor's enthusiasm for Buddhism and discussed it with him, as far as the patient's English would allow.

Hard cases, including a sizable number of patients subsisting on ventilators, went to Gellman 7. Todd was not sanguine about his patient's prospects. "My biggest concern with him was his unwillingness to come to grips with his diagnosis," he said. "It was the scariest thing for me, because I knew the outcome of this. It was never going to get better; it was only going to get worse. When I met him, the tumor was already too big to be surgically removed. Urology had said it would probably kill him to remove this tumor. Sarcomas do not respond well to chemo or to radiation, and this we proved."

Todd cared for Zen through an entire chemotherapy regime plus twenty-eight cycles of radiation therapy. "There's a fine line between acknowledging you're never going to cure the cancer versus getting the cancer to remit to a stage where someone can continue to have a pleasant life for a period of time," said Todd. "We were trying to extend the comfort of his life, though ultimately the finality would be determined by the tumor, and everyone collectively sort of knew that. No one held out false promises for him, and everyone was very clear about what they were doing, but I'm not sure he interpreted it that way, even though that's what he was told. Hope and faith are powerful things, and to a certain extent you don't like to get in the way of them, because they do keep the person motivated and their spirits strong."

One day I asked Chris Kam, the social worker assigned to the case, how to spell Zen's name, as it appeared in various ways throughout his medical record, a voluminous stack of notations contained in a thick binder. Only the emergency room was fully computerized.

"However you want," Kam said, then lifted a dark eyebrow as he added, with a smile that wasn't a smile, "That may not be a correct name, of course."

When Kam had asked Zen for a copy of his passport, Zen told him it was in his apartment, but his friends had been unable to locate it. Zen was a restaurant worker, who had come to the United States from Taishan, a coastal city in Guangdong province, China, best known abroad as a signficant launching pad for Chinese immigration. Taishan's official Web site advertised the exodus as a point of pride: "1.3 million overseas Taishanese distributed in 91 countries and regions. Therefore, Taishan is reputed to be China's first hometown for overseas Chinese."

Kam, a slender man with a broad, handsome Chinese face, was also an immigrant. Now thirty-nine, he had moved from Hong Kong twenty years earlier; he'd studied philosophy and psychology as an undergraduate student at Staten Island College and then continued his education at Columbia University, where he received a master's degree in social work.

Over the years he had had seen a lot of Mr. Zens. "We have many

Taishanese in Bay Ridge," he said. "They come for money. Because unless you are well educated or own a business or are politically connected with powerful sources and live in big cities like Beijing or Shanghai, there's not much opportunity in a rural area. You ask this illegal, undocumented group, the majority of them say, 'We earn more money here.' They pay seventy thousand dollars—that's the price tag now—to the smuggler. If you work in a Chinese restaurant, you don't get sick, you are a good worker, you pay off the debt in three years. Zen? He doesn't have any opportunity in China. He doesn't have a college degree, he is not a skilled professional. He's here because he earns more money."

Kam's sociology lesson continued. "You are a male, you work in a Chinese restaurant somewhere, in Florida, in North Carolina. Standard pay is two thousand dollars a month with room and board. Because you live there, you don't spend money. In three and a half years, you pay off the debt and then date the guy or girl you work with in the Chinese restaurant, and they get pregnant and come to New York City, pay three hundred and fifty dollars rent for a room, and come to our Eighth Avenue clinic. They get Medicaid under PCAP [during Governor Mario Cuomo's administration, New York State began offering Medicaid coverage for all pregnancies, regardless of immigration status], and after they give birth, they send the three-month-old back to China and send two hundred dollars back to China every month, and you are set."

Kam was unstoppable now. "After three, four years, your four-year-old is ready for school. She comes back, and your wife is pregnant again. This time you take care of the second child here. Your debts are paid off, you accumulate some money, you are working, maybe you open a small restaurant."

He stopped dramatically, raising his expressive eyebrows for emphasis. "You ask, 'Why is he here?' That's the attraction," he said, and then again laughed one of those mirthless laughs. "What a wonderful life!"

The wonderful life had bypassed Mr. Zen. After fifteen years of living in New York, now in his early forties, he had not acquired a wife or a child or a house. He had, however, acquired a sarcoma in his pelvis that was already too big to be surgically removed when he came into the hospital emergency room.

He readily settled in his room on the seventh floor of the Gellman building and became a favorite patient. His quiet gratitude was a welcome respite from the usual barrage of gripes and questions from patients and families.

"He was stoic to the point you'd have to push him to hear a complaint," said Dr. Todd. Besides being brave, he was gentle—and he stayed for a very long time, in a pleasant two-bedded room, where he was divided from a succession of roommates by a curtain. He would be there long enough to watch four seasons go by. His bed was by the window. From the view on the seventh floor, Brooklyn appeared surprisingly leafy, until winter came.

Eileen Keilitz, a nurse on Gellman 7, liked Zen immediately. "When he came to us, he was very virile-looking. You would never think he had cancer or anything like that," she said. "He was very independent. He would help turn himself and do things for himself. In the beginning, for many months, he used to get these pain patches, these lidoderm patches on his leg, and he would just cut them open and insist on putting them on himself. Anytime you asked him, 'Do you have pain, do you have this, do you have that?' 'No, no, no, no.'"

Zen spoke enough English to convey basic information: What did he eat? Did he move his bowels? How did he sleep? Had anything changed? If he had more complicated matters to discuss, he could talk to Chris Kam, who came to see him at least once a week at first, less often later on; in recent years the hospital had cut the number of social workers because of the budget. Kam worked for the hospital part-time. The oncologist who treated Zen— Dr. Yiwu Huang from the cancer center—was Chinese and willing to answer questions, but he was always in a hurry.

Keilitz stopped by whenever she was in the hospital, but, like most of the nurses, she worked 3 twelve-hour shifts a week, so she wasn't there many days. They always smiled at each other and chatted, mostly in monosyllables. *Nice day.* Yes. *How do you feel?* Fine. *Can I get anything for you?*

What could she know of him? Yet when Keilitz and other nurses and aides on the floors talked about Zen, their emotions were evident. Maybe they felt they knew him because cancer was the true melting pot. Unlike AIDS or diabetes, cancer was a democratic disease, distributing itself with cruel impartiality, disregarding sexual behavior, eating habits, exercise, income, age, or ethnicity. External differences became more and more irrelevant, because almost every cancer patient—educated or not, wealthy or not, citizen or not—eventually became fixated on the same questions: Has my tumor shrunk? Has the disease spread? Can you stop it? Is there hope?

Zen had a language barrier, but that was in some ways the easiest one to circumvent. Few cancer patients are exempt from feeling confusion and uncertainty, especially after exposure to an array of doctors and nurses with varying attitudes and skill when it comes to discussing prognosis and options. The medical people had a common vocabulary, but styles so different they amounted to cultural divides. Some were optimistic, some just stated factual data, some lapsed into medicalese, some simply said, "I am not God." The gifted ones could make strong connections no matter what language their patients spoke.

Keilitz said she felt such a bond with Zen, and the patient indicated that he reciprocated. For her he wasn't an ever-shrinking mass of flesh surrounding an ever-growing tumor, or the sum of his medications and symptoms. He was a man, a son, and a brother; his mother and sister lived back in China. She knew his eating habits. He showed little interest in the hospital food, not even the kosher Chinese cuisine the kitchen worked so hard to create at the suggestion of Joanne Quan, a member of the hospital board of trustees, vice dean for finance at Columbia University's Mailman School of Public Health. By the time the food was cooked, cooled, and reheated down in the labyrinth basement, then sat on carts, it lost its flavor, no matter how much seasoning was poured on in the kitchen. Keilitz also knew that Zen wouldn't starve. Almost every night one or two friends showed up with containers of Chinese food. Even when Zen underwent chemotherapy treatment, he could muster appetite for rice congee with bits of fish on top.

Chris Kam always knew that Zen was there for the long haul. As an undocumented worker, he was entitled to treatment only so long as he stayed in the hospital. Most illegals went to the city hospitals, like Bellevue in Manhattan or Coney Island in Brooklyn, which used Maimonides residents. St. Mary's in Brooklyn, which had served the immigrant poor for more than a century, was on the verge of closing; its parent organization was Saint Vincent Catholic Medical Centers, about to file for bankruptcy protection. But, by law, patients who came in through the emergency room had to be treated until they could walk out the door.

By the time I met Zen, he had been in the hospital seven months. His bill, which no one expected would be paid, had just topped $1 million; even the comparatively generous emergency Medicaid payments offered in New York would probably cover only about 10 percent.

One day, outside Mr. Zen's room, I joined Chris Kam and Lisa Keen, another social worker. She had arrived at the hospital thirty-five years earlier, reed-thin and always available for a satisfying protest march. Now a doting grandmother, she was no longer slender and walked with a limp acquired a few years earlier, when she was knocked over by a wave at the beach. Her method of protest was dark humor and dry commentary on the irrationality of the system, even as she kept trying to help patients. She often invited me to go on rounds with her.

Keen made a crack about working on Zen's discharge plan.

"He will be here until the last day," said Kam.

"Why?" I asked.

Kam answered matter-of-factly, "Because he has refused to leave the hospital, and there is no placement for him. He is undocumented."

"Can't you kick a patient out?" I asked.

"You can't? I don't know," said Kam. "Each time they give a different answer. What's the answer for today?"

Keen played along. "We do not actively throw anybody out. However, we try to encourage them if there's something that would be better for them, and occasionally . . ."

Kam finished her sentence: ". . . we do throw people out."

Keen laughed. "We walk them to the elevator and say good-bye. Like when we had a smoker who went out for smoking breaks even though she was told if she left the floor, she'd be discharged."

Kam offered another example. "I remember a Chinese, Mandarin-speaking, undocumented patient who had some kind of cancer, terminally ill, and she came to the hospital. I saw her the first time, and then we discharged her. It was very hard to discharge her. The only thing we could do was give her morphine from the pharmacy, and she came back two weeks later yelling at me that I did a poor job by discharging her because she is in so much pain. I said to her, 'That's the nature of cancer. If you need more medication, you should see your primary doctor.' But we checked her back in. That time she stayed for a few days, and when she got stable, my boss actually asked the security guard to escort her out."

He looked at me. "So we do kick people out if they are ambulatory."

I said, "Mr. Zen is not ambulatory."

"Right," said Kam.

· · ·

Mr. Zen was not the only enduring patient. Not by a long shot. The record went to the ninety-year-old man who had been on the Kronish 5 wing for three years; every time a bed came available in the nursing home where his family wanted him to go, he was too sick to move. The hospital had far more than a normal share (as many as eighty at a time) of "vent patients," those requiring artificial-breathing machines to stay alive. Melissa Turok was the hospital's ventilator-nurse case manager. She spent her days examining patients to see which of them could be "weaned" from vents and discharged, either to their homes or to long-term-care facilities.

Turok was middle-aged but still careened around on three-inch heels, examining patients and then negotiating with insurance companies. "Most managed-care companies do not want to pay for acute rehab if someone is standing on two feet and ambulating twenty or thirty or forty feet," she said. "They don't want to spend the money." She had to negotiate with families who couldn't imagine that their loved one was ready to leave the hospital directly from the ICU after open-heart surgery. I watched her talk to people who looked inert to me, like the retired police officer who clicked his tongue and rolled his eyes. "His brain is perfect," said Turok. "Imagine how he feels now that he can't communicate with people. Why is he still here? He had a colostomy, [is] a chronic smoker, his blood gases are horrible, his legs are swollen. He's going to end up going to a facility, and it's going to eat up his legacy to his family. So now he's dealing not only with being on a trach and a vent and a colostomy—can you imagine his body image?"

Many of these patients would never leave. A large proportion of this intransigent subgroup was elderly Orthodox Jews whose rabbis decreed they could not be unplugged. (Rabbis have varying interpretations of the law requiring life to be maintained, so families often search until they find the rabbi whose ruling matches their desire.)

The vent population, which was scattered all over the hospital, was not to be confused with another group, the "frequent fliers," patients who kept coming back. "They're the ones who never got their prescriptions filled and are returning in the same condition they were in three weeks ago, because it's just caught up with them again," said Todd, the Kentucky-born Buddhist securities lawyer–turned–physician. "For the want of thirty bucks' worth of pills, they'd still be home."

In addition to medical, financial, and religious reasons for lingering, the poorest immigrant patients often had a different understanding of what the hospital was for. "Some of our immigrant populations are used to different kinds of health care," said Todd. "You do have populations of patients who do believe they can effectively check themselves in to the hospital and stay as long as they want. And you have to battle with that process. They are used to a system that would never send them home, even though not much was done for them while they were there because they didn't have the resources. It's actually quite of a shock for them to hear, 'You have to go home. You can't stay in the hospital.' They look at you like, 'I don't want to.' This isn't about want. It isn't renewing your reservation at the Ritz."

He continued, "I tell them, 'Guys, I would rather spend the night at the base of a nuclear reactor than spend one night in a hospital that I didn't have to.' Frankly, the people at the nuclear reactor get more sleep. But you'd be surprised at the number of patients who want to stay here. My only question there, if you open up the heart of compassion, is to think how scary must their world be at home that this seems like a safe place. Hospitals are scary places to almost everybody. They must feel so alone and abandoned if a hospital feels safe, feels comfortable, feels home."

September 27, 2005
Daily Log—J.S.

The hospital at night. Maybe Marty Payson was right: It is like a movie set. The neighboring streets are dark, mostly residential, but the hospital is fully lit. Bright lamps beam down from the overpass connecting Eisenstadt and Gellman, turning street into glimmering stage, floodlights casting otherworldly glow on hospital workers standing outside grabbing a smoke, big Orthodox families trooping in to visit relatives.

Pam Brier has been holding town-hall meetings all day in Schreiber Auditorium for the staff. Tonight, more town hall. The politician in the policy wonk likes to mingle. At Bellevue she walked the halls late at night, like an old-fashioned chain-store president dropping in on one of his outlets to make sure the shelves were stocked and the help was friendly. She told me she took [Peter] Aschkenasy prowling Bellevue on one of their first dates. When she came to Maimonides, that's what they'd do on a Saturday night—take in a movie and then hang out in the ER or stop by nursing stations on patient floors. If the nurses offered, she tasted their food and ended up taking home goat curry for next night's dinner.

Now she limps. Walking around had not been easy for Brier even then, before the accident; she had scoliosis and related back problems for years. Since the accident, prowling has been out of the question for Aschkenasy and difficult for Brier, still hobbled two years after. The quarterly town-hall meetings gave her the chance to feel like she was communicating. Two in the morning, two in the afternoon, this one—8:00 P.M.—and one at midnight. She's letting Mark McDougle handle that one. Number two can stay up late.

The morning sessions had been packed, Brier's secretary told me, but only a couple of dozen people were there tonight.

Brier sat on the edge of the stage at the front of the auditorium, talking without a microphone . . . nice intimate touch for a small crowd. Good theater. She talked about how there were only forty-two days until Joint Commission on Accreditation of Healthcare Organizations, aka JCAHO—called Jayco—the nonprofit organization that evaluates nearly 15,000 health-care organizations and programs in the United States. [Maimonides had received a score of 96 out of 100 in the previous inspection.] The hospital was gearing up; "a readiness team" of fifty employees was on stealth alert, looking for soft spots in procedure for diagnosis, communication, teamwork, safety, lab results, HEICS, the Hospital Emergency Incident Command System—looking for dirt, junk piled in hallways and patient rooms.

Brier said that Maimonides had not been picked as a Magnet hospital, an award for nursing excellence given by the American Nursing Association. Only 150 hospitals in the country had won Magnet status, but Sondra Olendorf and her nursing staff had been working for four years documenting their case. "We missed by this much," Brier said, holding her forefinger and thumb close together.

A group of "environmental workers"—people who cleaned the hospital—gave a report on a yearlong study they were doing to improve procedures. Brier said, "When this group tells us what we need, we'll implement it—all we can pay for. We know, as Hillary Clinton is apt to say, it takes a village to keep Maimonides clean."

Someone asked about Katrina. Did Maimonides have an evacuation plan?

Brier gingerly scooted off the stage, as though preparing to escape. Maybe the Katrina question was too serious to answer sitting down. "We have an evacuation plan, but it wouldn't be sufficient for a complete evacuation," she said. "The Greater New York City Hospital Association is looking at it. Of course it's patients we have to provide for, plus health-care providers. We will take a look at the issue and follow the lead set by city agencies. We have drilled and practiced for other kinds of disasters."

The man nodded, as though he were satisfied, as though the answer had been more reassuring. Maybe people just want answers.

"I'm glad you raised that," Brier said, looking worried. "Sobering thought."

Her cell phone started ringing inside her bag.

She ignored the sound, which persisted.

"It'll stop ringing," she told the group. "I don't know how to turn it off."

Was there nighttime in cyberspace?

What time was it?

Administrators work nine to five unless they stay till midnight.

Surgeons come in at six.

Residents never sleep and always wear pajamas.

The emergency room gets crowded at 2:00 P.M., like clockwork.

Nurses come and go in twelve-hour shifts, three days a week.

Day for Night. *François Truffaut.*

Man, woman, birth, death, infinity. Ben Casey.

Which beep in the patient's room is the ticking clock?

Babies arrive, old folks hang on, people suffer, they heal.

Time stands still.

Premature death.

Endless waiting.

Jewish time, hospital time, resident time, secular time. Ramadan.

Time is of the essence. The tick-tock is people.

Ecclesiastes 3, a time to be born a time to die

For every purpose under heaven

What's that David Bowie song?

Time is senseless, the musician said.

A whore, a "sniper in the brain."

Checked his watch at 9:25 and thought
"Oh God I'm still alive."

It wasn't clear if Mr. Zen—illegal alien, undocumented worker, very sick man—was counted among the 47 million uninsured people in the United States, since he officially did not exist. But he was definitely part of the daily census at Maimonides, a crucial figure in the numbers game that obsessed the managers on the second floor of Eisenstadt, where the Maimonides executives were clustered. The "executive suite" was a humble row of little offices, many of them windowless, on either side of the hallways that intersected in the reception area, where the undistinguished portraits of former hospital presidents were hung at uneven angles. No feng shui there. Brier and McDougle had larger offices than the rest, but nothing fancy. Budget-conscious was the operating motif.

Maimonides managed to stay in the black—barely—without major benefactors because it almost always had an occupancy rate of 99 percent and because in the previous decade it had reduced the average length of stay from 8.24 days to 6.24 days. That was the magic equation: full house and not too many people allowed to overstay their welcome—not past the billing guidelines of the twenty-one insurers the hospital dealt with (compared with five or six in the days before the idea of managed care through competition took hold in the 1990s). The equation worked only if most of the patients kept moving through.

As Joseph Cunningham, chief of surgery, said, "You take any two hospitals, if I can do a coronary bypass and get a patient out into a secondary location—home, rehab, family—a day shorter than Lutheran, I've put another ten thousand dollars in my pocket. Every discharge across the board is at least ten thousand dollars to a hospital.

"It's all about turnover," he told me. "The more you can get in and out, the more times that cash register clicks. It sounds like business, and it is business, but the caveat is, you can't get them out if they're not ready. We're not kicking them out. But if you get them out two days later, for every discharge you lose, you're losing ten thousand bucks."

Everyone felt the pressure to build volume. "All these people crunch numbers every day," said Amit Schwartz, the young neurosurgeon who often showed up at the cancer center's interdisciplinary meetings. "You know when you're being looked at by Mark McDougle or Lillian, or Naldi [the chief financial officer], there's a number on your head of how many cases you did in the last month. They look at that number all the time. I can walk in the hall-way and the president of the hospital will say, 'Okay, you did ten operations last week.' They know everybody—who they did, how much they did."

Pam Brier acknowledged that this was true. "I look at the volume every damn day," she said. "I wake up every morning, I come to work, I read admissions and discharges. I read about patient discharges by service and by doctor on every single service. You sort of live and die by it."

Surgery numbers had been down over the summer, especially in cardiac; newer technology—stents, angioplasties—had steadily taken over. Waiting outside Pam Brier's office one day, I heard her yelling on the phone to Fraid-kin, "These fucking surgery numbers are keeping me awake at night!"

When I walked in, Brier was sitting at her desk, very ladylike, straighten-ing one of the already-very-neat piles of paper on her desk. "I love the syner-gism of my job," she said with a stagy smile as I pulled out my tape recorder. "Is the recorder on?"

Chris Kam wasn't joking when he said that his real assignment had been, as he put it, "to kick Zen out." Before Kam was assigned to the case, not long after Mr. Zen came to the hospital, Janice Yang, director of outreach to the Asian community, got a call from a social worker at the Brooklyn Chinese-American Association. Yang, a slender, pretty thirty-seven-year-old woman with straight black hair and an almost constant look of worry, had moved to New York from Canton (Guangzhou) when she was fifteen years old. She still had a heavy Chinese accent. When Yang learned that a friend of Zen's had complained that the hospital was trying to kick him out, she contacted the friend. Yang explained that the hospital wasn't meant for long-term care and that it was usual procedure to send patients home or to rehab or hospice or a nursing home. Yang tried to talk to Mr. Zen without success and then sent a series of interpreters, who got nowhere trying to convince Mr. Zen to move.

"He hesitated to talk to Asian faces," Yang told me. "Everyone is afraid they'll get a bill or we might ask them for money, so they try to protect themselves, they don't want to release information. It happens to a lot of the cancer patients, especially the Chinese patients. Either they are illegal here or have no insurance. Even people with insurance, not a lot of them do preventive care, so they end up in the emergency rooms. They've never been checked up, so once things happen, they go to the emergency room and find out it's too late."

She sympathized. She didn't speak English when she arrived in the United States. She and her brother and sister worked after school until eleven at night, because the family had no money. Her father had been a doctor in China but in the United States worked in an antique store staining and painting furniture. She remembered what it was like eating on the floor of an empty apartment because they couldn't afford furniture.

"I know it's not easy to be a new immigrant to this country," she told me. "We can't speak, we can't hear, we can't read. I want to help the community, because I went through the pain."

Patients like Zen clogged the system, curtailed patient flow. But Chris Kam seemed unconcerned about consequences for failing in his assignment to "kick Zen out," and Gregory Todd, the physician, said he never felt any specific pressure to discharge a patient before he believed it was time. Nevertheless, he said, "We all have the general pressure of shorter length of stay, which every hospital wrestles with every day. We always comment when we do it well—we don't know how we did it and how to reproduce it."

The tender care of Mr. Zen, spread over a period of months, was an anachronism. Old medicine. Social workers like Kam and Keen were replaced by nurse case managers, who had no leisure to spend time at bedside, because they were occupied with moving patients through the system. New medicine demanded cultural competency, clinical excellence, and psychological awareness, but not at the expense of efficiency, coordination, and speed (none of which conformed to the vagaries of illness, insurance compensation, and the availability of aftercare for the elderly and the infirm).

Every day, it seemed, a new study or book was published discussing the failures of the system, the pressures placed on health delivery by the domination of pharmaceutical and insurance behemoths—"How health care in America became big business—and bad medicine," to quote the subtitle of one of them (*Critical Condition* by Bartlett and Steele). But at Maimonides most people were too busy to ponder the larger forces that were making their lives difficult. Thinking about the big picture could crush you: Health-care expenses in the United States rose from $1,106 per person in 1980 ($255 billion overall) to $6,280 per person in 2004 ($1.9 *trillion* overall). Yet in 2005, 44.8 million in the United States, an appalling 15.3 percent of the population, had no health insurance.

"I don't spend a lot of time thinking about global issues," Robert Naldi, the chief financial officer, told me. He had curly graying hair and a rat-a-tat way of talking that seemed just right for a numbers guy. "When I hear Medicare is being cut six billion dollars over the next ten years, Medicaid cut four billion dollars the next, that ten billion dollars doesn't change what I do on a Thursday morning. I just don't get into that trap. I worry about our little hospital in Borough Park. . . . I have a luxury. . . . We have a very strong core business. People in the community like us a lot. It has its ups and downs, ebbs and flows. Me, I don't even read about it, to be honest. I don't spend any energy forecasting the next three or four years, because I don't think anyone can do that. We're lucky if we forecast the next six months, things change so rapidly. I just don't waste time on it."

Mr. Zen was part of "the bed-management problem," the bureaucratic way of referring to the fact it could take twenty-four hours and sometimes more for patients admitted through the ER to make it into a bed. Almost every day the scene that shocked Chuck and Carolyn Gregorius, Davey's parents, was reenacted in the emergency room that was Zen's entry into Maimonides. In the hallway leading to the ER, it was routine to find patients backed up like airplanes on a runway in lousy weather. Just in case any of the administrators up on the second floor of Eisenstadt forgot about the situation, Carl Ramsay, medical director of the ER, periodically held his cell phone aloft and snapped a picture, which he then transmitted to them by computer.

"The right leaders have to see it in real time," he said. "We have twenty-eight people waiting for beds, average wait time is twelve and a half hours."

When this digitized vision of chaos popped up on Lili Fraidkin's computer, she shrugged. "The emergency room is a pot of gold," she said in her unflappable way. That was Brezenoff's theory: Contrary to prevailing popular wisdom, that ERs were money losers, he recognized early on that the emergency room didn't just fulfill the hospital's civic responsibility, it offered a way to build volume. Sometimes the ER brought in those who couldn't pay at all, like Zen, but more often they drew in people with some kind of insurance—or for whom some kind of insurance could be gotten.

The variables may have been different, but the essential economic assumptions were the same in Lincoln, Nebraska. Chuck Gregorius, David's father, said the system reminded him of a popular bar and grill in Lincoln called P.O. Pears, with a menu that was decidedly not Borough Park, offering items such as the Jiffy Burger, a hamburger covered with peanut butter, bacon, and jack cheese. "You go up to a window to order, and the window looks like a big old pair of lips," he said. "On those lips it says, 'We lose a little on each sale but make it up in volume.' Sometimes in health care, because of the constraints on money, we have to spend on health care, sometimes it feels like they are using the P.O. Pears approach. Sometimes in health care, that's the way it comes out."

Fraidkin may have been unperturbed by the snapshots Ramsay e-mailed her way, but she didn't like the last part of his message: "We have three hours of diversion," meaning three hours in which patients were sent to other hospitals. For the ER to be a pot of gold, it needed constant refilling. But more patients meant more stress on the system.

David Cohen, senior vice president, clinical integration, whose office was just down the hall from Lili Fraidkin's, had come to Maimonides six years earlier, after a career in public hospitals, including ten years as the medical director at Bellevue. He and Brier were friends, and she urged him to come there to help streamline the hospital's unwieldy systems. Brier's husband, Peter Aschkenasy, called Cohen the living embodiment of "think Yiddish, dress British," by which he meant someone who was practical, smart, a man of the people, but who also aspired to a certain gentility. Cohen lived on Manhattan's Upper East Side and was a theater fanatic; he and his wife on occasion would fly to London for the weekend to catch the latest shows. In a hospital where everyone said what they thought as the thought occurred, Cohen revealed little.

Cohen saw the hospital, all of it—David Gregorius, Mr. Zen, the crazy ER, the pregnancies and deaths, the rabbis and the politicians—as Brownian motion. It was typical of his erudite sensibility to connect the glatt kosher institution in Borough Park with the nineteenth-century Scottish botanist Robert Brown, who found his place in history when, studying pollen grains under a microscope, he noticed they were gyrating in a strange, jittery way. Brown's name became linked to small, random movements that weren't apparent from the surface, a concept that became valuable to Albert Einstein in thinking about the atomic nature of matter and to David Cohen about the management of big-city hospitals.

Cohen had strong ideas about the hospital's place in the community, and he wasn't sure if Maimonides—if any nonpublic hospital—was right for him. But when Brezenoff and Brier beckoned, he went.

Shock number one: Unlike those at Bellevue, where almost all the physicians were employed by the hospital, a substantial number of Maimonides patients were treated by private physicians (like the Bashevkin group). "There seemed to be an awful lot of concern by the medical staff of finances in terms of their own compensation," said Cohen. "That was a surprise. I kind of felt that . . . I looked at the place as . . . this is so quotable I don't want to say it." But he did anyway. "It looked to me like a little factory for Jewish doctors to take care of their patients and make lots of money. I was much more interested in the role of a hospital in the community and advancing medicine and clinical practice and care. I just didn't think I was going to be happy or comfortable here."

Even Cohen, who kept his emotions under wraps, wasn't immune to the weird, compelling pull of the place. He began to see a desire to adapt and transform as the hospital struggled to find its place in the intersection between individual well-being and public health care, between expensive, efficient high-tech medicine and the human needs and demands of a community. "I think the place has changed considerably, and I know I have as well," he said. "It's hard to say which is which. I think it's both."

Cynicism and sentimentality are common enough in hospitals, but something about Maimonides brought it all to the surface. Winnie Kennedy, a senior nurse in psychiatry, told me she thought the exaggeration of all feelings had to do with jamming so many cultures into such a tight spot. "It's like the yeast in bread," she said. "It gives the place its rise."

Brier depended on Cohen to keep the dough from overflowing the pan, to rationalize an irrational system. He was in charge of the front end and the back end, checking patients in and helping them find care after they left the hospital—the transition points. He described how things had changed since he'd trained as a physician thirty years earlier. In those days the crucial nexus for patients and physicians came in the first twenty-four hours: get a history, make a diagnosis, set up a therapeutic plan, carry it out. Then everyone could take a breath, because the patient would stay for two weeks. Convalescence was still part of the plan. There was time for reactions to medication to manifest themselves, or for the patient simply to regain strength.

In 1983, Medicare began linking payment to DRGs, Diagnosis-Related Groups, about five hundred categories determined by disease, age, gender, and possible complications. This formula eventually became the standard payment for all patients. Reimbursement was set not by individual but by group. Thus began the push for hello/good-bye. Discharge planning began almost simultaneously with admission. It wasn't a bad idea in theory; hospitals were dangerous places full of infectious diseases, even when the staff did remember to wash hands. But, often, speed was achieved more readily than were efficiency and coordination. Even little things that got lost in the shuffle could have a big impact. For example, patients might come into the hospital taking one set of medications and, while in the hospital, be prescribed a similar medication with a different name. If the patients wasn't made fully aware before they left, they might fill the prescription for the new medication, the one with the different name, and then unwittingly double the dose when they get home.

The entire system had changed. More and more care took place outside hospitals—though patients ejected from hospitals often found they were stranded. As recuperating patients were shoved out the door earlier and earlier, hospitals increasingly resembled intensive-care units. The cottage-industry model, where doctors went back and forth between their patients and their offices, was becoming obsolete. Patients increasingly were handed off by their primary-care doctors to hospitalists like Todd. "Team approaches" and "interdisciplinary models" were meant to maximize efficiency, because everyone had less and less time to spend with each patient.

That's why the charts were so thick. Every new person who took a look also took a history and made a new notation. That's why the potential for mistakes increased. Who had time to read all that and get to the next patient in time? And that was assuming you could read the notations, which was rare. Even at a computer-savvy place like Maimonides—one of the one hundred "Most Wired" hospitals—electronic records (outside the emergency room) were still used primarily to relay lab results and to place orders for medication. Patient progress was still scribbled into charts.

"It's about teams, not lone rangers practicing anymore," Cohen said. "It's not even about who's the captain of the team anymore. It's about teams, one component of which is strictly medical care. There's no captain. Someone has to be coordinator, but at each point somebody else is going to have to take charge."

Cohen described his day.

"By about ten, ten-thirty, I get a list of expected discharges, and I can match them with patients coming in. Probably about sixty discharges a day, actually more. In medicine it'll be fifty-to-sixty range; that doesn't include critical-care units. Drop-offs on the weekend. Total surgical-medical discharges are in sixty-to-eighty range. Busy busy. If you consider a seven-hundred-bed hospital minus psych and maternity beds, you're talking about turning over about one-fifth of the hospital."

The potential for tension was there every step of the way.

"Before, it would take us ten minutes beginning to end to clear an admission. Now it's forty-five minutes to an hour," said Maria Ferlita, vice president in charge of admitting, medical records, in-patient insurance verification. Ferlita was another Maimonides character, Italian-born, a compact woman with long dark hair and dramatic eyebrows who wore snug-fitting skirts and spike heels. Her gravelly cigarette voice issued thoughts as decrees with the rapidity and punch of machine-gun fire.

"That's what's put tremendous financial strain on the hospitals," she said. "I would say on the patients as well. In the past we had five, six payers—Medicare Medicaid, Blue Cross, private, workmen's comp, and unions. Now you have myriads of HMO companies, mandatory enrollment of the Medicaid population, which has affected hospitals adversely, fiscally. Medicare and Medicaid, very simple. You have documentation guidelines you need to meet. You meet the guidelines, you get paid. With HMO companies, much, much, much more challenging. These are private companies. Their goal, or what we're finding—they deny a tremendous amount of admissions due to no authorizations. It's a method of postponing payment to the hospital, and if the hospital doesn't appeal these cases, there's a time element, money in their pocket."

No one was turned away if admitted through the emergency room, but Ferlita made sure her people did all they could for the hospital to be paid by someone. She knew that the system was a mess; her job wasn't to fix it but to game it. "If there is a discrepancy—a doctor has booked a patient as an inpatient and managed care says it has to be ambulatory—we contact the physician and say, 'If you want to book this patient as inpatient, you have to send more documentation.'"

NEW SUCK JOURNAL VOLUME A, ISSUE 7
OCTOBER, 2005

Dudes,

Ok. Sorry it has been awhile. A resident gets busy sometimes you know. I think I worked like every day for the past month. I guess I had a few days off, but they were fake days off—I really don't think you can count a day off after you just worked 27 straight hours (as you sleep the entire day), or when you have to go in to work that day at 7pm (as, again, you try to sleep the entire day). I just finished my month of Obstetrics, which I enjoyed, except for the fact I had to work (to some extent) every day, and had multiple 30 hour call shifts. Our hospital delivers 6,800 babies a year (about 20 a day)—the most in the country, so I was quite busy. But I gotta admit, Obstetrics is cool. For those of you who don't know (I hope not many), Obstetrics and Gynecology is the medical specialty of Woman's health/surgery/baby delivering, and such, and I nearly went into that specialty myself, as I really like it. I still think that it's possibly the coolest job in the world, with the exception that it sort of sucks. The hours suck at least. Also we all know that the greatest job in the world is being paid to fish. Duh. Either way, I am done with OB/GYN for now (and perhaps ever?). But I got to deliver a lot more babies, in a lot more languages than ever before. I learned transiently how to count to ten and say "push" in Cantonese, Mandarin, Russian, and at least two other languages that I'm not sure what they were. But that is done now, the times with young healthy pregnant chicks and their babies is finished—it's back to the ER and all the about-to-die old people . . .

Ok, until next time, carry on smartly

Love, Davey

"Fishing kills me exactly as it keeps me alive." The Old Man and the Sea

.   .   .   .

Hi Dave,
Could I meet you at the E.R. on Tuesday around 11-11:30 and hang out for a few hours, maybe find some time to talk, too?
Let me know.

Julie

.   .   .   .

Ms. Salamon-
If it is ok with my attending that day (not sure who it is yet), that would be fine. I'm not sure though. I think it would be fun. But if it is really busy and we start falling behind because i'm not seeing patients fast enough, i might get in trouble. I'll figure out who is the attending that morning and if i see them before tuesday, I'll ask them. If not, i'll ask them that day. And as far as just "following around", I'll warn you that probably 50-60% of my time is spent documenting on the computer . . . not very fun to watch.

Dave

Madeline Rivera, associate vice president for case management, reporting directly to David Cohen, told me about the three calls that preceded my visit one day. "I've got one patient that wants to be taken off the vent and get out and one who isn't ready to leave. The wife is upset. She's eighty-seven years old, husband not doing well, he has to go to a facility. The managed-care company has already told them they're denying. I've talked to our liaison from managed care, saying we have an eighty-seven-year-old who is trying to choose a facility and needs to take fifteen thousand dollars out of the bank, and she can't do that in one day. Let's give her until Monday to do that.

"There's a child who is handicapped and needs placement, and we're working with the mother, who doesn't speak English, to help her understand she isn't sending her child out to die, to reassure her she has visitation rights. She thought she would lose rights because she is of Mexican background, not legal. There are a lot of sad stories. Every day we deal with these things."

Rivera was a registered nurse, in her forties, pretty, with big, round, dark eyes and hefty from weight gained incrementally with the birth of each of her three children. Spanish was her first language; she didn't learn English until pre-K. Her parents were from Puerto Rico. They had one message for their three children: "You gotta go to school, you gotta go to school, you gotta go to school." One became an accountant, another a teacher, and Rivera, a nurse. "I went to Catholic school, Our Lady of Sorrow," she told me. "When I look back at my autograph book from eighth grade and it said profession, the answer was 'nurse.'"

None of her three kids spoke Spanish, and she spent most of her time moving patients through the system, but she wasn't a machine. Sometimes she needed to see firsthand that she was helping.

"Every day we collect clothes to give to patients who come in without clothing, or medication budget for folks coming through ER," she said. "I had a thirty-one-year-old coming in needing insulin he couldn't afford to pay for. He told me he survived on a can of tuna fish a day, an illegal, Mexican. My drawers are filled with stuff—glucose monitors I can give out as charity. This man would be compliant if he could afford to be. We charged him a sliding-scale fee, whatever he could afford, because he was working off the books. About five days later, he knocked on the door downstairs and carried in a floral arrangement the size of this table. I started to cry. 'Why did you bring this? You can't afford to eat, you shouldn't do this.' He said, '*Señora, yo quería.*' 'I wanted to.'"

. . .

Charity was random and unofficial. Getting paid kept the hospital in business. Enter the documentation specialist, whose job was to review charts and make sure doctors had filled in the diagnosis correctly—not for treatment but for reimbursement. The government issued thick manuals of diagnosis codes listing tens of thousands of code numbers, indicating diseases and their gradations.

Say, for example, a patient has a gastric ulcer. There are more than twenty variations on the diagnosis; the addition of specific details indicating severity could drastically change the amount paid to the hospital and to physicians. Precision was required. If you "upcoded" inaccurately about a diagnosis that was reimbursed at a higher rate, the government asked for its money back and could charge a fine as well.

When the documentation specialist taught residents, she brought a stack of charts from recently discharged patients—with patients' names and doctors' signatures blacked out—to protect the innocent (the patients) and the guilty (doctors who had screwed up the coding). Over and over she demonstrated the difference a word could make. For bacterial pneumonia, writing "staphylococcal pneumonia" instead of "pneumonia" meant a DRG (Diagnostic-Related Group) paying $14,690 instead of $9,453; noting the cause "TIA—transient ischemic attack, a slight stroke *possibly due to carotid stenosis,*" instead of just "TIA" changed the DRG to one reimbursing $8,851 instead of $6,498. Case by case not much, but making such changes had cumulatively increased hospital revenue by $5 million the previous year.

It seemed crazy. But when I talked to Michelle Spector, a documentation specialist at Maimonides, she said the coding requirements weren't just some sadistic bureaucrat's idea of fun. "The regulations are not insane but to make sure that the entire team has similar documentation," she explained. "The chart shouldn't look like it's a different patient on every page. That record is a business document, a legal document, and a big communications tool. You have so many people who don't speak the same language in this hospital. They have to understand each other's notes."

On the other hand, sometimes the reimbursement rules did seem crazy. "What's off the wall are some of the little decisions some insurance companies make, such as acute blood loss anemia is not reimbursed at the same rate as acute anemia secondary to GI bleed," said Spector. "You don't have to understand why, you just have to comply with it. That is part of the game."

I asked Sam Kopel, medical director, about the difficulty of keeping track. "The charts are so thick with everyone documenting, documenting, documenting, you can't make your way through them," he said. "I rely on nurses' notes, because their handwriting tends to be better, and I rely on the computer. I know all sorts of crap happens to my patients [that] I have no way of finding out, and I pray no horrible things are going to happen until the new computer system is in, in 2009. In the computer at least it's legible and it will be organized."

I first met David Gregorius after an early-morning lecture in a dimly lit, windowless room. One of the ER residency advisers had concluded the class by lamenting the disappearance of old-fashioned hands-on doctors. "We have lost the art of the rectal exam," he told a roomful of sleepy novices. "The eighty-year-old guy who taught you how to do it in school and could distinguish one thing from another by moving his finger around."

I was contemplating this thought when Steve Davidson, the department chairman, introduced me, telling the group I was writing a book about the hospital and it was okay to talk to me. After class Gregorius stopped by and asked if I would like to see an e-mail journal he'd sent his friends about his experiences. "Of course," I said.

I finally caught up with Gregorius again for a few minutes in the ER, not long after another lecture, this one from the documentation specialist. He was, as promised, typing into a computer terminal, eyes glued to the monitor, while talking to me, apparently tuning out the din around us.

"What did you think?" I asked him.

He lifted his eyes from the monitor for a second and laughed. "At first, we're all kind of like, 'Well, we get paid the same no matter what.' . . . I can see maybe we'll get a raise if the hospital makes more money. I ran into her a couple of times on the floor and showed her what I'd done. 'Check it out! I wrote "Diabetes Type Two" instead of just "Diabetes." An extra three thousand dollars.'"

Then, back to typing again, he got serious. "You have to learn how to bill properly," he said. "One of the reasons I wanted to go into ER is because in most other specialties you have to do more business. I just wanted to work at a hospital where you go in and work and then you go home, because I've never been really business-savvy. But we get the same thing in the ER. You do a procedure, log it on the chart, because then they can bill for it. If you just put in an IV, apparently, you don't even think about it, but if you wrote you did it in the chart, the hospital bills them for an extra fifty dollars, just by taking two minutes to write it down. I guess I'm getting better than that. I wonder if they keep track of how much we lost!"

They tried to keep track.

For several years Sondra Olendorf, head of nursing and hospital operations, had been trying to find the bottlenecks. Olendorf at first seemed to have no noticeable quirks; her unfussy short haircut, her manner of dress (conservative but feminine suits, often in bright colors) and way of speaking (vaguely Middle American) were cheerful and direct and would seem unremarkable anywhere else. She had grown up in West Virginia but had spent years working at a hospital in an upper-middle-class suburb of Detroit, where patients were predominantly white, Republican, and well insured and where the institution itself had, Olendorf said, "a kind of corporate culture." She fit in easily there.

At Maimonides, Olendorf started carrying around a Curious George lunch box. She said she wouldn't have felt comfortable doing that at her old job, but somehow this oddity now made sense. She explained that the lunch box prevented her from ever forgetting about patient flow.

How?

Olendorf had originally been hired at Maimonides as a performance-improvement specialist, responsible for understanding breakdowns in the system through data.

"There's a theory of asking why five times, and you'll get to something you can actually fix," she said when asked about Curious George, whose imprint wasn't limited to the lunch box. Olendorf's office had become a Curious George museum, filled with Curious George dolls, mugs, and clocks. "Early on, I got a reputation for asking, 'Why do we do it this way?

Why does that happen?' So the second year I was here, during the holidays, someone bought me this Curious George lunch box. So I carry it. It has pens and pencils and a calculator, Kleenex, markers, tape—management tools of facilitation. And now everyone brings me Curious George paraphernalia."

Olendorf had generally lived her life as the good girl. Her mother ran a grocery store, and her father worked at a steel company. Neither of them went to college, but they were ambitious for their children. She had no choice but to try to succeed. Yet after working her way through nursing school, Olendorf was burned out. She took a sabbatical from responsibility, packed her trunk, and headed for Aspen, to learn how to ski.

At Maimonides she saw the chance to combine responsibility and the thrill of the unknown, in a way that suited her in her fifties. "I need constant stimulation to get to the next good idea, and here everything was magnified and amplified," she said. "The place always feels sort of on the edge—on the edge of breakthrough of learning and improvement, on the edge of catastrophe because so many things can go wrong."

The hospital had hired a headhunter to find someone for the performance-improvement job in 1995. When the headhunter contacted Olendorf, an early adapter who had been doing that kind of work for a decade, she said no, she wasn't a city person. A conversation with someone who knew the hospital convinced her to take a look. She was fascinated by the different types of people, the lines queuing up at the clinics, the strange little brownstones (that weren't brownstones) that housed many of the administrative offices.

Her husband was ready to make the leap; he had retired from the building business and was making furniture at home. They surprised their grown children: "Hey kids, we're moving to Brooklyn, New York."

The door to her office remained open; at first glance the office usually seemed empty. A closer look would reveal Olendorf hunched in front of her computer screen, which provided the only light in the room. She puzzled things through in the dark, a way to shut out the static. It wasn't noisy on the executive floor, but there was a lot of nervous energy. "We're overstimulated, overinterested," said Olendorf.

Even sitting unobserved in the dark carried risks. Once, in the early evening, when it was already night outside, Brier came into Olendorf's office unannounced, with a physician, to steal some cookies sitting on a table by the door. The director of nursing sat in the shadows holding her breath, hoping they wouldn't notice her.

Olendorf had been instrumental in improving the nursing staff's performance and morale, which was at a low after the 1998 nurses' strike. She managed to be rigorous without insulting anyone, which Douglas Jablon—vice president for patient relations—interpreted as a kind of miracle. "With Sondra Olendorf, I feel she dropped from heaven, and I don't even think she got hurt," he said. "I say when God created her, God was just showing off. I remember before her we went through three, four nursing directors. I won't say they were all hated, but nurses didn't want to talk to them. Sondra walks on the floor and they throw themselves at her, kissing her."

In 2000, after she had become head of nursing, Olendorf asked a group of nurses to patrol the hospital to look for problems. They found several:

Patients would be scheduled for discharge, and then the doctors wouldn't pick up the lab work in time for the social workers to reach family members to pick the patients up. It was taking the cleaning staff eight and sometimes ten hours to get a bed washed, when the actual washing took about twenty minutes. Nurse-to-patient ratios on many floors were one to eight, requiring herculean effort on the part of every nurse; if a patient was discharged, there was little incentive to rush to fill that eighth bed too quickly.

Yet five years later, the problems continued, even after more nurses were hired and more social workers were replaced by discharge planners. Patients aren't fungible. They had to be distributed by disease and potential for infection, and available beds didn't necessarily crop up where they were needed. "You have to look at the entire picture," said Theresa Romanelli, a nurse on the telemetry unit who had been at Maimonides eight years and been chosen to become one of the "bed managers."

"We have twenty empty beds in surgery, no beds in medicine, and ten people waiting in the emergency room. We're not going to leave those beds empty. When it's really bad, in the winter months, we'll borrow beds from telemetry. But the next day they may be overwhelmed."

Being a bed manager took Romanelli outside her zone in the hospital and sparked a kind of existential awakening. She had never thought about her unit in relation to the rest, apart from maybe housekeeping and pharmacy. Who has time to reflect on all the links in any chain, how the envelope you put in a mailbox ends up at your mother's house a thousand miles away, or how freshly washed lettuce ends up in a sealed bag on a grocery shelf, or where electricity comes from, or how patients suddenly appeared in her unit? Suddenly she saw herself and the work she had done as both larger and smaller, part of a giant equation she hadn't even considered. "Coming from the floor, I was able to see the entire hospital," she said. "I just didn't think of anything outside my unit before. I just didn't. You go to work, you go to your area, you do your shift, and you just leave. You aren't aware. You have this notion you are working so hard, harder than anyone else. Then you start walking around and you see everyone working so hard. You're so consumed with your own thing."

The fact that Maimonides is a teaching hospital added to the complexity. As in most hospitals, the residents belonged to teams. The six medicine teams, for example, distinguished themselves by color: Purple, Yellow, Orange, Green, Brown, Black. Each color had a home floor, and patients were admitted on a rotating basis. So when a doctor from, say, the Brown team came down to "take report," to prepare for the handoff, the trick was to find that patient a bed on the floor where the Brown team was stationed.

The bed managers asked for and were granted an overflow unit, a grouping of rooms that could accommodate patients with a variety of illnesses. But every morning the infectious-disease team patrolled looking for "Contact P," as in pan-resistant, patients requiring isolation because they carried bacterial infections that had become resistant to commonly used antibiotics. The special precautions had begun in 2004, when there was a noticeable increase in patients infected with these supercharged bacteria.

"They'll call up to four P.M. and say, 'This patient is now Contact P. You have to move this patient,'" said Romanelli. "These biology majors ruin the bed manager's day. You think you have everything right, you think you can predict, you know what surgery is going on, then you get a call—'We have four new Contact P patients'—and it's chaos."

Romanelli often felt overwhelmed. "Sometimes I feel responsible, if someone is waiting in the emergency room for a day, waiting for a bed, [and] despite bed management, despite overflow, despite everything else, we just don't have the space, we don't have the room," she said. "You can have ten discharges planned, and within minutes ten discharges can be canceled. Things just happen."

When things just happened in health care, someone found a moneymaking opportunity. A company called TeleTracking Technologies created software to deal with the bed-tracking problem. In 2005, frustrated by its inability to speed up the flow, Maimonides management decided to spent the money—$408,000—for an automated system from TeleTracking Technologies.

The company's Web site explains how it is supposed to work:

> When a nurse requests transport for a patient who is being discharged, it starts a chain reaction. As the transporter leaves a room, he or she calls into Transport Tracking, which prompts housekeeping through Bed-Tracking. Then the housekeeper arrives and dials in. In the Patient Logistics department, staff members see that the room's status has changed to "In Progress" on the screen. When the housekeeper dials in that the job is complete, the system changes that room's color on the screen as it is designated "Clean." This allows all departments to easily view bed status.

Maria Ferlita was impressed by the new system, which had just been put in place. "Oh, my God, I'm going to go blind there with all these colors," she said. "But now we can look at that board in a snapshot and see which bed is empty, which one is being cleaned, which one is male, which one is female, and it will allow us in one view [to see] what is going on [on] each particular floor and everything else. This will help us produce the system electronically. This will help show us where the problems are. I think long-term what it's going to do is reduce the amount of dead bed time tremendously." She was willing to be hopeful.

A few months later, I checked in with Olendorf, who said the flow was better but the smooth transitions described by TeleTracking Technologies were still elusive. "I can be accused of a lot of things, but I won't be accused of kidding myself," she said. "If you want to fix things, you have to admit they're broken."

They had learned that for the bed-tracking system to work, someone at the nurses' station had to let the system know that a patient was ready to be discharged. This required punching a bunch of numbers into a telephone line. The job fell to the "information specialists" on the unit, who already had a long list of responsibilities. None of these duties involved clinical expertise, but they were the jobs that could make a hospital stay pleasant (that is, at least tolerable) or a nightmare.

The job description listed twenty-six tasks that included being receptionist and traffic cop for patient and visitor questions and needs; taking care of charts; notifying physicians, nurses, and dietary staff of arrivals and departures (via admissions, discharges, death); distributing mail; overseeing patient property; running errands. Now managing the bed-tracking system had been tacked onto the load of the lowest-paid people on the nursing staff, annual salary about $23,000.

"You have to be reasonable about what you can expect for what we're paying them," Olendorf said. Yet she was willing to raise expectations, hers and theirs, and made plans for yet another new training program. "People have to change their process to be watching instead of waiting for someone to call them or beep them. If we change that, it will greatly reduce potential errors. I think it's going to work, but you can't kid yourself about the implementation. You have to keep changing, and people have to change their practice."

The term "dead beds" had additional meaning in the hospital world in New York State. While Maimonides was overflowing with patients, about twenty other hospitals in the state had closed in the previous five years, for various reasons, including mismanagement and not enough demand, but all related to business. St. Mary's, for example, the hospital in Crown Heights that catered mostly to poor people, had been operating at about 57 percent capacity when it stopped operations in October 2005. A group called the Berger Commission, named after Stephen Berger, the former government official and investment banker who headed it, had been circling over the state's hospitals like the angel of death and eventually would announce its hit list.

About two and a half miles from Maimonides, another hospital was in trouble—Victory Memorial, whose very name now seemed like a portent of its own doom. This 250-bed hospital, which also had a 150-bed nursing home, situated across the street from a golf course and from the bucolic campus of Poly Prep Country Day School, conveyed the placid feeling of a hospital in a small city. Founded in 1900, Victory had not adjusted to the changes in hospital finances brought about by managed care; it had been operating in the red for the past two years. A number of doctors affiliated with the hospital had moved their practices; the hospital was generally running at 75 percent occupancy.

State and local politicians did not want the hospital to close; the institution employed 1,000 people and delivered 2,500 babies each year. But ob-gyn was a money loser. Reimbursements were low, malpractice premiums enormous. The only thing that might keep Victory alive was the fact that it had a middle-class constituency with political clout—unlike St. Mary's, located in Crown Heights, a poor neighborhood. Martin Golden, state senator for the Twenty-second District in Brooklyn, had been born at Victory. After a couple of failed attempts at partnerships with other Brooklyn hospitals, the state had asked Maimonides to get involved.

Brier was eager to do so. Victory and Maimonides entered into an uneasy partnership, overseen by state officials, under which Maimonides invested $5 million in Victory, mainly to cover payroll and other expenses. Maimonides was supposed to help Victory increase admissions and improve its finances, a task that fell to Fraidkin, Cunningham, and Robert Naldi, the chief financial officer. The return to Maimonides was murkier; the commitment was made in part to curry favor with public-health officials who wanted Victory to survive and also to fend off competition from other hospitals.

Victory became a major preoccupation for the senior staff, though most everyone else at the hospital was oblivious to the machinations involved. Like applying for Magnet status, trying to work out a deal with Victory was part of the hospital's big ambition, regarded with admiration by some and as overreaching by others. For Naldi, who had to shoulder much of the burden of the Victory deal, it was worth the effort. "As long as they're needed," he qualified. "If they aren't needed, they shouldn't be there."

But need by whose measure? Did the community need another hospital or more assisted-living centers for an aging population? What about all those babies being born at Victory? Maimonides didn't have room for their mothers or for them. What about turning Victory into a primary-care center, where inexpensive preventive medicine could be practiced, reducing overcrowding in emergency rooms all over the borough? I didn't envy the Berger Commission as it worked out its assessment of waste and need.

Both Maimonides and Victory were founded following the last great wave of immigration to the United States, in the nineteenth century. For Newman Dube, the founder of Israel Zion Hospital, which would become Maimonides, need was obvious, uncomplicated, and personal. Dube, born Nehemiah Dubovsky, came to America in 1888 from Minsk, at age twenty, because he was afraid of being conscripted into the Russian army. The Dube and Bashevkin families were part of the same chapter of U.S. history, in which impoverished greenhorn peddlers became prosperous American merchants. After the turn of the century, Dube moved his family to Borough Park, a fairly new community that had no hospital.

Two incidents convinced Dube that the health-care situation in his neighborhood had to change. The first occurred in 1916, when Dube's four-year-old son contracted croup diphtheria and barely survived the trip to the nearest hospital. The second incident, which took place almost three years later, was far more calamitous. The influenza pandemic of 1918, believed to have killed 20 to 24 million people worldwide and around 675,000 in the United States, found its way to the Dube home; the former peddler by then lived in a massive residence, with thirteen rooms to house him, his wife, and their six children. This time illness brought death. His fifteen-year-old daughter became part of the global statistic.

Would a local hospital have made a difference? It's doubtful, but Dube chose to believe so. Grief demands explanations. So just as Steven Cymbrowitz, a century later, would raise money for a cancer center in order to give his wife's early death some purpose, Dube the grieving father would became the primary force behind the creation of a hospital in Borough Park.

The dedication of the hospital took place in 1919, which seemed—in 2005—like a comparatively simple time. The $10,000 Dube collected was adequate seed money for an entire hospital. In 2005 that $10,000 would be worth roughly $112,890, using the consumer price index as a comparison. In adjusted dollars it would pay salary and benefits for one registered nurse, or three or four defibrillators, or 220 emergency room visits (less than a day's worth at Maimonides), or three bypass operations.

But paying for health care was a problem even then. "By the early 1900s, the annual deficits incurred by most hospitals in New York City became a generally recognized problem among the city's hospital trustees, administrators, and even charity workers," wrote David Rosner in *A Once Charitable Institution,* a book full of reminders that hospitals have always struggled with finances, with management, with determining their social mandate.

Was it ridiculous to try to connect this humble story of a father trying to cope with his daughter's premature death to present-day Maimonides—the multicultural patient flow, the feuds, the political wrangling over Victory, the cancer center, insurance reimbursements—to Mr. Zen?

Luckily—amazingly—I found a direct link, making me think that maybe it was true, *min zhong zhu ding,* "life is predestined." One of Newman Dube's children was still alive.

Douglas Jablon introduced me to Daniel Dube, who was about to turn ninety-seven years old when I met him in his office at Park Surgical Company, across from Moishe's Cleaners, under the elevated subway, a few blocks from the hospital. Park Surgical (named for Borough Park) sold all kinds of medical supplies, including wheelchairs, lactation aids, prosthetic legs, hearing aids. Newman Dube started the business in 1929, another legacy for his children and grandchildren, who seventy-six years later ran the business with their Uncle Daniel, the only living reminder of the past generations.

Dube was what my mother would call a "real gentleman," the type who stood when a woman entered the room. He was about five feet tall, had a thick, carefully trimmed white mustache, and was very natty in a sports jacket with tiny sky blue and white checks, plaid pants, and a striped tie. He spoke with the stentorian tones and elegant cadences of another era; he could have been a bit player in a Fred Astaire movie, part of the atmosphere. His precise diction was studied, not natural; he had found talking difficult as a child and eventually trained himself to speak, as he called it, "euphoniously." Hearing his melodious use of the language would have pleased his mother; she was an immigrant from Brest-Litovsk, famous for the treaty that got Russia out of World War I, and never spoke Yiddish with her children because she wanted to improve her English.

Dube gave me a tour of the business, pointing out an old sewing machine where, he said proudly, a gifted employee made prosthetic bras for women who'd had mastectomies. Then he told me his father's story, and his own, compressing a century's worth of social history into one family's memory. He covered the 1929 stock-market crash, the 1918 flu epidemic, the development of health care in southern Brooklyn, World War II, and elocution lessons. He also offered medical advice, urging me to take cod liver oil every day, as he had done for forty years, a prescription he felt certain had kept him from having arthritis. He endorsed bran powder as well, noting that too many people strain when they go to the bathroom.

As for the hospital, he told me he didn't know much about Maimonides anymore, though he spoke warmly about it. His father stayed on the board until he died in 1966 and insisted on going to every meeting, even though he was blind for the last three years of his life and needed his son's help to get there. Daniel Dube had been watching the construction of the new wing with interest but confessed that his company didn't do as much business with the hospital as it used to. "Hospitals don't pay their bills on time," he said. "It can involve a great deal of money, and if you want to be viable in business, you have to pay your bills on time or you lose whatever benefit you have in discounting."

I asked him how the hospital was regarded in the community. "It is well regarded, but the great difficulty is that the first contact is through the emergency room, and the wait is interminable to be admitted to the hospital," he said. "I can understand the difficulties, and I'm sure the hospital powers that be are doing the best they can. Before, the demands of the community were not as large."

I hadn't mentioned Mr. Zen—indeed, I hadn't yet met him—when Dube invoked his situation, if not his specific case. "Since the foreign element has come into the community, the undocumented element, where they have no private insurance and their only medical facility is the emergency room, that is the primary reason the hospital is burdened so strongly," said Dube.

Newman Dube's legacy extended beyond the medical-supply shop; Daniel Dube had inherited his father's sense of responsibility and his good heart.

"But what would these people do without it?" he asked. "Many of them are illegal, but you don't neglect them, you don't just disregard them. They're human. I don't think anyone would ever think of not doing what is right."

We chatted a while longer, and then Daniel Dube escorted me to the door, ever courtly, his hand lightly touching my elbow. As I was leaving, he asked me where I was going.

"I'm meeting Pam Brier," I said.

"Do me a favor," he said. "I once gave Pam a silver tray that was given to my father, thinking they'd have an area to show it. I don't think they ever did. Tell her I'd like to have it back."

I did ask Brier about the tray that morning, but neither she nor her secretaries could remember where they had put it. "I'm accused sometimes of getting mired too much in the details, but that elegant little detail eluded me," she said.

Brier told me she would pass along Mr. Dube's request to Derek Goins, senior vice president for operations. When I reminded her about the tray some months later, she replied, "The sad answer to your question is that we have not been able to track it down. I put Derek on the case, and his staff has searched about, with no tray in sight. Most of the other people who would know about it are dead or far away."

Five

The Fixer

ouglas Jablon's office, located a block from Eisenstadt, on the second floor of one of the little brick buildings, was headquarters for the Maimonides favor bank. His walls were covered with commendations and awards from yeshivas and monasteries, firefighters, police officers, and politicians. He was the fixer, the expediter, the goodwill ambassador, the Orthodox Jew frequently introduced by Nidal Abuasi, the Palestinian-born principal of the Muslim Al-Noor School, as "a colleague, a friend, and a brother." The imam Hafiz Mohammad Sabir of the Makki Mosque on Coney Island Avenue and the Pakistani American Federation of New York, when praising Maimonides for reaching out to his community, qualified, "The whole credit goes to Mr. Douglas Jablon."

Mark McDougle, the number two administrator and chief operating officer, learned soon after arriving at Maimonides that, when it came to community matters, the answer would be: Ask Douglas.

When McDougle first met with the leaders from the Flatbush Hatzolah in one of their homes, he asked them what they thought the hospital needed to do to satisfy their constituency. "They told me specifically how amazing Douglas is," he said.

One day I bumped into him in the hall before the Jewish High Holidays. He looked jazzed as he held up a typed list of names and telephone numbers. "I'm supposed to call these people to wish them a good Yom Kippur," he said.

The list was supplied by Jablon.

Every day McDougle learned something new about the neighborhoods that surrounded the hospital. Driving to work in mid-October, he noticed that the streets of Borough Park were empty and wondered why.

So he asked Douglas and learned about Sukkot, a harvest ritual known as the Festival of Booths. The holiday was rooted in Leviticus (23:42–43), where Jews are instructed to remember the huts God provided while they wandered in the desert for forty years, after the exodus from slavery in Egypt. That's why so many Orthodox men had suddenly been walking around the neighborhood carrying two-by-fours. These once-a-year carpenters, he learned, were preparing to build structures called sukkahs, where for seven days, they could take meals and even sleep, as commanded by their Torah.

McDougle was a rationalist, a midwestern WASP from Cincinnati, a spare, owlish man with a trim athlete's build and short gray hair. Crisp. He preferred to conduct business via succinct e-mails rather than long conversations. His large office was uncluttered and largely undecorated, except for family photos and a few architectural posters.

He was alternately perplexed and touched by the seemingly endless rules and rituals that surrounded Orthodox life in Borough Park. A siren followed by stillness heralded the Sabbath. Cell phones were turned off and automobile motors silenced every Friday evening at sunset, an exact but always shifting moment set not by the clock but by nature. The commandment to rest was at odds with the metabolism of a restless city, where meditation was something to be either avoided or accomplished efficiently—at lunch, in power-yoga classes, or, as McDougle did, by bicycling long distances on weekends.

The hospital worked on a 24/7 schedule; little was predictable, and the workload always outstripped time and resources. The early shutdown on Fridays and the unavailability of Orthodox physicians became another problem to solve. But for those who understood its meaning, the calm that fell on the hospital was different from the weekend slowdown at other medical institutions, marking a presence rather than an absence.

Almost two years into the job, McDougle was less surprised but still amused by administrative tasks that were particular to Maimonides and for which none of his earlier hospital jobs had prepared him.

Ask Douglas.

Just after Sukkoth I was in McDougle's office when Pam Brier popped in to ask him if he knew whether she had to cover her head when she entered a mosque.

"I'm still stewing over my outfit," she said. The imam of the Makki Mosque had invited her to speak after morning prayers, as Ramadan was drawing to a close. "Something long and something buttoned up," she said distractedly. "I have to be polite. I have to ask Douglas, but he doesn't even know the first names of the Hatzolah wives."

McDougle laughed.

"I have to call the right person, but I don't know who that is," Brier said.

McDougle replied, "Isn't there someone here who is Muslim?"

Brier said, "Someone I'm thinking about is Muslim, but she's not Pakistani."

"It is good to be polite," said McDougle noncommittally.

Brier raised her index finger up in the air. "I know who to call," she said "I'll call Douglas for the name of who to call."

With that she left. McDougle shook his head and lifted his eyebrows, ever so slightly. Sometimes the chief operating officer seemed like chief straight man to Brier's dizzy grande dame, and he accepted the part with good humor. "You have to deal with things here you don't have to deal with in Manhattan," he said dryly.

Two days later Brier headed for the mosque. After much consideration she had settled on a long-sleeved black blouse and an ankle-length black skirt decorated with hints of color. She carried a scarf she had pulled out of her large collection; long, silk, black with shiny piping, it had seemed just the right thing, stylish and respectful. (Though it was Lili Fraidkin, not Jablon, who had put her in touch with a Pakistani surgeon for a fashion consult.) I was along for the ride, this arranged by Douglas Jablon, Mitzvah Man, who joined us in the town car the hospital provided Brier, along with Leon, her Russian driver.

Jablon managed to be almost everywhere, but never out front. One hot summer night, a crowd of Hasidic Jews set fire to a couple of police cars and lit two dozen bonfires in Borough Park after two policemen arrested an elderly Orthodox man. He had been talking on his cell phone while driving and didn't pull over when the roof light on the patrol car behind him began to flash. One thing led to another: The seventy-five-year-old man was hand-cuffed and taken into custody, the Hasids protested, and Joseph J. Esposito, the local police chief, was accused of saying something like, "Get those fuck-ing Jews out of here." (The *New York Times* reported that the police depart-ment acknowledged Esposito's use of an expletive but specified that "quotes of his comments in the statement did not make any reference to Jews.") Jablon was one of a handful of people from the community called in to talk to Raymond Kelly, the commissioner of police for New York City. Jablon told the commissioner that everyone was overheated, it was a hot night, it was a misunderstanding, and Esposito was a great guy.

Jablon's conciliatory nature was linked to fears of authority and anti-Semitism and to demons he was reluctant to discuss, though he once men-tioned he was estranged from his brother over a matter of money. But if Jablon had a shtetl mentality, he was the first to acknowledge that the shtetl had gone multicultural. When Stanley Brezenoff declared the hospital's new policy of community engagement, Jablon turned his staff's attention there. "We never got any Chinese people, and we decided to dive into it," he told me. "Why should these people, God forbid, they get really sick, they have a terrible disease—cancer, heart problems—God forbid they get a heart attack and go to another hospital in New York that's more oriented to their lan-guages, that's a sin. God forbid a stroke, and here we are a minute away. Or chemotherapy? Why should they schlep?"

Born in 1950, Jablon grew up in Borough Park but didn't become obser-vant until he was sixteen years old when, as he put it, "the world had gone crazy." In reaction to the radicalism of the sixties, he became a student of Moshe M. Heschel (one of the many "biggest rabbis" in the neighborhood), stopping for religious classes on his way to public school. After college he sold "major appliances" at a department store and then quit to work for Dov Hikind, who became a New York State assemblyman in 1982, a position he still held twenty-four years later.

During his three years on Hikind's staff, Jablon was willing to overlook the assemblyman's impulsive behavior and radical politics. He studied—with admiration—how Hikind kept his constituency satisfied by making shrewd use of personal contacts and street smarts to deliver social services.

Jablon had been at the hospital for eighteen years before he was able to put what he'd learned from Hikind to use there. Opportunity arrived with Stanley Brezenoff in 1995. The new president found a community hospital with larger aspirations, a combative board of trustees, and a beleaguered chief administrator who understood hospital management but not local politics. He saw a hospital that had lost its connection to the surrounding community; the once-crowded ER had been suffering a decline in admissions as other Brooklyn hospitals recognized Hatzolah's power and catered to it. New York Methodist Hospital in particular recognized opportunity; the administration put in a kosher kitchen for the volunteer ambulance service and made them feel welcome, not like pests.

For Brezenoff local politics was the fun part of what he called "the swirl." He and Marty Payson agreed that the first job was to win back the loyalty of the Orthodox and engage the new communities that had grown up around the hospital. It didn't take them too long to identify their main man on that front. The answer was obvious.

Ask Douglas.

I asked Payson who specifically was responsible for unleashing Jablon. "Douglas will give me a hug and say, 'It's you Mr. Payson,' and he'll say the same thing to Pam and the same thing to Stanley," said Payson. "He'll say before we came, he used to hide his head from the community, because they had so many complaints and they took them all out on Douglas. As we began to build, he became a source of pride. So Douglas discovered Douglas. As we began to solve the problems and he saw what was happening, it gave him the nourishment to be Douglas. I can't say any of us created Douglas. We gave him the freedom to be Douglas."

In his best Brooklynese, Brezenoff explained that he made it clear there was one party line: "It's not okay to crack wise about Hatzolah, about the Pakistani community, or to regard yourself as superior [for] doing the community a favor. Douglas understood it, but before, he had to cajole and coax. I believe people quickly realized they couldn't cross me on this issue. Then, as it translated into success, people embraced it, because they liked being part of something successful."

Jablon's department grew from ten patient representatives to thirty. Their job was to interpret, mediate, and expedite matters between patients and doctors, nurses and everyone else. They came from many places, including

Haiti, Ukraine, Greece, Germany, Pakistan, Nigeria, Borough Park; they spoke seventeen languages and were in beeper contact with ninety volunteers trained in simultaneous interpretation. Some were Ph.D.'s; others had only high-school diplomas. They were notary publics, so they could act as official witnesses to Do Not Resuscitate orders and do favors for doctors who needed something notarized.

Jablon described his training method. "There's no monkey business," he said. "First of all, you gotta take care of patients. Number two, all this advertising is very important, but I believe the patient is the best advertising, especially over here. They sit outside in their chairs, outside the apartment houses, and if you treat them very well, they'll talk good about us. You do one wrong thing, they'll talk bad about us. I will not stand it from my department. My department has to have a hundred percent. I can't be responsible for everybody in the hospital, but we try to make a difference. Sometimes the doctors get stressed out, sometimes the nurses get stressed out, but we're not allowed to get stressed out. I say if you get stressed, you can come up and smack me in the face, hit the walls."

Brezenoff soon learned there were some things he could not ask Jablon to do—or not to do. The favor bank didn't extend to certain situations. If, for example, a child came into the emergency room who was hurt in a way that raised the suspicions of a social worker or clinician, the case had to be reported. "You have to make it clear to community leaders there's a line we won't cross," said Brezenoff. "Douglas couldn't do that."

Jablon's defining trait was his inability to say no. This insistent desire to help was both weakness and strength, and it often elicited groans inside the hospital.

Carl Ramsay found himself groaning a lot. The medical director of the ER—the beanpole, Dr. Ponytail—was part of the bed-tracking team. He saw the goodwill exerted by the patient-relations department as a giant stopper, backing up bed flow.

"Only sixty percent of those beds are controlled by medicine," he said. "The rest are controlled by all these fiefdoms: anything from patient relations to a cardiothoracic surgery nurse. I try to be polite. But when someone comes down and says, 'We have this person who just came in and needs this kind of bed,' and it's the middle of chaos, I let them know we've had five patients waiting for twelve hours each, some twenty-four hours, waiting for that exact type of bed. It's totally unfair. Then they say, 'What's wrong? Why are you getting so angry?'"

Still, Ramsay saw how useful the patient reps could be. They helped calm angry families, arranged for interpreters, discussed DNR and health-proxy orders. He asked Jablon to give them more hands-on responsibilities—to wheel patients to rooms if transportation was jammed up, to help track down lab reports and X-rays, to take away empty trays and deliver urinals.

John Marshall, the residency program director, went even further. "This is the first emergency department I've worked in that has actually had patient representatives in the emergency room like that," he said. "They're absolutely essential in terms of helping us—from the translation, dealing with families, everything else. If I ever went someplace else that didn't have patient representatives, I would push strongly to start a patient-representative program."

He continued, "Do they sometimes ask me to see patients who are more . . . let me say, who have more access to the administration than other patients? Sure, they do that. But they'll do it not just for those patients. It's not just that community, it's other communities as well. If they feel somebody is falling through the cracks, somebody has a lot of pain, they help, regardless of whose godson or nephew they are."

Jason Tache, a third-year oncology fellow, was not so enthusiastic about Jablon's apparently bottomless goodwill. "With Orthodox families you're dealing with seven, eight, nine children, which means when you have a patient, you have somebody who knows the vice president for patient relations," he said. "So many of them become VIPs automatically. The Pakistanis are VIP. The whole hospital is a VIP. Everybody is a VIP. And when everybody is a VIP, nobody is a VIP."

Driving with Brier and me, through residential neighborhoods en route to the Makki Mosque, Jablon pointed out the mosque that had been headquarters for "the blind sheik," referring to the Egyptian Muslim cleric Omar Abdel-Rahman. The blind sheik was serving a life sentence in federal prison for his role in the 1993 bombing of the World Trade Center. After that the FBI spent a lot of time in the neighborhood.

The atmosphere in the car became sober as Jablon, Brier, and I returned to a constant point of reference for New Yorkers in those years, the September 11, 2001, attacks. Not just the twin towers of the World Trade Center had been destroyed. The surprise invasion had shaken the sense of American invincibility that was the underpinning of its arrogance as well as its tolerance. Suddenly the large and growing Muslim population was no longer the latest colorful addition to New York's protean populace, but rather a potential menace. Whites, Asians, and black people eyed every Pakistani taxi driver with suspicion. Was he just trying to make a living, or was he a holy warrior eager to die for his faith? "Where are you from?" became code for "Do you want to kill me?"

We talked about what it had been like in the days, weeks, and months after. The city had felt under siege. Fear crowded out political correctness, unleashing incivility, suspicion, and violence. Reports were coming in of Muslim kids being stoned, fights breaking out. Someone threw pork chops in the backyard at the Al-Noor School; a Muslim teacher was chased up to the school's front doors; an African-American girl wearing a head scarf was pushed on the subway stairs.

Immediately after the attacks, hospitals all over the city were on alert for a massive influx of wounded people, which never materialized. Those who didn't escape the towers jumped to their deaths or were vaporized. Brier spoke of what it was like at Maimonides. The staff set up hotlines and help desks, following standard instructions for emergency preparedness, but it soon became clear that the wounded who needed tending were coming not from outside the hospital walls but from within. It seemed no one had been left personally untouched. Brooklyn provided a significant proportion of the Manhattan workforce, the secretaries, police officers, firefighters as well as the young executives, proud progeny of lab techs and nurses, and many of them worked at the World Trade Center, just across the river, an easy commute. The non-Muslim hospital workers, the vast majority, erupted in sorrow and bitterness, arousing feelings of persecution and anger among the Muslim employees. Brier saw that the institution was facing not the expected medical emergency but an emotional crisis that touched its core. How were halal and kosher, samosas and Irish stew, won ton soup and churros and goat curry going to mix now?

Brezenoff was in Italy on vacation, and he did what he could from a distance. As soon as the international telephone lines were up again, he called Nidal Abuasi at the Al-Noor School, just to make sure Abuasi and his wife were all right, a gesture that Abuasi later recalled with warmth and gratitude. ("That showed perception," Abuasi told me. "That shows care and sensitivity that we cherish.") It was up to Brier, however, to deal with the crisis, and she was scared. Walking around the hospital Tuesday night, September 11, she saw that the emergency-preparedness operation was missing something vital. She told her husband, who was there with her, "We're not really helping recharge people's souls." Brier decided to organize a series of prayer and reflection services in Schreiber Auditorium, the hospital's main gathering place, several times a day for the first week, then twice a day the second. With trepidation, she approached Avrohom Friedlander, the hospital's chief chaplain, a small, watchful Orthodox man outfitted with beard and broad-brimmed hat. "There can be no religious proselytizing or undue focus on Orthodox Judaism. You have to be restrained about this," she told him. She was relieved when Friedlander said he understood and agreed to lead some of the discussions, while priests took charge of others, and then Imam Hafiz Mohammad Sabir agreed to come.

The sessions were intense. Some people complained about supervisors who were not sensitive to the turmoil they felt, Muslim employees talked about being Muslim in a non-Muslim world, families of firefighters and policeman spoke of their concern for their loved ones. "We let everyone know that whatever goes on in the outside world, when you're in this hospital or one of our clinics, you are safe," Brier recalled, looking out the window at the heavy Friday-morning traffic. "I know this sounds touchy-feely, but I think it resonated with the staff—the Muslim staff, who are a minority, and the non-Muslim staff, who were really very distressed and angry about what was going on."

We all sat silent for a while until Brier dispelled the mournful feeling evoked by these memories and briskly asked Jablon if Brezenoff had spoken at the mosque. No, he said, Marty Payson had, but not Brezenoff.

Brier nodded without comment. She always spoke of Brezenoff neutrally or with praise; her former boss remained the measuring mark.

As the car turned onto Coney Island Avenue and reached the stretch known as Little Pakistan, kosher shops were replaced by halal. After passing several blocks of small storefronts, we came upon a police car sitting at the head of a long row of town cars parked in front of what appeared to be more storefronts, until the sign out front came into focus: There is no God but Allah, Mohammed is messenger of Allah, Help from Allah in approaching triumph in the name of Allah most gracious most merciful. This humble edifice was the Makki Mosque, where three to four thousand people regularly worshipped, as many as twenty-two thousand on a major holidays.

Only one of the town cars out front had been hired for a passenger, the representative from the United Nations delegation who was visiting that day. The rest of the cars were parked while their drivers prayed inside.

A smiling man with black hair and a lazy eye greeted us. Jablon whispered that this was Oscar, an important person (his real name is Asghar Choudhri, designated the "unofficial mayor of Little Pakistan" by the *New York Times*). As Brier stood on the sidewalk straightening her skirt, Choudhri said, "Of course you will be talking about the earthquake." Brier nodded, even though it hadn't until that moment occurred to her to mention the earthquake that two weeks earlier had devastated Pakistan; early United Nations estimates had put the dead at 73,000 and those left without homes at 2.3 million. Her intention had been simply to inform the Pakistanis about the free colon-cancer screenings and to speak generally to them about improving their health.

"They are waiting," Choudhri said as he opened the door, and she walked inside to find a surprisingly large hall; apparently the interior walls separating the small buildings had been removed. The imam, an elegant man wearing the traditional Pakistani *salwar kameez,* a long shirt over loose cotton trousers, stood at the front. Brier couldn't see the floor between him and her; it was carpeted with Pakistani men, kneeling or sitting, some dressed Western style, others in traditional clothing.

Brier slipped out of her delicate black velvet loafers and left them on a pile of men's shoes, then wrapped her scarf high on her shoulders until it swaddled her head. Only a bit of blond hair was visible as she followed Choudhri through a narrow path that opened in the sea of men, who moved to let her pass even as their eyes remained cast downward. Jablon and I followed behind. What were these silent men thinking as this elegant twig passed by with her head covered, followed by a giant Jew in a yarmulke and me, carrying my tape recorder, tiptoeing in stocking feet through throw rugs covered by Pakistanis?

The imam made the introduction in Urdu, which Choudhri translated for us. Referring to Brier as "The Pam," the imam said, "She is really concerned about the earthquake, and she wanted to come down and tell you that you are not alone."

Brier looked small in front of the microphone and began to speak in a quavering voice. Her words were strong, though, clear and focused in a way they often were not in meetings with her staff. Her impromptu speech began with a note of thanks, and then she said, "It has been a very sad and tragic time for the people of Pakistan and all of you. We at the hospital provide medical care to people, which we think is important. But we are not so blinded to the realities of the world that we think medicine alone helps make people healthy. Housing. Shelter. Enough food to eat. Freedom from the basic kinds of diseases that poverty and tragedy bring."

She spoke of how groups of hospital employees had been collecting blankets and supplies to send to Pakistan, then went on to say, "We became closer friends with the imam and with many people connected to him after 9/11/2001. It was a horrible time. We knew how much suffering there was going on and how much hatred there is that is surprisingly redounding in New York City in a way that we're ashamed of ourselves, really. And we decided, the staff at Maimonides—all of us, doctors, nurses, other staff— that when a patient comes to the hospital, if the patient speaks Yiddish, Hebrew, Arabic, Urdu, Chinese inside that hospital, inside those clinics, everybody is to be treated respectfully and everybody is to be safe. We think that is very important, and we welcome the people from this community. It's complicated for us to figure out how to offer people some financial assistance to pay for their care. In some cases we are able to make people eligible for Medicaid and other what we call special-service programs that carry with them financial assistance. In other areas we're not able to do so. But I do want to promise you we are committed to looking for ways of doing that."

The kneeling men now looked at her intently. Hard to interpret the gaze, which felt collective.

She encouraged people to come to the cancer center for information on the colon-cancer test. "I tell you about it not to drum up business while we're all here, but to tell you there are some services you can get if you have no money or some money, if you have no insurance or some insurance. I will not be so secular as to talk about it in the midst of a house of prayer, but I do want to tell you we will give you information on how you can be tested for colon cancer whether or not you have insurance, no questions asked. Right?"

She spoke for a total of nine minutes and then stepped aside. Some men began to applaud but were silenced by the imam, who said, "The Pam, we always welcome you here in the Pakistani community. Douglas Jablon, I love you a lot because you were the one who has taken us to the other leaders so we could have good relations with the priest, the rabbi. You are the best neighbor. Maimonides is the best medical center in Brooklyn. Not in Brooklyn, in New York."

Choudhri said, "In the United States."

With that he led Brier outside and told a young man to bring us next door to a Pakistani restaurant, where Brier ordered an abundance of take-out food. When the man behind the counter refused to accept money, she pressed it on Choudhri's helper and told him to give it to a relief fund for the earthquake.

A few weeks later, on a freezing day in December, Jablon took me to visit the imam and Choudhri. As he drove, he played a tape of the most recent broadcast of Dov Hikind's weekly program on WMCA talk radio. "I just want to mention one thing, and we're going to be very brief," the politician said to his sidekick. "This is amazing. We were both . . . ummmm, not shocked, but this was nice to read in the newspaper: 'Maimonides top hospital in survival rate,' one of the headlines in one of the major newspapers here in New York." He was referring to the annual New York State hospital report card, released by the Alliance for Quality Health Care and Niagara Health Quality Coalition, a nonprofit group, which gave the hospital "three-star" ratings in more categories than earned by any other hospital in New York.

With a note of surprise in his voice, Hikind said, "This is not Maimonides propaganda."

Jablon pressed the "off" button. "Forget about it," he muttered, clearly responding to something besides Hikind's words. "I don't know, people just aren't happy. Not at the hospital only, but in general. They like to complain."

He pulled up near the Makki Mosque, where the imam was waiting. We walked to an empty restaurant, but it was difficult for us to hear each other over the television set playing an Urdu soap opera. Choudhri, who had joined us, took us to his small, crowded office in a nearby tenement building, the smallness accentuated by the noise from creaky pipes. Like Jablon's office, Choudhri's was adorned with plaques and photos confirming that he was a personage of note.

The imam discussed his history with the hospital. Like many Pakistanis in the area, he was from the Kashmir region. He had arrived in New York twenty-two years earlier. In Brooklyn at the time, there were few Pakistani shops, so the imam's family, like most others, bought meat in kosher shops, because the rules of kashruth closely parallel those of halal. Until Brezenoff and Brier arrived at Maimonides, however, the hospital was regarded as off-limits. Contact was made; a clinic providing an Urdu-speaking staff opened on Newkirk Avenue.

But he confirmed that the event that cemented relations with the hospital was, paradoxically, September 11, the moment that had blown apart the Western and Muslim worlds.

"They were the only people who helped us through this time," he said. "Every day the FBI came to this area, taking six, seven families every night. No politician came to help us. None of them [were] returning our calls. The shops were closed, the shopkeepers were crying. The hospital called the whole staff and requested them to shop here."

Choudhri joined the conversation. "The politicians didn't know us, no one!" he said. He spoke about feeling betrayed by politicians he had worked to cultivate. "In 2000 there was a big fund-raising for Hillary Clinton [in her first campaign for New York senator]. I went with my wife, to the thousand-dollar room, I had a picture with her, with Gore's wife. Since the election Hillary doesn't know us."

Choudhri was on the community board of advisers at Coney Island Hospital, the public hospital that treated many Pakistani patients. "I said to them, 'There is no Urdu-speaking person in patient relations. Why don't you hire a Pakistani?' One day they say, 'Yes, we have someone.' I meet her, and I said, 'You are Pakistani?' She said, 'No, I am from Fiji.' I go to the director and say, 'You go to Fiji to find someone who speaks Urdu? That I do not like.'"

Another hospital hired a Pakistani department chairman, but then an Indian director came in and wanted to push him out. "We came here, this is our country," Choudhri said with a sigh. "We should not carry on the old stuff. The thing is, you cannot change everybody." For an instant I thought Jablon was speaking, but it was the Pakistani, echoing the same frustration and desire, just in a different key.

A few days after Brier spoke at the mosque, Jablon took me to Dov Hikind's office, a few blocks away from the hospital. Jablon dropped me off and, as usual, kept his opinions to himself.

"You'll hear what Dov has to say," he said with a short laugh before he left. "He'll have plenty to say."

As New York State assemblyman, Hikind was a go-to man for the community. He was called on to get park benches fixed; to yell at the MTA for having instructions on subway-card vending machines in English, Creole, Russian, Polish, Italian, Greek, Korean, French, Chinese, Japanese, and Spanish but not Yiddish or Hebrew; to lead blood drives by donating his; to help low-income people get heat.

He worked hard for his community. Yet when I met him in his office, Hikind struck me as a bully who thrived on insinuation and provocation, or maybe I just felt that way because I knew his reputation and I don't like zealots. He certainly didn't look fiery, with his trimmed graying beard, glasses, and cardigan sweater.

Hikind seemed to be Jablon's exact opposite. Jablon was conciliatory, Hikind was inflammatory. Jablon said things like "We're so stupid we only look at two percent of ourselves. Two percent of our body is skin. The rest is ninety-eight percent, and we don't look at that. We look at two percent, which is stupid. People look at color, which is stupid. They look at how you dress, who you pray to. God wants me to take care of everybody." Hikind was a Democrat who endorsed George W. Bush and who had been a follower of Meir Kahane, founder of the Jewish Defense League, a right-wing terror group. (Kahane, an émigré to Israel from Brooklyn, lived and died by fanaticism and hatred. He was assassinated in 1990, by El Sayyid Nosair, later convicted as a conspirator in the 1993 bombing of the World Trade Center.) Hikind's methods were more mainstream than Kahane's, but his politics were no less divisive. He had been repositioning himself for years as a more tolerant fellow than he'd been in his youth, when he was arrested several times as a Kahane disciple. But recently Hikind had urged the New York City police department to implement what he called "terrorist profiling."

Hikind invited me to sit at a table in his office and offered me his view on the cultural aspects of Maimonides. "I think what you should look for is a lot of negative feelings between nurses and patients, especially Orthodox Jews, a lot of resentment, latent anti-Semitism," he said, staring at me intently. "Many of the nurses at the hospital are minority. Catering to this community can be difficult. I think it would be very, very interesting to watch that. How does it play out in a hospital where, unless you're giving birth, people are very sick? How someone looks at you. Whether they smile or not. All these things can make a difference. That's where I think there are a lot of problems. Some of those things are difficult to address."

His father, he told me, had worked at Maimonides as a *masgiach,* making sure the rules surrounding kosher food were observed, and had died there. Dov Hikind's children, however, were born in Manhattan, at Mount Sinai, not at Maimonides, the neighborhood hospital that sponsored Hikind's weekly radio program. Hikind felt he and the Maimonides administration understood one another. "If they have me on board, Maimonides feels they're in good shape, because I can make the most trouble if I want to," he said cheerfully. "And they know I will do what I think is best, so if I tell them something, they take it very seriously."

He wished me good luck even as he shook his head. "To write a book how great Maimonides is," he said, "it would be a short book."

One night I ran into Dov Hikind again, unexpectedly. I had stopped by the emergency room one evening to see David Gregorius. He still looked like a kid in his green scrubs and bright orange Crocs, plastic clogs good for running around an ER. Yet he also seemed older, more self-assured than when I first met him just a few months earlier. Now he seemed almost oblivious to the scene around him. Without looking up from the computer monitor, where he was checking to see what patients were his, he said to a fellow resident, "I love working on Shabbos in the winter. The Orthodox leave early."

He was typing the words "penile edema" onto the computer. A twenty-year-old man had come in to the ER with a swollen penis. "Turned out he had masturbated too much," Gregorius said with a grin.

Next patient: a Russian woman with pain in her belly. As he examined her, the resident relied on her daughter, whose English was halting, to translate his questions.

Gregorius asked about what she had eaten, what her vomit looked like, had she had a bowel movement.

The daughter translated but then stopped at bowel movement.

"What?" she asked.

"Make cocky," said Gregorius, using an Eastern European expression he had picked up in the ER.

She blushed. "Everything as usual," she reported after asking her mother.

Gregorius learned that the mother had had an appendectomy and a gallbladder operation. He asked many more questions as he pressed on her belly, explaining gently what he was doing. During the examination he was jostled by Dr. Marshall, on the other side of the curtain, examining a patient in the next cubicle.

The daughter asked if he could give her mother something for pain.

Gregorius said, "I will gladly give her medicine for the pain."

A few minutes later, he entered the information into a computer and ordered morphine. "They dish out morphine here like it's candy," he said.

Earlier I heard Marshall explaining to a resident, "I'd rather err on the side of alleviating the pain of people suffering, even if we run the risk of some people abusing it." Marshall had come by and asked him to try to admit an elderly African-American man with cancer and pneumonia into the intensive-care unit. He had a bloody wound on his head from a fall on the floor at his nursing home. "They don't want him because he has cancer," Marshall said. The ICU people had a reputation for preferring to admit patients they thought they could save—or VIPs.

I asked him about his philosophy on administering drugs for pain. "The hospital does quarterly reports on how we've been doing with pain medication," he said. "That doesn't drive my practice. Some physicians here are more antiquated and think narcotics should be withheld." Before he could continue, someone called him away, too.

Stranded by both physicians, I felt that I was in the way no matter where I stood—until I realized there was no such thing as being in the way. People sidled, pushed, nudged, and otherwise adjusted to the stream of patients, equipment, doctors, nurses, visitors. A drunk insisted he wanted to be seen by the cute woman doctor with the ponytail. An elderly Chinese "environmental worker" gamely kept sweeping and disinfecting, but there were still pockets of stench, smelling vaguely of blood, bottoms, dirty feet, and God knows what else. Intimate exams took place out in the open. A young woman casually pulled off her hospital gown and sat in her underwear as she examined the flimsy piece of cloth, trying to figure out which way it should go. An old Orthodox man on the neighboring gurney watched and offered advice.

I needed an expediter and took refuge with Fabio Palermo, a young man with a shaved head, one of Jablon's patient representatives. The male patient reps were easy to spot. They stood out like FBI agents: tie, slacks, pressed dress shirt. Palermo was another one who came to Maimonides by default. He had a B.A. in communications and wanted to work in TV production but couldn't get a job. A friend said they were looking for a patient rep on the midnight shift. That had been five years earlier. "It's very stressful, but you get a rush from helping people," he said.

A man with a heavy Israeli accent came up to Palermo and complained. "I have chest pain," he said. "I've been here for an hour, and nobody cares. In a few minutes, I'm taking a taxi to another emergency room."

Palermo told the man he would see what was up. At a nearby computer terminal, he found the patient's record. "He's been here forty-one minutes," he said. "They already checked him out in triage."

Looking across the room at the man, who was pacing next to his gurney, he said, "A lot of them know the golden words: 'chest pain'."

At 7:00 P.M. Palermo's job was to ask friends and relatives to go to the waiting room for an hour, to lessen the pandemonium during the shift change. Dodging patients and clinicians, he moved around the room, politely asking visitors to leave. He squeezed by a bed holding a grizzled man with clear, beautiful blue eyes, who stopped the patient rep. "Could you take this tray?" he asked. "Does it take a resolution of Congress? It's been here for an hour." Palermo took the tray.

Palermo paused to reply to an urgent call on his beeper. "Dov Hikind's mother is in the hospital," he said. He told me he had to leave the emergency room and go up to see her in a few minutes and would take me with him.

While I waited, I stopped to chat with a group of PCTs, patient-care technicians, doing the job that once commonly was called nurse's aide. The elevated title didn't make the work any easier. Unpleasant jobs—like bedpan duty—fell to them. The educational requirement was a high-school diploma or equivalency plus completion of a course in a nursing-assistant program or EMS training. Marie C. Pierre, in her forties, originally from Haiti, was taking a break, sitting on the edge of a desk eating sunflower seeds. "They have more sophisticated things here," she said, comparing medical care between her old and new countries. "Some of the sickness in my country, we do healing with leaves. Here they have the same leaves, but as a pill. I've seen people come to the hospital with a hundred or hundred and one fever. In my country we do home remedies."

A tall, regal woman working on a nearby computer, Ethel Christopher from Trinidad, overheard the conversation. "We call pneumonia a bad cold back home," she said scornfully. "I think people here overuse the hospital. A woman came in the other day, she has a lot of pain for her period and she comes to the hospital! They have a headache and they come to the hospital."

Pierre spit shells into her hand. "I have a headache, I just lie down." Then she looked worried. "But sometimes you have a headache and it's a bleed in the brain."

Christopher nodded vigorously. "That's it," she said. "People are just scared. If you look at the amount of people they send home before the day is done. They want to make sure some vessel didn't bust. They do a CT scan, find nothing, go home. Then the headache comes back the next day and they come back. Because it's free."

They dispersed. I found Fabio Palermo and followed him past a line of stretchers parked in the hallway, through a maze of more hallways and onto an elevator, which took us onto a patient floor. The evening quiet was jarring, too much like death after the lively turbulence in the ER. Our destination was a bright-eyed, elderly Eastern European woman wearing a little cap around her pink face, lying alone in a bed in a large room meant for two. VIP. Her aide, a friendly woman with a Caribbean accent, lay back comfortably in a chair, her leg hanging over an armrest. Dov Hikind stood at the foot of his mother's bed.

"How's the hospital?" he asked me, and introduced me to his mother and the aide.

The two women joked with each other, both speaking with strong, if different, accents, and the aide said, "She's happy here."

Real or imagined, the easy affection that seemed to bond the women was so disarming I said aloud what I was thinking.

"How did you come to have such a nice mother?" I asked Hikind.

Hikind shrugged and smiled weakly at me. "A lot of people ask me that," he said. He looked weary and vulnerable. But then, hospital rooms have that effect.

His mother lifted her head. "A writer!" she said, smiling at me. "There's nothing to write bad about this hospital. You come in. They take care of you. Vat else do you vant ven you come in sick? I came in, they took care of me, and now I'm a new person!"

The Orthodox community had a love-hate relationship with Maimonides. The hospital could never do enough to please the 20 percent of its patients who considered it theirs. Because of the hospital's historic ties to the neighborhood, the locals had far different expectations for Maimonides than for any other hospital. It was assumed that the food would be kosher, that the gift shop would be closed on Saturday, that the hospital would indicate with a light at the front door that someone had just died so the *kohanim*, Jews descended from the priestly line of Aaron, brother of Moses, would know not to enter the building, because they aren't allowed to be in a room with a corpse. During the Passover holiday, all soda dispensers were shrouded and blowtorches blasted every last visible crumb of bread in the kitchen. In the gift shop, candy and chips disappeared from the shelves, replaced by Fruit Roll-Ups and kosher-for-Passover potato chips. In the cafeteria, food was served on cardboard trays and bread was replaced by little squares of matzo wrapped in plastic. Thousands of dollars were added to the budget to pay for the exorbitant markup on kosher-for-Passover foods. Yet even this was not enough for the most devout. The Bikur Cholim room, run by volunteers, posted a sign: WE HAVE A NON-GEBROKTS MENU (roughly translated as "*really* kosher for Passover") for those not satisfied with the hospital's purification process.

Borough Park was said to have the largest cluster of Holocaust survivors outside Israel; Dov Hikind's sweet mother was one of them. That history of persecution was often invoked to explain the community's behavior, but it clouded as much as it clarified, like trying to explain how one mother could produce twins who were opposites, one sweet-natured and responsible, the other squalling and self-absorbed. The Orthodox tended their own through an admirable, elaborate network of charitable and volunteer organizations like the Bikur Cholim (Guardians of the Sick) and Hatzolah, which led to charges of exclusivity and tribalism. But—when nudged—the community was willing to help others. Nishei Cares, an Orthodox charity, supplied the hospital with 130 volunteer doulas, women who offered help to any pregnant Maimonides patient—no matter what her background—during and after delivery.

Jablon accepted his role as punching bag, but he was unable to muster pure altruism. He wanted the acknowledgment from his own people that he felt he received from others. "The Gentiles come in, they love us," he said. "There's nothing we can do bad in their eyes."

He sighed. "The Jews complain," he said. "That's how they survive. But they also give. If somebody is in trouble, they will give. A person is in trouble and needs money, even if they don't have it they will borrow it to give to that family. If somebody needs a baby-sitter, they'll come in the middle of the night to help you. Someone gets stuck on the highway, they'll stop the car. But to get a pat on the back! Never!"

The mournful look on Jablon's face had become a semipermanent fixture. "You go into places, people curse the hell out of you about the hospital," he said. "They just have that feeling to bash Maimonides for no reason at all." He invoked the case of the ninety-two-year-old man who was in the hospital for three months with lung cancer. "We kept him going that way for weeks on respirators; no other hospital would do that. For weeks! Passed away. Ninety-two!

Jablon paid a shivah call (Judaism requires a seven-day period of mourning immediately after a funeral). He arrived a half hour before the afternoon prayers were recited and sat down to visit while he waited. One of the sons snapped at him, "Where did the administration learn how to run that hospital? From Auschwitz?"

Jablon didn't respond but stayed just long enough to participate in the short *mincha* service, one of the three sets of prayers observant Jews were required to repeat every day, to stay in touch with God while removing themselves from earthly concerns. Jablon couldn't concentrate, though the service took only ten minutes. He repeated the words by rote and then walked out. Another of the dead man's sons ran out after him. "My brother's crazy," he apologized.

Jablon tried not to sort and catalog the hurts, but he couldn't help it. He recalled a family who transferred a patient to NYU from Maimonides, about the same time Peter Aschkenasy, Brier's husband, was in the intensive-care unit there after the accident. Jablon was in the waiting room, about to go in to visit Aschkenasy, and saw the deserters. When the nurse came out and told the family members they could visit the patient, but just for five minutes, they meekly obeyed. "They came out like good little children," said Jablon. "Over here there would have been a war. They would have said, 'You're a dictator! Gestapo! The problem is, the administration made this open-door policy. The community has the ownership of the hospital."

Jablon was one of the first people I met at Maimonides, back in the early spring. I saw him again at the cancer center's opening, standing at the back of the tent, scanning the room like a hulking Secret Service man at a gathering of government officials. Occasionally he would seek someone out, lean down—no one was taller than he was—and whisper something, eliciting a nod or grin, and then resume his watchful post.

A few weeks later, before I'd really begun my yearlong stay at Maimonides, Jablon invited me to his son's wedding to Chaya Gitty Green. (Yitzy Jablonsky had reverted to the family's name as it was before his grandfather, Douglas's father, changed it.)

As I had never been to a Borough Park Orthodox wedding, I didn't know what to expect, so I asked Jo Ann Baldwin, the woman who had initiated my hospital adventure.

FROM: JO ANN BALDWIN
SENT: 7/11/05, 1:41
SUBJECT: HEADS UP!!!!

My husband Dan just called to remind me to let you know. Our first Boro Park event that we attended, the invitation said 6:00, so Dan and I got there at 6:00. The caterer was setting up . . . Douglas said that Chupa is at 7:30 and everyone started laughing that it would never happen that early . . . the earliest you should come is 7:30, and you should probably eat something. The last wedding we left at 11:00 and dinner was not served yet.

.   .   .   .

FROM: JULIE SALAMON
SENT: 07/11/05, 2:25
SUBJECT: HEADS UP!!!!

So am I to gather this isn't a sit down dinner???

.   .   .   .

FROM: JO ANN BALDWIN
SENT: 7/11/05, 2:37

NO NO NO. . . . it is a sit down dinner, there is a cocktail party that is supposed to start at 6, but that never starts until later . . . then the chupah (sp?) we go into a huge room, men on one side, women on another, and then the wedding cere-mony. which is really interesting, and kind of tribal, then we go back to the hall and have a sit down dinner, but the bride and groom don't come right away, people have told me that they are supposed to be consummating the marriage in a room in the hall, but I refuse to believe this. . . . Welcome to Boro Park. See ya later.

.   .   .   .

FROM: JULIE SALAMON
SENT: 07/11/05, 2:53

THANK YOU!!

Also, what about a gift? Are they registered? How does it work in Boro Park? Also, what are you wearing?

*   *   *   *   *   *   *   *   *   *   *   *

FROM: JO ANN BALDWIN
SENT: 7/11/05, 3:39

You just gave me a huge laugh . . . registered . . . Douglas had to pay the caterer extra to keep out the Schnoorers (sp?), the only reason I know what a schnoorer is, I had to get security to remove one from Beth Israel as he was trying to follow one of my surgeons into the bathroom to get money. A schnoorer is a religious person who begs for money, sometimes for an organization, but many times for himself. They are con artists, but that is not acceptable to say. I told Douglas that if they were outside the hall, I was going to call a local convent and get the little nun who sits in the subway.

So they are not registered anywhere. I just give money in a card, and I'm not sure that I do that right either, Connie (works for Douglas), told me I was a fool because many people put 18.00 in an envelope because that number signifies good luck. I said, so does 180, or 1800 and she laughed in my face. I'm giving what I would give to any friend who was marrying their child off, that's not you. You just met these people. I'm giving my gift for Douglas and our relationship, I love him. You don't have to do anything like that. If you have time to run out and get a gift you can do that. Who doesn't need a vase? . . . Do not feel obligated to give a big gift that will embarrass Douglas, You can pick something nice up. Yitzy (son) is pretty modern, he works for the police department, and the girl is a teacher.

CLOTHING: Okay this is important, forget the fact that we have reached temperatures of over 90 degrees and remember you have to have your arms covered and no pants. I'll either wear a suit or a dress, I also have my obligatory "old fart" dress that I have purchased just for these occasions, however, it may be too hot to wear that. Just no bare arms and no pants and you will be fine.

How to describe the scene at Ateres Chynka? That was the huge banquet hall on Elmwood Avenue where Yitzy and Chaya were wed on a hot night in July, in an intimate ceremony with fourteen hundred of their families' closest acquaintances. The guest list covered those who loved Jablon or owed him or who were owed by him. There were representatives from all his communities: Jews of course, but also Chinese, Haitians, Catholics, Muslims, physicians, nurses, firefighters, politicians, and policemen.

If I'm vague, it's because I don't remember much. That was my first introduction to a Borough Park scene, and I was overwhelmed. I was married under a chuppah, a wedding canopy, as required by tradition, and had attended many Jewish weddings, but nothing like this. Yitzy and Chaya's wedding—outsize, noisy, tribal, unabashed—felt authentic, the difference between white-water rafting on the Zambezi River and a ride at Disneyland (though the wedding also felt a little like both). Jablon, trying to please everyone, had followed Orthodox practice of separating men and women but wanted to accommodate the non-Jews and non-Orthodox guests— about half the people there, including much of the Maimonides administration. As people arrived, they picked up seating cards on a table in the entryway. My husband and I were seated at Table 2. Turned out, so was everyone else who wasn't Orthodox—a few hundred people. Table 2 was an entire subdivision, separated from the rest of the party by a partition. At Table 2, genders could mix.

It was a wild party, music supplied by Yossi Piamenta and his excellent hard-rock Hasid band. They played in the all-male section but were loud enough to be heard in the women's area and in Table 2. Jablon *had* paid the caterers extra to keep out the shnorrers, scruffy-looking religious Jewish beggars, but they sneaked in anyway and were hitting up everyone for money on the way to the restrooms. Sometime around midnight, just after the main meal had been served, Chief Joseph Fox, police commander of Brooklyn South (and Yitzy's boss), began dancing with two of his detectives.

About then my husband and I decided to leave. But first I wanted to pay my respects to Jablon's wife, Edy, whom I had just seen from a distance. I made my way to the women's section and then was immobilized by the mob of women talking, eating, and dancing, and mesmerized by the sight of hundreds of perfectly coiffed heads, all wearing wigs. Suddenly Jo Ann Baldwin appeared by my side and introduced me to a tiny woman. I told them I wanted to get through to Edy Jablon, but I was stuck. A small hand that felt like a steel clamp took hold of my wrist, and I found myself being dragged away from Baldwin, through the crowd, and deposited in front of the mother of the groom. She smiled politely when I thanked her for inviting me and said good night.

I didn't catch the name of my cavalier, the tiny, elderly warrior, armored and helmeted in her evening gown and wig, determined to reach her destination no matter whom she had to mow down. It was very noisy, and she had introduced herself in a mumble evocative of Marlon Brando in *The Godfather.*

Later, I saw her now and again at various meetings in the hospital. I could see she commanded respect, but I didn't learn exactly who she was until Alan Astrow took me to a gathering of physicians and rabbis discussing the religious protocols surrounding end-of-life matters. She pursed her lips and shook her head as someone talked about dealing with advanced directives, health-care proxies, and DNRs. "I am very against this idea," Miriam Lubling muttered in her thick Polish accent. "A doctor should say, 'May you live a hundred and twenty years.' The minute you sign, the nurse gives you up. As long as you live, you should get help. Even if you are not Jewish. You have a mother; you shouldn't sign, to give up. I don't like it. I don't like it. Even for goyim [non-Jews]."

In Borough Park there were many nonmedical people, most of them rabbis, who took it upon themselves to refer patients to specific physicians and hospitals. Some of them had become so powerful they could make a doctor's career and even positively or negatively affect a hospital's bottom line. Miriam Lubling was in a class by herself. She not only referred patients, she paid cash. If a person in Borough Park needed hospital care and didn't have insurance, Lubling would shake down local organizations and businesses. Jablon said, "At my synagogue where I pray, they have no respect for anybody. The rabbi walks in, everybody keeps talking. All of a sudden, *she* walks in and everybody stands up."

When I found out how important Lubling was, I asked Jablon to formally introduce us.

He sighed.

He said he would make the introduction because he just wanted everybody to be happy. He tried to love everyone, he said, so he would be the first to tell you Miriam Lubling was an angel of God. But he also tried to be honest, so he would also tell you how he'd almost killed her right in the hospital lobby—she made him that angry.

At the time Lubling was in her eighties (she never revealed her exact age), certainly more than old enough to be Jablon's mother—and half his size. Though she was feared and respected in Borough Park, Jablon said he couldn't help himself that day. Lubling drove him crazy. She was a fixer like him, but her loyalties lay elsewhere, even though Lubling believed otherwise. She insisted that she regarded Maimonides as Gan Eden, the Garden of Eden, paradise, and pointed out that her daughter worked there (for Jablon), and that the daughter had given birth to nine children at Maimonides, and one of those children had recently had a child. Lubling herself had been a patient in the hospital after she'd collapsed in her apartment (which was in the neighborhood) and had to go to the emergency room.

Yet she was an associate trustee of New York University Medical Center, though she was an immigrant nursery-school teacher of modest means. She had achieved a position usually reserved for wealthy philanthropists because she sent the hospital—NYU, not Maimonides—so many patients. Moreover, she made sure their bills were paid. What rankled Jablon was the source of these patients, which was Borough Park.

A doctor at NYU had saved Lubling's late husband's life, inspiring the unwavering devotion that instigated the screaming match with Jablon. The fight had to do with a patient's rather surprising odyssey through the hospital system.

"I had brought in this case from Mount Sinai, and she was hunting for this same patient to bring into NYU!" Jablon explained indignantly. "I stole a patient from Mount Sinai, and the administrator was about to call Brezenoff or Pam to complain about me, how I grabbed that patient. I told the family, 'That doctor operating is going to kill you.' The patient came here, and the next morning I go to visit and I find the patient is at NYU! Mrs. Lubling! She says, '*Mameleh, mameleh,* I send you patients.' What patients? I had such a fight with her. She's about three foot two and I'm nine foot seven, and I'm fighting with her. You can imagine, my size fighting with this little old lady in the lobby, and nobody said a word."

Jablon told me to meet Lubling in his office at noon one day and disappeared as soon as she showed up with her daughter, Peshi Drillick. Drillick was an attractive Orthodox woman, remarkably slender and unwrinkled for a mother of nine, recently a grandmother, outfitted in black down to her well-applied eyeliner. She had come along to interpret in case I couldn't understand her mother's Brandoesque inflections and Polish accent.

When I asked Lubling to explain what she does, she pulled fourteen pieces of yellow paper from her pocketbook, representing her morning's work. "This one couldn't get an appointment for two weeks," she said, studying one slip of paper after another. "I got it for today. Here's Mr. R., his kidneys aren't working, I made it for today."

Drillick smiled. "There's no waiting for an appointment when it comes to my mom. They know they have to please her. She brings them business. When she needs an appointment, she needs it done immediately. If they're not going to work with her, she'll go somewhere else."

Lubling handed me a printed roster of names, many with stars next to them, indicating Jewish patients. "NYU sends me the list every day," she said. "The stars telling me what I might have to do with."

Drillick said, "She goes room to room to see what the patient's needs are." Then added, "Nobody would make a list like that here. It's not allowed."

I was reminded of all the complaints I'd heard from doctors and nurses about the large Orthodox families that took up residence at Maimonides when family members became ill. Their devotion was admirable but problematic. They crowded into patient rooms and brought bags of food, making it difficult to keep rooms clean, then complained bitterly about how dirty the place was. Orthodox volunteers poked their heads into rooms and asked, "Jewish?" Kosher snacks were produced for those who nodded.

Drillick responded to my unspoken thoughts. "My mother's strength is that she's not embarrassed," she said. "She doesn't care what the doctor thinks about her so long as she gets what she wants done. Most people get intimidated. You don't want to sound pushy, you don't want to sound nudgy. Her attitude is, 'You don't like me, who cares?'"

Lubling came by her resilience by a means that was sadly common in Borough Park. On the eve of World War II, her family encouraged her and a sister to leave Poland for Israel, then the British protectorate of Palestine, while her father, mother, and other siblings stayed behind. They were killed in the war. In Israel she met and married her husband, built a business, and, at the age of thirty-six, he fell in the shower, hit his head on a faucet, spent two years in a hospital, and was given up for dead.

That was not an acceptable option for Lubling. She sold the family factory and took her husband and children to the United States, where a physician at NYU removed the clot in his brain. In appreciation she began a branch of Bikur Cholim, one of the Jewish charity organizations that offer help to the ill. That's when she began referring patients.

She assured me she wasn't exclusive to NYU. "Sometimes the child has hole in heart, Columbia has best doctor," she said. "And here, Maimonides, to Dr. Shani the cardiologist, and Dr. Rudolph and Dr. Jacobowitz. Lenox Hill when Rudolph was there."

What about the new cancer center?

"I was at the groundbreaking, a very beautiful, nice thing," she said. "Those doctors are very, very good."

Which doctor does she recommend?

"Dr. Bashevkin," she said—Kopel's former partner, the same Bashevkin whose refusal to participate in the new venture was making its growing pains much more severe than anticipated.

Jablon joined us after an hour had passed.

"So how's NYU?" he asked Lubling as he walked in.

She said something I couldn't understand and then smiled. "He has a wife, an angel," she said sweetly, nodding her head at Jablon, and then she was gone.

Six

Ability. Affability. Availability.

November 2005
Daily Log—J.S.

Saw this quote attributed to Abraham Heschel, who wrote the definitive biography of Maimonides the physician/philosopher, not the hospital:

"When I was young, I admired clever people. Now that I am old, I admire kind people."

I imagine that Heschel—especially when he was old—would have liked Alan Astrow.

This diagnosis would never appear on his medical chart. But you could argue that being considerate landed Alan Astrow in the emergency room at Maimonides.

It took nine stitches to stop the blood flowing from the gash on the doctor's forehead. He had to leave his apartment on the Upper West Side of Manhattan before dawn so he could make it to the hospital by 7:00 A.M. for the Tumor Board, a weekly discussion of complicated cases, involving surgeons, hence the early hour. He had tried to slip out of bed quietly and without putting on a light, so he wouldn't wake his wife. Fumbling in the dark, he smacked his head against the wall.

Being a nice guy always seemed to get Astrow into trouble. In high school, as coach of the intramural basketball team, he insisted on keeping one of the lesser players in the game for two quarters. He knew that his job was to make the team win, but that unruly compassionate streak refused to submit to common sense. Sometimes he wished the unpopular kids who glommed onto him would vanish, but why would they? He was trapped by his own sense of fair play.

When I met him at the cancer center three days after he hurt himself, he dismissed the large white bandage covering a wide swath of his forehead. "It looks worse than it is," he said sheepishly.

We were going to lunch at a Turkish restaurant across the street, at the edge of Chinatown: Russian music blared, and a Polish waitress took our order. On the way out of the cancer center, we walked by the large conference room on the main floor, which was still unfinished, six months after the hoopla of the opening and six weeks after the oncology group had finally moved in. The gleaming wooden flooring had been laid that week, but the wall separating the room from the lobby didn't yet exist. The other walls were in need of a final coat of paint. Astrow was not reassured when the painter explained he couldn't finish the job because there was no light. Wires hung from the ceiling, marking the place for light fixtures. The chairs hadn't yet been delivered.

The Joint Commission had just finished its inspection, a nonevent for the cancer center. "The whole place here was in a tizzy for months about this JCAHO visit," said Astrow. "Then they came over for forty-five minutes, took a tour, saw it was still under construction, and said, 'Nice facility.'"

He appeared to be remarkably calm, considering his worried nature and the fact that it was already Friday morning. In three days, for the first time, he and Daniel Sulmasy planned to hold one of their colloquiums, "Spirituality, Religious Wisdom, and the Care of the Patient," at Maimonides—in the conference room that was at the moment unwalled, unlit, unpainted. He had no choice but to trust Bill Camilleri, the man who had gotten the building built, who promised him that the job would be done by Monday.

Astrow was too exhausted by then to get upset by the construction snafu, and he was trying to convince himself that his other problems, like his injury, appeared worse than they actually were.

He hadn't been able to convince himself, with good reason. So far his attempt to organize a thoughtful public conversation about religion and medicine had generated nothing but anxiety and hard feelings. He had believed that the conference could be a good thing for a hospital with so many Jewish and Chinese patients. The speakers—Chun-fang Yu, a professor of religion at Columbia University, and Rabbi Shai Held, scholar-in-residence at the Jewish Theological Seminary—had impressive credentials.

Instead he had made people angry.

He ordered a mezza platter and brought me up to date: A week earlier he had merely been worried he didn't have time to publicize the event adequately. It would be embarrassing to have colleagues from Manhattan come to Brooklyn and find an empty room. He never knew how many people would show up, but this time the size of the crowd took on greater symbolic importance, as either ratification or rejection of his decision to come to Maimonides. Astrow was finding himself infected by the hospital's sensitivity to being on the wrong side of the bridge.

The earnest pondering of big questions wasn't his primary consideration now. For the first time in his career, he had to consider the bottom line. His job was to run a division. The young woman administrator he'd hired during the summer was very bright but had been alienating almost everyone—especially Sam Kopel. She regarded her ideas and attitudes as necessary antidotes to hidebound thinking; they saw cocky youthful certitude and condescension. While the radiation-oncology business was still slow, adding to the financial pressures, the hematology group was getting busier all the time. Astrow was finding it hard to return calls to patients as quickly as he would have liked. He needed to recruit new doctors before the group could handle too many more patients. He needed a nurse-practitioner but had received almost no response to the ads he placed in nursing journals. The receptionists complained that the indirect lighting meant to make the place more attractive made it impossible for them to see. The previous week he had been summoned to a charity function honoring Pam Brier and Edward Lichstein, chief of medicine. That same week he met with several rabbis and other doctors and social workers to discuss how they could work better together. It was at this gathering he met Mrs. Lubling, who mumbled her objection to Do Not Resuscitate orders before excusing herself to answer her cell phone.

With so many practical and political tasks already competing for the energy he had left for patients, Astrow didn't need extra work. But for years now, the spirituality conferences had helped him to combine his inner and outer worlds, the technical, tangible functions of being a doctor with the more ephemeral concerns that made him feel alive. Bringing this conference to Maimonides was risky, a public revelation of something personal and precious that could easily be dismissed or rejected. Now that he had set it in motion, he wanted it to succeed.

He invited all the private hematologic oncologists affiliated with the hospital. He took a stack of flyers to the hospital's bioethics committee, which met the first Tuesday of every month, to discuss exactly the kind of morally fraught issues the spirituality conferences addressed. How should they deal with an Orthodox family, grieving over the death of a child hit by a car, ready to break the Orthodox taboo against donating organs but wanting to restrict the gift to Jewish families? Should they discourage the pregnant mother, diagnosed with metastatic breast cancer, who wanted full-blown treatment, knowing that fetal defects could result from scatter effects of radiation but also knowing that without the treatment the mother would likely die before the baby's birth? Should parents be permitted to select the gender of their unborn children? How long should life be sustained by machines?

Two days later he got an urgent call from Marcel Biberfeld, a regular participant in the bioethics committee. Astrow could feel Biberfeld's anger trembling through the phone, though Biberfeld's voice was controlled. "He was very angry," said Astrow. "Not yelling, but very angry." Biberfeld asked why Astrow had invited Shai Held, someone who didn't represent the Orthodox community. A powerful board member had expressed his displeasure. What was Astrow going to do about it?

As Astrow told this story, he paused and grinned. "You might ask, 'Why did I do this?' I'm starting a new job. I'm trying to meet people. I'm trying to get along with everyone. Why would I do something which might get people all upset when I'm just trying to get started in a new job and have good relations with people? You might well ask that question."

Before I could respond, he said, "But you're not a psychiatrist."

Biberfeld wasn't either, but he was the hospital's vice president for psychiatry. I had seen him watching me warily around the hospital. He was a thin, hovering man with a D.S.W., a doctorate in social work, whose function at the hospital was only partly indicated by his title. When I finally met him for an official (taped) interview, I said, "I see you play many parts here."

He nodded. "Some of them are very tangible roles and some are not," he said. "The largest department I run is the psychiatry department. It's a full-time job, really. We have seventy inpatient beds. In any rural area, this would be a hospital by itself. The other big piece on paper is religious observance. All religious observances from Jewish, Catholic, Protestant, Muslim . . . Jehovah's Witnesses. That reports to me."

After offering me a bottle of water, he left the table we were sitting at for a minute and then returned with a piece of lined paper. He drew a Venn diagram and explained. "I sometimes draw a picture to explain Douglas and me," he said. It took me a minute to realize he was talking about Douglas Jablon. I had heard that Biberfeld was envious of Jablon's influence with the executive office.

"Douglas has a very specific area he runs, and there are a lot of areas we overlap." He pointed to the area marked off by the intersection of the two circles. "This area, I spend at least almost as much time as the other. That is dealing with community-board members, community leaders, and rabbis at large. How does that differ from patient reps and stuff like that? In certain significant ways and certain ways that overlap. As a professional and a clinician, many of the people look to me in that level. That's one aspect. The other level is just being in my capacity as community member living a block away, I'm convenient to come over and expedite something. I work through the patient reps, but as a senior management person you can get certain things done. Certain Orthodox board members call me about something dear to their hearts."

Added to my mental Venn diagram: Both Biberfeld and Jablon were polite hosts. But Biberfeld offered his guests water, Jablon put out cookies.

When Astrow's flyer found its way to Aaron Twerski, the dean of Hofstra School of Law and a member of the board, Biberfeld moved to expedite. He called Astrow to let him know that Twerski was upset, so naturally Biberfeld was upset, too. Not, as Astrow would have thought, about the presence of a Buddhist speaker. The name that caught Twerski's attention was Rabbi Shai Held, summa cum laude graduate of Harvard University, former director of education at Harvard Hillel, adjunct lecturer in Talmud at the Jewish Theological Seminary, the academic arm of the conservative Jewish movement.

Only one of Held's pedigrees mattered in Borough Park, and it was the wrong one: He was a Conservative, not an Orthodox, rabbi.

Astrow's first reaction was to get angry back, though he tried not to reveal his feelings to Biberfeld. He didn't sleep most of Thursday night, trying to figure out what to do. He had run into this kind of problem before. At a conference at New York–Presbyterian, a prominent faculty person walked out on a pro-abortion Catholic speaker Astrow had invited. An Orthodox rabbi he brought in to speak at Sloan-Kettering irritated secular Jews in the audience. What did he expect? The world was inflamed—again—because of religion. Bringing religion into medicine had become controversial—even just religious thinking, not religious dogma. So he couldn't complain if people were agitated.

A year later Daniel Sulmasy, Astrow's collaborator in the spirituality series, the Franciscan friar who was a doctor, would write in *Tikkun,* a liberal Jewish magazine, "Even when I attended medical school in the early 1980s we were at least taught to ask a perfunctory question about the patient's religious preference. Now, even that question has disappeared from standard textbook instruction in taking a medical history. Religion and spirituality have been effectively purged from medicine."

When he was a child, other boys rebelled against going to Hebrew school, but Astrow loved the Bible stories with their violent, lusty narratives and their ethical riddles. Connecting body and soul, medicine and theology, had been the centerpiece of his academic pursuits for much of the previous decade, beginning with the first spirituality conference he organized in 1998 at St. Vincent's. The hospital auditorium couldn't hold the crowd. More than 250 people came to listen to four people—a Jew, a Jesuit, a Muslim, and a Protestant—discuss "What does it mean to be a healer in your tradition?" Over the next six years, more than twenty conferences took place in different hospitals, drawing as many as four hundred doctors, nurses, chaplains, social workers.

Astrow was contemplative and often seemed lost in an alternate universe of thought, beyond matter. He was in his fourth year of medical school before he discovered he had a lisp. Strange as it seemed to him, now a parent, he had gone through life mispronouncing his *s*'s and no one had done anything about it—or even seemed to notice. But in medical school he became friends with the family of his roommate's fiancée, whose mother taught public speaking. One day she told him he had to do something about his lisp or no one would take him seriously as a doctor. He decided that by the time he went to Boston for his training at Boston City Hospital, where no one knew him, he would speak a different way. That's what he did. He went to a speech pathologist and diligently did his exercises. He lisped his way through the rest of medical school until he became an intern, and then he stopped.

No one could accuse him of acting in haste, but he did eventually take action.

Now he wondered if the most decisive action would be to follow the path of least resistance and move the conference to St. Vincent's. He took a poll. Bill Camilleri said the whole thing was ridiculous, that of course they should have the conference at Maimonides, but the decision was Astrow's. Douglas Jablon just laughed and said he planned to be at the conference. Kopel told him not to worry but urged him to call Twerski. McDougle agreed and offered practical advice. He told Astrow to explain that the event was a secular, medical conference for physicians and nurses, who could get continuing-education credit for attending. It was never intended to be a public forum for the community.

The affirmation didn't make Astrow less nervous. "They may be supportive," he told me. "But administrators don't like problems. They have budgets to meet. They can be supportive but also annoyed with me because I've caused a problem."

Astrow put off calling Twerski until the following week. He wanted to be calm when they spoke, not agonizing over why he always felt compelled to stir things up in the name of doing what was right. The distinction between righteous and self-righteous was perilously fine, he knew that.

Astrow was a product of the Long Island suburbs, post–World War II, a particular moment of naiveté and optimism in U.S. history, at least among the new professional classes. Born in 1954, he was the middle child of Depression-era parents who bought into the mythological view, who preferred to link technological advance with hopefulness and a promising future rather than with the horror of the recent past, the efficient wholesale slaughter of European

Jews and millions of other people worldwide, or with doomsday scenarios of nuclear meltdown and environmental catastrophe. They believed generally in the progress of humanity and specifically in their right—their duty—to participate in the then-popular vision of the American dream. They moved to Woodmere, part of the Five Towns on the south shore of western Long Island, where former residents of cramped apartments in Brooklyn, Queens, and the Bronx spread out in suburban manors, with easy access to bowling alleys, the beach, drive-in movies, and amusement parks. The hardscrabble life associated with immigration, the urban shtetl, was behind them. Martin Astrow was an engineer, a rocket scientist—literally, for Sperry Gyroscope, manufacturer of Sparrow air-to-air missiles. Ruth became a teacher. Unlike their parents—his father a florist, hers a tailor—they were professional people, modern Conservative Jews, observant but flexible. Ruth bought kosher meat until she had an argument with the butcher. Even then she still forbade pork or shellfish to enter her home. Shrimp cocktails and lobsters eaten in restaurants, however, were given special exemptions from the dietary laws, according to her (nonrabbinic) interpretation.

The Astrows appreciated the chance to live well while endorsing social responsibility within the confines of respectability. In other words, they wanted the child designated the brightest one to become a doctor, an ambition widely shared by the other Jewish parents in the Five Towns. The desire was expressed openly and often. In fact, Ruth, a slender, long-legged woman from the Bronx who posed like Betty Grable in seductive girlhood photos, once said, "I used to joke to Martin, my husband. Martin, I said, you've acquitted yourself as the perfect Jewish husband. You got me a mink coat. We have a Cadillac. We have a son who's a doctor. You've done everything you're supposed to do."

As with disease (and goodness), finding the root cause of choices we make is often hard to untangle from misleading symptoms and wishful thinking. But Alan Astrow always returned to his father. During the Vietnam War, when Astrow was in high school, he and his father had many heated discussions about the ethics of earning a living from the military-industrial complex. The arguments never diminished Astrow's love for his father, nor did they stop the future doctor from having his education financed by said military-industrial complex.

But the dilemmas posed by those discussions would always reverberate for him. Later he would direct the same fervor at debates about a new enemy of idealism, the *medical*-industrial complex, accused of preventing universal health coverage to benefit corporate coffers, of imperiling basic health care by creating a profit motive to focus on costly procedures. Yes, there had been tremendous advances in remedying heart disease and certain cancers, but Astrow found it hard to defend the millions spent on cosmetic surgery, the financial disincentives that discouraged young doctors from going into primary medicine, pediatrics, obstetrics.

How was an idealistic physician supposed to contend with the pharmaceutical companies that, with the insurance behemoths, had come to dominate medical treatment? The drug companies sponsored research that produced the drugs that cured previously fatal diseases and lifted the death sentence off so many others, like AIDS and certain cancers. They paid for speakers at educational conferences. They helped physicians filter the mass of information that was churned out by medical researchers in overwhelming volume. A diligent social worker could *hondle* with them to obtain free drugs for indigent patients. But those same companies had a vested interest in determining which studies were supported, which diseases got attention, which populations were served, how many drugs they could sell. Their executives made unconscionable amounts of money.

Those questions continued to bother him. "I was thinking this morning about Leslie Wexner," he said. "Do you know who he is? He funded this deluxe Jewish adult-education program, and he gave all the people in the program a talk about how his father had owned a department store in Columbus, Ohio, and how he, Leslie Wexner, got his M.B.A. and came back to work in his father's store. He noticed the only department that really made money was women's sportswear. He said to his father, 'You know, the only thing making money is women's sportswear, and that is what we should focus on.' His father said, 'No, we're a department store. We have to do everything.' So Wexner raised the money on his own and opened a chain that sold women's sportswear, which is the Limited, and became a billionaire as a result."

He shoveled a piece of pita piled with hummus into his mouth and then apologized. "My wife says I have terrible eating habits," he said, hastily rubbing a napkin across his lips before getting back to his retailing analysis.

"That's fine in the department store, but what's happened in medicine is that people have applied the same reasoning to hospitals," he said. "They are almost like department stores, where some departments make money and some don't make money or lose money. If you decide to take a profit-and-loss mentality for the whole system, you focus on the things that make money. That's why people have opened these cardiac hospitals or orthopedic hospitals. If you're looking at the system in that way, how you maximize profits, that makes sense. But you would think that in health care you wouldn't want to look at it that way. But the whole market ethos has become so dominant that people don't really have another way of understanding what health care is all about, and it causes all kinds of problems."

Astrow liked to argue and debate, but he wasn't at heart a rebel. He reconciled himself to working within the system. "I don't really have any solutions," he said. "You have to focus on the individual patient and hope that someone is looking at some of the larger policy issues in a way that really reflects the public interest," he said. He hoped to develop clinical trials to use what he and others at Maimonides learned from individual cases for greater knowledge, but mainly his focus was micro. "As a doctor you have to do the best you can for every patient," he convinced himself. "You get involved with these larger social issues, and you can't."

He sometimes wondered whether medicine had been a calling at all, or whether he had simply complied with what was expected of him. In eighth grade Astrow asked his father, who was widely read, for help with a school assignment, to write a report on three books with related themes. The books his father suggested were *Arrowsmith, The Citadel,* and *Of Human Bondage,* all novels with protagonists who were physicians. The message was readily received by the sensitive boy. A year later Astrow was sitting in his friend Jason's basement, vehemently arguing that medicine was different from other fields because it wasn't primarily about making money. Being a doctor was about being an ethical person—someone like his father, who was so honest he insisted on paying full price for Alan at the movies the instant his son turned twelve.

At age forty-nine, when Alan was sixteen, Martin Astrow became sick with Parkinson's disease. It seemed impossible. He was a fine physical specimen. Look at the old photos of him—handsome, bare-chested in the sun, his tall, slender bride on his arm in one shot; Martin wrestling with a fish in another. Then Parkinson's, with its terrible symptoms—the shuffling, the drooling, the muscle contractions, the gait freezing.

The son couldn't remember his father ever complaining about the degenerative illness, the tremors and rigidity imposed on an athletic body. What might have seemed a cruel joke to someone else, a mockery of a life devoted to scientific mastery, Martin Astrow seemed to accept as biological fate. On occasion, however, there were outbursts that were at odds with his gentle nature—slapping Alan for returning a library book late, hitting him with a belt when he was mean to his brother. Ruth Astrow simply denied that these events had happened, whereas her son later attributed them to the disease. What causal links could be made between these irrational episodes, shocking at the time, and a shy boy's attitude to authority figures, later manifested as a desire to both rebel against and please them?

Astrow recalled his father with love and a sense of frustration. He wanted to help him. One summer he worked in a Parkinson's research lab. Though later he linked his decision to become a doctor with his father's illness, when he entered Yale University in the fall of 1972, he declared himself a history major, not premed. He wrote for the *Yale Daily News* and studied literature. He played the clarinet. He loved theater. He was interested in politics and law. Maybe he could be a reporter. He was smart—summa cum laude, Phi Beta Kappa. He had always excelled at everything he tried, except art. The possibilities were vast.

Yet in the spring of his sophomore year, or maybe it was fall of junior year, he decided to go to medical school. He couldn't remember when or exactly why, but he did remember where. Walking across the plaza by the Beinecke Library, he realized it was time to accept his fate. The compassionate streak that sometimes got him into trouble was his destiny after all. He wasn't outgoing enough for politics, nor tough enough for law. He would become a doctor.

Iatrogenic. Literally, "brought forth by a healer" in Greek, referring to complications or sickness resulting from misguided medical treatment.

Paraphrased by George C. Scott, playing a doctor in the 1971 Paddy Chayevsky satire *The Hospital,* a movie Astrow loved:

"In short, a man comes into this hospital in perfect health," says the doctor played by George C. Scott in disbelief, on hearing about a patient's
progress through the system. "In the space of one week, we chop out one
kidney, damage another, reduce him to coma and damn near kill him."

Did modern medicine cause more disease than it cures? Astrow didn't
really think so, but he knew that something was missing, a philosophical and
spiritual dimension to taking care of patients that seemed to have become
incidental. Call it healing.

At Yale School of Medicine, the students learned to draw blood on one
another. At the time, his second year, Astrow had been sick, not sick enough
to miss a day of school, but sick. He lost five pounds, had low-grade fevers,
GI symptoms. The blood work showed he was anemic. Tests followed, and
he was diagnosed with Crohn's disease, an inflammation of the intestine. The
prognosis was devastating: He could be chronically ill or need surgery.
Crohn's disease—very common among Jews—was thought to be psychoso-
matic, like irritable bowel, linked to worry, anxiety. Though this wasn't accurate, the association itself was enough to provoke worry and anxiety.

The diagnosis made him angry. An iatrogenic illness. If they hadn't drawn
his blood, maybe he wouldn't have been sick. He would have been fine. He
knew that his reaction was irrational, that he was lucky, and that the doctors
hadn't caused the disease but found it. A year on sulfasalazine and the
Crohn's symptoms never reoccurred. Even so, the experience left him with
an enduring skepticism about overtesting patients. He remained acutely
aware of the ramifications of giving a diagnosis; the worries, frustration, and
anger it could trigger; how simply articulating a disease could disrupt a life.

Ability. Affability. Availability. Patients often don't distinguish among
these, warned an associate dean at his graduation from medical school.
Remember that.

Astrow remembered. He also remembered the angry critiques of the
medical system he read as a medical student, as relief from the crush of data
he had to memorize. Books like *Medical Nemesis* by Ivan Illich, the former
Roman Catholic priest (whose mother was Jewish) whose fierce antiestab-

lishment books and articles grabbed the imagination of baby boomers in the 1970s and then were largely rejected or forgotten.

Much later Astrow would often reread an essay called "The Patient as a Person" by Abraham Joshua Heschel, the rabbi who wrote learned, emotional treatises on Jewish law and marched with Martin Luther King Jr. Astrow especially liked one section of the essay, originally delivered as a speech at the American Medical Association in 1963: "The truth of being human is gratitude, the secret of existence is appreciation, its significance is revealed in reciprocity. Mankind will not die for lack of information; it may perish for lack of appreciation."

Heschel gave that lecture in an era when paternalism was the accepted relationship between doctor and patient. By the time Astrow became a doctor almost twenty years later, openness prevailed, an attitude Astrow believed in and practiced. But he found that honesty could be more treacherous than deceit. Cancer forced patients and doctors into the realm of philosophy by bringing the uncertainty of existence into sharp focus.

Another lesson from Astrow's medical-school years: His father had been taking bromocriptine, a medication used in the treatment of menstrual and fertility problems that had been found useful in controlling Parkinson's symptoms. Martin Astrow was under the care of the leading expert on Parkinsonism at Columbia Presbyterian, who urged hospitalization when the patient began having strong dystonic reactions to the medication— causing him to flail wildly. The doctor told him to come into the hospital to have the dose readjusted. By the time Martin arrived, he had broken into a cold sweat and was in pain so severe that the admitting doctors decided not to do an EKG. He was given a private room and assigned a fourth-year medical student to look after him.

Three days later an EKG revealed that the pain attributed to a drug-reaction muscle spasm had been a major heart attack. He survived, but with severe heart-muscle damage.

As Astrow received this immediate education about the frustration and fallibility of medical science, he also began wondering about the source of character. Why was his father able to cope with his illness with such courage?

For several years Martin continued to work, until the Parkinson's made it too difficult for him to walk. But he didn't despair, or at least he didn't reveal any despairing feelings he might have had (except for those occasional displays of anger). Astrow's mother remembered Martin's answer to the doctor they saw at Mount Sinai, a man close to his own age at the time, about sixty-five, who looked at her husband pityingly, as he asked his patient how he passed the time.

Martin seemed surprised by the question, his wife recalled. He had been immersed in reading the works of Einstein, contemplating modern physics. "I have plenty of things to do," he told the doctor. "I read. I watch television. I exercise."

When he was sixty-seven years old, on Valentine's Day, he put all the family photographs into albums and organized the bookshelves. His wife went shopping for a new television set to replace theirs, which was broken. They were going out for dinner that night to celebrate Valentine's Day, as they always did. While at the store, Ruth heard her name being paged. It was Martin calling to say he'd fixed the television; she didn't need to buy a new one. That evening they went to dinner at a seafood restaurant, as planned.

Maybe the fish they ate was from the ocean, Alan Astrow speculated. A heavy salt load would explain the pulmonary edema that killed his father that night.

Martin Astrow had lived to see his son become a doctor. He had celebrated Valentine's Day with his wife. He'd arranged the bookshelves and fixed the television. He had left his house in order.

Would he have lived longer if someone had done an EKG on him that first night at Columbia Presbyterian, a decade earlier? Undoubtedly— maybe—if he had been struck by the disease just a little later, when treatment of heart disease had progressed, much of his heart muscle might have been saved. But back then? Astrow couldn't say.

Much of Astrow's job would be helping people live with uncertainty, even those with an optimistic prognosis. Hopefulness was less likely to be a lie now—far less than when he had begun to practice oncology. But cancer continued to be an elusive disease. Could he ever say with certainty there would be a remission, even when it was likely for certain kinds of cancer after certain kinds of treatment? Some other disease could come into play, as it did with his father. The prospect of death was always present for everyone, but cancer made the inevitable hard to ignore. The only real variable was timing.

The more experience he acquired, the larger the questions loomed.

Where did goodness come from?

Was it possible to be truthful and kind?

Could you be kind and command respect?

Those were the things Ruth and Martin Astrow's son thought about.

Jill Nathanson grew up without religion. Her mother was a classical musician, a pianist. Her brother Roy Nathanson became a saxophonist of some renown. Jill painted. Art was the family's theology.

Autumn 1988: She was in her middle thirties, living in her studio on the Lower East Side, pregentrification, cooking on a hot plate, when she picked up a book called *Major Trends in Jewish Mysticism,* written by the Kabbalist scholar Gershom Scholem. She didn't know how the book had wound up on her bookshelf. Someone may have given it to her, or maybe she'd bought it, thinking it was cool—she couldn't remember. For years she had been trying to understand unknowable things, like the depth of suffering that led her mother to commit suicide. Attempting to make an inchoate universe more comprehensible, Nathanson had scaled down her work, from big splashy paintings to smaller pieces that made her feel better, closer to finding hopefulness in the mystery of strange, shifting colors.

Things still felt dicey. While her art comforted her, the art world seemed cynical and shallow. Her life devoted to creating art hadn't created an orderly existence. She sought redemption in color but found she wanted more.

One day she picked up Scholem on her shelf, hoping to find an answer in the intricacies of Jewish mysticism. But to her devoutly secular eyes, the words on the page seemed just as tangled—and perhaps even more incomprehensible—than earthly existence or the depths of blue.

No help.

Not long afterward Marshall Meyer entered the picture—literally, she saw him on television—and changed her life. Meyer was a rabbi, born in Brooklyn, raised in Connecticut, who had spent years in Argentina. He became a vocal adversary of the military government that had imprisoned or killed thousands of people, known as *los desaparecidos,* "those who have dis-appeared." He tried to save lives of the persecuted and visited hundreds of them in jail, including a well-known journalist, Jacobo Timerman, who later dedicated his record of torture and humiliation, *Prisoner Without a Name, Cell Without a Number,* to Meyer. In 1985 the dynamic rabbi was asked to take over B'nai Jeshuran, a Conservative synagogue on the Upper West Side of Manhattan that had shrunk to eighty families. In short order he revitalized the congregation, eventually drawing thousands of people with his message that life could have meaning, urging social responsibility across religions and borders.

Suddenly Nathanson found coordinates for her sense of urgency: the book on her shelf and the rabbi on her television. It was time for action. She went to B'nai Jeshuran one Saturday morning but stood frozen outside when she realized she had a pocketbook with her and remembered vaguely that you weren't supposed to carry money on the Sabbath. She returned a week later and still was uncertain about how to enter. This time she saw something on a flyer that might offer a possible antidote to her ignorance. She decided to return yet again on Wednesday night, for a course called Introduction to Judaism.

That night she walked in, only to find that the class was, as she said, "extremely boring." So much for karma. She sneaked out and was standing in the hall, about to leave, when someone beckoned her into another room. She obeyed. As she sat down, an imposing figure strode in. He was the rabbi she had seen on television, even more impressive in life, who actually fit the description "a bear of a man." He began his lecture on Rabbi Abraham Joshua Heschel. Nathanson was again mesmerized by Meyer. This was no theoretical lecture. Meyer had been Heschel's secretary and translator, his successor in a quest to translate learning and theory into justice and decency.

Despite the power of his rhetoric, she couldn't stop herself from glancing around, from evaluating the aesthetics of her surroundings. "I was a decora-tive painter at the time—for money—and the room was very dingy. It had these crummy walls," she said. "I found myself in an ugly room with the world's worst sponge-painting job." She also noticed her fellow classmates— a few elderly couples and eight youngish men who were so incredibly square-looking that she couldn't believe she was sitting in this dreary room with such conventional characters. But when they began to talk, she was bowled over. "The class was fabulous, just amazing," she said. Though her intent hadn't been to meet a guy—at least not her acknowledged intent—suddenly she saw a roomful of very interesting, possibly single men.

One of those men was Alan Astrow, wearing corduroys and Hush Puppies. He introduced himself after class, and when they discovered they both lived downtown, they rode together on the subway. His shoes kept coming untied. He said maybe they could have coffee sometime, but then he never called.

Nathanson stayed in the class. She and Astrow didn't speak further after that initial subway ride, though she always noticed when he walked into the room, head bowed, dragging his coat on the floor. As the weeks passed, she found herself paying special attention when he talked in class. At first she thought his thinking was simplistic, because his manner of speaking was so straightforward, almost childish sometimes in its directness. Then she listened. "Weird," she said. "Smart. Weirdly brilliant, the things he would say. He would just be able to pull things from past reading but say them in such a simple way they would sound strange."

She believed that this dorky man with the carefully combed brown hair, sweet smile, and sleepy blue eyes was truly an original thinker. Wednesday after Wednesday she listened as unique observations poured from his mouth, footnoted with references to obscure texts, reaching conclusions that transcended the usual divisions between conservative and liberal, platitudinous and radical.

Six months after he said they might have coffee sometime, he called and asked her to go to the theater. "I'm going to say it was *Twelfth Night,* but if I'm wrong and he finds out, I'll be chopped liver," she said. "He remembers everything. Every play we've ever seen. With me, I don't like it, gone."

She laughed. "Even if I do like it."

They joked that they had nothing in common. She was slight and fast, unafraid to climb forty feet in the air to work on scaffolding, splattered with paint, arguing with construction workers. He was cautious, wore white doctor's coats, and pondered metaphysical matters. She was happy with take-out Chinese food; he liked fancy French restaurants. She knew nothing about religion; he seemed to know everything.

But she felt comfortable with him. They were the same age. They had lunch together and liked each other. "He was so careless, so absentminded about himself, so unprecious," she said. "I was comfortable with him because I'm not that orderly."

He also seemed innocent, strangely pure—until she found out he was dating someone else, a woman even more countercultural than Nathanson considered herself to be. She was conventional enough to decide, at thirty-five, that she wanted marriage and children, so she did the conventional thing for a woman who chose to succumb to the biological imperative. "I gave him an ultimatum," she said. "I told him we couldn't continue to go out if he was dating her."

They married. They had children, a boy and a girl. They moved to the Upper West Side, to an apartment big enough to encompass this new life—a life that outwardly may have had the predictable trappings of the New York Jewish intelligentsia but which for them was a surprise, daring and experimental.

Without Marshall Meyer she doubted they would have found each other. "Reading this text together brought out something original in both of us," she said, and then corrected herself. "'Original' is the wrong word. Something deep and unconventional. We spoke our souls in some ways in this setting that we would not have if we had met without the class." Meyer touched what they had in common: a fundamental inability to pass through life lightly, a willingness to stand apart, a desire to search for the sacred in beautiful and terrible things.

Everything about being a doctor changed for Astrow during a hematology elective when he was a resident at Boston City Hospital. It was late fall of 1982, or maybe early winter 1983. He drew blood from a patient with a rare diagnosis, and after that nothing was the same.

Later the memory was embarrassing, in the light of the disaster that followed, but Astrow's first response to the diagnosis was excitement: toxoplasmosis of the brain, a disease a doctor-in-training might read about but would never expect to witness. Pregnant women would come to know about toxoplasmosis, the disease spread by cat feces that could result in severe damage to babies in the womb. Caused by a single-cell parasite called *Toxoplasma gondii,* its presence goes unnoticed by most people infected with it. "Severe cases are more likely in individuals who have weak immune systems," explains the Web site of the Centers for Disease Control and Prevention (CDC), the U.S. government agency assigned to promote and protect public health. Back then, however, there was no CDC Web site. There was no Internet. The CDC had only recently classified a mysterious outbreak of symptoms and infections related to a collapse in immune systems as AIDS, acquired immune deficiency syndrome. That summer, July 1982, the CDC reported 413 cases of the new disease in the United States with 155 deaths; a year earlier the CDC had reported seeing 108 cases.

Astrow was only dimly aware of these cases when the man with the toxoplasmosis of the brain died, followed by a Haitian patient with tuberculosis, and then a pronounced number of young men showed up who were deathly ill with aggressive lymphoma or Kaposi's sarcoma (KS)—another disease so rare a resident might expect to see one or two over an entire three years of training. By the time Astrow began his fellowship at New York University, in 1983, KS had become an epidemic; all three hospitals serviced by NYU residents and fellows were overrun with young men suffering from fevers of unknown origin or from atypical or fungal infections.

When he entered medical school, AIDS didn't exist, at least not as a known disease. When he entered the field of hematologic oncology a decade later, it became his life's work. In 1986 he joined the staff at St. Vincent's in Greenwich Village, the heart of the gay community in New York. The hospital turned two entire floors over to HIV units, trying to cope with the onslaught of KS and AIDS-related lymphomas. The hospital's residency program suffered. No one wanted to come to New York to train because of AIDS.

Astrow was surrounded by death—grisly deaths submerged in pain, stigma, disfigurement—early death, imposed on his peers, men in their twenties and thirties. The dead included his best friend, a surgeon at St. Vincent's. They included a sweet young hairdresser, a patient, who gave Astrow a blue sweater someone had given him from Bloomingdale's. Twenty years later, after more than 550,000 people had died of the disease in the United States, after protease inhibitors had tamed the plague and transformed it into a chronic illness, Astrow still wore that sweater. He thought of that young man every time he put it on, like a ritual blessing for the dead. A kind of kaddish.

By comparison with those grim days, Astrow's dilemmas at Maimonides were minor, which didn't stop him from worrying about them. He realized he had to repair his unwitting breach of etiquette, caused by inviting a non-Orthodox speaker to his spirituality conference at the cancer center. He sent Dean Twerski a polite e-mail to say he understood there was a problem.

Twerski could be fearsome, with his haunted eyes and deep, resonant voice that harmonized with his intellect. Biberfeld had convinced him to join the board because he was Hasidic and lived in the neighborhood. Twerski had seen great improvement in the medical care at Maimonides over the past decade, but the community was always ready to pounce. "What happens in the hospital in fifteen minutes will be known in every synagogue," he once told me. "That's a very hard way to run a hospital, where everyone knows everything. There's been a slipup, I'll get calls, eleven, twelve o'clock at night: Someone is in the emergency room, and things aren't moving. I will go over, and things will start moving."

But he called Astrow in response to his e-mail and was sympathetic to the doctor, if not to his predicament. Twerski didn't buy Astrow's proposition—that the yeshiva-educated minions in Borough Park would be eager to hear alternate views from another branch of Judaism. He told Astrow it was a bit of an insult, to bring an outsider to a community where there were so many scholars. What Astrow saw as a chance for discussion, Twerski saw as a slap in the face.

Twerski also seemed skeptical about the whole idea of a debate between religions, and he questioned the validity of the distinction between ethics and spirituality and religion. Astrow explained he wanted to demonstrate that you could disagree with another person and yet listen respectfully to him or her.

Listening to the silence on the other end, Astrow realized he hadn't convinced Twerski and probably wasn't going to. So he took Mark McDougle's advice. He explained that the conference wasn't about ethics or religion but about spirituality, which was different. He said it wasn't really for the community but a continuing-education program for the doctors and nurses, for which they would receive credits. In other words, the conference could be explained to the touchy rabbis as hospital business, not a competition for the souls of Borough Park.

During the conversation Twerski remembered that Astrow had taken care of one of his relatives. He told the doctor he and his family were grateful and suggested that in the future Astrow should consider checking with the religious-affairs committee of the board before inviting lecturers to speak on such sensitive subjects.

Later Astrow would say that the whole episode was a blip, maybe because happiness evaporates while disappointment lingers—the way months or weeks or even days of illness inhabit memory more powerfully than do years of health.

But Jill Nathanson was a witness to her husband's happiness that night. She looked at him and saw the self-assurance with which he wore his nice dark suit. The bandage had been removed from his forehead, which showed no trace of the stitches. Someday he might shrug it off, but that night there was no mistaking the expression on his face. He couldn't deny it. He was happy.

There was a fruit platter and wine and cheese. The chairs had been delivered—seventy-five of them—and they were filled. The light fixtures were in place, and the walls were painted.

Jay Cooper even cracked a joke. "This room didn't exist just a few days ago," he said by way of opening the first conference at the cancer center.

Astrow stood up to introduce the speakers. First, though, he explained why they were there.

"As physicians, nurses, and other health-care professionals, we may recognize that caring for patients involves several dimensions," he said. "The most obvious is the technical, the scientific, the biomedical—to diagnose and treat illness with thoroughness, attention, and skill. A second dimension might be termed the emotional, or the psychosocial, in which we try to engage with our patients as whole human beings. Who are our patients? What do they care about? What worries them? How do we show our concern for them as unique individuals? Here in the heme-onc division at Maimonides, we attempt to address these interlocking realms with our fellows in our weekly biopsychosocial rounds, organized by Dr. Allan Novetsky with the assistance of Dr. Sheldon Berman."

He may not have been smooth, but he could be eloquent. "There is a third dimension, which for want of a better term I'm going to call the spiritual, which may underlie the other two. By spirituality I refer to the unseen, often unspoken, values that motivate us. In the contemporary world, when we speak of an invisible hand that drives us, it is often assumed that we are referring to the marketplace and the invisible hand of economic self-interest. But most physicians and nurses, I think, want to see themselves as more than simply one party in a financial transaction. Why do we do what we do? What keeps us going? Not just that we ought to care, but why? Faced with a suffering or demanding patient whom we might prefer to avoid, where do we find the strength to enter the patient's room? What is the conception of the human person and the role of the physician and nurse that medical practice relies on?"

That night Alan Astrow was in his element.

Seven

We Speak Your Language

On the home page of the Maimonides Medical Center Web site:

SPANISH, RUSSIAN, CHINESE, ARABIC, YIDDISH, AND MORE . . .

At Maimonides Medical Center, providing culturally sensitive care for patients who aren't fluent in English is important. One of our priorities is facilitating better health care access for non-English speaking patients and their families. To achieve this goal and to serve our culturally diversified community, the Medical Center has been recruiting multilingual physicians, nurses and staff, especially for patient care areas. A prime example of this effort can be seen in the emergency department. As a result of an increasing Chinese, Russian, Spanish, and Arabic patient population in the emergency department, we now have coverage twenty-four hours, seven days a week by multilingual patient representatives who are available to assist patients and their families who speak languages such as: Arabic, Chinese, Czech, German, Greek, Hebrew, Hindi, Italian, Polish, Russian, Spanish, Ukrainian, and Yiddish. Informational brochures and relevant hospital forms have also been created in many of these same languages to assist patients.

اللـغـة العـربـيـة

中文

по-русски

Español

ייִדיש

. . .

More than a quarter century had passed since Arthur Kleinman, the Harvard medical anthropologist, began promulgating the importance of cross-cultural awareness in the 1970s. Kleinman understood that the potential for misinterpretation went beyond words. The language of healing had to encompass gestures, fears, desires, superstitions, beliefs. But it was only in the last decade that aiming to achieve "cultural competence" had become a national, institutionalized goal. In 1998 the Association of American Medical Colleges recommended that medical schools teach "knowledge of the important non-biological determinants of poor health and of the economic, psychological, social, and cultural factors that contribute to the development and/or continuation of maladies." That same year the National Council on Interpreting in Health Care was established to help health-care providers learn how to speak to patients from different cultures.

As research and symposia on the subject proliferated, and the study of cultural competence itself became an industry, one conclusion was indisputable: Language was easy; comprehending was hard.

Sometimes Kathir Suppiah thought it was all just crap. Suppiah was one of the ten fellows in hematologic oncology, doctors who had completed their residency and were M.D.'s but had decided to specialize, requiring an additional three years of training. Son of a diplomat from Malaysia, he carried himself with the confidence of privilege. I thought of him as "the Prince."

"I hate to say it, this is horrible to say right now, but I'm going to say it," he told me one day. "I have lived around the world and thought I was the least prejudiced person you'd ever meet. Since coming to Brooklyn, I've become, believe it or not—I shouldn't even say this—I've become a lot more prejudiced. I actually feel bad sometimes. I say, 'How did I come to this?'"

Whom did he dislike the most? I asked him.

He was hard-pressed to choose.

The Orthodox Jews?

He nodded. "Maybe," he said. "They become so demanding and are actually so derogatory when they speak to you that you think, 'Remind me again why should I help you?'"

Maybe the Chinese?

"They're very rude people," he said, nodding. "Go to Eighth Avenue. They don't listen to anything you tell them. They don't talk to you unless you're Chinese. They don't even look at you."

Russians?

"Oh, God, take it back. The Chinese aren't so bad. Not compared to the Russians."

What about Sam Kopel or Alan Astrow, two of his mentors?

"No! No! They're very very different," said Suppiah. "I don't consider them Jewish. I don't think of them that way. They're the more modernized Jew, very decent people, I don't care whether they're Jewish, Chinese, whatever."

Dr. Huang?

"He's very different," said Suppiah. "He's one of the people who makes you feel bad about saying bad things about Chinese. You say, 'Damn. He breaks the mold.'"

This unvarnished analysis had been triggered by a case presented at a biopsychosocial meeting, involving a patient who didn't speak English. These weekly meetings were part of the fellows' training, where they discussed the nonclinical aspects of cases—ethics, behavior, feelings.

One of Alan Astrow's responsibilities as chief was to moderate this weekly meeting, whose purpose wasn't to arrive at a diagnosis or treatment plan. He had inherited biopsychosocial from Allan Novetsky, who had begun the oncology fellowship program in 2001, in anticipation of the new cancer center. Novetsky saw these sessions as the place the fellows would learn "to be doctors," the humanistic counterweight to the bulk of their training, which was devoted to the impossible task of keeping up with the latest research; according to the Institute of Health, the number of clinical drug trials conducted had grown to nearly ten thousand a year at the turn of the twenty-first century, roughly three hundred a day.

Novetsky said he loved these theoretical, humanistic discussions, but his own rules of practice were inflexible. God forbid one of his patients should show up late for an appointment. He told them at the outset he expected them to arrive on time or he would cancel.

Novetsky had come to Maimonides from Brookdale Hospital, to help lay the groundwork for the new cancer center. The hospital's interest in Novetsky wasn't purely academic; he had a large practice, and it was hoped that this would help fill the referral gap left by the departure of the Bashevkin group. That hadn't happened, which contributed to the decision to hire Astrow, who would take over the fellowship program as the new chief. Novetsky's final months and Astrow's first months at the hospital overlapped, adding another undercurrent of tension masked by forced civility—and unwittingly adding another layer to the idea of training fellows "how to be doctors."

Whatever Astrow's other feelings toward Novetsky, he was grateful for biopsychosocial. The physician he respected most was Howard Spiro, who in 1983 had started the Program for Humanities in Medicine at Yale's medical school, the purpose of which was to help physicians think about the spiritual and ethical components of medicine—the things that obsessed Astrow. Spiro was the only teacher from medical school with whom Astrow remained in touch.

Suppiah, who usually was quick to jump in with a question or a joke, had sat out the session, doodling furiously in his notebook. I could see that his guard was down and tried a gentle poke to see what it might provoke. "Why so quiet?" I asked him.

"I had to assimilate to this country," he told me. "I had to assimilate to Switzerland. I had to assimilate to France. Wherever I went. This disrespect for our country is what I hate. And this is my country now. We cater to this disrespect. Our health-care system completely embraces this kind of stuff. We can't expect these people to change because we do nothing to change them. When I was in France, they didn't bend in any way. You either learned French or else. Nothing. They can speak English, but they won't. Even if you go to a hospital, they expect you to speak French. Here you get translators. That kind of catering is why people have this attitude they can do anything they want."

Theme and variation of the biopsychosocial meetings was the failure to communicate. Every week the Maimonides cancer fellows brought up daily frustrations that required interpretive skills far more subtle than knowing the rules of grammar and syntax. Using specific cases, they discussed how to deal with angry families, doctors they disagreed with, nurses who annoyed them, chart notes they couldn't read, religious and cultural differences, the essential antagonism of the system. They contended with their own behavior— sometimes indulging in relaxing trivia (how patients liked doctors to dress, for example) and sometimes confronting sources of anguish (how to acknowledge the futility of treatment). The fellows were required to attend. They were often joined by social workers, a psychiatrist, the pain-management team, occasionally one of the oncology attending physicians, sometimes a nurse, sometimes a resident.

They complained about the patients from all over the world who came to the hospital directly from JFK Airport, looking for free care in the emergency room. Maybe soon there would be a special air-traffic-control system just for sick people. While the indigent poor from "over there" were coming here, hospitals in India and Thailand had begun courting U.S. patients with no medical insurance, promoting "medical tourism packages," combining vacation and surgery for bargain prices.

The fellows met every Monday morning in a dining area in the back of the Maimonides cafeteria, just behind the tables where the *mashgiach* hung out with the guys who cleaned the tables, usually young men from Caribbean countries. (The *mashgiach* were the bearded men in charge of making sure the kitchen observed the Jewish dietary laws; Dov Hikind's father had been one.) While careful planning went into patient menus, healthy cuisine didn't seem to be a priority in the feeding of staff. The grill turned out delicious french fries, cut thick and deep-fried. But the laws of kashruth prohibited providing yogurt at lunch when meat was served (except on Tuesdays, dairy day). The separation of milk and meat was taken so seriously that the dairy refrigerator was padlocked during non-milk meals. You could get matzo brei during Passover, and kosher Chinese food and sushi, but it was futile to even think about a cheeseburger.

For these residents and fellows, discussion of "cultural competency" wasn't a matter of us and them. They were themselves part of the cross-cultural stew. Besides the Malaysian Prince there was the Russian Princess, Inna Sominsky, the second-year fellow with the streaked blond hair, two small children, parents, her own immigration experiences, and a kind heart. Mendel Warshawsky, an opinionated South African who wore a yarmulke on his shaved head, was competing for a permanent job on the faculty staff with another third-year fellow, Mohammad Razaq, a quiet Pakistani.

Mendel the Jew versus Mohammad the Muslim.

The choice would be Astrow's.

Besides the Malaysian, the South African, the Russian, and the Pakistani, there were the Indians—Sirisha, Sushma, Ranju, Nagander, and Sramila. And there was Jason Tache, prematurely middle-aged in his thirties, born in the U.S.A., at Maimonides Hospital.

Many of them would be dispatched on graduation to hospitals and medical practices around the country. (Suppiah was already signed on with a practice affiliated with a big regional hospital in Wilmington, Delaware. Sirisha Perumandla was heading for Iowa.) Better, worse, or indifferent, they would take the lessons they learned at Maimonides with them.

The Prince rubbed his black-rimmed glasses and grimaced. "If I have to pick the two patients I'm most prejudiced against . . ."

He paused, looking like a man who had taken a leap off a cliff and realized halfway down that the pool of water he was diving into was a shallow hole.

"This is so bad, right?" he wailed. "I've gone from someone who was open-minded to this. Okay, the Russians are the worst. Even though they can speak English, they refuse to do it. They say, 'No, I don't speak.' I say, 'I know you can speak English. Can you speak a little bit? I can't speak Russian, so I'm just going to take a guess at what you have.' Then you can see the fear start. They go, 'No, no, no, no,' and then words start coming out." He lowered his voice to a whisper, imitating the patients. "They go, '*Heart, heart, heart.*'"

He shook his head. "This kind of collision is not necessary. It shouldn't have to be a battle."

Then he turned his dark eyes directly at me. "My question to you is, Why would you subject yourself to that when you don't have to?"

I asked, "Are you saying we can be happy only if we don't mingle?"

No, he said. "But to mingle you need some unifying way of behaving, a language. If you don't speak the language, bring someone who does. You're coming into a fricking hospital. You have to give your entire history. How do you think that's going to happen? I have so many relatives who came to this country and got citizenship status. Do you know how many English classes they went through? They suffered. They went to work; at night they went to their English classes. They don't expect someone to speak Hindi or Tamil for that matter."

Suppiah had grown up in France, Switzerland, Malaysia, the United States, and had learned a new language with each move. When he was fifteen years old, his family settled in New Jersey. His father enrolled him in a Catholic high school, though the family was Hindu, so Suppiah could learn something about Christianity, his new country's dominant religion. The idea was to adapt, to accommodate, to become so comfortable that people would overlook the dark skin, the accent, the strange religion. It was useful at Maimonides, the ability to adapt. Suppiah had completed his residency there and was now in his third and final year of the hospital's fellowship in hematologic oncology.

His parents had tried to dissuade him from medicine. He preferred playing tennis to studying. They told him to talk to family friends who were doctors. They, too, tried to discourage him. "It sounds glorious, but it's quite painful at the end of it all," one of them said.

Suppiah ignored them all but almost quit after his first year of training. Then providence intervened, or maybe he simply found a story that explained his own secret desire.

Providence in this case arrived at a party, thrown by his brother. Over drinks, Suppiah talked to a friend from college who asked him what kind of specialist he was going to be. Suppiah told him he wanted to quit. The friend was shocked. Why, he asked? Suppiah said he didn't think he was going to help anyone, that he didn't see the point of medicine anymore.

The friend sat down and told Suppiah a cancer story. When the friend's mother got sick, he flew back to India to visit. No doctor wanted to take care of her. They said she was terminal and there was nothing to be done. She was forty-two years old, and she died. The friend looked at Suppiah and said, "I didn't want treatment," he said. "I wanted someone to take care of her."

Suppiah was angry. "Go have a drink," he said. "Go relax."

The friend persisted. "You could have been that doctor," he said. "You have that quality. Trust me. You can take care of patients. Do it."

Suppiah didn't immediately appreciate the declaration of faith. "Who the hell are you? What is this about?" he said. "I know what you're doing, this guilt crap."

But long after the friend walked away and the party was over, Suppiah couldn't stop thinking about what he'd said. Did he, Kathir Suppiah, have some special quality? Could he be one of the gifted ones who could help a patient heal, even when there was no cure? He returned to his residency and applied to specialize in the hematologic-oncology program. One day (to his surprise) he found he was feeling much better about his profession, about life in general.

"Yes, it's depressing, but it's the best job in the world," he said. "Yes, it's heartbreaking almost every single day, but it also gives you newfound meaning. Have you ever heard the saying 'One man's misery is another man's happiness'? Horrible as it sounds, seeing how unfortunate other people are actually allows me to live."

Idealism was one casualty of his medical training; his marriage was another. One more lack of communication. They met in college, and she, too, became a physician, specializing in ob-gyn. He admired her. "I try to be her," he told me. "She is very, very good. If you want a physician, that's what you should have. Very, very smart, incredibly dedicated." But after eight years of marriage they split up, he said, because her dedication surpassed his.

"She clocked in one week at a hundred and twenty hours," he said. "I clocked her. I don't know when she defecated and urinated. She was more than obsessed. She just couldn't let go. She didn't stop talking about it when she came home. She couldn't stop. She had to be the best. Number one in high school, number one in college, number one in medical school. She strived so hard to be the best she couldn't stop. I'm the opposite. When these doors close behind me, you'll never hear me discuss a case outside of work. I deal with the difficulties my private way."

I think in your book you have to have a whole chapter on diversity," Lilia Colon told me. "We focus so much here on diversity, but in this country people do not have the smallest idea of what diversity is. They think it is black and white. But you have culture, you have race, you have age, you have position, you have education, you have so much to it."

Colon was Puerto Rican, willowy, gorgeous, stubborn, smart, and impatient, with flashing black eyes sparked by an electric intensity that could attract or repel. She was a nurse by training and had spent years as a clinician before becoming a consultant on labor-management issues, one of Pam Brier's abiding passions and a significant component of care in New York's unionized hospitals.

Colon's office was tucked off a ramp leading away from the second-floor administrative offices into an odd little alcove, part of the hospital's haphazard design, which often seemed more archaeological than architectural.

"I am not from this country, and so I come already with a whole understanding of diversity and tolerance, and sometimes I don't have it," she said. "Sometimes I'm human, and in the heat of the moment I'm not that . . . tender. But I see awareness here, more than other places—even if people don't have the skills."

Awareness didn't require great skill; it was impossible to avoid. "The community here changes every three blocks. The Hasidic, the Hispanic, the Asian—even between Latinos you have different types of cultures and they are right here, and they are segregated," she said. "Walking here from patient accounts upstairs, I passed a Mexican group, a Dominican group, a Cuban group, a Puerto Rican group."

But she must have seen diversity at the other hospitals she worked at in Manhattan, hadn't she?

Colon leaned forward, exposing a bit of décolletage, unusual at Maimonides, where everyone tended to cover up—except patients, forced into immodesty by the open flaps of hospital gowns.

"Don't forget we have a visual reminder of diversity, and that's the Hasidic population," she said. "We are in a very melted pot, though we're not melted, we're segregated, but we're so close together we look melted. I've worked in the city all my adult life. You see black, white, yellow, Latino all over. But here you have something unique. You're in the heart of a Hasidic community. Eighty percent of our patients are Hasidic."

I thought I had misinterpreted. Her English was impeccable, but perhaps her Spanish cadence had altered a syllable.

"Eighty percent?" I said. "You must mean eighteen." The actual percentage was more like 20 to 25 percent.

Colon looked genuinely surprised.

I said, "Think of what it would be like if it were eighty."

Many nurses commented or complained, depending on their inclination, that the Orthodox received so many visitors from family members and rabbis and charitable groups that it was often a struggle just to make it to the patient's bedside. For the cleaning staff, known as environmental workers, the visitors' goodwill translated into another obstacle to hospital hygiene. Hard to sweep in a crowd.

Similar thoughts must have occurred to Colon, because she nodded vigorously. "You're right."

She knit her eyebrows together, trying to analyze the Freudian slip.

"I guess it's because of the observances," she said. "The elevator is blocked on the weekend. You need to provide them a place for their prayers. The cafeteria accommodates them."

We both understood that she had touched on something significant with the 20 percent who felt like 80 percent.

"Play this out a little," I asked her.

She was game. "I'm speaking for myself, okay? For me, the visual of the attire is a big part of it," she said. "The same happens when I see the Middle Eastern women with their veils. The visual is a reminder that I have to stop and understand that I am not going to speak from a different language perhaps but from a different perception, and I have to be sensitive to that. I don't know how they perceive us. I don't know if they see us as different the way I see them as different. Going back to the eighteen and not the eighty. Change the equation. They are making the eighty percent stop and think. It is the visual and tangible awareness that I have to be more tolerant of, because his faith and culture have to be respected just like mine."

Her office was filled with graphs and flow charts, so it was natural that this numbers game appealed to her. "I don't know, when I said eighty, if this was a slip or my real perception," she said. "It feels like an eighty, because the eighty percent is the STOP sign to stop and be sensitive. At this moment in history, we are hating each other, especially the Muslim and the Jewish groups, but I think the history is more at a political level than individual. Just like black and white in the United States. Blacks sometimes pull the race card on me and say, 'You just say that because I'm black,' and I say, 'That's not even funny.' But at a different level, you can go to labor and delivery here and have the Muslim woman sit next to Hasidic and be worried about the baby of the Hasidic and vice versa."

(Actually, the hospital didn't ask people what religion they were, but patient-satisfaction surveys did inquire whether they kept a kosher home. Between 2003 and 2006, the percentage of patients who said they kept a kosher home varied between 20 and 25 percent, except in obstetrics, where 70 percent of the babies delivered had mothers who kept kosher homes.)

Maimonides had hired Colon to work on staff development, which meant she spent most of her day wrangling with managers and employees over rights and duties while trying to make them *appreciate* one another—and while trying to create systems that made the hospital run more efficiently and deliver higher-quality care to patients. All on a tight budget. No wonder she usually felt frustrated.

"I am a vehicle to create a culture of mutual respect, collaboration between two groups that historically have seen themselves as adversaries," she said. "In utopia, in the ideal world, you will have a whole curriculum where employees are required to attend classes on how to work with each other, and there will be a staff to run it. They would learn how to use conflict rather than avoid it. How do we use information that gets dumped on the table? How do we hold multiple realities so we can accomplish our goal while we are listening to each other and understanding how we are different from each other?"

Colon felt that Brier's message was not filtering down through the system. "We have limited resources," she said. "We don't have money to hire people to make sure each department gets these classes on how to build a team and how to solve conflicts. We always say 'the developers,' but I am *the* developer. So this is very far from utopia."

Her impatience extended to the man who had been instrumental in developing the labor-management collaborations at Maimonides. Peter Lazes, an old friend of Brier's, had been working as a consultant to the hospital for almost eight years. Lazes, a faculty member at Cornell University's School of Industrial and Labor Relations, was an idealist who believed in the concept of a civil society that centered on meaningful work. "If people have more responsibility—no matter what level the job or pay—the more they become involved in civic participation," he told me. He believed that union participation would create systems that would increase patient safety and improve patient care.

"It's very practical," he said. "Most people want to be consulted in decision making about their work. There's research about that. I don't think it has anything to do with whether you're well educated and well paid or less educated and less paid. And in health care it's much different than working in a factory. People go into this because they have some compassion for people. A hospital setting in general has a better ability to engage people—as opposed to, say, a Xerox plant. They want to feel they are contributing to someone else's well-being."

Before taking on Maimonides as a client, Lazes had tested his central theory—that union participation could improve workplace results—at the Xerox Corporation, Bell Laboratories Works, Levi Strauss, and the World Bank. In 1995, when the Warnaco Group said it would close the Hathaway shirt plant in Maine unless costs were brought down, Lazes helped the union workers and management cut costs by working in teams and changing job roles. The factory stayed open—for another six years. But the worker triumph ended when a new owner moved the manufacture of the shirts overseas, where labor was cheaper.

In the eight years Lazes had been advising the hospital, Maimonides had established forty-two joint hiring committees; employees helped hire managers and directors of departments. The hospital had several departmental labor management committees (DLMCs), described by Lazes in a report as "a forum for labor and management to share critical information about their department's performance and labor-management issues."

Maria Ferlita, the vice president of finance who was in charge of medical records, recalled the initial response to the DLMCs in her department. "I'll never forget. I met with the medical records staff and told them this is what we're doing, not just 1199 [the hospital workers' union] employees but management as well, and they looked at me: 'Okay, what have you been smoking?'" Twice a month the group met to discuss the problems. "Work-related issues like, 'We can't do our work because we don't have enough chairs,'" said Ferlita, ". . . problematic employees calling in sick time, not accepting responsibility for their work, blaming their shift for their lack of productivity."

The medical records department was a mess, with something like six hundred feet of unfiled documents containing information on patient care and reimbursements. The employees worked out a system to increase productivity; the department's delinquency rate dropped to 4 percent, far superior to the Joint Commission's requirement of below 15 percent.

In cardiology, strategies developed by labor and management were credited with reducing response time to cardiac-patient alarms and monitors to less than one minute, from an average response time of between three and eight minutes.

But too often, Lazes complained to Brier, the DLMCs never got past communication to action. The Environmental Service DLMC was set up in 2002 to help the hospital meet the Joint Commission's standards of daily cleanliness. Three years later, after dozens of meetings, visits to other hospitals, endless discussions, Maimonides was substandard in that respect. The lobby in particular had a shabby air; the door leading into the volunteers' room run by the Bikur Cholim, right by the main elevator bank, was especially scruffy.

"I don't understand it," Lazes told me. "We're trying to systematically get rooms up to speed, get everyone trained, get equipment. They look for brooms and mops, so people steal each other's mops. You go to a floor and want to do a good job and don't have a mop. You learn through the grapevine, go to this other unit and steal it."

In August 2005 a new manager was hired, after being interviewed by a joint management-labor committee. Almost a year later, Michael Yohannes, born and raised in Ethiopia, was still mystified by Maimonides.

"The employees feel free to go all the way to the top," he said. "It's good and bad. It's good because the employee has another venue to vent, but it's bad because it doesn't send the right message. I feel employees are taking advantage of that. Not all of them, just a few. But it makes it difficult for management to run. It isn't an easy path."

Colon echoed his sentiments. "So much waste of time, money, resources, energy, and yet Maimonides is still the most advanced hospital in this area," she said. "Though in the entire industry they are furthest ahead, after eight, nine years very little has been accomplished. That's no way to engage in a mission."

In Mendel Warshawsky's view, the social experiments taking place at the hospital—both the purposeful and the unintended—had created fertile conditions for a kind of anthropological graft-versus-host disease.

From the Web site of the National Marrow Donor Program:

Graft-versus-host disease (GVHD) is a common side effect of an allogeneic bone marrow or cord blood transplant (also called a BMT). An
allogeneic transplant uses blood-forming cells donated by a family member, unrelated donor or cord blood unit. In GVHD, the immune cells
from the donated marrow or cord blood (the graft) attack the body of the
transplant patient (the host). GVHD can affect many different parts of
the body. The skin, eyes, stomach and intestines are affected most often.
GVHD can range from mild to life-threatening.

"You get pissed off," said Warshawsky, the Orthodox oncology fellow
from South Africa. "People want to think there's this utopia of cultural
acceptance. It just doesn't exist. Doctors are the same as everyone else—same
prejudices, perhaps even worse."

Fierceness emanated from Warshawsky, who had a boxer's stance and
pugilistic verbal style, his intellectual jab and thrust sharpened at the
Lithuanian yeshiva where he studied Talmud in Israel for three years. Behind
thick glasses, his eyes were unblinking and had a red, rabbity look, which
made him seem wary and combative. Warshawsky, who had once considered
devoting his life to Torah study, was competing with Mohammad Razaq for a
full-time job after graduation.

Warshawsky was a man of many interests and many opinions. He'd given
me a few chapters of a book he was writing about his experiences in the medical world of South Africa. The manuscript revealed a good eye for detail
and—his yeshiva years notwithstanding—a lusty sensibility.

Warshawsky's ferocity was genuine, but his aura of physical robustness
was misleading. A decade earlier, at age twenty-three, he had stared down
death from leukemia. His dry-eyed gaze was a physical condition, the residue
of a bone-marrow transplant undergone while he was a medical student in
South Africa.

For him the graft-host analogy wasn't theoretical. He had endured many
variations of the disease. His lungs had been so weakened that it was an effort
for him to climb a flight of stairs. Infertility problems had almost kept him
and his wife—another cancer survivor—from having a child; it took eight

years of fertility treatment to produce their baby. Perhaps worst of all, for someone whose livelihood depended on keeping up with research, he suffered from Sjögren's (SHOW-grins) syndrome, a chronic disease rooted in many causes, including transplants, in which white blood cells attack the moisture-producing glands. The inability to make tears had damaged his corneas, the sensitive membrane covering the iris, the colored part of the eye. His corneas had become scarred; light caused exquisite pain.

He hadn't been able to read an entire book for two years, serious deprivation for a Torah scholar and cancer-specialist-in-training. He had heard of patients who suffered so much from the condition they had their eyelids sewn shut. He felt he had almost reached that point when Douglas Jablon—the Mitzvah Man, the fixer—told Warshawsky that Edy, Jablon's wife, also had been debilitated by dry-eye syndrome; after years of misery she had found relief. Dr. Perry Rosenthal, a cornea specialist who taught at Harvard Medical School, had developed a special lens—called the Boston scleral lens—filled with a fluid that merged with the eye's own tears and provided a protective coating for damaged corneas.

Thanks to Jablon's intervention, Warshawsky had recently returned from Boston. For the first time in years, he could endure light without pain. He no longer needed glasses.

"I had given up hope, and then I went to see Dr. Rosenthal, this elderly guy, and he put in this lens, and I could see clearly," he said. His sense of excitement was palpable. "It was a miracle. He's been on *Oprah,* on ABC, but the medical establishment has not promoted him the way he should be promoted. The first reason is that doctors, myself included, they can't believe that such a simple, elegant thing would actually work. The second thing is egos. You've got people who have invested their lives in corneal transplants—big high-tech things—they don't want to give that up so quickly. It makes no sense to modern doctors that something so simple could overtake something so high-tech."

I'd cornered Warshawsky in the cafeteria to talk about another low-tech aspect of medicine—the competition between him and Razaq to fill one of the new positions opening up at the cancer center. Each had played his own race/ethnic card with Astrow. Razaq was a soft-spoken Pakistani Muslim who pointed out to the new chief that the Muslim community in the area was growing. Razaq spoke Urdu and Hindi and felt he could draw a different set of patients from an emerging population to the cancer center. Warshawsky, backed by Kopel, knew that his strength was as possible conduit to the Orthodox patients who were not using the cancer center. "I have to see if I can get the Orthodox vote," said Warshawsky. "I have to compete with Bashevkin."

"I think Astrow has this idealistic vision that Bashevkin will come here," said Warshawsky. "He doesn't understand old rifts and old feuds. Everyone looks after their own, that's how it works. You scratch my back, I'll scratch yours."

What did he think about his rival, Razaq?

"As a physician I respect him," said Warshawsky slowly. "But at the end of the day, we are separated by our cultures. Not our cultures. By our race. Our nationality. You can't deny it."

When he was in medical school, he told me, he shared a cadaver with an Indian Muslim. They got along fine until Al Quds Day, the last Friday of Ramadan—designated by the Ayatollah Khomeini after the 1979 Iranian revolution as a day for Muslims worldwide to unite in their support of Palestinians and denunciation of Israel. (Al Quds is the Arabic name for Jerusalem.)

"Come Al Quds Day—where they moan how they lost Jerusalem and are going to reconquer it—I would punch the guy in the face and he would punch me back," recalled Warshawsky with satisfaction. "And then the next day we'd be sitting in class working together again. Muslim-Jewish fights on campus were the big thing. We would call in the big boys from the JDL [the Jewish Defense League], and they would come in with their gangs, and the other side would come out and say, 'Death to Israel.' You'd smack a guy, and the next day this is the same guy you'd have a conversation with about the biology of cancer cells."

He grinned a little wildly. "It's crazy," he said. "It is. It is the same thing here." He lowered his head and glanced around. The tables were occupied by mixed groups of various ethnicities eating and chatting.

As noted, Warshawsky had a good sense of drama.

He modified.

"It's simmering," he said. "It's undercurrents. I tell you straight out, there's a lot of complications in physician-patient relationships precisely because of this. Because physicians don't understand other cultures, and a lot of these cultures do a lot of things that are very distasteful to a lot of physicians. I can only say for myself, as a Jewish physician, I've struggled, and there have been times I've asked someone else to take care of a patient.

"Like when an Arab guy came from Ramallah, got off the plane, got an angiogram that showed he needed an operation, and came to this hospital thinking he could just walk in and get it, and I found that very very disturbing.

"Picture me in Lebanon, say—if I was allowed to go into the country, which I would not be—or Saudi Arabia, breaking my leg and needing medical attention in the hospital. What are my chances of coming out of that hospital alive? I'd say zero. And yet with impunity those same people walk into this hospital dressed up in traditional gear expecting charity in a Jewish hospital.

"But this is America," he said. "You're not allowed to turn someone away from the emergency room."

He nodded his head toward a group of Orthodox doctors who sat at a nearby table. "A lot of things upset me here as well," he said conspiratorially. "But I can't really talk about it, because you can't talk badly about your own people, even though they are guilty of many things that are despicable. It doesn't look good on you to talk badly about your own nation."

Only a few months were left until the fellows were to be graduated. Warshawsky was frustrated with Astrow's delay in making a decision. The young doctor wondered aloud if Astrow was too soft to be chief. "He isn't narrow-minded like most of them," Warshawsky said. "He's incorporated the humanistic side of medicine, which is very unusual. I see that with patients. But administration is a different animal. You can either do it or you can't. You need single-mindedness, the ability to detach yourself from feelings."

Warshawsky continued. "Dr. Astrow is a universalist. He sees things in terms of multicultural, including Christianity, Buddhism . . . we can all just get on. He's missing the point. Because we can't. Astrow, I don't think he understands it that well."

He shook his head. "I don't know if Kopel understands it completely," he said. "I don't know if I understand it completely."

. . .

Lisa Keen, social worker, the former sixties radical who often took me on rounds with her, always seasoned her observations about hospital life with peppery commentary about the doctors and nurses. The Prince, she told me, was a good one, compassionate.

What about that not-so-compassionate stuff he said?

Watch him, she said.

A few weeks later, I caught up with him sitting at a nurses' station on Kronish 7, looking at the chart of a fifty-nine-year-old woman from Bangladesh.

"She's gone," he was saying brusquely to Keen, who was the social worker on the case. Suppiah showed her Mrs. Devi's CAT scan on a computer screen. Cancer of the colon had spread to her liver, abscesses measuring seven centimeters.

"That's what you are going to tell her?" Keen asked. "She's gone?"

Suppiah shook his head, but still, there was no avoiding it. "This is a death sentence," he said.

Keen wanted Suppiah to talk to the family about the prognosis. She was concerned that the doctors parading through Mrs. Devi's room had been so preoccupied with the immediate issues of lab tests and treatment plans, with the patient's progression through the system, they had forgotten to tell the family the true meaning of all this activity. Through the patient-rep office, she found someone who spoke Bengali, a technician in the blood bank, who agreed to meet Suppiah in front of the patient's room.

Keen felt a duty to patients and their families, to provide hope (when there was none), to make them believe that someone cared about what happened to them (which someone did, at least in an abstract way). She knew that the impersonality of the hospital lent a certain futility to her mission, but she persisted, even though she was scheduled to retire in June and could have taken it easy.

Suppiah arrived shortly before the interpreter and peered into Mrs. Devi's room. She was curled up in her bed like a child. She was tiny, even tinier than her husband, a slight man with a weathered face, wearing a red-and-white checked scarf around his neck. He was a contractor who worked with his son. The son, in his thirties, had acquired American heft; he had a sweet, chubby face. His English was minimal, though he had lived in the United States for fourteen years. His father followed him ten years later. The mother had stayed in Bangladesh, caring for the rest of the children, arriving in New York two years before she showed up at Maimonides.

Suppiah agreed to talk to Mrs. Devi's husband and son. Keen and I joined them outside the patient's room, where we smiled and nodded awkwardly at one another, waiting for the interpreter to arrive. His name was Asm Rahman, a slender man in a shirt and tie, with brown skin and black hair worn slicked back, who had studied medicine and wanted to become a physician. For five years he'd been working in the Maimonides blood bank. There was no private room for family conferences on that floor. Suppiah—and Rahman—had to deliver Mrs. Devi's death sentence under a fluorescent light in a busy hallway.

Suppiah fixed his gaze on the family as he explained in great detail what he saw. Certain phrases popped out. "Large mass sitting on the colon . . . multiple areas of infection . . . probably why she has fevers and belly pain." He paused every so often, and the son and father turned their attention to Rahman, as he interpreted word for word, as Suppiah instructed him to do.

"Do they understand what I just told them?" Suppiah asked Rahman.

"I understand," the son said sadly, in English.

Suppiah looked at him gently. "Could you tell me what I said?"

The son nodded, turned to Rahman, and spoke at length in Bengali.

Rahman nodded. "He says he knows there is a large mass in the colon and liver and an infection. He wants to know what they can do about it."

"First is to get a biopsy," said Suppiah, "To take a piece of tissue and analyze it, but this is complicated by the infection. I haven't seen her yet, but from what I see on the CAT scan, she is very, very sick. I cannot stress that enough. She is very sick."

As Rahman interpreted, apparently taking Suppiah at his word, skipping nothing, it was clear that the message had been received. Both son and husband looked stricken. Their eyes reddened. They seemed oblivious to the movement in the hallway: an old man walking by slowly, trailing his IV drip; orderlies wheeling someone on a gurney.

Suppiah said the disease looks like cancer, very advanced. The son and the father began to weep.

Suppiah said he understood (from Keen) that the family didn't want Mrs. Devi to know the details of her illness. Could he ask why? The son replied, "That's what she wants."

Suppiah said, "I'm not going to tell her anything, but I need to examine her. Does she speak any English?"

No, said the son.

Suppiah smiled. "That works out very good," he said. "I don't speak Bengali, so I won't be able to tell her."

The son and father looked blank, not comprehending the weak joke.

Suppiah explained that Mrs. Devi should sign a health proxy form, giving her husband and son the right to make decisions about her treatment. He touched the son's hand and offered more details about controlling infection, antibiotics, chemotherapy.

The son asked, "What is the prognosis? What is the best and the worst?"

Suppiah hesitated. "The problem with this question is her infection," he said. "If I give her therapy now, she will die from the therapy. If this is cancer, people who have this type of cancer and no infection, the average life survival is a year, a year and a half. Because of her infection, this can be much shorter than that. I'll know more when I get the results of the biopsy."

Suppiah and Rahman went inside to examine Mrs. Devi.

Keen held the son's hand and urged him to tell his mother everything.

He shook his head. "I tell her she has an infection."

Keen said, "My guess is, your mother knows."

The son shook his head. "She don't tell me nothing," he said in English, his face twisted with grief. "If she told me something, I'd bring her right away. Only now she said she had a pain over here." He pointed toward his lower torso.

Keen asked him if he would like an imam to pray with. He said he would ask his father, who had followed the doctors into the room.

When Suppiah emerged, rubbing Purell on his hands, the son pressed him for answers. Suppiah again was gentle. "I know you are looking for an answer," he said. "I wish I could give it. We will do what we can."

Rahman, a Muslim like the Devis, told the husband and son that the hospital would do everything that could be done, and they responded, "What happened is God-given," and he said the doctors would use the latest technology. Later he told me, "I feel sad because this is a great loss for them, but I don't know how to console them."

The hurt and love in the eyes of the son, the tender helplessness of the young physician and the blood-bank worker required no translation. Transcendence one minute, frustration the next. The convergence at Maimonides distilled the sweet and sour verities of humanity into a heady, combustible brew that could expand consciousness or cause it to implode.

As a child I was inculcated with unwavering belief in the miraculous nobility of America-the-refuge, country of immigrants. In our small rural town in Ohio, my Hungarian-speaking Czech-Jewish father was welcomed as a hero for his willingness to set up a medical practice in a poor, remote place that was not attractive to most American-born doctors.

No one seemed to consider him a threat. But nostalgic appreciation of immigrants—an appreciation easy to come by when there weren't many of them—had diminished to the vanishing point in recent decades by the large influx of newcomers, many of them illegal. Their willingness to take tough jobs for low wages had made them objects not of gratitude but of hostility. Their untaxed wages didn't contribute to the cost of running schools or hospitals—though they did fatten the bank accounts of those who employed these desperate, hardworking people.

Immigrants were dispersed throughout the country, but New York remained a major gateway. The public hospitals were the mainstay for people who had no coverage (and no documentation). Many of them ended up at Maimonides.

Location, location, location.

Under the Brezenoff-Brier regime, Maimonides moved its primary-care clinics out of the hospital into smaller offices located in the surrounding neighborhoods. This was both a marketing and a social-services decision: Go where the patients are. Urdu was the main language on Newkirk Avenue, Spanish in Sunset Park, Russian at the Fifty-seventh Street site, and Chinese (in several dialects) on Eighth Avenue, a few blocks from the new cancer center. About eighty-five thousand patients a year—more than double the number who were admitted to the hospital—were treated at the clinics. The hospital made an effort to install doctors and staff who spoke the same language and, when possible, were from the same background as the patients.

Bing Lu, a native of Wushi (now Wuxi), a coastal city near Shanghai, was the medical director of the Maimonides Primary Health Service in Brooklyn's Chinatown. He estimated that as many as 80 percent of his patients there were Chinese. We met in his small office at the end of a hallway that led to several examination rooms; residents periodically interrupted to ask questions about the treatment for respiratory ailments. The weather had turned cold.

Lu, who was forty-seven years old, wearing a dark suit, a white shirt, and a tie, looked like a prosperous Chinese businessman, a common sight in these heady days of commercial globalism. He apologized for his garrulousness. When I heard his story, I was glad he didn't skimp.

He told me that he had studied traditional Chinese medicine, including acupuncture and herbal remedies, as an apprentice to a famous physician. He learned the four main diagnostic methods: *wang* (inspection), *wen* (listening and smelling), *wen* (asking), *qie* (touching). "Touching the pulse is very important," he said, "and so is looking at the tongue. Today, for most patients I still look at their tongues."

He continued, "Once you gather this information, the processing is based on a very elaborate or complex hierarchy of theorems we call *bian zheng lun zhi,* almost like a therapy based on dialectical analysis of syndrome, juggling within the mind of the physician."

Yet his teacher encouraged him to study Western medicine, telling him he could always return to Chinese-style practice later. Bing Lu entered medical school in the spring of 1978, at the end of the Cultural Revolution. For almost ten years much had been stalled in China, including university studies. Bing Lu became merged with a driven generation, the so-called class of '77, the first group to take entrance exams in a decade, a class whose slogan was "We have to catch the time back."

He had big ambitions—the biggest, and most secret, to win the Nobel Prize. He had it all planned out. First step was coming to the United States to study. In China he was doing research in medical biology on the hepatitis B virus, probably the direst illness for Chinese, with a chronic infection rate of between 5 and 15 percent. He arrived in New York in the spring of 1986, to begin his career as a Nobel-aspiring researcher—studying the hepatitis virus—at Albert Einstein College of Medicine.

When he told me about his youthful dream, Lu laughed with embarrassment. Eight years into his quest, his wife was on his back to be more practical. They already had one child. Being a clinician was secure; research was quixotic and paid poorly. So he took the qualifying exams to become an FMG, "foreign medical graduate"—now known as the more politically correct IMG, "international medical graduate."

Even after being away from the trenches in the lab for so many years, he was surprised at how much he remembered from medical school. "I'm accustomed to working very hard, not a problem," he said. "Some residents would turf patients, and I would say, 'Fine, turf to me, I'll learn something.'" (Definition of "turf," from *House of God,* Samuel Shem's frisky bestselling novel about life as a medical intern: "to get rid of, get off your service and onto another, or out of the House altogether. Key concept. It's the main form of treatment in medicine.")

Bing Lu trained at the Miriam Hospital, affiliated with Brown University's medical school in Providence, Rhode Island, another Jewish hospital. I asked him about his religion, a question that didn't seem impertinent at Maimonides.

"Nothing official," he said. "I kind of believe in a somewhat abstract higher being," he said. "I don't think it's Jesus, not Buddhist per se, not exactly God. In Chinese we call it *tien,* which is actually 'sky' in Chinese. If you are puzzled, don't know why life is unfair, you look to the sky and go, 'Oh, sky, why does this happen to me? Why is this injustice?'"

At Miriam he often questioned his decision to leave research. One day a doctor who had become his mentor asked him, "Don't you see life as a series of compromises?"

Lu paused in his story. The room was quiet except for the buzz outside of patients and staff moving around. The practice was constantly growing; in a couple of months, it would move to the old Kopel-Bashevkin faculty practice offices a few blocks away, near the new cancer center.

"I like to talk, my wife says," said Lu, who wore his discontent cheerfully. "If you like, we can visit her. Her office is nearby."

We went outside and walked past a bubble-tea place. We stopped for a minute to say hello to Cheng Neng Fang, a doctor of traditional Chinese medicine, a skinny man with a wispy beard, whose shop was packed with all kinds of teapots and drawers filled with herbs and roots. Lu said something to him in Chinese. He nodded and handed me his business card.

Bing Lu's wife, Xiaoxi Hu, also a doctor, had just opened her office, a lovely converted storefront space where everything was new, including acupuncture tables with curtains for privacy. Hu, a brisk, friendly woman, stopped by to say hello, told us to make ourselves comfortable in her office—still largely unfurnished—and then vanished.

Bing Lu had gotten permission from his department chairman and Pam Brier to begin doing acupuncture in his wife's office. The hospital clinic didn't offer it for the usual reason—money. Most Maimonides patients were covered by Medicare or Medicaid or by HMOs that based reimbursement on the government insurance rates, which did not cover acupuncture. Private patients either had insurance that covered the cost or were willing to pay for it on their own. The hospital could offer the same deal, but acupuncture treatment required different beds from the ones used in medical examination rooms. For the hospital the economics (revenue versus cost) didn't make it worthwhile.

Lu found himself reconnecting with his old teachers as he began combining old and new, using herbs and acupuncture in the context of conventional—Western—medicine.

"Western medicine is good at treating organic problems like pneumonia, heart failure—structural failures," he said. "Chinese medicine is better in milder functional disturbances rather than organic disturbances. You have to weigh the evidence. Let's say a middle-aged woman, married, with children, taking care of family, taking care of career, stressed out, very busy, always has tightness. Tylenol or Motrin does help, but she doesn't sleep so great, sometimes feels nervous, et cetera. As an alternative to Paxil or Prozac, you have acupuncture. Another alternative: healthy lifestyle. These are real alternatives."

The conversation wound back to the subject of compromise.

"After finishing high school, I had the option of going into a family business, to learn how to manufacture watches, or to medicine. When I decided to study medicine instead of being a watch man, it's because I felt with medicine you could go to the end of the world, discover the cure for cancer."

He smiled wistfully. "I told you my childhood wish, the Nobel Prize."

He remembered that his father, who had been a farmer, kept a map of the world in their house. "When I am punished, I am sent to the wall looking at the map. He, for a farmer, had a very broad worldview, was very open-minded, and encouraged me to do these things. When I was six, I read a series of books called *One Hundred Thousand Questions.*"

Bing Lu had reached the opposite end of the world. Many questions were still left open, and his laboratory days were most likely done.

"I tried to do some small research initially," he said. "But now I'm kind of not just New Yorkerized, I'm Brooklynized. I'm more of a practitioner, not making innovative findings. In that way I feel I wasted all that time. I compromised too much. I feel I made a balanced choice. From that point of view, I'm making a compromise. I have a private practice on Staten Island. I have the luxury of taking my younger son to school every morning. Balancing everything. This goes into my series of compromises."

He showed me a photograph of his children. "Besides being a scientist, I am a Chinese immigrant," he said. "I have to do what I'm doing now in many ways to help my children have a better launching pad, and I think I'm doing that fine."

November 23, 2005
Daily Log—J.S.

It's cold today, ice on the street, day before Thanksgiving. Clutching the railing, trying not to slide down the slippery steps from the elevated train platform to the street. I was supposed to talk to Sam Kopel today. He was all caught up with the JCAHO inspection. Then I got a voice message from him: "Hi, Julie, Sam Kopel. Sharon just called. She's not feeling well. I'm rushing home, so I don't know if you and I are going to be able to meet later on this afternoon." I called him back, and he said she's disoriented and has a fever. Not much of a Thanksgiving. We made a date for after the holiday. After I hung up, I couldn't stop shivering. What is it like to be the oncologist always identified as "you know his wife is dying of cancer." As though it is somehow his fault, something he dragged home from the office.

This morning I met Sushma Nakka, first-year fellow in Gellman. She's small and pretty and generally accessorizes her white doctor coat with nice earrings and necklaces. Nakka told me she always celebrated Thanksgiving. "It's an American holiday, no religion." When her seven-year-old son turned four, she also began doing Christmas, because he likes presents. Shopping, the American religion.

She trained after medical school at Mahatma Gandhi Memorial Hospital in Hyderabad, India, and then moved to New York to meet her fiancé, who became her husband ten days after they first laid eyes on one another. It was an arranged marriage. Nakka worked as a resident at North General Hospital in Harlem and then completed a two-year fellowship in pain and palliative care at Memorial Sloan-Kettering, where she stayed an additional year as house staff. She said she thought the people in Harlem were "more appreciative." At Memorial, she said, the patients were more educated and much more demanding.

She told me her father is a family physician. Her mother is a physician in India. Her brother is a physician; he's coming to America, in the middle of visa-application process. She speaks Hindi and Urdu. Lots of Muslims where she comes from, and she speaks Telugu. Muslims ruled her region for four hundred years.

For a minute I couldn't remember. Which building is Gellman? The hospital is a maze, cobbled together from era to era as the place expanded. I go into the main lobby in Gellman, which is pretty nondescript, quiet today, pre-Thanksgiving. Even though it is Wednesday, I take the Sabbath elevator, which stops on every floor so religious Jews don't have to "work" by pressing buttons. The walls are grimy, despite Pam Brier's cleanup campaign. Yesterday she canceled our interview to go to the hairdresser. I saw her later in the day with Leon the driver trailing her, weighed down by the giant cardboard boxes he was lugging..

I told Pam her hair looked good. She opened one of the boxes and handed me a chocolate turkey wrapped in colored tinfoil. Happy Thanksgiving.

Nakka had agreed to take me on rounds, where she would check in on the hospital cancer group's patients and consult on patients for other doctors who saw indications of cancer or weird blood counts. I found her in the lab, where she was piecing together a diagnosis for a seventy-six-year-old Chinese man who had been admitted two weeks earlier for repair of his aorta. He was in the ICU. She had been asked to do a consult for anemia and was looking at his blood under a microscope.

"Let's go," she said. We walked down several hallways and took an elevator. On the way I asked her what she thought was the biggest difference between being a doctor in the United States and in India.

She smiled.

"Back home my sister works for a veterans' hospital. When she goes shopping or to the movies, they look at her as the doctor and they bring her free sodas," she said. "She is treated like a celebrity."

And in the United States? I asked.

She laughed. "Here, no."

We arrived at the ICU. A pale, bony resident with beard stubble and a Russian accent told her that someone from renal had seen the patient, but he wanted a hematology consult because the old man was anemic and had spiking fevers.

We went to see the patient. His throat was swaddled in bandages; he'd had a tracheotomy, a hole cut through the skin at the neck into the trachea (breathing tube) when someone is unable to breathe without help. His eyes were wide open but revealed nothing.

Nakka introduced herself and began to ask questions.

A young Orthodox Jewish nurse, wearing gloves as she examined the settings on machines, said, "He doesn't speak English." Nakka walked out to the nurses' desk and called out, "Anyone speak Chinese?" A tall young Asian man said, "Give me a minute."

David Kho entered the room a short time later. The patient fixed his eyes on the tall young doctor with the Asian face as the doctor interpreted Nakka's questions: "Have you had anemia before? Have you been treated with iron tablets?"

The old man couldn't speak because of the tubes in his throat, but he nodded and blinked.

"Did you have a transfusion before? Did you ever smoke? Any family member with anemia or cancer?"

The word "cancer" popped out from a stream of Chinese. The old man looked frightened, though interpreting emotion is even trickier than language, especially with someone breathing through a hole in his neck. Nakka made notes in the patient's thick chart, observing that his skin was oozing, his extremities were swollen. Was he suffering? I asked. She said he was taking morphine, and then ordered several tests.

David Kho, the resident interpreting for Nakka, told me he would be glad to talk to me later. When we met, he told me he had been born in Singapore and moved to the Bay Area of San Francisco when he was nine. He had been willfully oblivious to his Chinese heritage. "You just wanted to fit in," he said, "just to be a regular Joe." His father was a biochemist and his mother an accountant—not quite regular Joes. "I tried very hard to fit in," he said. "You lose a lot of your culture and your heritage as a result of that, to be assimilated. It's not something you see as a strength, to be able to speak other languages."

Being at Maimonides was, for him, part of an awakening that had begun when he was a medical student at the Columbia University College of Physicians and Surgeons, working in the clinics in poor neighborhoods. Most of his classmates were like him, well-to-do, confronting poverty for the first time. The school made a big effort to integrate the students. They ate meals with host families, worked in the clinics. They were taught statistics and theories about why blacks and Hispanics were excluded from good health care. They understood the reasons: No insurance. Poor access. Language. Yet few of the medical students spoke passable Spanish.

"To see it happen at a world-class institution where people come from all over the world to get treatment and people who live two blocks away can't get care, that's something else," he said. "To see it right in front of you is pretty powerful."

His experience there made him think about being Asian. "Being Asian and what have I done for the Asian community?" he said. "Which was absolutely nothing." He came to Maimonides hoping to reconnect with his roots, which he had done with mixed results. "When I was a kid, it was a curse to be different. I wanted to be the same," he said. "Now, all of a sudden, this is, 'Wow, you're so special; you speak so many different languages.' For me it's odd to integrate all these experiences together."

Though many young doctors were perplexed or offended by the demands of the Orthodox, Kho appreciated the powerful urge to protect one's own. "To me a place like Maimonides arose because the Orthodox or Hasidic people said, 'They'—other people—'don't understand anything about Shabbos. We're going to build our own hospital.' It's odd, crazy that a minority group, albeit a very influential and powerful one, were able to organize themselves to build a hospital to cater to those needs. It seems that's how it's going to have to be until everyone's on equal footing to get medical care."

Kho was a sophisticated and sensitive man who had been trained in the gospel of Arthur Kleinman, the Harvard medical anthropologist. In medical school at Columbia, Kho had heard lectures on cultural competence, ethics, and philosophy. He had studied the biases that could distort communication between patient and physician.

For David Kho these questions weren't academic. His wife was half Jewish, half Catholic, had grown up in Puerto Rico. He met her when he was doing research in Boston, before medical school. They both were accepted to the College of Physicians and Surgeons and married while in medical school. He learned Spanish, he said, "in recognition of her heritage." The perfect Maimonides couple.

He was gratified by the efforts Maimonides was making to hire Chinese-speaking doctors, nurses, patient reps, and social workers. Yet despite all these efforts, he wondered how much improvement there could be in health care for new immigrants without their assimilation. "Just to hear about the cultural mind-set of patients when they come into the hospital is crazy," he said. "A lot of cultures don't have the concept of preventive care. They don't go to the doctor unless they're deathly ill. That's the way the Chinese community is. We throw all this money at it—and that's a good thing, to have people who speak the language and understand the culture. But it's only half the equation. If the patient has the mind-set 'I'm only going to come to the doctor when I'm on my deathbed,' then they are going to die. I can't see that patient reps or having doctors that speak Chinese or making inroads in the community will change the mind-set of these people," he said. "The only thing that will change the mind-set is themselves. More education. Whether the something that is preventing them from coming is our point of view or their point of view, it is reality."

He seemed like someone who could cross the gap. But when I asked him his long-term plans, he looked sheepish. He wanted to be a radiologist, he confessed and explained why. X-ray scans could be beamed anywhere on earth via computer. He spoke with envy about a world-renowned radiologist who lived as a recluse. Kho's dream was to move to Hawaii and read X-rays on the beach, far from patients.

"Patients break your heart," he said.

NEW SUCK REPORT, VOLUME 7, ISSUE 2

Dudes,

Sorry it has been awhile. Not much new to report from The Brooklyn. The battle with the roaches is escalating, as you might guess . . .

I am not currently working in the ER for the month. I am doing my EMS month, which basically is playing paramedic and riding around in the ambulance. The medics call us the "special truck", as during my shift, we are the only ambulance in Brooklyn with a doctor aboard. I have decided that paramedics have a way cooler job than ER doctors, as they still get to save lives, but they also get to take lots of naps during their shift, not to mention eat. It has been so wonderful to eat lunch everyday the last 2 weeks, i think I might quit the whole doctor thing and become a paramedic, as I think sleeping and eating while at work are the two qualities that I seek most in a job. The one drawback of the EMS job is when you have to pick up dead people from their apartments, especially when the person has been dead and rotting for like a week. I swear, you haven't smelt nasty until you've met a week-old rotten dead guy. Uggh.

In other interesting news about my new home, I was running today and my iPod stopped working . . . just plain stopped. I couldn't figure it out, so thinking I'd find a store that sells them, I Googled "iPod Brooklyn" and to my surprise i did not find any stores. But the top 10 results from the search were DIFFERENT stories like "Brooklyn teen shot by police after stealing iPod", "Brooklyn Man slain over iPod", and "Another Brooklyn iPod murder" or something like that. Awesome. This is my new home. Maybe I should listen to my mother and carry ID while running at night. Naaaaw . . . . . . "No Guts No Glory" I always say.

Ok. I close with the picture of the Verrazano Bridge taken from my balcony. Pretty huh? It's no Colorado Rockies, or Grand Canyon, or Harvest sunset in Nebraska, but it's all i got for now.

love, davey

For some time I had been trying to talk to Davey—feeling guilty for pestering him. I could see from his e-mails he was exhausted. But we all had our jobs to do.

Julie

unfortunately, i am working night shifts from Saturday thru tuesday, from 7pm to 7am each night. by 10:45am on Monday i'll be sound asleep, as it is during "my nighttime" for the next week. i think i am back on day shifts on Thursday (7a-7pm) and off the next day but on all weekend, and back to nights the next week think? you can actually access our schedule on the internet. . . .

When I finally found him, I tried having the multiculturalism conversation with Davey in the ER. Big mistake. Hard to deconstruct the Tower of Babel when you're standing in the middle of it.

"The whole term 'multiculturalism' has always been kind of weird," said Gregorius as he scanned the computer screen looking for his next patient. "You don't have to define people all living together. It happens anyway. It's probably been going on forever, and in the last twenty years or ten years they're saying, 'Oh, we're multicultural now.' We always were multicultural. So I don't know. People are just bringing attention to the fact. 'Oh, look at us, we're doing great stuff.' I'd have to think about that one."

He raised his eyes for a second and gave me a pleading look.

"My girlfriend, Jenn, is here, visiting for a month," he said. "She's ten times smarter than I am. Want to talk to her?"

Sure, I said.

He pulled out his cell phone and called.

"She'll meet you in the lobby, where the ATM machine is," he said. "She is five ten, blond, pretty, she'll be wearing a black puffy coat, jeans."

"That's enough," I said. "I'm sure I'll find her."

Jenn Pfeifer sounded like just another attractive young woman in Los Angeles—or Manhattan, for that matter. In Borough Park she would be as hard to spot as a pink flamingo trying to go incognito in a flock of geese.

We walked over to a nearby bagel shop where young Orthodox neighborhood matrons—no older than Pfeifer—hung out wearing long, shapeless skirts, their hair tucked into wigs, chatting while their babies lounged in strollers. Like many of the kosher food places in the area, the shop had décor that was functional, like the basement social hall in a church or synagogue without an endowment. You came, you ordered, you sat, you ate. The women were diverted for a minute by Pfeifer and then went back to their conversations.

She noticed their reaction. "I come out to visit about every month," she said. "In the summer when I first came out, I went running around Borough Park in my little running shorts, and it was a very weird experience. I was just doing what I'm used to doing. Walk out the front door in Santa Monica and you go for a run and you pass a dozen people doing the same thing. You're not used to being the person who sticks out like a sore thumb."

Maybe it was the way she ended her sentences with question marks, but she seemed oblivious to her own slightly crooked beauty. When she told me that her last name was Pfeifer, I said, "Like Michelle?" (The movie star.)

"Yes," she said, "only with two *f*'s, not three."

"You must get that a lot."

"Yes," she said. "Isn't it ridiculous? She's probably the most unique-looking person on the planet. I don't look anything like her."

Her modesty wasn't false, but she was not an accurate judge of her own appearance. The comparison to the beautiful blond actress wasn't as ludicrous as Pfeifer insisted.

I told her about my visit to the ER that morning. "I was following Dave, and first he checked out this skinny little Jewish man wrapped in his phylacteries, and next to him was an eighty-year-old man from Trinidad. Has he talked much to you about what it's like for him?"

She swallowed a bite of bagel sandwich.

Jenn's diagnosis:

"It's pretty difficult," she said. "Did you get his e-mail about learning to count to ten when he was doing ob-gyn rounds? He learned to count to ten in Mandarin, some words in Russian, probably can't remember any of them now, but at the time he could do that. It's a frustrating experience to feel you're competent at doing something but then all of a sudden the language barrier is in the way and you can't do what you know you can do. Sort of disempowering."

As she talked I could see she was preoccupied by the logistics of their relationship. He had two and a half years to go in his residency, and he was always tired. She was considering trying to transfer to Columbia or NYU, so they could live in the same city—something they hadn't really done.

"He calls me every day and makes all this effort, but he's missing the energy that he had a year ago," she said sadly. "The exhaustion is breeding some sort of apathy. You're so tired you don't want to make yourself feel better about anything. Then he gives these temporary glimpses into something being really good, really elating. He tells me about cases he has that sound so exciting, pretty awesome, miraculous. But then it immediately gets squelched by the day-to-day reality of, 'Oh, I have to go back in there again, and I'm really tired, and I'm losing weight.'"

He was disappointed by his first performance review. Marshall had told him, "You're doing fine, but people are worried you're a little too laid back."

Pfeifer's eyes looked weary as she defended her man.

"That's an additional dimension of culture I hadn't thought about, that there's this New York way of doing things," she said. "He's not that way. He's not intense and quick. Not that he's not quick. He's laid back and nice and compassionate and relaxed, and I think he's getting the feeling that's not acceptable. Maybe when they're evaluating you as a resident, they take being laid back as meaning you're hesitant, you don't know what you're doing. It never means that to him."

She sighed. "I thought he might feel better if he could get some food he likes." Trying to help, she scanned the Internet and found several online services that delivered organic food. The prospect of whole grains seemed like manna from heaven, until Pfeifer found that every local zip code she tried was rejected. None of the health-food people delivered to Borough Park.

"It's definitely harder than I thought it was going to be," she said, the "it" clearly encompassing more than the availability of tofu.

The next day an e-mail from Gregorius:

Julie,

I'm sorry I couldn't talk more yesterday. There really never is time to stop in this ER. I didn't even eat my lunch Jenn made me, and I never went to the bathroom all day! And yep, i'll be on Medicine for the next month and then Medical ICU after that. I am not sure how much down time there is but I'm sure it's more than when you are in the ER. I am told that the Medicine month really sucks, but the MICU month is cool, and not so bad. We'll meet up again sometime for sure.

DAve

I didn't see him for a while but then received another e-mail that made me think that Davey was starting to feel at home.

Hi Julie-

Dave Gregorius here. We had an ER "happy hour" today and one of the Pediatric ER attendings, Dr. Garcia, and one of the nurses and myself and another resident were discussing one more interesting aspect of our hospital and community (which we think we could write up for a paper actually) but mentioned to Dr. Garcia that this is part of the observational stuff you might like for your book-

anyhow-

Dr. Garcia and our most veteran Peds nurse have observed (and this is so true), you can pretty much predict which babies will come into the Pediatric ER at which hours. for example at 11pm-12 midnight you see a bunch of Chinese babies all come in at the same time (this apparently because that is when the Chinese restaurants close, and sure enough, they usually smell like they have been in a restaurant all day), then between 3-5am, suddenly you get a bunch of pakastani babies (when the cab drivers get off work)
and the Chasidic Jewish babies seem to come in at 10pm usually, but we are not sure of why.
i know this seems like we are being ethnocentric or stereotyping- but it is true. At least that is when we get a sudden rush of babies each night.

interesting. i thought you'd find it amusing. once again . . . . only at Maimonides.

Dave

Eight

No Margin, No Mission

From: Lillian Fraidkin, Senior Vice President & Chief of Staff

Date: December 29, 2005

Subject: Budgetary Restrictions

Please be advised that due to major budgetary constraints, there will be no approval of the following until after the first quarter of 2006:

- Monetary support for employees to attend conferences outside of the hospital
- Temporary or agency usage
- Catering, unless approved by the SVP

In addition, there must be a <u>dramatic</u> decrease in overtime usage.

These requests are our last attempts at avoiding layoffs. If we are unable to fulfill them, I will be forced to request a layoff list from each of you.

Thank you.

January 5, 2006, dawned with a crisp burst of light that was soon overtaken by a damp, gray chill. When Pam Brier met with her department chairs and administrative staff at 8:00 A.M., the weather had already shifted from promising to grim, matching her mood.

As usual, the hospital president had chosen her outfit carefully—a pink sweater and an old pair of pink shoes, reserved, she told me, "for occasions that require extra fortification."

"Happy New Year to all of you," she greeted the group gathered in 2C, an austere conference room lit by unforgiving fluorescent lamps. "Sorry about this." She nodded toward the hospital's preliminary budget, being passed around the table where two dozen of the top physicians and managers waited, glum and hungry. The apology extended to the small table in the corner, usually laden with breakfast pastries, fruit, and coffee, now barren as per Fraidkin's directive.

No one spoke of the medical matter dominating world news that morning. Israeli prime minister Ariel Sharon had suffered a massive stroke at age seventy-seven, threatening fresh chaos in the Middle East, another potential front in the U.S. war in Iraq. Brier had more immediate concerns, her own parochial crisis, the $8 million gap between the hospital's projections and the actual budget.

"You've heard, I'm sure, of hospitals around the city laying people off, but it can't be solved by layoffs," she said. "Union layoffs take forty-five days, so don't even think of it."

Bob Naldi, the terse financial chief, explained the problem succinctly: Expenses had gone up 5 percent, and reimbursements had gone up 2 percent; the $8 million lay in that 3 percent differential. Anticipated increases in surgery hadn't materialized, while the cancer center had produced far greater start-up costs than expected. Naldi looked exhausted; his group had spent the last month narrowing a $30 million budget gap, but even with a hiring freeze, the hospital was $8 million short.

"We need eight point five million dollars over the next two weeks," he said. "You look at every single item to see if you guys can find more cash."

When Brier spoke, her voice was steely, but underneath the table one slender leg was bobbing with nervous energy. A few minutes into the meeting, she left the room to call one of her assistants, who soon appeared with a cappuccino in hand.

Brier's message was unequivocal. "It is the fifth of January, and we don't have a balanced budget," she said. "And that is my one fundamental professional fear in life—that we won't have a balanced budget. It is what allows us to do what we do. We *are* going to have a balanced budget."

Though he wasn't seated at the table, Stanley Brezenoff hovered in the room, a spectral presence, a reminder of the glory days, when things might have been worse—much worse—but were improving at a swift and measurable pace.

There was a budget crisis every year, but this one felt more ominous. Lili Fraidkin referred to it as "the perfect storm," a calamitous confluence of events. "Normally we might have, for instance, a decrease in surgical admissions," she told me shortly before the meeting. "This year it's the combination of so many things it's horrendous. Reimbursement is down. Cases are down. Expenses are through the roof—and a lot of that is because of new docs coming on board with their needs for staff, their own equipment, salaries. All of this coming together this year."

In October the hospital booked its first operating loss since Brier had been there. How could this be? Only six months had passed since Maimonides posted its most successful—financially—month ever. Less than two months had passed since the doctor in charge of the Joint Commission inspection told Brier and the management team, "You're way ahead of the curve. You're an outstanding organization and can really hold your head high." But construction on the new building, containing the new ER, was progressing more slowly than expected. She'd signed on an expensive Manhattan ad agency to promote the hospital, at a hefty cost of $3 million. All these modernization and promotional projects were based on optimistic budget projections that were not coming through.

Was this to be her legacy, the chief executive who ended an eight-year run of prosperity?

Like Fraidkin, she could recite all the reasons: recruitment costs for new doctors, greater expenses for nurses' salaries and training, fuel, malpractice insurance. Length of stay had been creeping up, and yes, she could blame that on the abundance of old, sick patients. The beds were full, but the hospital didn't get paid according to the number of patients who checked in, rather by how many left.

"Every hospital administrator has a reason why their patients are sicker, take more resources, are the oldest of the old," she told me. "I never met a hospital administrator who didn't say, 'Oh, mine are sicker! Mine are sicker still!'" Brier could rattle off all the excuses, but she wouldn't—not to the board. She knew that this flinty crew wasn't interested in hearing excuses.

Neither was she—not from the group at the table, not even from one of her pets, Steven Shelov, head of pediatrics, who had capitalized admirably, in her view, on his aura of avuncular wisdom. He was a populist academic, whose credentials included coauthorship of the *American Academy of Pediatrics Child Care Book for Parents* and appearances on *Oprah, Good Morning America,* and the *Today* show. "Some of the vacancies [from the hiring freeze] are physician vacancies," he said. "Who's going to see those patients to increase the volume? It becomes Catch-22."

Brier shook her head. "Save all your tears and Washington Monument moments for somewhere else," she said. "At least the number isn't twenty million dollars now. This is the most up against it we've been since I've been here. I'll be damned if we don't get it right."

The most significant drain on the budget was the cancer center. Year-end losses were projected at nearly $8 million, almost exactly the amount left of the $30 million budget gap. Jay Cooper, head of the cancer center, sitting across the long table from Brier, complained about the finance department's decision to break out the center's operations as a separate budget line— ironic, since Cooper, who showed up at as few hospital meetings as possible, generally tried to maintain a clear line of demarcation between his bright new outpatient treatment center and the frenetic, messy institution that owned it.

He revealed a certain attitude during a discussion about Medicare patients and the hospital's dependence on Hatzolah ambulances, which brought in a disproportionate number of old, sick people to fill Maimonides' beds.

"We don't want more of the elderly, complicated patient," said Cooper, looking imperturbable in his *Father Knows Best* cardigan. He then brought up just such a case, a person whose treatment took four times as long as a younger, less complicated patient's would have. He didn't have to say, "Time is money." Everyone at the table knew it, though they preferred the altruistic spin, "No margin, no mission."

The cancer center was still the favored child, so Brier overlooked Cooper's impolitic truth. She defended the losses by invoking Murphy's law in relation to start-up costs and then proclaimed the importance of the service with a little speech concluding with the party line: "There is no reason to go to Manhattan for cancer care unless it's some esoteric something or other."

The meeting continued. Brier batted aside suggestions she considered obvious but unhelpful, such as Enrico Ascher's observation, "We must concentrate on increasing volume." Ascher, a slender, elegantly dressed vascular surgeon, was known as "the $3 Million Man"; he routinely made the top of *Crain's New York Business* annual survey of the city's highest-paid doctors. Ascher may have looked like a Thoroughbred, but he was a workhorse. Brier called him "the indefatigable among the indefatigable, never met a patient he wanted to give up to another discipline." He lived and breathed surgery. But even Ascher's production—still astronomical, still far greater than that of any other doctor in the hospital—had dropped. He'd been credited with discharging 717 patients in 2005, compared with 832 in 2004.

"Our budget is based on volume increases," she told Ascher, and then looked around the table. "To the extent you have a tangible, let's hear about it. Believe me. We don't want to be shortsighted."

Someone asked whether the hospital's $5 million investment in Victory Memorial Hospital had brought more referrals. Because Fraidkin and Cunningham had been dealing with Victory, Brier looked in Fraidkin's direction and barked, "All I know about Victory are referrals to another institution, and that has to stop, Lili. That has to stop *now*."

Fraidkin didn't comment. She knew how to use silence as a reproach. Fraidkin and Cunningham might be handling the day-to-day at Victory, but Brier had been the advocate of the deal. She had the backing of the board, but it was the president's baby, her bid to be a wheeler-dealer in the game of hospital roulette being played out in New York. If logic ruled health care, divvying up services between overstuffed Maimonides and underfed Victory could well result in better care for the people who lived in southwestern Brooklyn. But money and politics, not logic, determined the allocation of resources. Victory had to stay alive long enough to come up with a new configuration, and the hospital was short of cash. Fraidkin, Cunningham, and Naldi had spent hours each week at Victory, trying to help turn things around. Their task wasn't made easier by the fact that Victory's elderly chief executive—who had been at his hospital more than forty-five years—couldn't stand Brier. (One of his secretaries told Fraidkin he turned beet red every time he heard the Mai-monides president's voice on the phone. Fraidkin told Brier to stop calling.)

The Maimonides board had agreed to the investment when the hospital felt flush (just a few months earlier). It was understood all along that helping Victory was a gamble, and a long shot at that. Brier was well aware that an act of noblesse oblige (the board's) could feel like a dumb mistake (hers) now that money was tight.

A few minutes after snapping at Fraidkin, Brier seemed to realize she'd been harsh. "The Victory issue is a conundrum," she said, well after the sub-ject had changed. "That hospital is half full. Figure it out. They are going to make it or not." She forced a smile and added a compliment that was both sincere and perfunctory. "Despite the herculean efforts of Lili, Joe, and Bob."

To wrap it up, Brier tried to lighten the tension with a maternal gesture, but it was awkward, like an idiomatic expression being mangled by someone unfamiliar with the language.

"You have to eat right," she said (though not on the hospital's dime). "Ten steps. No one can get sick here."

Yeah, yeah, shuffle, shuffle.

"I'm serious," Brier said, flipping from mom to drill sergeant. "No one can get sick. We have to get this done."

Sondra Olendorf, head of nursing and hospital operations, who had kept quiet throughout the meeting, now made use of her peppy, schoolmarmish charm.

"Before you put on your green eyeshades, go discharge some patients," she said briskly. "We have thirty people waiting for beds right here, right now."

Olendorf had sat through the meeting with her hands folded on the table alongside her Curious George lunch box/briefcase. She wasn't fooled by Brier's bravado. Brier had confided to Olendorf that Marty Payson, the chairman, was not happy with the numbers, a concern Brier interpreted as a lack of confidence in her.

Olendorf thought her boss seemed weary. There was doubt there, some-thing new. Olendorf was concerned about Brier. Did she have the stamina to wrestle all the forces pushing and pulling this big, unruly organization? "Stan is a hard act to follow," Olendorf told me not long afterward. "Pam knows that. I sense vulnerability in her. I don't want her to appear weak.

"Our successes are all tied together," said Olendorf. "We want the institution to look good. We want her to look good. We want ourselves to look good. She's so different. If I would run into her in a classroom or something, I wouldn't seek her out to be my friend. You have to spend time getting to know her. If you just saw the quirkiness, if you just saw the behaviors, you wouldn't get to the depth of her, that depth of caring. She's very sensitive. She's very, very mission-driven. She lives out her idea that people should not be underserved and that we should be taking care of them, that they should get what they need, whatever that means."

Brier was tired and uncertain and vulnerable, but damned if that tough cookie would let anyone see her as weak. When I stopped by her office for a debriefing the day after the budget meeting, she was determinedly insouciant.

"I'm sick and tired of not having the first baby of the year," she said, and she wasn't kidding: The New Year's baby guaranteed good PR. "Peter and I were in the labor and delivery room on New Year's Eve. I said to one of the nurses, 'I don't get it,'" she continued. "We are the biggest deliverer of babies in the state. Where are those babies? She said to me, 'I've been here every year on New Year's Eve for thirty years, and we've never had the first one.'"

Then, absently, Brier said, "Peter and I always go to labor and delivery on New Year's Eve. We only missed that one year."

She rarely talked about the accident, mainly by inference, but it never went away, the chronic condition that flared up when other pressures came to bear.

Brier, sitting behind her large, immaculate desk, raised a manicured finger. "I have a new plan," she said dramatically. "The first baby for the *Jewish* New Year—we could do the Chinese New Year."

In case I missed the joke, she said, "We have to have some fun."

The telltale phrase lingered.

We only missed that one year.

When she met Peter Aschkenasy, she was closing in on fifty. They were introduced by a mutual friend. Brier's marriage to Steven Brier was over, after almost thirty years. Aschkenasy was still married to his second wife, but that marriage, too, was nearing the end.

Hospitals had been part of their romance. When they began to see each other, she took him to visit Bellevue. When Aschkenasy—a marathon runner—was hospitalized for hip surgery, he called Brier from the hospital to tell her he had a craving for ice cream. She was cooking Thanksgiving dinner but left her guests to take him dessert.

Then followed the dates that often ended with midnight jaunts through hospital corridors. Aschkenasy, drawn to the chaotic excitement of restaurants and politics, the not-nine-to-five, was comfortable in the all-consuming hospital world. (Too comfortable, some people complained; there was a feeling among some on the senior staff that Brier relied too heavily on her husband's opinions.)

They were well into middle age, still energetic and ambitious, youthful enough to dream about making an imprint, old enough to think about legacy.

We only missed that one year.

Two and one half years had passed since the accident. Aschkenasy would be classified as an invalid if he would allow it. His right knee didn't bend at all, and the left could move sixty degrees at most. He couldn't put on his socks by himself.

Aschkenasy was far more easygoing than his wife, but they shared a forceful desire to resume life as it had been. He had his car specially outfitted so he could drive. He worked every day, across the river in Manhattan. They figured out which movie theaters had handicapped seats that could accommodate not just his wheelchair but the leg that stuck out straight. They ate at restaurants they knew would have room for the chair.

Aschkenasy was determined to bend his knees. In October they had visited an orthopedic specialist about a procedure called a quadricepsplasty that could increase the mobility of the knees but could also leave his legs too weak to support his body weight. "I am not risk-averse," the doctor told them, "but there is not much to be gained, and the risks are great."

He recommended physical therapy, which wasn't what Aschkenasy wanted to hear, though he followed instructions and bought a treadmill the next day. He remained fixated on finding a surgical remedy—a *remedy,* not a stopgap—so they continued to doctor-shop. In November they found an orthopedist who thought he could take out some of the extra bone that had grown in his right knee and the quadriceps area. In December, having looked at additional X-rays, the same doctor told them they would also need a plastic surgeon. The skin over Aschkenasy's knee was very tight, and the surgeon worried there wasn't enough skin to close the wound after he opened the leg and took out the extra bone. The plan was to add a large skin graft, called a free flap, over the knee at the same time the leg was opened up, so extra muscle and bone could be covered.

The surgery was scheduled for February. Brier knew too much about hospitals and surgery to feel sanguine.

She always tried to accompany her husband to doctor appointments. "You have to have someone with you to take notes, to ask questions, to hear," she said. "Even if you take notes, it's hard to focus. I hear so many patients say, 'What did he say?' when the doctor walks out of the room. That's why hospitals are scary. For all the care organized around you, when you're in the hospital bed, I won't say you're dead meat, but you're really in a vulnerable position."

For Sheila Namm the budget cuts were just part of the ongoing disaster drill she prepared for every day. Namm's title was "vice president, professional affairs," a general description of her responsibilities as whip-cracker-in-chief. A nurse and an attorney, Namm was in charge of screwup prevention, officially known as organizational performance, risk management, medical staff peer review, regulatory affairs, bioethics, credentialing, JCAHO readiness, and claims management.

A couple of days after the budget meeting, Namm told me what was on her mind now that the hospital had survived Joint Commission inspection. "Terrorism, bioterrorism, internal and external emergencies," she said. "That gives you a flavor of the list of things that are going to consume us."

It had been Namm's responsibility to implement the recommendations of the Institute for Medicine, an advisory group chartered by Congress to advise on scientific matters. In 1999 researchers for the Institute issued a report called "To Err Is Human," containing the estimate that ninety-eight thousand people died each year in the United States because of preventable medical errors. Surgeons occasionally chopped off the wrong leg—or took out the wrong kidney (that had happened at Maimonides a few years back).

The report also found that medical technology may be amazing, but patients were putting their fate in the often unwashed hands of doctors and nurses, who were like forgetful children when it came to basic rules of hygiene. In response, like hospitals all over the country, Maimonides began "hand hygiene observations"; between June 2003 and September 2005 the hospital went from a 69 percent compliance rate to 80 percent. Hardly perfect, but there was measurable improvement, though how depressing is it to think you have to have a management team and charts and graphs to get medical people to wash their hands in a hospital?

Namm, who was approaching sixty, was a kind of institutional spy. She even altered her appearance regularly and dramatically, showing up with short hair one week, long hair the next, color always to be determined. Her wardrobe was equally unpredictable: business suits one day, cowboy boots and cowgirl skirts the next. Underneath the costumes were tattoos, not available for hospital viewing.

The budget cuts took away an unfilled position in her department just as she was dealing with new pay-for-performance requirements for Medicare reimbursement. For the past eighteen months, the hospital had been submitting data to CMS (Centers for Medicare and Medicaid) related to the treatment of patients with certain conditions, including congestive heart failure and pneumonia. Beginning in 2007, CMS would be paying hospitals according to how they stacked up in comparison to one another, with full reimbursement going to the best performers.

Namm approved of the public report card, but now she had one less person to collect and sort the data. Her small office, just down the hall from McDougle's, looked like a storage closet, jammed with piles of paper.

The data collection forced the hospital to constantly reevaluate its procedures and practices. Maimonides often got high marks (but some low and many average) from organizations that rated hospitals, including the Niagara Health Quality Coalition, a nonprofit that evaluates New York State hospitals (www.myhealthfinder.com), and HealthGrades (www.healthgrades.com), the for-profit national rating company that offers paid membership services to hospitals.

What did it really mean for a hospital to measure up? What was the bottom line?

Atul Gawande, a surgeon and author who writes regularly for the *New Yorker,* wrote an article called "The Bell Curve" in December 2004, in which he discussed the question of grades for doctors. "It used to be assumed that differences among hospitals or doctors in a particular specialty were generally insignificant," he wrote. "If you plotted a graph showing the results of all the centers treating cystic fibrosis—or any other disease, for that matter—people expected that the curve would look something like a shark fin, with most places clustered around the very best outcomes. But the evidence has begun to indicate otherwise. What you tend to find is a bell curve: a handful of teams with disturbingly poor outcomes for their patients, a handful with remarkably good results, and a great undistinguished middle."

He continued, "It is distressing for doctors to have to acknowledge the bell curve. It belies the promise that we make to patients who become seriously ill: that they can count on the medical system to give them their very best chance at life. It also contradicts the belief nearly all of us have that we are doing our job as well as it can be done. But evidence of the bell curve is starting to trickle out, to doctors and patients alike, and we are only beginning to find out what happens when it does."

Sam Kopel, the medical director at Maimonides, once said to me, "What are the right statistics to use for outcomes? You treat a patient for pneumonia, and they go home and have a horrible course. They get readmitted, but the patients survive, so the mortality figures don't look that bad. Patients leave here with a lousy life, to nursing homes, with tubes, with trachs. There's no way to measure that. Outcome measurements is the black hole."

He went on, "Some things are easy to measure. Death. That's easy to measure. Readmissions. You have an electronic way of counting something and assume it's a proxy for the real thing. But how much happiness are you producing? Who the bleep knows? Think about it. It is very, very hard to measure. How do you measure outcomes of hip replacements? Thank the Lord we are designed, however we got here, whether Lord Darwin or the Creator, that most things tend to fix themselves, and it takes a lot to really fuck someone up. Most things do get better."

But, as he knew too well, some things only got worse.

Sharon Kopel had been admitted to the hospital the weekend before the budget meeting. No one expected her to go home.

. . .

Steve Davidson, the chair of the emergency department, one of Sam Kopel's closest friends, sat through the budget meeting unable to concentrate on the numbers. Hatzolah was on his mind. He was trying to piece together how, in the past few days, he had managed to simultaneously antagonize the Orthodox ambulance corps, his most important provider of patients, along with two of the most powerful people in the hospital, Douglas Jablon and the president herself. What had he been thinking?

Later he told me he finally grasped the farcical nature of his situation that evening, when his thought processes were aided by a clarifying glass of scotch: *Hatzolah didn't work for him, he worked for Hatzolah.*

How had he missed this salient point until now?

He confessed he regarded the Hatzolah volunteers as "whackers" (the nickname in some quarters for volunteer firemen or EMS technicians). "The guys from Hatzolahs are like volley whackers everywhere," he said. "They're enthusiasts about their thing. They've got a little bit of—I don't mean this at all disparagingly, and I hope it doesn't sound like I'm dissing them—but volunteers everywhere have the I-want-to-be-a-hero-complex thing."

As the scotch worked its magic, Davidson remembered his grandfather, a cutter in the garment industry. "He was a labor organizer. I knew about equity and legacy. I knew the community owns the hospital. I believe it in my bones. But that's extraordinarily hard to live by day to day, in a very challenging environment where many a day you realize your aspirations for yourself are not being met by you. That is humbling."

Davidson would be well cast as a distracted, curmudgeonly, brilliant, arrogant, amusing (or irritating) academic; he once told me he had imagined himself in exactly that role. "At the end of the day, I wanted to play pontificating professor, puff my pipe, drink my tea, have a little less crazed existence, compete on the intellectual front, and get some of the recognition I perceived my old man got walking down Spruce Street by Pennsylvania Hospital [in Philadelphia], big fancy hospital. Everybody in the neighborhood knew my dad," Davidson said. "He was in clinical practice, he did teach, he was on the faculty at the graduate school of medicine at the University of Pennsylvania until he died."

Davidson intended to become a research chemist but went to medical school, like his father. At heart he remained a data guy, not much on bedside manner, preferring to improve patient care through systems that built efficiency. Self-aware, though. "I'm not the smoothest, most sociable kind of fellow," he said. "I can be a prickly, opinionated kind of character." He went to Wharton Business School. He read studies of how Disney World used an engineering approach to help the park deliver fun more systematically and profitably. He read about combining management and medical measurement tools. For eleven years he was the medical director for the City of Philadelphia Emergency Medical Services System.

In 1995 he got a call from a headhunter and went to New York to meet Stanley Brezenoff, who had then been at Maimonides all of four days. "I met Stanley at lunch, and within ten minutes I knew I could work for this guy," recalled Davidson. "He said to me, 'Steve, I'm here four days, and all I've heard is how terrible the ER is. The community, the medical staff, my administrators. Not only are my administrators telling me how terrible the ER is, they're telling me how to fix it. If they know how to fix it, why is it so fucking terrible? We're going to fix it, because it is so important to this community.'"

Davidson saw opportunity in Brezenoff's determination. Hospitals had finally discovered W. Edwards Deming, the management guru, and his "continuous quality improvement" model, with emphasis on interdisciplinary teams. Japanese car companies started using it in the 1950s and 1960s and went on to lead the industry. Davidson wanted to try Deming's methods at Maimonides.

Davidson understood hypothetically what Brezenoff meant when he said that the ER was "so important to the community." Davidson did not understand, however, that in the ER, Hatzolah *was* the community. Or rather, the Hatzolahs, plural: Borough Park, Flatbush, Williamsburg all had their own branches with their own leaders.

"Stanley didn't make it plain how much working with Hatzolah was my responsibility," said Davidson. "He buffered that from me greatly. There were times he suggested I make more phone calls to them. I did. Stanley calculated correctly that my general motivation to make things better would deliver what they required, so he didn't emphasize the courting of Hatzolah. If that had been said to me in February, March, May, of 1995 while I was negotiating, it would have been a turnoff, and I wouldn't have taken the job, and that would have been a mistake."

In the ten years he'd been chief, emergency-room volume had increased almost 70 percent. In just the first year, without an increase in the budget but with rearrangement of shifts for doctors, nurses, and clerical staff, the number of ER admissions grew to 68,000 from 50,000. By 2005, the number was 82,000.

Davidson associated the increase in numbers to continuous quality improvement, the triumph of his systems, but the Hatzolah coordinators believed they controlled the switch. Davidson admitted he didn't know how to concede the point, even a little.

"I'm a logician," said Davidson. "It's my impression that when I talk about how we did it, people's eyes glaze over. I used to enjoy going out to Hatzolah and these other community groups and watch Stan Brezenoff do these great spiels. It was admirable, and I'd be so envious. I just can't do that shtick. I'm pretty proud of what we've accomplished, but the challenge I face right now is the expectation of comparable improvement. Well, I've squeezed the rag drier sooner. It's getting a lot harder."

Barbara Sommer, a calming, eye-in-the-hurricane presence, longtime director of nursing for the emergency room, had been promoted the previous July and hadn't been replaced. Her absence represented a double disappointment. For three years Sommer had been in charge of the hospital's application to be accepted in the Magnet Recognition Program, developed by the ANCC, the credentialing branch of the American Nurses Association, to recognize health-care organizations that provide nursing excellence. Only 4 percent of health-care organizations achieve Magnet status, whose prestige was an invaluable attraction in an era of chronic nursing shortages. The application process is long and arduous, requiring volumes of documentation covering patient-satisfaction surveys, nursing research projects, and peer review. Once a hospital is part of the Magnet program, someone has to be in charge of maintaining the standards that got it there. Sommer was designated that person.

Sondra Olendorf, head of operations, had cause for optimism when she promoted Sommer. The hospital's lengthy narrative analysis was deemed sufficiently excellent by the ANCC to take Maimonides to the final round, a site visit. Eighty percent of the hospitals that get this far become part of the Magnet program. But once again Maimonides was relegated to almost-as-good-as. The hospital didn't make the final cut. Now Sommer had a better title but no clearly defined job, and the emergency room didn't have Sommer.

Davidson had recently hired a nursing manager, a position that had been vacant for two years. He considered himself lucky to get anyone who was qualified. With a national nursing shortage, candidates were not knocking down the door to take over an emergency room jammed with acutely sick patients speaking numerous languages. Davidson said he thought Ann Marie Ceriale had "some great leadership chops." When he tried to intimidate her, she didn't let him. "She got red as a beet and pushed back," he said. Guts she would need, he said. It would be rough for her, especially because, with Sommer gone from the department, he had no one to train her.

"We are at a very important transition time for nursing in the emergency department," said Davidson. "There is a large cadre of staff who has an intimate relationship with Barbara Sommer, built over many, many years. They know each other's families, the way each other thinks, their failures and heartbreaks. At the same time, there's a new, young, eager nurse manager who will be quite challenging for the staff, and the staff is going to be quite challenging for her. And the most important mentor for her, a nursing director, is nowhere to be seen."

In December, Davidson thought he had finally found someone willing to take Sommer's place, someone who could train Ceriale, among a million other things. The candidate was a nurse director at another big Brooklyn hospital's ER. Sommer interviewed her and thought she could handle the job. When questioned as to what she knew about Hatzolah, the woman said no problem, she and Hatzolah got along well.

Davidson decided to hire her. But when he told Douglas Jablon, Jablon told Davidson he should call Bernie Gips, one of the coordinators of the Borough Park Hatzolah. Gips would later say—with sharp-pronged tact— he felt she wasn't the right choice. "She's a very nice person, competent, but two and two doesn't always add up to four," he said elliptically. He felt he had conveyed his message to Davidson, and nothing more needed to be said.

This courtesy call, as Davidson thought of it, became the opening volley in a round of accusations and counteraccusations that wound up with Davidson withdrawing the job offer and eating a large piece of humble pie, washed down with a big gulp of scotch.

Douglas Jablon was furious because Davidson hadn't consulted him about the delicate diplomacy required to approach Hatzolah. Bernie Gips was insulted that Davidson hadn't listened to him about the nursing-director position. Davidson thought he had fulfilled his obligation by putting in a call to Gips.

When the contretemps blew up to the executive offices, Brier was not pleased.

"Stupidity," she said. "These ER people really don't get it. Well, they get it, but they don't get it. This has been true since Stanley was there. Steve Davidson will tell you the day I sat him down after I took over and said, 'You are not doing X and Y and Z. If you don't do that plus ABC, you are not going to make it here.' He said, 'Stanley never told me that.'"

In her view, Davidson needed remedial training in community management. She recounted the story.

"Whereupon I called Mark McDougle and said, 'Mark, Douglas is in meltdown. Can you call Douglas and calm him down?' So he did. Meanwhile, I talked to Steve and said, 'Steve, Douglas is very upset.' 'Why?' he said. 'I love Douglas!' I said, 'Steve, you went and chose the ambulance person after Douglas told you Bernie didn't like her,' and Steve said, 'I guess the lesson is, I should just take matters into my own hands.' I said, '*No,* actually, the message is just the reverse. You've got to make Douglas feel like the player that he is, because he's working his little heart out to smooth things over and make things good, and to the extent you don't go through him, you make him look bad. He found out about the supervisor-person hire from them! That's bad. He shouldn't. Could you just call him?'"

She concluded, "When I talked to Douglas a while later, I asked, 'Did Steve call you?' He said, 'I didn't return his call.' I said, 'You must return his call. You must let him apologize.'"

Jablon felt betrayed by Davidson, but his sense of betrayal paled next to his fear of Brier. "In front of both of my bosses, he let them believe I didn't take care of the situation, which I did. I would never treat anybody like that," Jablon told me. "But then Pam said [he paused] Steve apologized [another pause], and I kissed him [long pause], and that's that.'"

Later I asked Bernie Gips and Elliot "Lazer" Rosman, the Borough Park Hatzolah coordinators, about the incident. Rosman, a gray-haired, intense man, was director of disabled students at Queensborough Community College; Gips, who tucked his side curls behind his ears, was president of a commercial air-conditioning business. (They both exuded the excitability that once led me to ask a Hatzolah volunteer why the Orthodox always seemed so nervous. Without hesitation he replied—grinning, "Because God gave us nerves!") Jablon was the liaison for our meeting. He invited us to use his office, made introductions, left, and then returned briefly to deposit a box of cookies on the table.

"In the same breath I'm criticizing, I want to defend," said Gips, who spoke so rapidly he wheezed as though he were running, not sitting. "They have a very good computerized system. But you have to have the doctors to go on the computer and check it. What good is it if the doctor doesn't enter the order in the computer, the nurse doesn't read the orders, and then the patient doesn't get the right medications? The system is overwhelmed."

How would he fix the emergency room?

Gips hesitated, just for an instant. "Couple of things," he said. "I would change certain personnel."

Who?

"You're putting me on the spot. Certain personnel."

Who?

"You know what they say?" asked Gips. "The fish stinks from the head. Let me just say that."

Rosman chimed in. "That person, for example, he has certain expertise. He is a computer genius, and this makes him look good. This is very nice for patient information, but it doesn't relate to what we call in Yiddish *nisht mayn a'khaver* ['not my friend']."

What was this, a Harry Potter story, talking about Lord Voldemort, "He Who Must Not Be Named"?

Neither of them corrected me when I asked if either of them had told *Davidson* directly that they didn't approve of the nursing director *Davidson* wanted to hire.

"Not me personally, but someone let him know there might be a problem," said Gips, whose face was flushed; he had a reputation as a hothead. "I want to ask you a question. Anyone trying to work with the community—and we bring five hundred patients a month, four hundred patients, which turns into big dollars—is it worth it to take on a fight? Is there only one person to take her place?"

Gips shook his head. "He talks to us without respect."

When Brier called McDougle to deal with the situation, he once again was reminded that Maimonides was not like other places he'd been. "Everybody knows everything about everybody," he said. "It's very bizarre."

"I'll never forget Bernie's first comment to me," he recalled. "He said, 'I'm going to be a pain in the ass.'"

Gips fulfilled his promise, but McDougle didn't really mind. He admired Hatzolah. "Other ambulance drivers come, it's their job," he said. "Hatzolah are volunteers, and they are like advocates for the people they bring. It's like everyone comes with an advocate. 'Why is the doctor taking so long? Why are the lab techs taking so long? Why is the medication not being given? Why is the radiology exam not done?' They stay there. It's the difference between being not just an ambulance person but an advocate. And they felt that this person [the nursing-director candidate] hadn't been sufficiently sensitive."

But he was also sympathetic to the pressures in the ER. "I do believe that everybody who works there is part saint," he said. "When things don't go perfect, there's a lot of blaming. So not only do these people have to deal with sick patients, old patients, not enough space, too much noise, they have people running around blaming everybody for why it's that way."

"Bernie said Steve didn't call, and Steve said Bernie didn't return my call," said McDougle. "They don't like each other, so they don't communicate and they blame each other. Who's right? I don't know who's right. There are times you have to draw the line, and this didn't seem to be one of those times. So now we're back to square one with trying to hire a nurse director."

McDougle looked at me poker-faced. "But square one is better than negative three."

I sent Davey Gregorius a note asking him what he thought about Hatzolah. His reply:

I mostly have had good experiences with Hatzolah. it is unfortunate that they sort of get a "bad rap" from the other EMS/Ambulance crews. i think they got bad reputation 1. some people infer that they only run Jewish patients (which i do not think is true . . . . but certainly 95% of the people they bring in are Jewish). so i think it's a sort of counter-discrimination. 2. (i am told) they respond faster than any city-wide (private or government) EMS "company". not sure of the exact times, but i was told something to the effect of average response time for Hatzolah was like 3-4min vs. 8-9 minutes when calling 911 . . . . so if this is true, i can see why FDNY and Maimonides EMS workers would be "jealous"

you'd have to ask some people a little more close to the program than i

one thing i do recall is that they usually gave a very professional presentation of the patient they brought into the Resus [Resuscitation] room

and 3. the other thing was they were notorious for "Hatzolah-fications", which is a unnecessary "notification" called in by Hatzolah. a notification is when the ambulance crew (regardless of company) calls ahead to the ER to warn of a life-threatening condition (stroke, heart attack, bleed, etc), and thus all Notifications were immediately triaged to the Resus room, instead of waiting in that line at triage and then waiting however long to be seen. the general consensus is that Hatzolah calls in some Notifications that did not need to be notifications. that the Hatzolah members would call in a Notification for an elderly Jewish patient that they just wanted to get seen faster instead of waiting 1-2 hours, although they really were not sick enough to require "jumping the line", if you will . . . . i think overall, Hatzolah is great and if i was injured or having a heart attack, i'd call Hatzolah. also i wouldn't want to piss anyone off. Ha

January 8, 2006
Daily Log—J.S.

    A couple of months ago, Steve Davidson told me about Ann Marie Ceriale, a youngish nurse he'd hired to be a nurse manager in the ER. The nurse manager's main job is handling discharges, organizing the floor nurses to make sure each patient has been seen, diagnosed, and then sent home or to a hospital bed. Nice and orderly job description in the abstract. Davidson hadn't been able to find anyone willing to take the position for the past two years. Before that the department regularly ran through nurse managers at a rate of one a year or so. Ann Marie sounded like someone I should hang around with, to see if she survives.

Davidson agreed but asked me to wait until January. "Yeah, January sounds good," he said, looking worried. "Barbara Sommer, who's been in the ER twenty years plus, is becoming associate VP of nursing as of January 2, and I won't have a nursing director, just this new nurse manager. She's a nifty young woman. She's been a charge nurse on the cardiac-cath recovery unit and worked a couple of ER's in Westchester. She's got some great leadership chops—she wouldn't let me intimidate her. I like her. She pushed back."

The other day I reminded him about introducing me to Ceriale, and he said he would see how she felt about having me tag along with her. "I don't want her to feel too much on the spot," he said. "She might . . . I don't know how I feel about it. Her success is pretty important to me, I don't want her to pull her punches." Then he shrugged. "She's a grown-up, you should talk to her."

I called Ann Marie. "Sure," she said, "you can follow me around. Just don't go into shock."

On January 9, Ann Marie Ceriale came to fetch me at 9:00 A.M. in the pleasant-enough waiting room at the walk-in entrance to the emergency department. She was thirty-four, had long brown hair and big dark eyes, pretty, Italian-American, a little chubby, assertive. She told me she lived in Yonkers, four blocks from her parents, and that she's lost more weight in the six weeks of this job than on any diet, including the twenty pounds she'd dropped on Jenny Craig. In the hallway leading to her office, I read the advisory posters on the wall and felt a mild panic at the implications in these instructions on what to do in case of stroke, chemical terrorism, smallpox.

On the way we passed through the emergency room, which appeared calm, with patients neatly deposited behind curtains and doctors and nurses walking rather than careening. I noticed a woman doctor with the unlikely but momentarily appropriate name of Placid Bone.

"Just wait," said Ceriale. "Two o'clock. You can set your watch."

"What?" I said.

"Chaos," she said. "You can set your watch by it."

Ceriale stopped to snap at a nurse who was reading the newspaper. "There's no time for this," she muttered.

For six weeks she'd been trying to connect Dr. Davidson's continuous quality improvement model to reality. But almost every day of the six weeks she'd been in the ER, Ceriale had been short of nurses. She usually spent the first couple of hours at work trying to find subs. She had six open positions, all on nights, and depended on the staff she had to do overtime. One of her jobs was to solve the staffing problem. She was thinking of using more travelers, who worked on contract. She had been a traveler and loved it. She'd seen California that way, Sonoma County. If you don't show up, you don't get paid, while the Maimonides nurses were unionized. "Call in sick and you get paid," she said, adding quickly, "I one hundred percent support the union."

When she first walked in from the street to the ER, her impression was that it was a "complete disaster." She said, "I thought, 'I would never want to be a patient here nor would I want to work as a nurse,' and now I'm a nurse manager."

But she came to see there was both method and madness. "There's actually a very organized and systematic way we're doing business here, but from the outside it looks like a complete disaster," she said. By then we were in her small office, decorated only with a photograph of a sunset taken by Ceriale at Club Med in Mexico.

"We'll get a massive amount of discharges today, because it's Monday and a lot of beds open up on the floors, because doctors don't do a normal amount of discharges on Saturdays and Sundays," she said. "Meanwhile, the ER is backing up throughout the day, so by the time we get the beds available, we have a flow list of fifty or sixty and one or two transporters."

She said it was ironic that she took this job, because what she loved about nursing was the clean slate at the end of the day. No matter how grim or hard or tense, her duties were finite. "At the end of the day, it was the end of the day," she said. "At the end of the day, you handed off patient care to someone else. Now there's no end of the day."

The ceaseless demands, the unending pile of loose ends, reminded her of the seven years she spent working at an insurance company. "I had files of injury cases I had started at the beginning, and when I left seven years later, I had the same files," she said. "Instead of taking up one single file folder, they were taking up a drawer in litigation. They had a life of their own. There was never a time I could say my desk was completely cleared off. This is very similar. My desk is never going to be clean. The end of my day is never going to be a fresh start or the end of the day. Your days off are not your days off."

At 11:00 A.M. we went to a management meeting led by Carl Ramsay, the medical director, Dr. Ponytail. The head of the ambulance service said the fire department's new computer terminals with GPS tracking weren't working and screwed up the entire system over the weekend. Lab problems, staffing problems, a stab wound in pediatrics. Ramsay told the group that the new nurse director hadn't worked out, though he didn't mention the Hatzolah veto. "We'll do fine so long as we are talking to each other, respecting each other," he said wearily.

Next time Ceriale and I walked through the ER, the earlier calm had evaporated. I checked the clock. As Ceriale had predicted: It was 2:00 P.M. Chaos time.

We walked by an Orthodox man on a gurney surrounded by women praying. A blond young man on a stretcher in the hall complained he'd been waiting too long. Dr. Huang and one of the cancer fellows swooped in to press the belly of an African-American woman. I saw Dave Gregorius beelining it for the "resus," or resuscitation room, reserved for possibly about-to-die patients needing swift attention.

Back in Ceriale's office, she showed me the tracking board on her computer. She was starting to get the hang of it, using this snapshot to find hangups in the system. She could see that at 2:28 P.M. there were seventy-three patients in the ER, none of them in pediatrics. A sixty-seven-year-old female with complaint of chest pain had spent eleven minutes with a nurse and was now with an attending physician. A report was given to the doctor on the floor, patient admitted to telemetry. Team One. They'd requested a telemetry bed. Here on the cardiac monitor, her EKG. Lab orders. Blood work, vital signs, history.

But between "patient admitted" and "they'd requested" lay the gap between "continuous" and "quality improvement." Minutes could quickly become hours. "It's a very busy emergency room," said Ceriale.

Her beeper went off. She stared at it. "The beeper, the beeper, the beeper," she moaned. "I already had my first dream of the beeper going off. I got up Saturday at five in the morning searching for the beeper, which was right next to my bed."

When she found it, she realized that the beeping had infiltrated her inner consciousness. It was only a dream. The beeper hadn't gone off.

For a moment Ceriale's entire being seemed to sag with weariness. "I started at the busiest time of year without a mentor and came into a situation that was a big mess," she said. "I've been here for six weeks, and three days out of five I've gone home crying. It's not something you can show either. You don't want them to see you sweat, like they say on the deodorant commercial. Every other day I'd like to quit, but then on the in-between days I think it was a good move and I'm happy to be here."

She straightened herself. "Now the holidays are over, staffing is starting to get a little bit better, my job will start to get a little bit better," she said. "I have a lot of confidence in myself. I think I can do the job. Not even think— I know it."

On that hopeful note, we said good-bye and agreed to meet later in the week.

Four days later—Friday the thirteenth—when I stopped by the ER, someone told me that Ceriale was gone. No one knew where she was or if she was coming back.

Nine

The Code of Mutual Respect

MAIMONIDES MEDICAL CENTER
Department of Perioperative Services

You are invited to the first
Crucial Conversations training session
Topic: "Getting Unstuck"
Learn: How to recognize what Crucial Conversations are, and the
consequences of not having them!

DATE: Friday, January 13, 2006
TIME: 7:00 A.M.–8:00 A.M.
PLACE: Schreiber Auditorium (Admin Bldg., 2nd floor)

I t had been a long time since Alan Astrow had thought about the former colleague at St. Vincent's he once referred to sarcastically as "Mr. Doctor" (as in, "He thinks he's so great he calls himself Mr. Doctor"). Three years earlier Astrow was covering the oncology service when one of Mr. Doctor's patients was about to go into surgery, to have his spleen removed for a cancer biopsy. The patient was elderly. Before the surgery, pathology reported to Astrow that the lab already had tissue that showed metastasis of cancer, making the biopsy unnecessary. Unable to reach the patient's doctor, Astrow spoke to the surgeon, and they decided to call the surgery off. When the family asked why the procedure had been canceled, Astrow told them. The cancer had spread.

The next day, just before his daughter's fifth-birthday party, Astrow received a call from Mr. Doctor.

"You asshole," the conversation began.

You asshole!

Mr. Doctor continued, "You shouldn't have talked to the family."

Astrow couldn't believe it. They might have killed this patient in the OR. Okay, maybe the surgery wouldn't have killed the patient, but it wouldn't do any good. Why should an old person with serious hematological malignancy run the risk of major surgery for no good reason?

And his thanks for preventing what could have been a disaster?

You asshole!

So he gave it right back to Mr. Doctor.

He spoke softly as usual, but his words were riposte, not reply.

"You almost killed this patient," he said. Even as he spoke, Astrow knew he had gone too far. Mr. Doctor's recommendation for surgery hadn't been unreasonable with the information he had. He was angry with Astrow not because he'd called off the procedure but because he had delivered the upsetting diagnosis to the patient's family instead of waiting for Mr. Doctor to return.

Astrow's empathetic self knew that Mr. Doctor was concerned for the patient's family and for his own reputation, and that hundreds of cuts and slights and deliveries of painful diagnoses had turned him into the brittle, rigid, wounded individual that he was. Astrow knew he should apologize, because someone had to bend.

But sometimes he got tired of bending.

The bitterness ruined his daughter's birthday party for Astrow. For weeks he agonized about the nasty exchange, alternating between anger at Mr. Doctor and frustration at his own inability to ask forgiveness even if he did think the other man was a self-righteous jerk.

The patient received appropriate treatment—chemotherapy—but the relationship between the two doctors was terminal. Neither apologized, and the department chief declined to get involved.

Astrow had suppressed the memory of Mr. Doctor. At first he didn't connect the incident to the e-mail about Crucial Conversations that showed up in his mailbox just after the New Year. In fact, he had forgotten about the meeting, which he didn't plan to attend. But that Friday morning he'd gotten up early. He was happily engrossed in something he was reading when he remembered the e-mail, which he had been sent as a courtesy, as a department chief. The meeting was mainly intended for the surgery department.

"If you want the surgeons to use the cancer center, you have to show up," his overdeveloped superego lectured him. "It's a matter of showing respect for other people." He groaned as conscience and sobriety pried him from his comfortable chair.

Maybe he could have ignored the internal prodding if the cancer center's numbers were better. But they weren't. Face time with his colleagues, many of whom still didn't know him, would be politic as well as polite.

So he took a quick shave, rushed to get his car from the garage a couple of blocks away, and drove to Brooklyn. When he walked into Schreiber, he was twenty minutes late, but not the last straggler in the crowd of about 250 tired-looking souls, many wearing green scrubs, some in white doctor's coats, others dressed in street clothes. These doctors, nurses, medical students, and technicians came from the various surgical groups—cardiac, orthopedics, vascular, neurosurgery and so on—as well as ancillary services like anesthesiology and radiology.

Astrow arrived in the middle of a bizarre piece of theater. On the stage in the front of the auditorium, Stephen Lahey, chief of cardiothoracic surgery, was screaming at a tough-looking nurse with short, iron-colored hair.

Lahey, a full-bodied Irishman with a curly mop of gray hair and that unmistakable Boston accent was yelling, "This is not a hernia! This guy is going to die! When I have to send this guy home in a box, I'm going to tell the family it was your fault! So when you're finished here, you can go straight to the goddamn medical-malpractice lawyer!"

The nurse glared at him and folded her arms.

He yelled some more.

Finally she yelled back, "How dare you!"

The improvisational skit had the bite, if not the brutal poetry, of a David Mamet play. Big applause. The venom spewed by the amateur players clearly resonated as something familiar and true.

A broad-shouldered, balding man of looming height, with piercing eagle eyes, about fifty, with a mustache and goatee, took over. Standing at a podium and then striding up the aisles like a television talk-show host or motivational speaker, he began to speak in the soothing yet provocative tone common to both.

David Feldman, former chief of plastic surgery, had for the past eighteen months been in charge of perioperative services. He was responsible for how patients were treated from pretesting—the labs or X-rays and case histories required to evaluate their ability to safely withstand surgery—through discharge, either to home or to a hospital bed. That antiseptic description didn't reflect the messy reality of the job, which was handling the complaints and hysteria of distraught patients and their families, impatient doctors and nurses, and beleaguered technicians. Operations were delayed for understandable reasons, like emergencies, but just as often for paperwork foul-ups and administrative errors.

"We know what the problems are at Maimonides," he said. "How do we know? Because you are all calling Pam and me every four days to tell us." Pamela Mestel, his nursing counterpart, stood nearby, nodding.

Feldman had acquired another, more ephemeral job. He had become the hospital's dean of deportment after writing the Code of Mutual Respect that every doctor had been required to sign.

They signed it and then forgot about it. Pam Brier didn't forget, however. She decided to make good behavior an official hospital goal, part of the strategic plan, part of her overall desire to civilize her willful troops. Eighteen months earlier she had hired Kathryn Kaplan, an organizational-development specialist, who had helped design programs to prepare physicians to become leaders—instead of simply promoting them—at Mount Sinai and NYU. Brier had already picked Feldman as a physician leader, so Kaplan became his partner. The Code of Mutual Respect was part of the arranged marriage; the project became her baby, too. It was the perfect assignment for Kaplan, a smart, apprehensive woman with a singsong voice, not young but girlish, a gentle person who wrote poetry and wanted to believe in the sweeter, softer side of human nature. She held on to this belief even after spending a year in operating rooms as a consultant and witnessing a great deal of bad behavior among doctors. "The people who bring in the most money can be the most abusive," she once told me, sounding sad and disappointed at this unsurprising observation.

In "The First Five Years of the 21st Century," Brier's progress report to Marty Payson and the board, written in November, she emphasized behavior. "The code's implementation has now been transformed into a hospital-wide priority with structured skills development for doctors, nurses and support staff. Our expectation is that Maimonides will become recognized within the next few years not only for its outstanding and humane patient care but also for the way staff treat each other, as well as our patients and their families."

There were plenty of people who snickered. There were mutterings of, "Madam President, heal thyself," referring to what Sondra Olendorf politely called Brier's "behaviors." What next? Spankings for cursing? Time-outs for littering? Was this political correctness run amok?

Feldman's cynical humor and tough-minded reorganization of the operating rooms helped him subdue the cranky and the skeptical. He had been willing to take on this quixotic assignment because he had reached the stage of disillusionment that can be liberating. He was able to say frankly that he wanted to recapture the satisfaction he'd once felt at just being able to help, before he spent his time worrying about whether he was being nickel-and-dimed by insurance companies. That he missed the collegiality, when doctors came in twice a day to make rounds and then stopped in the lounge to grab a cup of coffee or a smoke—you could smoke in the hospital then. Who had time to do any of that anymore?

"In the hospital we get so caught up in what we're doing—mostly in the service of patients, I will say—we get nasty to each other," he told me. "But the way people get treated is every bit as important as what they are being treated with. I believe this."

There was a tendency to sentimentalize bygone days of warm relations between doctors and patients. But rudeness was nothing new to the medical profession. The men who drafted the charter of the American Medical Association, approved in 1847, felt it necessary after all to warn physicians to "avoid all contumelious and sarcastic remarks."

The AMA's early concern about etiquette was a matter not just of manners but of salesmanship. In *The Social Transformation of American Medicine*,

Paul Starr observed that in an era when their financial status was precarious, "physicians were much concerned to maintain a front of propriety and respectability." Not a lot of time had passed since the days when medical practice required supplemental income. Starr offers examples of one eighteenth-century doctor who also sold tea, sugar, olives, grapes, anchovies, raisins, and prunes; of another described as a surgeon in his obituary but as a wigmaker in his will; and of a midwife who cured ringworm and piles but also made dresses and bonnets.

By the twentieth century, these stories had become quaint history. Sophisticated procedures and new drugs elevated the status and mystery of doctors, as well as their incomes. Medicine became a lucrative profession, and doctors became a staple of popular mythology, centerpieces in endless television episodes depicting dramatic collisions of life, death, and sex. One generation was reared on shows like *Ben Casey* and *Dr. Kildare;* the next tuned in to *M*A*S*H,* and then *St. Elsewhere, E.R., Scrubs, House,* and *Grey's Anatomy.* Reality television brought the operating room home. You could watch liposuctions being performed and babies being delivered without leaving your couch.

Medicine-as-entertainment was thriving as the twenty-first century began, but real-life relationships between doctors and patients were suspicious and confused. Like everything else in the world—from the balance of global politics to the way people communicated—medicine was in flux. The familiar bulwarks no longer held fast, not even the nuclear family. The 2000 U.S. Census reported that the percentage of married-couple households with children under age eighteen had declined to 23.5 percent of all households, compared with 45 percent in 1960. The family doctor, treated like a second-class citizen by insurance companies, became another endangered species. Low value was placed on the generalist who saw not just a patient but recognized a person with a history, a place in the community, a functional part of a larger system.

Specialization had led to superior technical results but also to a fragmentation of care that injected an element of distrust into even the friendliest relationships between doctors and patients. Physicians felt embattled by the rising cost of malpractice insurance, cumbersome insurance reimbursement, and regulation. Patients felt incidental, like inconveniences to be dealt with between computer entries.

The Internet had revealed the secrets of the medical profession, opening once-shrouded information reserved for a highly educated elite to anyone who could plug in a computer. Patients felt free to question the wisdom of their doctors and to shop around when they didn't like the answers. Yet the increased availability of information didn't lead to a greater sense of power. Even as cures were found for more diseases and new drugs proliferated, a sense of frustration prevailed. Almost every day brought pronouncements of a medical advance, many of which were soon modified or retracted, creating a fearful atmosphere of unrealistic expectations followed by disappointment. There was more data about cure but also more reports of failure, like the aforementioned 1999 Institute of Medicine report with its estimate that as many as 98,000 deaths a year could have been avoided were it not for the mistakes of medical professionals.

Each medical advance made death seem less like an inevitable, natural part of existence and more like an insult, a cop-out, a failure. But medical science had not yet made humans invincible. Sometimes people simply died. They died too young, they died mysteriously, they died despite receiving the best medical care possible. Too often they died feeling abandoned and alone, shielded from fear by neither science nor God nor the reassurance of a doctor who seemed to care about them. In turn the doctors struggled with their feelings of guilt, anger, or shame at failing and, worse, with the emptiness they felt when they recognized their own indifference.

Eric Scalettar, vice president for planning at Maimonides, said it well:

"Can I quantify whether the doctors are better or worse than my father's generation?" he asked me. "They're clearly more educated today than in my father's generation. Do they care as much or invest as much of their time or energy? That I doubt. Do they bring the same dedication and devotion to their practice? I don't know. I don't think so."

He continued, "Why would they? We don't treat them as well. We don't hold them in as high esteem. We chastise them in the newspapers and watch their every move to see if they're conducting themselves right or wrong. It's real different today."

This combative atmosphere forced physicians to consider their presentation as well as their medical practice. In 2001 the AMA made idealistic additions to its principles of ethics, encouraging physicians to consider patients' rights as well as their dignity, and to participate in activities that contribute "to the betterment of public health." The threat of sexual-harassment suits and the rising numbers of female doctors had made outright crude behavior less acceptable among medical colleagues. But flirting and sexual innuendo were inevitable in a profession suffused with physical and emotional rawness. A macho ethos prevailed in many places, particularly among surgeons—"the big-dicks-swinging school of management," in the words of Holly Hartstone, a hospital consultant who worked for Maimonides.

All over the country, hospitals were writing codes of behavior, as the medical profession tried to win back the confidence that had been eroding for decades. At Maimonides the task fell to David Feldman. He became an expert in behavior modification in the same way he had become an expert in pressure sores—for reasons that perplexed him. "Am I that interested in it?" he said. "I don't know."

He had an impulse to organize and rationalize. When he was a resident in plastic surgery at Duke University Medical Center, he was assigned to give a talk on decubitus ulcers, or pressure ulcers, dangerous wounds that can result in uncontrollable infections and death. Commonly known as bedsores, they result from immobility, when people lie in one position for a long time or suffer from diabetes or other circulatory problems. "We saw them when the patient had already developed them, and they're horrific," he said. "The care is very complicated for the patient and family. The purpose was to prevent them from ever happening, which is not usually the realm of a plastic surgeon." He did research on the subject and suddenly found he had developed a specialty.

His interest in ethics and communication evolved the same way. Feldman was an organization man. His father was a dentist and his mother a professional volunteer. When he was growing up in the suburbs of Long Island (not far from Alan Astrow), Feldman's parents decided to get their M.B.A.'s together at night. Their son helped them with their calculus homework. So even as a young surgeon, Feldman wasn't satisfied with writing book chapters on pressure sores; he organized a Committee on Pressure Sores. He started a program at Duke on the business of medicine. Plastic surgery paid the bills, but what fascinated him was the organism of the hospital.

He understood that hospitals confront the same issues that come up in any organization—rivalries, jealousies, envy, people feeling that their bosses are dumping work on them or giving them crummy assignments. There are always unpleasant jobs that have to be done and people trying to shift those jobs onto somebody else. But there's a crucial difference: The doctor's job is dealing with disability and frailty, with life and death. The emotional stakes are huge; the consequences of a misstep can be irreversible.

Cunningham recruited him to Maimonides in the early nineties, and the plastic surgeon soon became active in medical-staff politics. Surgery had become routine; skin grafts, wounds, scars, skin cancer made up 75 percent of his practice; breast reductions and augmentations the other 25 percent. Cosmetic surgery had become a $15 billion industry, putting all plastic surgery under special scrutiny by insurance companies. "Plastic surgery is borderline. Is it cosmetic or not?" said Feldman. "We tend to do multiple procedures at one time, and they reimburse for one and not the other. It drives you crazy."

He decided to follow his parents' footsteps and get a business degree. "I could see what was happening in medicine," he said. "I still love taking care of patients, but a lot of things were bothering me. My back started to bother me. I thought, 'How long can I take this?'"

He entered an M.B.A. program at New York University designed for midcareer executives; there were five physicians in his class of one hundred, which included a man who owned a photography studio and a woman from Benjamin Moore paints who had written books about picking out paint. Feldman found it invigorating to see how people outside the cloistered world of medicine thought.

Pam Brier recognized Feldman's ambition and wanted to keep him happy. She felt he would leave Maimonides one day, to become the chief executive of a hospital, but she wanted to delay the moment as long as she could. Sondra Olendorf offered to relinquish management of the operating rooms to Feldman. He had the right personality for the job. He was affable but formidable, idealistic but hard-nosed enough, a combination that made people want to please him because they liked him and because they were a little scared of him.

In 2002, Olendorf told Brier she wanted to attend a conference called the Trust Initiative, about to take place at the Harvard School of Public Health. Organized by David A. Shore, an associate dean there, the conference was designed to confront the poor public perception of medical care. This spoke directly to Brier, who firmly believed that good behavior wasn't a mere nicety but a crucial part of taking care of patients. She asked Feldman to join Olendorf and Warren Wexelman, a former president of the medical staff, at the conference.

The conclusions reached at the conference were summarized in the fall 2004 issue of the *Harvard Public Health Review* in an article by Cathryn Delude, a science and health writer. "Across the United States, trust in institutions that guard the public's health and provide care has fallen to an all-time low. Patients mistrust insurers and pharmaceutical companies, and lack complete confidence in their doctors; physicians, in turn, are skeptical of clinic and hospital leaders. Citizens doubt government's ability to protect them from epidemics and bioterrorism, deriding each new 'orange' or 'yellow' warning as an empty scare."

The message resonated with Feldman. "What's been lost is the ability to separate all this technology from just taking care of people," he told me. "How does this stuff relate to what I do in the operating room? The OR is a crucible for this sort of stuff. There's a lot at stake. Things happen quickly; there's an urgency about things. Surgeons grow up in medicine understanding the need for urgency. It's a natural place for people to lash out. If people are afraid to say something, patients suffer."

The Maimonides group was so impressed that they returned for a follow-up session a few months later. The next conference's name indicated how completely business was entangled in modern medicine, even when the subject was ethics—Building Clinical and Administrative Trust: Advance Your Mission and Improve Your Margin.

Feldman used the following example of a case at Maimonides to illustrate the relationship between respect and result. A patient had been prepped for a knee operation. The medical people had followed the Universal Protocol for Preventing Wrong Site, Wrong Procedure and Wrong Person Surgery, required practice in all JCAHO-accredited hospitals since 2004:

Step 1—Verification (of the patient, procedure and site)—This is conducted independently by each of the following: Surgeon, Anesthesiologist and Nurse, preferably with the patient awake and involved and is the information matched to what is written on the consent and/or OR schedule.

Step 2—Marking the operative site (in cases where there are issues of sidedness (Left/Right) or levels (e.g. spine))—Presently, the Surgeon marks at or near the site of incision (or insertion) with a "YES". In March 2007 we will mark with the Surgeon's initials. This marking must be visible after the patient is prepped and draped.

Step 3—Time-out—Just prior to the time of incision, the entire operative team does a time-out to reverify the patient, procedure, side, site, positioning and the availability of any needed special equipment.

Curtain up—until someone asked loudly, "How come the knee being prepped isn't marked with a 'yes'?"

The room went still. Who had dared to speak? It was a medical student—lowest on the hierarchy, except perhaps for the patients themselves, or maybe family members.

The "yes" was on the other knee.

What went wrong? At the root-cause analysis, the closed-door meetings where medical people dissect their mistakes, it was discovered that the "time-out," the final check, had taken place too soon. The equipment had not yet been formally placed on the operating side, and everyone assumed that the leg next to the equipment was the object of the surgery. After that, the time-out was the last thing to happen before the scalpel was ready to fall.

"You can't stop these things from happening unless people are respectful to one another," Feldman explained. "There has to be enough respect so a medical student can raise his hand and say, 'You're operating on the wrong knee.'"

With a convert's zeal, the new perioperative chief volunteered to take additional responsibility for an ambitious plan, to not only change the way people behaved in the hospital but to make them considerate of one another. As he pondered the title of the document he was drafting, he decided he didn't want to call it a code of conduct but rather wanted something that signaled a fundamental shift in attitude as well as behavior. At Maimonides, pragmatism was poetry, an attitude reflected in Feldman's blunt Code of Mutual Respect:

On Professionalism. The Staff recognizes that acting professionally entails treating others with courtesy and respect, and refraining from the use of abusive language, threats of violence, retribution, or litigation, and actions that are reasonably felt by others to represent intimidation. The Staff also recognizes that it is unproductive to make inappropriate remarks concerning the quality of care being provided in front of others or to make such entries in the medical record. Finally, the Staff agrees to address concerns about clinical judgments with associates directly and to avoid favoritism or sidestepping rules.

On Language: All members of the Medical Staff agree not to use language that is profane, vulgar, sexually suggestive or explicit, intimidating, degrading or racially/ethnically/religiously slurring in any professional setting related to the hospital and the care of its patients.

On Behavior: The Medical Staff agrees to refrain from any behavior that is deemed to be intimidating, including but not limited to using foul language or shouting, physical throwing of objects . . . .

The admonition against "physical throwing of objects" caught my attention. I brought it up during an interview with Allan Strongwater, former chair of orthopedics. "I've worked in lots of hospitals where surgeons have thrown instruments; they get a scissors that don't cut, they fling it across the room," he said with a shrug. "I don't think behavior was worse at Maimonides." Then he added, "Of course, there were isolated incidents that were very bad. Like the physician who pushed a nurse and another who threw something at a nurse. On the other hand, I was at a hospital where the resident accused the attending surgeon of breaking her wrist."

Things had improved at Maimonides in the past decade, he said. He recalled receiving a disturbing telephone call from the head of academic affairs a few weeks before he went to Maimonides in the mid-1990s. She wanted to warn him about what he might find. She told him about two chief residents who got into a fistfight and knocked a patient off a stretcher; about a surgeon who carried a gun in the operating room; about residents who were secretly tape-recording conversations with attending physicians, so that when things didn't go well, they had deniability.

When I talked to him, Strongwater had recently resigned from the hospital under pressure from Brier, after months of unhappiness. When I asked him to explain their differences, he said, "Everyone has the right to health care, but when you buy a Volkswagen, you don't get a Bentley," he said. "It's not that they don't both work and they aren't both good cars—they just don't have the same luxury. The level of expertise of the physician should be the same, but people who pay for health care don't want to sit in a room with fifty other people. They want to be seen in a timely manner. I think that's very reasonable."

Pam, he said, wanted everyone to sit in the same room.

(When I asked Brier about this later, she agreed and she didn't. "We had differences of opinion about how to accommodate patients with managed-care coverage, which is in some cases lesser coverage," she said. "I wanted to make sure there was some access for people with insurance. That's what the neighborhood consists of. He felt he could not tell his people to accept managed-care insurance at all. That was one issue."

She was hesitant to elaborate. "I was concerned about growth in the department," she said. "We had differences about management. That's about all I would say.")

Strongwater and I met in his office in lower Manhattan, across the street from the NYU Hospital for Joint Diseases, where he had joined the staff. He told me he had thrived at Maimonides when Brezenoff was there, but he and Brier hadn't gotten along since she became president. "I had a great relationship with her as chief operating officer," he said. "But as president she is a politician. She would like her hospital to be the model for public health. That's okay. But she seems to take things more personally than Stan. If something doesn't work out, she gets really angry. Business is business, and you have to have a business attitude."

For example?

Strongwater was emotional. He had not wanted to leave Maimonides.

"For example, the Victory game," he said, referring to Brier's decision to put money into the struggling hospital. "We sat around, the leadership— Pam and Mark, Sam Kopel, the chairs, Lillian—talking about Victory. I said, 'Why don't we just let it close? It's in its death throes. It's substandard. The state wants to let it close.' She looked at me and said, 'Don't you get it?'

" 'Don't I get what?'

"She said, 'If we don't do this, some other hospital is going to go in there and buy it up.' She'd gotten word Methodist had put money on the table. So what? Is Methodist going to run that hospital on the other side of Brooklyn? No, they'll suck everything out of it, and then it will close. But she was going to put money on the table and outsnooker them. But the game of snooker is a tough game, and the one who got snookered was her."

At first, Strongwater had refused to sign the code. "I thought it was pathetic," he said. "I thought it was pathetic that you have to tell professionals at that level how to behave."

He told a story about an operation he performed several years earlier on a young woman who had been in an accident and suffered from hip dysplasia, a shallow hip socket, a condition that caused severe pain and an inability to walk without limping. Strongwater had been an early user of a relatively new procedure called a Ganz osteotomy, named after the Swiss surgeon who developed it in the 1980s. It is a difficult surgery that rebuilds the hip socket with the patient's own bone, and it has become a good alternative to hip replacements, which almost always have to be repeated if patients are young.

The operation was likely to take six hours and require 3,000 cc's, or 6 pints, of blood. The family had been adamant that the girl receive blood they donated. She'd had bad reactions to banked blood in the past.

Blood was taken from the family and stored. The girl was admitted and prepared for surgery. After she was anesthetized, Strongwater made the incision and told the nurse to call for the blood. Normally this step would have come two hours into the procedure, but that day, for reasons he couldn't remember, he asked for the blood early.

He heard a rustling on the phone. He waited. The wound was open. He asked the nurse, "What's the problem?" She said, "They're looking for the blood." Strongwater packed the wound and got the head of the blood bank on the phone.

"What's going on?" he asked. This was a difficult operation, he had a nervous family on his hands, and he had no blood.

She told him there had been an emergency over the weekend, and they had used the blood the family had so carefully set aside.

He told her to explain this to the family.

He heard her reply, "You're the doctor, you tell them."

He reddened as he recalled the moment. "At this point I'm not calm any-more," he said. "If I could have reached through the phone and ripped her throat out, I would have. So here's your Code of Mutual Respect."

He composed himself. "I don't care they used the blood. That's okay. They saved someone's life. Good. That was on the weekend, and this was Monday. Why the hell didn't someone call me and say, 'Dr. Strongwater, the blood for your patient was used emergently'? Or say on Monday, 'Don't do the case, the blood's not available'?"

He had to face the mother. He offered her options: They could do the operation and use banked blood or close the wound and do it another time. She said close the wound. Strongwater did the case a month later at the Hospital for Joint Diseases. "So look at the mess," he said. "Here I am with all this experience, all this education, all this training, and look at this *twit* in the pipeline, the clerk who never made the call to notify me. You are relying on people with all levels of training, all levels of skill, all levels of commitment."

So why didn't he want to sign the code? In theory, the system of confrontation and conversation was meant to help prevent situations like this from happening. The hope was that the code would force a discussion, illuminate the weak links, improve the system. The case he used as illustration, which took place in 1999, had led the hospital to tighten its procedures for segregating designated blood.

"I didn't sign it initially because I thought it made a comment on the medical staff at Maimonides, that it was so bad it needed a written document for behavior," he said. "I thought it was atrocious the physicians needed it."

Then he changed his mind. "I told David [Feldman], 'This is great.' People needed to know the organization was serious about working conditions. Not just OR, not just doctors, but across the board. This only works if you implement this across the board," he said. "That means the guy who does six thousand cases a year has the same responsibility to that charter as the guy who does two. That's hard to do from a financial standpoint. I have a running bet with Kathryn Kaplan [the development specialist who worked with Feldman on the Code]. The first time one of the high rollers crosses the line, the organization will back down."

I heard that same skepticism many times, including from Pam Mestel,

the executive director of perioperative services, Feldman's nursing comple-
ment. Mestel's father was in the garment business, and she had a streetwise
sense of how the hospital's sociological system produced perfect conditions
for spikes in foul language and rude behavior.

"I have nursing attendants who make twenty-eight thousand dollars a year
working elbow to elbow with these attending doctors who come into work in
Jaguars and take these magnificent vacations," she said. "When you're in the
room for three hours, you chat, you get to know someone. Some of the nurses
have been here twenty years and knew these doctors when they were residents.

"Think about it," she continued. "You can't do surgery without your
instruments. Our instrument techs make thirty thousand dollars a year, and
we expect them to be these highly skilled, ambitious people who are going to
make sure the tray is going to be built exactly the way the surgeon wants it.
But they don't have the same drive the surgeon has. It's not the same drive
even a nurse may have. I say this to doctors all the time when they tell me
these nursing attendants aren't working hard enough or fast enough. I tell
them, 'They're not going to work like you work. They're not going to stay for
twelve hours for the good of the cause or the good of the patient or 'This is
why I came into health care.'

"How do you motivate someone who makes twelve dollars an hour? By
saying, 'Your next raise you're getting another twelve cents'?" she asked. "I
think what beats them down is the hierarchy, the respect they're given or not
given. Everyone beats down on the one below."

While Mestel had been eager to help Feldman with the training program,
she was both hopeful and doubtful. "There's a lot of skepticism," she said.
"The nurses say, 'Sure, they're going to tell Dr. Cunningham to stop being
rude. Sure, that's going to happen to Dr. Felicia. He does almost three hundred hips a year. Sure, he's going to say to the nurse, "Fuck you," and they're
going to do something to him. Sure.'"

I first heard about the Code of Mutual Respect four months earlier, at the
beginning of my sojourn, on September 12, at a "leadership team" meeting
in the conference room next to Brier's office. Much of the discussion was
devoted to housekeeping and various plans—ranging from new solvents

to new management structure—that could improve cleanliness. Brier reported on a meeting she had with a group of environmental workers, aka janitors.

"They specifically talked about doctors," she said. "They didn't say they were pigs that throw things on the ground—"

David Feldman interrupted. "Yes they are."

Brier continued, "But they are not-nice non-pigs throwing down things and getting grouchy and maybe a little retaliatory. We need to work on this. This is not the hallmark of a mutually respectful workplace."

A few minutes later, Feldman and Kathryn Kaplan, the organizational specialist, introduced their strategy for giving the Code of Mutual Respect some bite—or at least some recognition. For the pilot program, they selected perioperative services, in part because Feldman ran it and also because it was a hospital epicenter for frayed nerves and robust tempers (vying for top place with labor and delivery and the emergency room).

Feldman and Kaplan had been trained in Crucial Conversations, the trademark of VitalSmarts, a company based in Provo, Utah, that specialized in helping organizations—mainly corporations, a handful of hospitals—instill what might be considered rudimentary social skills in managers and employees. Clearly, the World Wide Web, with its magnificent, instantaneous transferral of information and ideas, had not made it easier for people to communicate. VitalSmarts published two handbooks, *Crucial Conversations* and *Crucial Confrontations,* both of which were *New York Times* bestsellers and had been translated into eighteen languages.

Feldman and Kaplan laid out the plan.

In January they would begin a customized version of the training for the perioperative staff. The department chiefs had agreed to relinquish one Friday a month, for a total of eight sessions, one of the weekly morning slots reserved for surgical conferences. The training sessions were the theoretical part. The practical application: Those who misbehaved would be called in for an accounting with Feldman, along with the person who felt offended. Each could bring an ally. The sessions sounded like a cross between an administrative law proceeding, couples counseling, and a nursery-school time-out.

There would be two preparatory stages. Four days after the leadership meeting, on Friday, September 16, at the quarterly perioperative-services meeting, Feldman, Kaplan, and Pam Mestel would introduce the plan. Most important, they felt, was that Brier would come to the meeting to endorse the Code of Mutual Respect.

In December, they explained, forty-five volunteer members of the hospital staff—including nurses, clerks, and physicians—would receive training that would allow them to be Code Advocates—the "influencers," Feldman called them, chosen because they were believed to have the respect of their peers.

The marketing jargon grated, inviting uncomfortable associations from the wider world, past and present, raising a Stalinist specter of institutionalized snitching. But then Feldman said something that made me think again. Did bullies always have to win? "People know something is happening, but there haven't been any major changes," he said. "The people who yell and scream are still yelling and screaming."

"Code Violators," someone wisecracked.

Feldman smiled. "I like that. Yes. Code Violators. I want to put up a plaque with this quote—it isn't mine: 'Respect is like air. When you lose it, nothing else matters.'"

Brier muttered, "No plaques."

That Friday Feldman addressed a packed house in Schreiber. He reminded the audience that the Code of Mutual Respect had been endorsed by the hospital's medical council in 2004; all members of the medical staff were given a copy and asked to promise to abide by it.

Facing a wall of blank faces, he asked, "How many of you have heard of the Code of Mutual Respect?"

Six people raised their hands.

No one responded when he asked, "How do you feel about doctors' respect for one another? If you're a clerk, how do you feel about how doctors respect nurses and other doctors? How do they respect you?"

No one responded when he projected the Code of Mutual Respect on the big screen at the front of the auditorium.

"Other institutions call it a code of behavior," he said. "I think that's too punitive. It is not a bylaw or a policy but a way of life."

The crowd did come awake when he asked, "How many of you have been treated disrespectfully in the last week?"

Encouraged by the noticeable ripple in the sea of scrubs and suits, Feldman continued. "Sounds like an epidemic," he said. "How many times have you been in a situation where someone starts yelling or insulting?"

A wave of appreciative giggles.

He told them how, earlier in the year, a court had ordered a doctor to pay three hundred thousand dollars for bullying.

Another wave.

He played a video showing two nurses talking.

"Remember Dr. So-and-So's parting shot?" said one of them. "He said baboons could take better care of his patients. I see one of the good doctor's patients has an elevated temperature. Ninety-nine point five. Maybe I'll call him."

The other nurse widened her eyes with the exaggeration of a sitcom character. "It's two A.M.!" she shrieked. "You wouldn't!"

The other nurse picked up the phone, and the screen went dark.

By then the mood in the room had shifted from dutiful to interested, from listless to attentive.

With new confidence, Feldman became fervent. "We need a culture change," he said. "Our patients are savvy. They see what's going on. You can't tell me they won't get better quicker if the staff is more respectful. This is Day Zero. It is no longer okay to act disrespectfully in the operating room."

He paused and looked out over the room. "I know what you're saying," he acknowledged. "This is the way it's always been here, and it isn't going to change. Well, this is like psychic surgery."

He explained about Crucial Conversations, and Kathryn Kaplan explained that sometimes the conflicts would be among peers. "We're going to have interventions when there's an unfriendly exchange between a physician and an anesthesiologist," she said.

Someone in the audience muttered, "An anesthesiologist *is* a physician."

Feldman accepted the challenge. "How many of you think this is *not* going to work?" he called out.

Almost every hand in the room went up—the converse of the showing for who knew about the Code of Mutual Respect.

Feldman decided it was time to introduce Brier. She peered into the auditorium and noticed Enrico Ascher, the $3 Million Man, who had walked in late wearing a sleek suit, sitting in the back of the room. "Dr. Ascher," Brier called out to him. "Don't be afraid to come to the front."

She then turned her gaze to the room at large. "What is a good workplace?" she asked. "It's a place where people know they're going to be treated respectfully. Without it you're sunk. We're piloting this program here in the OR because it is the hardest. It's a tough one. But let me be really straight with you. No one in this hospital is so good, so special, so talented, that this doesn't apply to you."

Big round of applause.

"Hopefully, it won't come to that, where people don't get it and don't get it," she said. "You can hold us accountable."

Everyone was asked to fill out a survey. Then the session was over.

Survey results: Almost 85 percent of the respondents felt that the Code of Mutual Respect would positively enhance the workplace, though only 76 percent said they had a clear understanding of what it was. Thirty-seven percent believed that leaders handled disrespectful behavior effectively, and 62 percent felt that physicians were held to the same standards of professional behavior as were staff. Almost 90 percent of the respondents felt they treated others with respect, but only 61 percent felt they were treated with respect by fellow workers.

Sixty-seven percent of the people in the room answered the survey; of these, 53 percent were physicians, 27 percent were nurses or technicians, 3 percent were ancillary/clerical staff, and 17 percent were "other."

Doctors were the worst offenders in every category. It was believed by 46 percent of the respondents that doctors treated other doctors with respect; only 39 percent felt that doctors treated nurses and technicians with respect.

My acquaintance with the Code of Mutual Respect deepened three months later, in early December. On a drippy, gray morning, I trudged through the slushy residue of the previous night's snowfall to the hospital's "learning center." It was located ten blocks from the main campus, on a weary residential street of small houses stuck behind elevated train tracks. Antiseptic fluorescent-lit classrooms shared the building with the Maimonides ambulance corps employed by the hospital, not to be confused with Hatzolah, the Orthodox volunteers.

Waiting for the train that morning, I'd heard a woman tell her companion why she loved her doctor: "I saw this old lady on the street, and her skirt and underpants fell to the ground. Dr. K. was walking by, and he just reached down and pulled up her underpants and buttoned her skirt," she said in a Caribbean accent. "He's an old-lady magnet. They all love him. He's gay, but all the old ladies come to him. You have bad news to hear, you want him to be the one to tell you. He is kindness itself."

I was ready for Phase Two, training the forty-five Code Advocates, the "influencers," the missionaries enlisted by Kaplan and Feldman to spread the Gospel of Mutual Respect. I joined one group of these influencers—doctors, nurses, techs—for the first day of what would be a sixteen-hour cram course in the art of Crucial Conversations. Each of us found a Crucial Conversations Participant Tool Kit on our tables. There were chapters on "How to Spot the Conversations That Are Keeping You from What You Want," "How to Speak Persuasively, Not Abrasively," "How to Listen When Others Blow Up or Clam Up."

My tablemate was Irving Pineiro, a doe-eyed young man whose job was to keep track of nurses and aides and help orderlies set up for surgery. He told me he had come to work at Maimonides as a janitor, nineteen years old, newly arrived from Puerto Rico, no English. Now he was an administrator, wearing a shirt and tie to work, dating the secretary who worked for Steve Lahey, chief of cardiothoracic surgery. The hospital had been good to him. He told me he believed he'd been chosen to become a Code Advocate because he had complained about nurses being rude to families of patients undergoing surgery.

Pam Mestel began. "We work in a high-stress environment," she said. "We know it's not one person's fault a screw isn't in a tray, the blood work isn't there. The system isn't what it should be, and we tend to take it out on the person who is there. The question is, how can we change the culture? And the doctor is the most notorious offender. We're taking you out of work two days in a row, and David's spending numerous hours with chairmen, talking them into giving up their precious M&M's [morbidity and mortality meetings] once a month."

"I know you're sitting here thinking, 'Oh, yeah, we did this five years ago.' But this is serious. Will it happen in a week? No. But we're calling people on the carpet. Our vision is that in the future you'll be able to take care of these situations. It's like Dr. Feldman said: 'It's just respect. Who doesn't want respect?'"

Kathryn Kaplan asked, "Do you know how long a culture change takes?"

Someone called out, "One hundred years?"

Kaplan laughed. "Wow, this isn't going to sound so bad," she said. "Five or six years."

The group learned that they would have to distinguish between rudeness, incivility, and bullying, which were Code of Mutual Respect matters, and sexual harassment and racial discrimination, which were union issues.

Paul McMurray, the consultant leading the sessions—chubby physique, preacherly style—told people to introduce themselves. Meanwhile, sitting at a table near the front, a taut man dressed in blue shirt, slacks, and necktie opened his laptop computer and began receiving and sending e-mails. Steven Konstadt, the new chair of anesthesiology, looked tightly wound as he typed furtively, his almost-hairless head glistening under the lights.

McMurray the consultant asked Elvia Johnson, a feisty nurse with long braids, "How do you stay in dialogue when a doctor has yelled at you?"

She laughed. "This happens to us all the time," she said. "They yell at us, we tell the doctors to call Dr. Feldman. He calls us, we tell him what happened, he calls them, and then they are pussycats."

Marion Contino, a nurse with short hair and "don't mess with me" body language, chimed in, "They respect the doctor's word more than the nurse's, so we say, 'Call Dr. Feldman.' The doctor sees the doctor on the same level."

Pineiro said, "I don't personally have a problem with this, because I respect them, but I see what happens. If someone has a little higher rank than you, they'll scream or yell. The doctors yell at the nurses. The nurses yell at aides. That's how I see it."

Konstadt kept typing.

Another nurse asked, "What do you say to a doctor who says, 'I wish the patient would die so I could sue you'?"

Soon McMurray was barraged with lively examples of conversations gone wrong. The gripe session bubbled along, complaints flowing like champagne, gathering festive momentum until Elvia Johnson brought the proceedings up short with a nod toward Konstadt, still typing.

"I hear what you're saying and appreciate that this institution is committed to this," she said to McMurray, Mestel, and the other group leaders. "Then I see Dr. Konstadt sitting using his laptop through the whole thing, and I think that's very disrespectful. I don't want to sit here for two days if this is just lip service. There is still a hierarchy here. If this is to work, everyone should be committed, not just us front-liners."

Konstadt froze, no longer typing, staring straight ahead. The incriminating laptop remained open.

McMurray jumped in with the enthusiasm of an acting coach whose student has just opened a vein. "Before I let him talk, let me respond," he said. "What you see is a doctor with his laptop open. You see laptop open: *disrespect*. My path, I see something different! I see a doctor who says, 'I can't be here today. I have pressing matters beyond my control. I can't be here.' But he is here. If he brings his laptop, he can participate at some level. I'd rather have him semiengaged than not here. I tell myself I'd rather have a doctor with a laptop than no doctor at all."

Johnson was not impressed. "You see, he gets away with it and I don't!" she said with a theatrical shrug.

McMurray changed tactics. "What is going on here?" he asked rhetorically. "Why is the doctor more important than me?"

Contino said, "We did confront. We went to Dr. Feldman during the break."

McMurray continued, "You can see from body language and tone: 'I am here, I don't count, I've got emotional issues and work issues, but I am frustrated as hell. I am pissed and want to bring a computer tomorrow.' Or maybe he doesn't want to be here either, but he can do what he wants because he's a doctor."

Konstadt clutched his knees and then absently pecked at the computer while McMurray went off on a long story about his fears of riding the subway. Pineiro leaned over and whispered to me, "Do you see what's so bad about him being on the computer?"

Lunch.

After the break, before doing damage control with Konstadt, Feldman discussed the mechanics of how the mass training was going to be conducted, once a month in Shreiber.

A nurse asked, "There will be attendance taken?"

Feldman looked pained. "There are hundreds of people," he said. "I'm not sure. The idea right now is, we passively support bad actions. If they see everyone else talking differently, we hope they'll change. I have Pam Brier's support. I run the OR. We don't want to get to the point where I say, 'I won't book rooms for you.' We don't want to do that, but we want that threat to be there."

Konstadt was back on the computer.

McMurray nodded at him. "Now we're going to hear from the other side."

Konstadt stood and spoke. "I want to apologize to anyone who took my computer as a sign of disrespect," he said mechanically. "I'm going to be here four days this week, and I have things to do before the weekend. My beeper is disruptive, so I arranged with my secretary to e-mail me things. Seven years ago I finished an executive M.B.A. program, and I was looking up my notes about negotiations. For *this*. On a personal note, I have a psychology that could be called multitasking or ADD; it's part of my learning style. I don't want to be disrespectful, and I apologize if this ancillary tool is causing any disruption."

Feldman explained that Konstadt had already been involved in a trial crucial conversation involving an anesthesiologist and a gastroenterologist. Each of the doctors brought the chairs of their department to meet with Feldman. "That's the first problem," said Feldman. "To put five doctors in a room takes three weeks of scheduling."

The case involved a patient who spoke only Italian, who entered the hospital with a minor problem and ended up with a cardiac stent, very sick. The anesthesiologist began to discuss the case with the gastroenterologist immediately after the surgery, but he said, "I can't talk about this now," and left without explanation. The anesthesiologist was upset and complained to Feldman. He forced a meeting. At this conference, the doctor explained that the patient's family was sitting outside and wanted to talk to the gastroenterologist. "It didn't help that one is Syrian with a thick accent and the other is Chinese with a thick accent," said Feldman.

They discussed the Maimonides Method: "One of them screams at me, and I scream back louder, and he says, 'Why are you screaming?' and I say, 'When you stop, I'll stop.'"

Class dismissed.

Maimonides had a history of freewheeling behavior. Old-timers spoke nostalgically of the giddily righteous tumultuousness of the 1970s, when a group of social workers from psychiatry, angry at cutbacks, stormed the executive office and took the hospital president hostage for several hours. The young union mental-health worker who led the charge, a striking African-American man named Clarence Davis, wasn't punished but was recognized as a leader. Now, thirty years later, Davis was an executive, director of hospital safety and security, still trim and muscular, still on the move. Every time I saw him, he was racewalking from building to building. I would run to catch him and ask if I could schedule an appointment to talk about emergency preparedness.

He always nodded and then pulled ahead, leaving assurances in his wake. "I can't do it right now," he said. "Later." And I would make a note in my calendar for the next month, when the scenario would be repeated. My calendar was filled with notations, spaced about a month apart: *"Call Clarence D. re evacuation plan, weapons of mass destruction, biological warfare, chemical disaster, etc."*

Davis was always dressed in a smart suit, the picture of officialdom. When I heard of his earlier, rebellious history, I was reminded again of the words of Carol Kidney, the nursing director of obstetrics: "Everybody believes they can and should speak up."

The right to disagree was as basic a tenet in the hospital as any principle in the Hippocratic Oath. This belief and practice led to the eruptions creating the need for a Code of Mutual Respect but sometimes resulted in a remarkable willingness to accommodate. Coincidentally, Carol Kidney turned up in scenarios illustrating both aspects of the hospital's unruly persona, one side bent on contention, the other on compromise. Kidney had signed on to be one of Feldman's Code Advocates. She also found herself part of a national battle over a late-term-abortion procedure being fought by some with acceptable partisan fervor and by others with unpardonable nastiness.

Kidney and Howard Minkoff, the physician chair of obstetrics, brought

the abortion issue to the Maimonides bioethics committee. It involved a procedure called D&X, dilation and extraction, usually performed after the
twentieth week of pregnancy. The method, recommended by the American
College of Obstetricians and Gynecologists in certain cases, requires the person performing the abortion to dilate the woman's cervix, pull the fetus
through feetfirst, and then puncture the head so the skull won't cause damage as it exits the cervix. "Certain cases" might involve a fetus that was so
damaged it was no longer viable or a teenage mother who, through ignorance or denial, didn't realize she was pregnant until late in the game. The
procedure was almost always reserved for instances when the alternative—
pulling the fetus out whole—could be dangerous to the mother's health,
causing severe blood loss and cervical damage significant enough to prevent
future pregnancies.

It was a procedure rarely used at Maimonides or nationwide. In 2000 it
was used in only about 0.2 percent, or 2,200, of the estimated 1.3 million
abortions in the United States, according to the Guttmacher Institute, a
nonprofit research and public-health-policy organization that focuses on sexual and reproductive rights. Though the procedure was rare, its mechanics
made it a powerful visceral weapon for antiabortion forces, which dubbed
the method "partial-birth abortion" and vilified the physicians who termi-
nated pregnancies in vivid, gruesome language, like "baby killers."

Pop-ups on the National Right to Life Web site:

"the *abortionist jams scissors* into the baby's skull"—they are pulled feetfirst from the womb and *stabbed* through the back of the skull"

In 2003, President George Bush signed the Partial-Birth Abortion Ban Act,
a bill that used the politically charged and nonscientific name for the procedure.
The bill had twice been vetoed by his predecessor, President Bill Clinton. However, since Bush's endorsement almost three years earlier, the procedure was still
legal because of numerous court challenges that were keeping the ban in limbo.

That was the political situation when a physician newly affiliated with
Maimonides scheduled a D&X and Carol Kidney could not find a nurse in
the hospital willing to participate. She and Minkoff brought the matter to

the monthly bioethics meeting. Alan Astrow and Carl Ramsay were among the nurses, doctors, and legal people gathered in the boardroom as a bright, early-morning winter sun illuminated the Empire State Building in the distance.

Minkoff, a vocal advocate for the rights and health of pregnant women, had clear opinions and let them be known. For example, when local Orthodox women proposed a doula program for the hospital, Minkoff agreed, but only if the doulas operated strictly on a first-come, first-served basis, regardless of whether the new mother was Arab, Chinese, or Jew. In Minkoff's view, Maimonides had an ethical obligation to offer legal abortions to its patients, even if a particular method offended someone on the nursing staff.

"The procedure is much more humane for women," he told the group. "You dilate the cervix, and instruments extract the fetus in pieces. More humane for the patient, less pleasant for the nurse. I don't object to individual objections. I do object to institutional objection."

A nurse at the table spoke. "Many people don't object to patients' right to have an abortion, but this involves the removal of body parts of a human body. Whether you are pro or against abortion, it is an unpleasant landscape. It is a scene many have trouble with."

Carol Kidney elaborated, "It's pulling the fetus out in pieces."

The ensuing conversation covered moral and aesthetic objections, medical and ethical rebuttals. Alan Astrow expressed sympathy for the nursing staff and suggested that greater effort be made to explain why the procedure was necessary. Minkoff acknowledged sympathy for the nurses' reluctance and then commented that some people might think it was unethical to keep elderly people alive in a persistent vegetative state on ventilators. An Orthodox doctor whispered, "It's not at all the same."

Marcel Biberfeld mused, "Maybe so few doctors do this because they don't want to do it either," to which Minkoff replied, "They don't want to get shot. There used to be more of them, but they didn't want their homes to be picketed or to be shot."

Yet Minkoff said freedom of choice included the right not to participate. "It would be a Pyrrhic victory to tell nurses they have to be there when they object," he said.

Biberfeld tried the other side of the argument. "Isn't that a slippery slope?" he asked.

Kidney answered. "I agree it's dangerous to have nurses object to one procedure or another, but this is unique."

The final decision came later, an agreement to compromise. Next time the hospital would hire nurses from outside to assist in the procedure. Quirky, rambunctious Maimonides managed—this time—to find a reasonable arrangement that respected opposing views without forcing one to capitulate to the other. They agreed to live with unease, with the recognition that fairness and mutual respect meant struggle and uncertainty.

Five years earlier the hospital had brought in a group of airplane pilots to talk to surgeons about how to reduce errors, making comparisons between the mistakes and miscommunications that led to runway collisions and mistaken amputations. They talked about the importance of emergency checklists and an atmosphere that encouraged communication. The pilots told stories of an airplane en route to Florida trapped in a circling pattern because of a thunderstorm. When air traffic control told the plane to return to Atlanta for a forced landing, the pilot threw a tantrum. But the copilot remained calm and brought the plane down.

The surgeons hadn't been convinced. "It's a beautiful analogy, except the captain can control it," Richard Lazzaro, a Maimonides surgeon, told me. "That copilot was this cool guy. He said, 'You have to be cool, you're the captain, you take it up, you fly, you land.' But if you're in the middle of an elective case and the carbon dioxide tank goes out and your circulating nurse isn't in the room and you're putting a stitch in some big blood vessel and the belly's totally deflated, a minute might seem like an hour. You have this pause that's beyond your control, and then you find out someone is out talking to their boyfriend on a cell phone—you want to drill them. But if you drill them, that person is going to say, 'God, what a prick.'"

Lazzaro was one of the hospital's bad boys, a surgeon known about equally for his fierceness on behalf of his patients' well-being and his nastiness in the operating room toward those who dared to show less enthusiasm for the work than Lazzaro thought they should have. His father and grandfather had been doctors, and he grew up in their offices, knowing this was what he wanted. "I feel there's no greater glory than what we do, and I expect that from my team," he told me. "Our job doesn't end at five o'clock. You have to be willing to say, 'I can't go to that wedding or some family event,' or you're not going to help your patients."

Lazzaro was one of five brothers in a Brooklyn Italian family who pounded one another playing football and basketball and then forgot about it. Still chubby-cheeked and impish in his forties, he described his own behavioral flaws with the same sheepish charm he probably beamed on his mother when he announced he'd knocked out the living-room window with a baseball.

Lazzaro had become an expert in laparoscopic surgery, using tiny cameras that allowed surgeons to do precision work, reducing the area that had to be cut, sutured, and stapled. It made hospital stays shorter and recovery faster, and the procedure had become commonly used for gallbladder removal, hernias, and cancer. But as Americans got fatter and fatter, the fastest-growing field for laparoscopic surgery was gastric bypass surgery, which reduced caloric intake by shrinking the size of the stomach and the length of the intestine. In 2006 the Public Health Service estimated that medical spending averaged $29,921 for obesity surgery (and as much as $65,031 if there were complications that required hospitalization) and six months of follow-up care.

When Lazzaro was at about 120 cases, he told me, and very comfortable with the procedure, he was operating on an obese patient—huge, a body-mass index (BMI) of more than 40, meaning the man was carrying at least a hundred extra pounds. The surgeons had penetrated the dense flesh and the camera was in place when the senior resident asked a question:

"Why are we here?"

Lazzaro, trying to concentrate on the tiny incision, couldn't believe his ears. This was not the moment for existential angst. The resident elaborated. He'd read a paper that had come out of Long Island Jewish Hospital reporting that in twelve out of forty cases where patients had a BMI of over 40, the cases took too long and patients suffered a lot of complications.

Lazzaro recalled his reaction. "I said to him, 'To be honest with you, that's the stupidest thing I've ever heard, because if it were true and you knew it prior to the operation, why didn't you bring it to our attention beforehand?'"

he said. "You've got to be an idiot if you think something that important, grade-one evidence—you should be shouting it from the rooftops, saying, 'Guys, you shouldn't be doing this!' But not in the middle of the case to try and impress somebody."

Is that really what he had said?

No, said Lazzaro. "I screamed at him and called him a fucking idiot, and then I sent him out of the room," he said with a grin, remembering for an instant how satisfying it was to take that smug idiot to task for asking a question appropriate for a naïve college student, not a senior resident.

But the explosion didn't make Lazzaro happy. He was aware of his hothead reputation, and he didn't like it. He had heard that people who worked with him in the hospital said they respected his ability and would send their families to him for surgery, but they also thought he was a jerk. "I was a mean person," he said plaintively. "It wasn't me, it was part of me. They never saw me outside of the hospital, with my patients in the office, with my family. They knew me from a surgery standpoint, and they thought I was a nasty guy."

Something was wrong. He was forty-two years old, the proud father of the adorable children whose photographs sat on his desk. He had a job that was also an avocation, a passion—and yet he wasn't happy. He smoked. He was overweight. He was tired all the time.

It didn't make him feel better to know that others were nastier than he was. He recalled the surgeon who said to his residents, "Your mom must have taken thalidomide when you were born," suggesting they had no arms and their hands were like flippers. At least he'd never been that bad.

Maybe it was because his wife was nagging him to get some exercise. Or because he got tired of people telling him he looked like he hadn't slept in a week. But Rich Lazzaro decided to change. He began doing yoga. He quit smoking. He lost weight. So he was primed for the perioperative-services meeting on Crucial Conversations that met January 13. Lazzaro was sitting just a few rows from Alan Astrow when the surgeon stood up and said, "Hi, I'm Rich Lazzaro, and I have to say, from my standpoint, sometimes we don't think about the view of the team."

Not exactly a thunderbolt from beyond, but startling enough for Lazzaro to be surrounded by colleagues after the meeting was over, asking him to sign their copies of Crucial Conversations, and only partly as a joke.

"I felt if I'm the poster child for being the tough person, and I wanted to make change, I needed to stand up and say so," he told me later. "So I did."

Lazzaro's enthusiasm was infectious. Astrow raised his hand for a microphone and spoke in a humble tone of recognition. "There's a part of the Jewish liturgy where you ask forgiveness," he said. "And at St. Vincent's I'd hear the Lord's Prayer over the loudspeaker: 'Forgive those who have trespassed against us.' To have a conversation, you have to recognize your own fallibility and to forgive others from that place."

By then hosannas wouldn't have surprised me. None erupted, but many people did applaud. On the way out, I bumped into Steve Davidson, still smarting from his misadventures with Hatzolah and Jablon and the executives. I couldn't decipher the odd expression on his face. "It's so reenergizing to have someone like Astrow bring that kind of thinking back to this place," he said, and disappeared into the crowd exiting the auditorium.

Strange that in all this talk about the Code of Mutual Respect, no one ever mentioned the Oath of Maimonides. It was displayed on the wall next to the receptionist's desk in the Gellman Pavilion, alongside a brief historical accounting of Maimonides, the twelfth-century philosopher and physician for whom the hospital was named. Sometimes, especially when sleep deprivation left my emotions raw, I would find in these noble sentiments from long ago an exquisite connection to the people surrounding me in the small lobby: the family murmuring in a mixture of English and Russian about a parent's prognosis; a black man reading a book on Islam; a Pakistani woman in bright silk pajamas running after the little boy playing hide-and-seek by the cash machine.

When I asked Feldman about the oath, he said he had a copy in his office, a gift from an aunt, but he thought of it as décor more than inspiration.

THE OATH OF MAIMONIDES

The eternal providence has appointed me to watch over the life and health of Thy creatures. May the love for my art actuate me at all times, may neither avarice nor miserliness, nor thirst for glory nor a great reputation occupy my mind; for the enemies of truth and philanthropy could easily deceive me and make me forgetful of my lofty aim of good for Thy children.

May I never see in the patient anything but a fellow creature in pain. Grant me strength, time and opportunity always to correct what I have acquired, always to extend its domain; for knowledge is immense and the spirit of man can extend infinitely to enrich itself daily with new requirements. Today he can discover his errors of yesterday and tomorrow he may obtain a new light on what he thinks himself sure of today.

Oh, God, Thou has appointed me to watch over the life and health of Thy creatures; here am I ready for my vocation, and now I turn unto my calling.

Moses ben Maimon (Rambam)

During my year of immersion, a new biography of the medieval scholar was published. It was written by Sherwin Nuland, another physician and author, who focused on the sage's place in medical history. He explained the significance of the prayer of Maimonides: "the testament of the ideal—and idealized—healer. It has rivaled the Hippocratic Oath as the statement by which a young physician pledges fealty to his art, his principles, and the trust of his patients.

"Unfortunately," continued Nuland, "it is also like the Hippocratic Oath in that it was not written by its putative author." Scholarly research indicates that the prayer most likely had been written in the eighteenth century.

Nuland decided not to let the question of authorship stand between him and his desire for illumination. "The prayer's final paragraph elevated my sense of worthiness to the task I had chosen," he concluded. "Had Maimonides ever read it, I feel certain it would have done the same for him. I would have preferred that these were indeed his words, but it hardly matters. This prayer is a credo for the life that was his, and has been mine. Any thoughtful physician might say the same."

Ten

A Good Death

8:40 A.M., Monday.
Winter
Daily Log—J.S.

Transcendence . . .

Davey G. (Gregorius) told me he'd just seen a forty-one-year-old pregnant Hispanic woman who came in with vaginal bleeding. First baby. He grinned, reached into the pocket of his white coat, and pulled out a photo of the ultra-sound. "Baby okay," he said, wide grin, slipping the photo back into his pocket. "I'm giving this picture to them," he said. "They're really scared. I want it to work out for them."

He continued toward a pretty woman on the other side of the room; she wore a running suit, sat on a gurney, and held on to her husband, standing next to her. They clutched hands and watched the young doctor approaching, fear in their eyes.

I saw Davey show them the photograph and their expressions soften as he reassured them, "Baby okay." Then I resumed my conversation with Yevgeniy Lukyanenko, one of Douglas [Jablon]'s patient reps, a compact, square-faced Ukrainian who looked so much like a youthful version of Nathan Lane, the actor, that I half expected him to break into a song-and-dance routine. He told me to call him Eugene, his English name—it was easier. A nurse came along and told Eugene that the patient in 13B, one of the curtained slots that lined the ER perimeter, wanted to make a phone call. I followed Eugene to #10. He unplugged a telephone and took it a few cubicles down to the gaunt, stubble-faced old man lying on the bed in 13B. The old man whistled a little when he talked—he was missing a couple of front teeth—and told Eugene he'd already made the call on his cell phone. He wasn't sure he was allowed to use it inside the hospital but got tired of waiting.

Eugene wished him good luck and turned to leave.

The old man stopped him. "I don't want good luck," he said. "I would like to die."

No! said Lukyanenko—Eugene—and returned to the old man's side. "That's wrong. You'll be fine."

The old man weakly shrugged and said, "You don't want to listen."

The young man waited, and the old man began to talk.

"My first thirteen years were in Germany under Hitler. At thirteen I came here. For forty-seven years I had a perfect marriage. I know you may think that is hard to imagine. But it's true. Most people might argue over money or children. Children we didn't have; money I didn't worry."

The hum of the emergency room seemed to recede as the old man's story gained momentum.

"I worked at something that paid very well," he continued. "Not that any-body needed it, what we made, but it paid well. At thirty-five I was making a hundred dollars an hour when people were happy to make a few dollars. I had a perfect life. I am eighty years old. In forty-seven years I didn't say no to my wife once, or vice versa. If she wanted to do something I didn't want, I just gave a look and she knew. And vice versa."

He watched me scribbling in my notebook and paused, maybe to let me catch up, maybe to catch his breath.

"Children we didn't have," he repeated. "We had a house up in the moun-tains. A condo in Florida. Even though she was sick twenty-seven years, it was good. Four years ago my brother died, and then my wife died. I don't want pain. I want to go to sleep and not wake up. It could be tonight. I wouldn't mind."

Eugene said with sweet earnestness, "You have many good years ahead of you."

The old man shook his head. "You wouldn't understand," he said. "You don't know how it feels to lose a wife. Children are even worse, I hear, though I don't know. I never had any. I wanted to die the day after my wife. I had the pills. . . ."

He stopped and looked at Eugene. "Are you Jewish?"

The patient rep nodded.

I didn't know why it mattered until the old man continued. "I had the pills, but if I took them, I couldn't be buried next to her. (Then I understood: Jewish law traditionally prohibits suicide, and those who commit it are not permitted to be buried in Jewish cemeteries, though rabbis make many exceptions, including suicide resulting from mental illness.) Before she died, she said to me, 'I suffered with you thirty-two years, so I want you to suffer with me for eternity.' So when I buried her, I walked out of the cemetery and threw the pills away."

He looked miserable. "I just don't want pain," he said. "I only have my niece who lives in Buffalo, a nephew who is good for nothing, and my other brother, in the hospital. So now, give me an answer, why should I live? Today I figure maybe today's the day. I choked, I couldn't breathe."

Eugene was studying to be a nurse, and he was young. The wish for death was anathema to him. In his strong Ukrainian accent, he said, "If you are Jewish, you know the rabbi said, 'You must weep for those who are born and smile for those who are dead.'"

The old man clucked. "You are talking to the wrong man," he said. "I am an atheist."

Eugene smiled. "So am I," he said. "But what the rabbi says is true. We must feel sorrow for our children at facing the difficulty of life."

The old man said, "I have a religious friend I gave money to say kaddish for me. I don't remember how to say kaddish anymore. . . ."

He waved his hand in dismissal. "He's all right, but I don't like most Hasidic Jews."

Eugene said, "That makes two of us." Then he resumed his insistent defense of hopefulness. "You still have life ahead of you," he said.

"No, I don't," the old man said glumly.

Eugene sighed and glanced at his watch. "While you're here in the hospital, if you need anything, call me." He gave his extension.

As Eugene began to move away, again, the old man touched his arm.

"You want to know something?" he said. "You're the first pleasure I've had since I'm here."

They seemed to be somewhere else, no longer closeted in an emergency-room cubicle, separated from sick people on either side by curtains, yet still exposed. I, too, had drifted. Dan Sulmasy, Astrow's Franciscan friend, told me about moments like this. "Sometimes I feel I should take my shoes off before I enter the room of some patients," Sulmasy said, "because what's going on there is sacred in

a real transcendent sense. So much faith, so much hope, so much love. Whether
they're dying or going to recover almost doesn't matter, because something bigger is
going to happen."

On January 30, Lisa Keen, the social worker, brought a difficult case to biopsychosocial. She wanted information about a twenty-four-year-old woman, undocumented, unmarried, two children, Hispanic—we'll call her Ms. Hernandez. Mendel Warshawsky, the third-year fellow and cancer survivor from South Africa, said he knew the background: An initial workup had shown a negative breast exam. This was not, as one might think, good news. The cancer had metastasized.

"The prognosis in the case is dismal," said Warshawsky. The sun shining brightly through the cafeteria windows seemed at first to mock this grim forecast but on reflection seemed the perfect backdrop for the specter of unseasonable death. Why was it sixty degrees in January? The persistence of unnaturally warm weather was creepy, a portent of doom, heralding the end of seasons as we had known them for the past many centuries.

Warshawsky was still waiting to hear from Astrow about the oncology job and was angry about the delay. "Astrow doesn't have the balls to make a hard decision," he told me before the meeting. "I don't know if he's going to last here."

Warshawsky tried to concentrate on this difficult case, which left open many questions that he summarized for the group seated around the cafeteria tables they pulled together for the session, since there was no conference room for the fellows. Should the patient receive chemotherapy, which would not cure her and almost certainly make her feel sick but could prolong her life long enough for her to get her affairs in order?

What did it mean to get her affairs in order? "We have an undocumented woman, limited English," Keen summarized, challenge in her eyes, as usual. "Boyfriend of three months, the only one who knows she has cancer. She's entitled to nothing, working as a cashier in a supermarket off the books."

Alan Astrow sat with his hands clasped on the table, his head slightly bent. "Probably not a big chain," he said. "She'd have to have papers." He seemed distracted. He had told me his mother had checked in to Sloan-

Kettering with chest pain and was angry with him for not interceding with her doctor.

"Probably an Indian store," said Sushma Nakka in her lilting Indian accent, her makeup flawless and tasteful.

Keen said, "We're going to have to send her to Coney Island. Who's going to follow her?"

"Where's the father?" Astrow asked.

Keen said drily. "Somewhere."

Warshawsky finished his diagnosis. "She has metastasis to every part of her body."

Keen shook her head. "She doesn't have a clue."

Warshawsky straightened the yarmulke on his hairless head. "Maybe we shouldn't just talk about chemotherapy but that she should start thinking about taking care of her kids, about going home. If we start her on chemotherapy, she'll be so involved with that, and then she'll be so sick she won't be able to do anything, and then she'll die in the hospital. There isn't that much we can do for it."

Sheldon Berman, the psychiatrist with the shaggy gray hair, several years older than Astrow, chimed in. "We know we have a young woman here. Mendel brings up the context of how we interact with the patient. How do you implement your plan? We have a patient we assume is going to die in the next year. I'm reading between the lines—physicians will talk about treatment without talking about imminence of death."

Jason Tache, another third-year fellow, always spoke as if making a conclusion. "You're talking about prognosis," he said.

Berman shook his head impatiently. "No, not prognosis," he said. "We're talking about a young woman, limited English, how do we help her?"

"Help" in this conference meant something different from in the interdisciplinary meeting.

Berman was an old friend of Novetsky's; they had developed the group-therapy style of this biopsychosocial conference together. Like Keen, he had a sensibility shaped by the 1960s, rebelliousness worn down to an attitude of weary cynicism, righteous fervor mellowed but intact. This would be one of his last sessions. He had told Astrow he wanted to leave as soon as another psychiatrist could take his place as provocateur.

Berman repeated, "How do we help her? What do we do?"

Keen laughed shortly. "Run away?"

Tache sighed. "We are not prepared to give her the psychosocial treatment you are talking about because of the patient's financial and social situation."

He looked at Warshawsky. "Has it spread quickly, or did she ignore it because she didn't have the money? We can't give her long-term care—"

Astrow interrupted. "I thought she would be referred to Coney Island and a fellow will follow through." The Maimonides fellows did rotations at Coney Island, a public hospital four and a half miles away.

"They don't have social services," said Tache.

Astrow nodded. "They don't have a Nella."

Nella Khenkin was the cancer center's social worker, who usually came to the meetings, but not that day.

"They don't have a non-Nella," Tache replied. "There is no one to help with social aspects."

A woman in her forties, wearing a wig arranged with pageboy smoothness, entered the conversation. "She's going to have to think about child support," said Beth Popp, the hospital's pain-management specialist, who was Orthodox and often wore headbands that matched her clothing over her smooth wig. She was eating oatmeal out of a Styrofoam container. She had told me she'd lost a hundred pounds before having her fourth child and was careful.

"Giving her some suggestions about things she can do that are helpful is better than telling her she has terrible cancer and we'll know how bad after the test results," Popp said. "We should send off some warning shots, and it has to be done with social workers who speak her language."

Tache shook his head. "She has no insurance," he said. "When she leaves this place, she has nothing."

Popp raised her voice. "But she's here now!"

Berman stepped in. "Listen to Jason's approach," he said. "He's saying she is up the creek without a paddle."

Tache smiled. "I'm not saying she's there, but she's on the way," he said. "I speak the language, and it's common these people come here and have three, four children at home."

Keen stared at Tache. "Her mother is here," she said.

"Is she a responsible human being?" Tache asked. "You think she has two kids and someone has to tell her she has to take care of them? Why do I have to figure out what to do with her kids?"

Astrow spoke. "No one is asking you to solve her social problem."

Exasperated, Tache replied, "That's exactly what Lisa wants and Shelly, too," referring to the social worker and the psychiatrist.

Berman shook his head. "I'm trying to emphasize we are a team," he said. "When you become an attending, it's not just taking the temperature."

Astrow listened, his hands folded on the cafeteria table.

"I agree with you, Shelly," he said. "Let me reframe the question, because Jason has thrown down the gauntlet. People often want us to solve their social problems. Jason is suggesting it's a limited role."

Tache shrugged. "I have a limited amount of time to expend my energy," he said. "What's the most useful way to do that? In our system I don't see how to help."

Sramila Aithul spoke next. She was a second-year fellow who spoke with calm authority, a personality trait that had been reinforced during her tenure as chief resident. "Sometimes if you just talk to a patient in a way that gives them ideas of how to handle the situation . . . ," she said. "You may not tell them what to do, but just talking to them, showing some compassion—"

Tache interrupted. "With all due respect to Sramila, compassion is not going to raise her two kids."

Keen said, "I don't have a problem finding services for people. My problem is dealing with a twenty-four-year-old who is dying. Somebody with two kids; my daughter's age. I was half serious about wanting to run away. I need help."

Inna Sominsky, the second-year Russian fellow, said she had the same situation with another patient, a thirty-year-old with colon cancer, stage three. "Was told about her disease and prognosis by the surgeon, but she has never asked about the future," she said. "She doesn't ask any questions, and I am avoiding."

Astrow synthesized. "When a patient doesn't ask," he mused. "Sounds like this young woman—Ms. Hernandez—is not going to ask Mendel, and he's raised some good questions. Does she want to go back?"

Keen shook her head. "She doesn't," she said. "Her mother and sisters are here."

Astrow said, "Her country doesn't have the services?"

"It depends what kind of services," said Berman. "Loving care, kindness . . . it may be better. For me the most significant thing is pain management and end-of-life care, which, God knows, we don't do well. Let's think of this as a team. We are totally impotent to be able to stop the disease. Death is going to occur. This has to be part of our thought. Everybody dies, including us. If our goal is to help this woman, let's deal with the fact her kids are going to grow up without her, go to elementary school, to high school, get married, have children, and she's going to miss all that. The most important thing for family members is to know that you are there. Have any of you sat by the bed of a family member when they died?"

The discussion drifted in that direction for a few minutes, and then Astrow interceded. "The woman is not actively dying," he said. "We haven't finished the diagnostic workup. What is Mendel supposed to do?"

Berman said, "I'm suggesting that part of what we do is to be a human being, to be there in the moment, knowing we can't make it better other than to say, 'I am here.' "

Astrow tried again. "In the spirituality series, a priest talked about getting out of the fixing mode," he said. "Instead of worshipping Jesus, he said, you should follow Jesus into the vale of tears. But before we follow this patient down the vale of tears, we have to help Mendel with the medical diagnosis and what to tell the patient."

There was more conversation, and then Keen said, "This has made me feel better. Being in the room and caring is the most important thing. We shouldn't underestimate the power of hope."

Tache muttered. "Just don't overestimate it either."

Astrow glanced at his watch. They were reaching the end of the ninety-minute session. "It is important to be aware of your feelings," he said. "Not whether you like or don't like the patient, but helping them figure out what's best for them. Part of being a good doctor is self-awareness."

Popp turned to Warshawsky. "Think about this woman and having to face this huge challenge in a month or twelve months. She hasn't had an easy life. Many of us have faced a number of challenges, but probably nothing like hers. She is twenty-four, doesn't speak the language, eking out an existence while living here illegally. She has faced a bunch of challenges—yes, many of them of her own making, and of which we may or may not approve. But people like this often do better than middle-class people."

Astrow picked up that thought. "They don't have the illusion that the world is there to please them."

Popp replied, "It doesn't mean we shouldn't do what we can do."

Astrow looked at Warshawsky. "When you go in to see her, Mendel, take Dr. Popp's suggestion. Go in humbly. There's a lot we don't know about her. We don't even know her prognosis. We think we do. We should go step by step. This person is not you. She's had a different life. Maybe she wants chemotherapy. I know you see what's down the road for her and don't want her to make a bad choice."

Berman offered an example. "Choose chemotherapy when it might leave her unable to say good-bye to her children."

Warshawsky sounded exasperated. "I chose this specialty because I thought I'd cure cancer," he said. "We treat cancer, but how often do we cure cancer? Almost never!"

Astrow looked surprised. Warshawsky was a walking example of cure.

"Never?" asked Astrow. "Why do you say 'never'?" (Did he mean, *How can you of all people* say '*never*'?)

Warshawsky laughed. "I retract," he said. "It's just that when someone comes in with acute cancer, we rarely cure it. We're not purveyors of medicine. We're basically their doctor until they die, despite everything we do."

Astrow replied gently. "A lot of patients live," he said.

Warshawsky was combative again. "What cancer do we cure?"

Guptay Ranjiv, another fellow, said, "We give them five years."

Mendel was impatient. "Colon? Lung? We don't cure them. The focus can't be on curing the disease. How do we make life better?"

Time was up.

Most of the 40,262 patients who were admitted to the hospital that year would leave alive, most of them in better condition than when they had entered. But more than 1,000 of them would take their last breath at

Maimonides. The social workers and the chaplains tried to create the illusion of sanctity for families and friends, but it was difficult. The hospital was a pulsing organism whose reflexes were programmed to keep moving, the way a chicken continues to run after its head has been cut off.

A few hours after the Ms. Hernandez discussion, I accompanied Lisa Keen to a patient's room where a Chinese man in his fifties lay dead on his hospital bed. He had died unexpectedly that morning during an operation in which a Greenfield filter was inserted into a vein. Keen said she didn't know what caused the death—a blood clot, a heart attack, or the procedure itself.

Keen had talked the nurses into keeping him out of the morgue until one of his children could drive to Brooklyn from college in upstate New York, which would take several hours. The man's daughter held his hand while his wife wept. In the hysterical sadness of the room, only the dead man appeared calm. Keen told the daughter she was looking for a Mandarin interpreter to talk to her mother, who didn't speak English.

When we returned to the social-work office, two women in their forties wearing hospital badges were working the phones, weeping. I was touched at their empathy for the dead Chinese man until I learned they were weeping for themselves. They were surgical physician assistants who had been laid off because of the budget cuts. They introduced themselves as Josephine and Lisa.

Josephine was saying, "Feldman has done nothing but fuck up everything since he's been there."

Lisa said, "They didn't even call to say good job. Nothing."

Josephine chimed in. "It should have been done differently. It should have come from Cunningham, not from the administrator. He brought me in. We've been here ten years and twenty years. I would not have expected the man to do it this way."

Death shouldn't come as a surprise, certainly not in a hospital, definitely not when its imminence is a foregone conclusion. Yet a week earlier, on January 23, when I arrived at the cafeteria's back room for Monday-morning biopsychosocial rounds and no one was there, I was shocked to hear the mes-

sage I found on my cell phone. Alan Astrow called to let me know Sharon
Kopel had died Sunday, yesterday, the funeral was today at one, and biopsychosocial was canceled.

It was a gloomy morning drenched in rain. I decided to walk the twenty
blocks to the cancer center, figuring I could catch a ride to the funeral. Feeling chilled and empty, but not ready to talk to anyone just then, I factored in
a stop at a Chinese bakery for tea and the comfort of solitude among
strangers. On the sidewalk outside the Eisenstadt building, trying to open
my umbrella, I bumped into a man wearing a black leather jacket. It was
Steve Davidson, the ER chief. We exchanged awkward mumblings of sorrow,
and he told me he had practically lived at the Kopels' his first seven years at
Maimonides, when his family remained in Philadelphia and he commuted.

Davidson said that Sharon fed him physically and emotionally during
those years. He said she had come back from the brink of death many times
in the past two years, since September 2003, the date of diagnosis. He said
Sam, like anybody, was devastated at the loss but also relieved that the ordeal
was over.

The words stopped. Time stopped. Rain fell around us, but we were dry
beneath the underpass connecting Gellman and Eisenstadt, neither strangers
nor friends, bound and separated by our very different relationships to
Sharon Kopel, our professional concerns vis-à-vis one another, our private
thoughts of death. I had spent many hours talking to Davidson, learning
about his past and his travails with Hatzolah, connecting his impressive mass
of charts and data with the mob scene in his emergency room. We had gos-
siped, joked, and philosophized. I had become enmeshed in his world, but I
was also suspect, witness, and judge, always watching and recording. Even in
this instant of suspended reality, hyperaware of the collective sorrow
unleashed by one death, intellect swamped by feeling, we were walled in by
our own mass of data—not unlike the relationship of doctor and patient, or
patient's family, it occurred to me later.

He reached toward me and patted me on the arm—a clumsy, doctorly
pat. We turned in separate directions into the windy spray, he toward the
ER, I toward Chinatown. On Eighth Avenue, I walked past the big church
that advertised services in English and Chinese, past hair salons and grocery
stores, past the man selling hot noodles with sauce from a cart covered by

plastic. A thicket of umbrellas turned the sidewalk into a maze. I angled mine to squeeze through. A few blocks from the cancer center, I took refuge in a crowded bakery, sitting knee to knee with other damp people, almost all Asian. As they stared at the television showing news in Chinese, I watched a man scratch a Lotto ticket and then throw it on the floor. I drank hot tea from a Styrofoam cup, sweet milky solace for seventy cents, blissfully unable to understand a word being spoken around me.

I thought about Alan Astrow's spirituality conference in November. Chun-fang Yu, the Columbia professor who specialized in the effect of Buddhist thought on Chinese society, had invoked the concept of the "good death." Yu's subject was not mercy killing, not euthanasia, another kind of good death, derived from the Greek words for "good" (*eu*) and "death" (*thanatos*). There the object was to help a dying person escape suffering through active intervention, the actual termination of life. Yu described "the good death" as a state of being similar to the final stage of acceptance postulated by Elisabeth Kübler-Ross in her classic treatise *On Death and Dying*. For Yu the good death meant "being at peace with oneself," of facing death without fear.

The professor, a solid woman of about seventy, with close-cropped hair, spoke in a heavy accent with a reassuring blend of humbleness and authority. She said her own parents, who had remained in China, both died of colon cancer and were never informed of their illness or prognosis. "Not knowing makes it hard to prepare," she said. "Buddhism says we are one. We are interconnected, and we suffer when we feel there is a separate self. If you see only a cloud, you are very sad. You forget the cloud becomes rain. But many, many Buddhists are not ready. Many people are not capable of dying a good death."

After Professor Yu spoke, a psychiatrist discussed hope and paraphrased Václav Havel, the absurdist writer who became a political activist and then the last president of Czechoslovakia and first president of the Czech Republic. Later I looked up the quote in *Disturbing the Peace*, a collection of essays by Havel, including the pertinent one called "The Politics of Hope."

"Hope is definitely not the same as optimism," wrote Havel. "It's not the conviction that something will turn out well, but the certainty that something makes sense, regardless of how it turns out. . . . It is also hope, above all, which gives us strength to live and to continually try new things, even in conditions that seem as hopeless as ours do, here and now."

I thought about meeting Sharon Kopel, three months earlier, on a gray October afternoon, in the Kopels' rambling, comfortable Victorian house, fifteen minutes by car from the hospital. They lived in Prospect Park South, an idyllic, leafy enclave in Flatbush, conceived at the turn of the twentieth century by Dean Alvord, a visionary real-estate developer. Describing the community as *rus in urbe,* or "the country in the city," the real-estate man wanted to leave his mark on the present and the future, with houses of architectural distinction and a landscape that reflected the cycle of life. "Alternating every 20 feet were Norway maples, for permanence, and Carolina poplars, for immediate shade," explains the American Institute of Architects' *AIA Guide to New York City.* "The short-lived poplars, Alvord and his architect, John Petit, reasoned, would die out as the maples reached maturity."

The maples had grown large; the poplars were gone. Sharon Kopel was wasting away. Her emaciated body barely made a ripple on the overstuffed chair where she rested and watched television, mainly cooking shows. She was an accomplished cook. The chemotherapy made her too sick to eat much, but she could dream. Sam greeted me and gave me a quick tour of the house. That's when I saw the piano he'd traded up for from the one given to him by his former partners, now the antagonistic Bashevkin group. I saw toys belonging to the Kopels' two young grandsons. I had seen Sam only at work, aloof, dressed in a white doctor's coat or jacket and tie. Now I saw him as the patient's husband, wearing jeans and a look I interpreted as heartbreak. He brought Sharon a nice snack of focaccia with mozzarella cheese, tomato, and olive oil—a lunch she barely touched—and left us alone to talk.

Her voice was thin and quavery. Her breath was short. Occasionally she apologized for forgetting certain words—a side effect of the chemo, she explained. Though she insisted that she was in denial, she discussed her diagnosis and treatment—and the history of the cancer center, including the feud with the Bashevkin group—with fierce and funny Brooklyn articulation.

"It's about two years right now since I started chemo," she said. "I found out about the cancer and started the chemo all in the same week, not a luxury most people have. You can sometimes wait two weeks for an appointment and another two weeks for the test results; you may have to go to

Manhattan or the Bronx, and by that time you might as well be dead you're so aggravated."

I remembered Sam's description of her. "Fierce," he said. "'Fierce' is a good word. A really good word. Fierce and uncompromising. I would say unforgiving, but that's too harsh. She could forgive. But she was a tiger in defending me."

Maybe that explained why she had been willing to talk to me, despite the obvious effort it cost her. Even then, shrunk by half from her heaviest self, when she tipped the scales at 182 pounds, she was watching out for Sam, as she always did. "On top of everything else, Sam is having to take me around, taking care," she said. "I'm in denial most of the time. I don't think about it. I watch television and just pretend. I can't even think what this has done to him."

The cancer center had led me to Maimonides. Like the feuds at the hospital, Sharon Kopel's illness was built into the cancer center's core, as surely as the steel and cement that encased Jay Cooper's linear-accelerator radiation machines. Remember, Sam's interest in building the center a decade earlier became obsessive only after his wife's first round of cancer, when he was awakened to just how unpleasant the hospital's radiation facilities were. She encouraged him as his first and second and third efforts fell apart. She kept the grudge with his former partners alive; nothing that hurt Sam could be overlooked. Then she volunteered to help with an organization collecting smoking data for a cancer project. There she met Steven Cymbrowitz, the Brooklyn assemblyman whose wife had recently died of cancer. Sharon told the assemblyman about Sam's many failed attempts to start a cancer center at Maimonides. Cymbrowitz met Sam and came on board with the promise of some public money at a time when the hospital was ready to make the commitment. The groundbreaking ceremony to announce the beginning of construction was set for September 25, 2003.

For almost a year before that, Sharon experienced a steady barrage of swarming pain in her lower back and abdomen. The sensation resembled powerful menstrual cramps, but she had already gone through menopause. She said she was annoyed because she was unable to help her daughter, who had just given birth to her second child, as much as she had hoped. Sharon said she wasn't alarmed. Illness had been part of her life since she was a teenager and learned she was diabetic. Her adult life had been punctuated by periods of sickness, often related to complications from the diabetes, which damaged her eyes and almost destroyed her feet. In addition there were angioplasties for cardiac damage and a long history of back pain, including one bout, when she turned fifty, so severe that she couldn't walk for weeks.

She didn't ignore the pain. "I'm very diligent about going to the doctor," she told me. Her mother had died of a rare form of cancer that had eluded doctor after doctor, test after test. Sharon was careful. For her back pain, she went to her chiropractor and physical therapist. Sam arranged for a pelvic sonogram, which was followed a few months later by a CAT scan. The pain widened from her back to her right side to her left side. A neurologist examined her, and a pain specialist told her she had a pinched nerve. The painkillers he gave her helped for a while, but by the summer of 2003, she was miserable again.

They didn't go to the Berkshires that summer. Sam was consumed with the cancer center, working seven days a week. Sharon was consumed with pain. Over Labor Day weekend in September, they finally went to the country, where Sharon spent the weekend lying on the couch. Back in the city, more trouble: Sam's mother, suffering from Parkinson's and dementia, was taken to the hospital; though a Do Not Resuscitate order was prominently displayed on her refrigerator, she had been intubated and died in a coma a few days later.

The following week, after the Kopels observed shivah, the seven-day mourning period, Sharon had another MRI for her spine. She had postponed the test for a week because of her mother-in-law's death.

That night after dinner, Sharon said, Sam told her she had to go for another test the next day, and she said she couldn't, she had a dentist's appointment. He was insistent, she recalled. "You're not going to the dentist, you're going to drink this stuff," referring to the barium solution, which she described as "banana-tasting chalk." She told this story with a wistful look of amusement, as though recalling a romantic moment rather than the prelude to her death sentence.

"Which goes to show I did teach him something," she said. "No bad news before dinner is over."

The next morning she recalled taking a change of clothes, because after the test she and Sam were going straight to the groundbreaking ceremony. "You don't want to look like you've been to the doctor," said Sharon.

She recalled Sam saying, "You have ovarian cancer," and her asking, "How? They looked behind every nook, every corner, every cranny—how?"

She didn't remember much after that, except that she did change clothes and went with Sam to the celebration of his triumph—their triumph.

Pam Brier told me that the instant she saw the Kopels arrive at the groundbreaking ceremony, she knew that something was wrong. "I could just tell by the looks on their faces that things were not good," she said. "I remember looking at Sam and Sharon and thinking, 'Maybe they had a fight.' They just did not look good, and they definitely came in later than other people."

Brier always had sensitive radar for the placement of people and things, but her antennae were particularly alert that day, less than three months after the accident that had almost killed her and her husband. Peter was still in the hospital, and she had just come back to work. This was her first public appearance, and she was determined to give the impression that she was in control of the hospital. She left her wheelchair in the car, out of sight of the gathered local officials and hospital personnel, and used a walker to make her entrance.

"I was really focused on trying to move one foot in front of the other and get through the thing, because it was really hard," she recalled.

Later, after she learned why they looked stricken, a thought occurred to her, a thought that stayed with her throughout her recovery and that revealed much about Brier's intricate psychology. "It was like you look at two planes intersecting in the air, and you see that for one the trajectory goes one way and for the other, something else," she said. "I thought, 'Here you are, Pam, and your trajectory is so positive, and Sharon's is so negative. Listening to accounts of Sharon getting sicker and sicker was so significant to me—aside from the irony of the whole thing, and the tragedy of the whole thing—she was the person I kept in mind as I got better and better. As I got strong and stronger and more and more back in the world, I stopped thinking about it so much. But in those first months, that first year, you can believe she was in my mind as the possible other course."

. . .

In 1961, 90 percent of the doctors responding to a survey by the *Journal of the American Medical Association* said they would not tell their patients they had cancer. By 1979 almost all the physicians responding to a similar survey (97 percent) said yes, they would tell their patients. In 1977, reflecting on this sea change in attitudes, an oncologist named Franz J. Ingelfinger delivered a lecture at the Harvard Medical School shortly before he retired as editor of the *New England Journal of Medicine*. In that lecture he defended the physician's right to treat patients with "authoritarianism, paternalism and domination."

Ingelfinger used his own experience as a cancer patient to support his position. After he was diagnosed with a glandular cancer, which was removed surgically, he faced the decision of whether to receive prophylactic chemotherapy and/or radiation therapy. His surgeon saw no visible evidence that the cancer had spread, but it was possible that it had. Both chemotherapy and radiation therapy could produce debilitating side effects. The physician/patient was bombarded with well-meaning, contradictory advice, all of which made him more indecisive. One day a friend told him, "What you need is a doctor."

"He was telling me to forget the information I was receiving from many quarters," said Ingelfinger, "and to seek instead a person who would dominate, who would tell me what to do, who would in a paternalistic manner assume responsibility for my care."

Ingelfinger followed his friend's advice. "My family and I sensed immediate and immense relief," he said. "The incapacity of enervating worry was dispelled." Ingelfinger recognized that paternalism was a form of arrogance and that "a physician can be beneficially arrogant, or he can be destructively arrogant." He defined destructive arrogance as "accentuated by insolence, vanity, arbitrariness . . . lack of empathy."

The *New England Journal of Medicine* published Ingelfinger's lecture as an article called "Arrogance" in December 1980, eight months after the author's death. Sam Kopel sent me a copy when I asked him what his philosophy of medicine was. "I can't say I have a philosophy," he told me, "but the way I practice has been heavily influenced by something I read twenty-odd years ago. You must present the options as honestly, fairly, and effectively as you can, and you have to frankly admit to what you don't know. But you can't dodge the responsibility for making a recommendation."

I remembered Estee Altman's evaluation: *Dr. Kopel is very brilliant but very rational, scientifically makes the decisions about what needs to be done.* He could seem cold.

"Some people think I'm too arrogant," he acknowledged, as though reading my thoughts. "Because I will actually voice an opinion and strike out in a direction and say, 'Here's what I think you ought to do.'"

He tried to be deferential to Sharon's physicians, but he didn't allow himself the relief of relinquishing responsibility. He couldn't. When Sharon and Sam began dating and it was obvious to her they might marry, she sat with him on a bench in a garden by a pool on the Brooklyn College campus. She told him she had something very important to tell him.

When she told him she had diabetes, he didn't fully comprehend the gravity of her condition—he hadn't yet started medical school—but he recognized that it was serious. Instead of being scared off, however, he found himself drawn by her need. It was an attraction as vital as her cute face and deceptively insouciant reddish pixie haircut. Sam told me, "I grew up in a household with a father who was a double amputee. I was used to taking care of someone. Sharon being ill . . . somehow made it more compelling."

Over the years he abdicated to her physicians—and he didn't. He was Sharon's husband but also her medical adviser and medical director at the hospital where the fatal illness was discovered. When she went for the spine MRI the day before the groundbreaking of the cancer center, the radiologist didn't call the patient with the results; he called her husband, the medical director, with his report: The radiologist saw some kind of growth, involvement of the right kidney.

Sam Kopel and I discussed many things over the next few months following Sharon's death, but more than a year would pass before he sat in his office in the cancer center and showed me his wife's CAT scan on his computer screen. It was one of a few dozen images of Sharon's insides that had been taken over the years; some part of her was now stored in the hospital's hard drive.

First we looked at a CAT scan taken in February 2003. On the computer I saw a swirling bunch of lines, resembling a satellite radar map on the Weather Channel, settling into definable shapes. Sam pointed. "Now, liver looks perfectly okay. Vena cava, normal bile ducts." He pointed to splotches. "That's fat." Then: left kidney, right kidney, guts, aorta, pelvis, uterus, fibroids, rectum, bladder, vagina. Click. Click.

Then he brought up the fatal picture, taken seven months later, on September 25, 2003. Kopel showed me what he saw when he stood behind the technician and watched the computer monitor as sixty-four X-ray detectors beamed in on his wife, integrated the data, and generated a high-speed image in maybe ninety seconds.

First he saw tiny speckles in her lungs, which didn't worry him. Seconds later the pulsing picture came into focus as her liver. "To my horror I see these big lesions, and they're instantly recognizable," he said, pointing to the screen. "A normal liver looks smooth, like a slice of pâté," he said in a professorial voice. "The lesions are actual holes, like Swiss cheese."

"Were you anticipating what you saw?" I asked. We both kept our eyes on the screen.

"I deliberately made myself blank," said Kopel. "I've been in this business long enough to know that in an individual patient anything can cause anything. You can jump to conclusions about a population of patients, but not an individual." He told me, "I knew there were ten benign things it could be. A large fibroid or a kidney stone or a band of adhesions from a previous appendectomy. But it also could be malignant."

He knew the possibilities, hopeful and dire. Yet he said, "I was not anticipating what I saw next."

The screen showed a large mass. "Almost the size of a grapefruit," said Kopel. "A large orange." He had little doubt. This was cancer.

He was honest with Sharon and he wasn't. "I didn't tell her everything," he said. "I told her there was a mass. I wasn't going to lie to her. I told her there was a mass blocking the kidney and we'd take some steps to take care of it."

During this conversation Sam Kopel said, "If you were to write it the way it was, it would seem too operatic." That's when he talked to me about Violetta, the doomed heroine in *La Traviata* and why he loved opera. *You know she's a striver, that she's good, that she is doomed by illness,* Sam said. *In the first minutes of the overture. Those high violins, those dissonant notes. Go home and listen to it. That is a musical depiction of tuberculosis, of disease. It's perfect.*

"Forget the opera," I said. "What was your life with Sharon like in real life?"

His thin face seemed to shrink behind his glasses. "We had our ups and downs," he said slowly. "We were very different people. I had a very difficult time getting used to her circumscription. She was afraid of going out and daring to do things—hiking, skiing, exploring. She was more into people and relationships, and I was into new adventures. So that was a friction. On the other hand, she kept me safe and I provided whatever I did for her."

He leaned forward to turn off the computer. "I had one major regret, in the distant past," he said. "Because of the diabetes, she didn't want to have any more kids after Lisa. That was a big problem. The pregnancy accelerates complications of diabetes, that's true. You can minimize that by taking very tight control of the diabetes, also true. But she never took tight control of the diabetes until very late in life. She ate whatever she felt like. She gained weight, so be it. That was a friction."

I looked at the photograph on the wall, showing Sam leaning in to kiss Sharon's neck on his fortieth birthday, his eyes closed dreamily, a big grin on her face.

A false positive?

Kopel was trained to keep a poker face but his voice trembled. "In some ways she was my lightning rod," he said. "She was all emotion. I'm all analysis and intellect. We fought. But we were partners. She could sense who was good and who wasn't. She really, really hated folks who took advantage. She was a rock through all those hassles with the cancer center, completely and unambiguously my compatriot. She could hate, but good."

"Was that a good thing or a bad thing?" I asked.

He paused for just a second. "I think it was overall a good thing," he said.

The afternoon of the cancer center's groundbreaking, Sharon and Sam stayed in his office in the old oncology practice, a block away from where the new center would be. Sam called a Maimonides surgeon to arrange for a stent and a chemotherapy port. He called a former colleague of Jay Cooper's at NYU, who agreed to manage Sharon's treatment. They decided she would have the chemotherapy at Maimonides, by Dr. Huang, for convenience, because sometimes it would take all day for the chemo to drip into her veins. Beth Popp handled her pain; Sharon's internist took care of her diabetes. Sam Kopel acted as intermediary.

What about Ingelfinger and his recommendation to relinquish responsibility?

"I have to straddle," Kopel said. "I saw to it she had doctors rather than a million doctors. I tried to step away, but you can't do it. She expected me to give her advice. I went with her to the oncologist to remind her of the side effects she wouldn't mention. I might tell him about a new symptom I had seen or that she wouldn't tell him about. Most patients don't tell their doctors bad news."

He prepared a detailed history for the NYU doctor:

Diabetes since teenage; complications include:

CAD with multiple angioplasties & stents. Most recent in 2000.
Retinopathy treated successfully with laser, mid 90s.
Charcot's foot, now stabilized, 2001.
No renal, peripheral vascular or neuropathic issues of note.

Medications:
Cardizem, 180 mg daily
Zestril, 10 mg daily
Atenolol, 25 mg bid
Imdur
Plavix
Lipitor

Insulin: lantus, 25 u hs. Humalog 5,5,10 before meals; 0–5hs prn.
Breast cancer, stage I, Aug., 1996. Lumpectomy, RT & Tamoxifen for
    5 years.
Vaginal bleeding, 2000, while on TMX & Plavix; D&C neg.
Low back pain; severe in 1996 (12 weeks bed rest); intermittent since.
Acupuncture & physical therapy, ongoing. Bextra, 20 mg. hs prescribed 2003.
Irritable bowel diagnosis, 2002, based on spasmodic pain with defecation, constipation etc. Never clear whether pain related to bowel,

GYN, or lower back. Workup included colonoscopy (6/02), AP
CT (2/02), AP MRI 7/02, pelvic sono 1/03. All non diagnostic.
Consultation with anorectal surgeon 11/02—confirmed spasm &
uncoordinated peristalsis. UGI/SB series 3/03 "to complete the
workup of irritable bowel"—negative. No hint of a pelvic mass.
Treated variously with Bentyl, Elavil, stool softeners etc.
Consultation with pain specialist 3/03; Bextra prescribed with partial
   relief for 2–3 months.
Unprovoked sweating since Jun '03.

Sharon had described her progress under treatment. "The first few treatments were pretty good, because I weighed 182 pounds, so I looked healthy
for a while," she told me. "Then the heavy-duty vomiting started. I swear to
you, one morning I looked in the mirror and I was green and had no hair
and the clothes were hanging off me and I was scared. I looked like a
concentration-camp victim. Not a survivor, but a victim.

"We tried four or five treatments," she said. "Should I count the ways
they've been trying to kill me? The first one I had my head in the toilet. Then
I had a pulmonary embolism. They got me to the hospital, and I felt, 'This
really is the end.' Little did I know bigger and better were in store for me.

"They took me once to the hospital in an ambulance, because Sam
couldn't wake me up," she said. "I had gone into diabetic shock. That was a
horror. I didn't know what was happening. Vomiting, rashes, dizzy, then
nonstop diarrhea. Why do people do this?"

I asked Sam whether he thought Sharon was prepared for death.

"She was always asking me if there was something else to be done," he
said. "But she was prepared."

I asked him about the concept of "the good death."

He replied without hesitation. "The dignified death is a myth," he said
flatly. "Unless you just keel over and drop dead, and there's not much dignity
there either. People dying of chronic illnesses like cancer or Alzheimer's, it's
an awful process. Evolutionarily, the body wants to keep going. The struggle
can be mitigated by judicious use of medications and not overdoing the
medical procedures. But it's always a struggle."

. . .

On the day of Sharon Kopel's funeral, after finishing my milky tea at the Chinese bakery, I went back into the rain and continued up Eighth Avenue to the cancer center. I found Nella Khenkin, the cancer center's social worker, in her small office filled with books and paraphernalia—wigs, makeup, pamphlets—meant to help cancer patients deal with the indignities of treatment. A full-bodied woman of fifty, Khenkin had immigrated to the United States fifteen years earlier from the former Soviet Union, where she taught Russian language and literature. Steeped in her ancestral home's appreciation of suffering and melancholy humor, she was a wise and comforting presence.

"Friday was his birthday," she said by way of greeting. Kopel had turned sixty two days before his wife's death.

Unlike Sam Kopel, who spoke with both the sorrow of a man who has lost his wife and the sense of failure doctors often express when patients die, Khenkin saw aspects of a "good death" in Sharon Kopel's final days.

"I understand that she suffered a lot, so for her it is the end of her suffering," she said. "It is amazing she let him have his birthday on Friday. Didn't spoil it. Didn't make it sad. Can you imagine if it had happened on Friday? At least he will be able to celebrate his birthdays many, many years—and then a couple days later, of course, it will be a memorial day."

Khenkin told me that her own husband had died almost exactly three years earlier. "I remember when we came to the funeral home, Kopel was the person who met me there. Dr. Kopel," she said. "It was very important to me he was there with support, though he didn't know me very well. And then later, when I was sitting shivah, he took time, the medical director! I just came to the practice at that time. I was amazed to receive such respect. I expected the little people would not be interesting to someone in that position, but he took the time."

She told me car pools were being organized for the Kopel funeral. "A lot of people want to go," she said. "He brought her here to the New Year's party in a wheelchair. She was very frail, but I'm glad she was here, able to see the center. It was his baby; he was building this center and thinking about it all the time."

She sighed. "So how are you?"

I rode to the funeral home on Coney Island Avenue in a car with Alan Astrow and Jay Cooper. I met Astrow in his office, and he told me that his mother had given away her jewelry and informed her children that she'd prepared a will. She told him she was going into the hospital for a cataract operation. Astrow called her oncologist to see if she was well enough for surgery. "The disease is progressing slowly," he was told.

In the car the two doctors avoided mention of where we were going and why. Instead Cooper complained about American Airlines changing his flight on the way to a conference in Florida and losing his luggage on the way back. They discussed a story on the front page of the *New York Times* about a breakthrough in ovarian cancer and how misleading drug trials are. They avoided the obvious connection between the news and our destination. Cooper gave directions to the cabdriver and said he grew up three blocks from the funeral home. We passed a cemetery; he told us Mae West was buried there. When he leaned forward to instruct the driver further, the driver raised his hand and said, "Stay calm, sir, I'm born and raised in Brooklyn."

"So am I," said Cooper tersely.

The funeral home had capacity for 315 and was overflowing. The Maimonides crew was there in full force, from Marty Payson on down. Lisa Kopel-Hubal, Sam and Sharon's only child, spoke. Then Sam Kopel stood at the podium, poised and elegant in his black suit.

I didn't take notes, but I remember the speech as a kind of aria, composed by a man who appreciated operatic emotion but rarely showed it.

If you were to write it the way it was, it would seem too operatic.

At Sharon's funeral he made a joke about how his computer had a virus, not cancer, so his speech was handwritten.

He said he and Sharon loved opera and ranked individual ones according to hankies needed. *Falstaff* zero, *Madame Butterfly* off the charts.

He noted that his grandsons were the first in his family to be born in the United States; Lisa, their daughter, was born in Italy, when he was in medical school.

He said Lisa was Sharon's masterpiece, her *capolavoro,* and he used both the Italian and the English. Sharon's product, not his. He had missed every parent-teacher meeting—not proud of it, just reporting.

(Lisa later told me that this wasn't true, that she remembered him home for dinner every night, that he taught her how to ride a bike, he took her to see *The Magic Flute* at the movies, he took her ice skating.)

He said Sharon had taught science for years at a Jewish day school and that she was beloved. That when the principal once asked the children who the most famous Jewish scientist of the twentieth century was, the children did not, as you would expect, offer up the man who declared that *e* equals *mc* squared. No, the children said, the most famous Jewish scientist of the twentieth century was Mrs. Kopel. The audience laughed through tears.

Sam described their meeting, at summer school. He was there because he'd flunked a course; she was merely industrious. He copied her papers. For thirty-six years she took care of him, he said: investments, shopping, everything. He went to an ATM for the first time three months earlier, he said. He was still afraid of supermarkets, he said, but he guessed he would have to get over that.

Then he paused and said dramatically that he wanted to say it publicly, that Sharon never resented her late diagnosis. She never discussed recrimination.

(Later Sam told me he saw one of Sharon's doctors walk into the funeral home just then, and he wanted to reassure him. I remembered Lili Fraidkin once whispering when she was irritated with Kopel that Sam felt guilty for not diagnosing his wife's cancer earlier. When I asked him whether he felt guilty, he said, "When I said Sharon never resented the late diagnosis, was I subconsciously giving myself absolution? Probably. My analyst would probably say yes. I don't reject that. Why didn't I see something the others didn't see. Like everyone else, I rationalize.

"Ovarian cancer can be cured, even in late stages," he said. "When it's the sort of typical ovarian cancer, presents with fluid and swollen belly, those patients respond to chemotherapy beautifully. I have lots and lots of patients like that. Every oncologist does. Sharon's cancer was different. This was a variant, and it behaved in a more malignant fashion.

"If you're asking, do I have sleepless nights about it? I would say no. Was it the subject of analytic sessions? Absolutely.")

He said taking care of her the last three years was a privilege.

Sharon always came through for him, he said. After being in a coma for a week, she woke up for a few hours on Saturday, the day after Sam's birthday. "I don't know how or why," said Sam. He corrected himself. "I do know why, but not how." She wished him happy birthday. That was the why.

He concluded by repeating something he said often: that the four years they spent in Italy in their youth were the best years of his life.

Three weeks passed. After a balmy interlude, winter asserted itself, with the biggest snowfall ever recorded in New York, 26.9 inches in Central Park. By the next day, the sun came out, melting the snow, leaving the streets a mess. The hospital felt dank, dispirited. Brier's husband had had yet another operation, another attempt to restore mobility to his knee, at New York–Presbyterian Hospital/Weill Cornell Medical Center. On her daily visits to Aschkenasy, Brier tried, unsuccessfully, not to be overcome with envy of the clean hallways, the beautiful rooms, the unscuffed elevators, the hospital's $1 billion capital campaign. Plus, HealthGrades had just issued its 2006 report; after receiving the Distinguished Hospital Award for Clinical Excellence for three years in a row, achieved by only 5 percent of the country's hospitals, Maimonides was dropped from the list because of an uptick in mortalities. And January surgery numbers, in Brier's words, were "in the toilet."

At the biopsychosocial meeting, Ms. Hernandez was back on the agenda.

Astrow walked into the room carrying a banana for breakfast. As usual, he was last to arrive. The fellows looked at him expectantly.

"We have a twenty-four-year-old with metastasized lung cancer," he began. "Even if she smoked like a fiend, that wouldn't explain this. She's from Mexico."

"Dominican Republic," said Keen.

Mohammad Razaq spoke. "We gave her one dose of chemotherapy."

Razaq was the quiet Pakistani who had told Astrow, along with Warshawsky, that he would be interested in staying at Maimonides for a full-time position after his fellowship was completed that spring. Like Warshawsky, Razaq was growing impatient with Astrow's slowness in making a decision.

"Why is she still in the hospital?" Astrow asked.

Sramila Aithal, a fellow, answered. "She doesn't have insurance."

"She's very sick," added Inna Sominsky, whose blond hair was streaked slightly differently that morning. She looked tired. Her two young children seemed to wake up earlier and earlier.

"Failing," said Razaq.

"At four we're having a family meeting," said Lisa Keen. "Her mother she hasn't told, because the mother has high blood pressure. The father of the children, who has legal rights, is coming, supposedly."

Astrow nodded. "What is the patient's understanding?"

Keen replied, "That she has a limited time to live, but that God and a miracle will save her."

"Does she have English?" Astrow asked.

One of the fellows nodded. "She does," she said.

Keen shook her head. "No, she doesn't."

"She doesn't have an understanding. . . ." Astrow seemed to be talking to himself. Then he looked at Keen. "What do you plan to say to the family this afternoon?"

Keen didn't directly answer. "Dr. Rubin said if she doesn't respond to the chemotherapy, she'll die in the hospital. If she does respond, she has maybe six months."

"What's happening to the children?" Astrow asked. "Is the father involved?"

Again Keen shook her head. "No, but the boyfriend and the grand-mother are."

"The mother needs to understand she has to think of the welfare of her children," Astrow said. "That has to be brought up."

"We've started," said Keen.

Warshawsky raised another question. "What happens if you're illegal and suddenly the children come to the attention of the authorities?"

"They are citizens by birth," Aithal said.

"Even if the parents are illegal?" asked Sominsky.

"Born in the U.S.A. Yes," said Astrow.

Sominsky's words sounded more cynical than her tone. "So everyone can come here and have children born here and apply for services?"

Razaq returned to medical issues. "She became tachycardic," he said. "Afterward I spoke to the sister. The patient knows she hasn't got a good prognosis. I haven't spoken to her about time."

Astrow asked, "How do you plan to talk to her about her children?"

Razaq looked pained. "The children. The oldest is five years old," he said. "Can you tell them?"

No one answered.

"The children are now staying with whom?" Astrow asked.

Keen replied. "Mom and her boyfriend," she said. "The patient's boyfriend of three months."

"There's a whole literature on how to talk to children about their parents' illnesses," Astrow said. "It would be good for us to review this whole topic."

"This meeting is to look at what the family dynamics are and how they can support her," said Keen.

"I'm going to tell the family they need to take responsibility immediately," said Razaq. "Even if she survives a few months, she won't be in shape to take care of children."

"How will she get to Coney Island?" asked Keen. If Ms. Hernandez got well enough to be discharged from Maimonides, her treatment would continue at the public hospital. Then the social worker moved from practical matters to spiritual. "She's an ecumenical Christian and looking for spiritual support. We called around and found a priest who came over Saturday to pray with her."

Astrow asked, "Who do we have in this hospital for patients who aren't Jewish?"

"Deacon Tom," said Keen.

"Episcopalian?" asked Astrow.

"Catholic," said Keen. "We have all kinds of churches on call, and there's a priest regularly on Wednesday and Friday. Jewish support is hard to get unless a patient is dead."

"It's surprising in this hospital there's very little religious support," said Warshawsky.

Astrow laughed. "I see all these rabbis floating around here," he said. "What do they do?"

Robert Rosenblum, another social worker, middle-aged with a beard and yarmulke, smiled slightly. "They float," he said.

Astrow was about to change the subject. He looked at Keen. "It's very important for the mom to think about her children and how she wants them to remember her," he said. "A fairly tough discussion."

At 3:00 P.M., the time scheduled for the meeting, Regina Tarkovsky was waiting outside Hernandez's room. Tarkovsky, a Russian with pensive eyes and short blond hair, was a firm director like Gregory Todd, a full-time staff physician who had her own patients and, along with a nurse manager, supervised clinical care of all the patients on her floor.

While we waited, Tarkovsky brought us up to date. "It's a very interesting case," she said. "She's so young, and it is not likely for a young person to present this way, stage-four lung cancer. Plus, she has no insurance, and we're all thinking, 'What is going to happen? How will she get treatment?' She looks better, she just got chemo. But the five-year survival rate is almost nonexistent."

God help the interesting patient. "We have teaching rounds at one-thirty; ten A.M. morning report on interesting cases," she said. The floor was full of them.

She told us about another patient she had, metastasis to the brain, no hope. Her group collected money to send him home to Ukraine.

Tarkovsky sighed. "Sometimes I think there is too much teaching." I noticed she wore frisky boots with skinny high heels and pointed toes, and I wondered how she managed to get around; the doctors never stayed in one place very long.

"This patient can't get treatment in our cancer center if she leaves the hospital," said Tarkovsky. "She can go to Coney Island. The resident already talked to her about advanced directives, Do Not Resuscitate. But she's in denial."

Tarkovsky explained that she was in charge of Hernandez but felt that the oncologist should talk to the family. Suddenly a dizzying smell oozed into the hallway from the room on the other side. Tarkovsky and Keen seemed oblivious to the stench and its source, an elderly man walking in small circles, and periodically lifting his gown, exposing his naked rump. He grabbed some plastic gloves from a container and leaned over to swipe at something on the floor but missed the fresh turd he had just deposited there.

Tarkovsky finally noticed and called out to the nurse's aide—the "patient-care technician"—a slender black woman walking down the hall. Smoothly the PCT shifted course and quickly cleaned the mess, while gently talking to the man.

The Spanish-speaking student social worker couldn't come to the family meeting Lisa Keen had scheduled because of the snow. Keen decided to proceed with another interpreter, a resident who spoke Spanish.

The family arrived shortly after the hour. It was a modern family, nonnuclear, ordained by neither religion nor state, held together by blood, passion, children, culture, and now necessity: the patient's sister and brother-in-law, the father of the children, and the new boyfriend of three months. They were young people, in their twenties, outfitted in jeans, a baseball cap, stylish boots, but apparently ready to assume this grievous responsibility.

The resident who had offered to interpret appeared. It was David Kho, the Chinese resident born in Singapore, married to the half-Jewish Puerto Rican. Last time I'd seen him, he was interpreting for a Chinese patient. Now he was needed for the Spanish he'd perfected working with Dominican patients while a resident at Columbia's medical school.

While the group waited for the oncologist, Phil Rubin, Keen explained the purpose of the meeting. "Dr. Rubin is coming to talk about chemotherapy," she said. "But the reality is, you have a limited time to be on this earth, and we want to help the family use this time in the best way."

Kho interpreted carefully. The sister began to cry, as did the children's father. The boyfriend looked dazed. Only Hernandez herself, ethereal in her hospital gown, thinner and paler than when I last saw her, was composed, despite the breathing tube in her nose. She handed tissues to her sister and to the father of her children.

Rubin arrived. He was a bulky, awkward Orthodox man whose yarmulke always looked ready to slide off his head. Bangs added to the impression of a big, gawky boy, even though his hair was graying. He was known for his thoroughness, an unwillingness to rush that contradicted every impulse of hospital momentum, and for a desire to cure so fervent that it compelled him to put a positive spin on the direst situations.

He looked like he wanted to hide behind his bangs as he explained that the cancer in the patient's lungs had spread throughout her body by the time she entered the hospital. Fluid around her heart had been drained so she could have chemotherapy, which had begun the previous Friday. "If no treatment was given, she would not be alive today talking to us now," he said, looking at Kho, with an occasional sympathetic nod in Hernandez's direction. "We hope the chemotherapy will fight the tumor around her lung and allow her to breathe by herself."

Rubin paused periodically, giving Kho time to interpret, in careful textbook Spanish. Rubin explained that the chemotherapy, which would be given intravenously once a month, was a poison, so it would affect healthy cells, too. It would take one or two weeks to recover her blood counts and at least two cycles of chemotherapy to test the overall effect.

Rubin tried to use language that was hopeful. "If over the next week or so she has improvement in her breathing, that is a good sign and an encouraging sign," he said. "She is not ready to leave the hospital until she recovers from the effect of the chemotherapy."

His young audience listened with petrified faces.

Keen whispered something to Rubin.

Dutifully he said, "The chemotherapy will not be able to get rid of all the cancer, but it can help her feel better and live longer. If it works, she can do as much as six cycles."

Keen interjected, "There is also the possibility she may not respond."

Kho interpreted. Rubin looked miserable. "Yes, as she says, you can only know if the patient will respond to chemotherapy by giving it," he said. "It is possible she may not respond. If she responds, this may . . . it could give her many months, even years. The only thing to do is support her and see if she responds."

Once again Keen prodded. "We should mention the same people who follow her here will follow her at Coney Island."

Rubin nodded. "When she leaves here, that will be a good sign. Some of our doctors will follow her at our affiliate, Coney Island Hospital," he said. "With God's help we'll pull her through this."

As Kho interpreted this, Hernandez smiled. Her sister continued to weep.

Keen talked about the children and the need to make some formal arrangement for their care, even temporarily.

Then, for the first time, the family spoke. The children's father said, in English, "I can take care," he said. "They ask mother if that's what she wants. She says yes."

Keen asked Hernandez, "You don't want them to come see you?"

She nodded.

The brother-in-law, leaning on the windowsill, volunteered to take her to and from chemotherapy at Coney Island Hospital, before and after work.

Rubin said, "I hope it will only be a few times a month," he said. "Two or three times a month. She has to be there five hours."

Keen asked about telling Hernandez's own mother, but the brother-in-law said she suffered from high blood pressure. The news could be dangerous.

Keen asked Tarkovsky, who had been standing by silently, to discuss the health-care proxy. They gave the sister brochures in Spanish from an agency that helps children.

Keen said, "You can call on any of us for help. Me, Dr. Rubin, Dr. Tarkovsky."

Kho said, "And me," reminding them he was a doctor as well as an interpreter. He then repeated in Spanish Keen's offer to find someone to pray with them and stumbled on the word "*religioso.*" For the first time, Hernandez's sister laughed, as she corrected his pronunciation.

Keen looked at Hernandez. "We appreciate how brave and strong you are, but there will be a time you want to cry and carry on, and that's okay," she said. "At some point you'll want to tell the kids, and if you need our help with that, we can do that."

February 15, 2006
Daily Log—J.S.

Three days after the meeting with the Hernandez family, my cell phone rings. It is eight-fifteen in the morning. I am walking home from dropping [my son] Eli at school. It is Lisa Keen.

"Ms. Hernandez died," she says.

Once again that feeling of doom. Dr. Rubin was talking months and possibly years—everyone knew that this was overly optimistic, but I thought at least weeks. The family meeting took place on Monday, and now it is Thursday, and that young woman is dead.

Why am I surprised? She was so wan. And the next day, on Tuesday, when Lisa Keen and Dr. Tarkovsky were going to meet with Ms. Hernandez again, she canceled the meeting because she felt so sick.

Was it the chemotherapy or the illness? Lisa K. wondered.

This is one of those cases, Lisa K. said.

Her mother never saw her in the hospital, she said. Her children didn't come.

Lisa K. said Ms. Hernandez told the doctors she wanted to try everything to fight the disease. She wanted the chemo. Lisa K. was impressed by how earnest and responsible the young men were. Ms. Hernandez was not a beauty, but she had a sweet, eager smile—until she became too sick to smile. I remembered her pulling tissues from the box to hand to her sister, who was crying at the family meeting. The old woman in the next bed was hooked up to tubes.

They had to intubate Ms. Hernandez, Lisa K. said. Like the old woman. But it was the young woman who died in the night.

I told a friend the story of the family meeting, and she was touched, just as I had been. But did it matter to the family? Was that gathering—that acknowledgment of their collective and individual responsibility—important to them?

What will happen to the Hernandez children? Will they remember their mother? Was some part of her, as Solzhenitsyn wrote, "indestructible, some tiny fragment of the universal spirit"? Had she become part of the soul of Maimonides? Does a hospital have a soul?

Nothing—not even bad behavior or dirty floors—preoccupied Pam Brier as much as the area of patient care referred to as "pain management." At Maimonides the pain program was combined with palliative care and directed by Beth Popp, who had trained in oncology at Sloan-Kettering. Helping patients deal with pain strained the budget. Anesthesiologists in private practice, with a different reimbursement structure, could make money at it, but hospitals dedicated to pain management were forced to treat it as a luxury.

Alan Astrow often returned to the theme of the dictates of the payment system. "All the things that are really good—diabetes care, asthma care, taking good care of cancer patients—you don't get paid for that, no way," he often repeated in one form or another. "You get paid for radiating people, doing complicated surgery, giving them chemotherapy. That's what you get paid for. You don't get paid for taking care of people." What set him off that time was an article in the *New York Times*, about how diabetes centers were all going bankrupt. "Well, I could have told you that," he muttered. "People think doing good will lead you to doing well. Absolutely not!"

Brier and I had a long conversation about pain one day. It was a typical Brier tour de force, which began with a story about constipation. Specifically, she told me about a telephone call she'd made to Vincent Calamia, the endocrinologist who had taken on the thankless job of running Victory Memorial Hospital while the Berger Commission decided whether to close it. Calamia and Brier had a cordial relationship, quite different from the one she'd had with Victory's previous chief executive.

It was during this phone call that Brier declared to Calamia, "I want you to know I'm considered one of the great constipation experts in the borough of Brooklyn."

He was recovering from ambulatory surgery, which took place the day before Brier testified to the commission about the relationship between Maimonides and Victory. When she called to see how his recovery was going, he told her he wasn't feeling well.

"I presume, like everyone else in the world, you're having a lot of trouble with your bowels," she replied, and made a few suggestions on how to solve the problem (Metamucil regularly or Senokot-S; if more serious help was needed, "check with your doctor"). At the end of the conversation, he said to Brier, "I can't tell you how much better I feel," to which she replied, "Well, you're a doctor, can't you talk about this with your doctor?" According to Brier, he simply groaned.

"So the guy was constipated. What else is new?" she said. "I go on this seeming tangent because it is part and parcel of pain management. If you went down the hallway at Rusk [the Rusk Institute of Rehabilitation Medicine at New York University] and asked every single patient what their biggest problem was, they would tell you it's their bowels. But people just pretend like it isn't happening, and doctors don't talk about it with their patients. It makes me crazy!"

Pain, both its management and its side effects, had been part of her life for years. Every so often her narrow face looked frozen and her eyes glazed, as if she were holding in something fearsome. The pain had begun not, as I thought, with the accident but long before that, with flaring back pain in college. It wasn't until she was fifty that she learned she had an advanced case of scoliosis. Over the years she had tried it all, at the best hospitals: physical therapy, acupuncture, surgeries, and had dealt with a gruesome assortment of side effects, including nerve damage. She had taken revolting drugs that made her mouth feel dirty and painkillers that knocked her out or made her throw up. Percocet turned her into Mr. Hyde, she said, so out of control and obnoxious she decided she would rather be in pain.

Finally she found relief with an anesthesiologist who was director of pain management at NYU. Every eight to ten months, he injected Botox, the drug often used to relax facial lines, into her lower back. "It's not very pleasant and not all that scientific," said Brier. "He pokes around with his finger and tries to find the spasm, and when he does, he buries deep, marks it with a pen, and then sticks in the needle and wiggles it around to get the Botox in there. Very gross, and it does hurt. I must have very relaxed buttocks, I'm sure."

For the past eight years, she had regularly taken methadone. "To say I'm addicted to pain medicine is to state the obvious," she said. "David Cohen told me, 'You are so crazy to say you're addicted, because you're going to need it for the rest of your life.' No one in their right mind would bother to get addicted to methadone, by the way. It's not very pleasant."

She explained why she wanted this on the record. "Too many doctors are Calvinist and cover-your-ass-ish. I had a very good surgeon who called me and begged me not to take anything for pain. I just said, 'Don't you think there's some correlation between having your pain managed and being able to walk right away and walk so much? I am a hawk about it, and it has influenced what we do. This is a big problem and a big cause of dissatisfaction among patients. It is fundamental. So I have set money aside to begin a pain service."

I thought of a complaint about Brier—that she started many projects that couldn't be followed through because of lack of resources. As if she were reading my mind, she said, "I don't care if it can't be everything, but we will start where we can afford to start."

Pam Brier was one patient of Beth Popp, the hospital's specialist in pain management and palliative care. Another was the immigrant Chinese restaurant worker known as Mr. Zen. By early April eight months had passed since he was admitted to the hospital with a cancerous tumor. His unpaid medical bill had crossed the $1 million mark months earlier. His attachment to this earth was growing weaker by the day.

I began spending time with Popp and her team as they became a crucial part of the final phase of Mr. Zen's life. His arms had become skeletal; his eyes were large and haunted. The bones of his face stuck out in sharp relief against his black goatee and mustache. The only part of him that was thriving was the enormous tumor pressing on his pelvis. PLEASE WEIGH PATIENT DAILY, said the sign on the wall behind his bed, a reminder to check the growth or shrinkage of the appendage as a ratio of the patient's body size. A computerized PCA pump (patient-controlled analgesic) dispensing pain medication was attached to an intravenous line. Mr. Zen could push a button to release more of the drug when he was in pain, but he rarely did, even when he was suffering.

Popp had come by with Nagander Mankan, one of the Indian oncology fellows, a slender, dark-skinned man with a thick mustache, and Anita Kaminer, the nurse-practitioner who specialized in pain management and palliative care. Mankan said he believed that the tumor weighed somewhere between five and ten pounds. After he finished his oncology fellowship that summer, Mankan planned to move to Georgia, he said, where it was quiet.

Before entering the room, Popp talked to the team. "He has been in the hospital since August and has undergone all kinds of treatment," she said. "He has no family here, sends money to his mother and sister back in China. He communicates with his mother by cell phone and wants her and his sister to be his health-care proxy. His oncologist speaks Mandarin and he speaks Cantonese, so it's only a little better than me. Last time we had a speech pathologist who speaks Cantonese who translated. Mr. Zen's condition is getting worse. We will continue to treat his pain and keep him comfortable."

Kaminer, the nurse-practitioner, about to become a grandmother, wore flouncy skirts and shoes that looked like ballet slippers. She was an attractive woman who carefully tended her makeup and smooth, dark hair. She was a quiet, sympathetic presence at Popp's side. Kaminer told me the nurses were worried because Mr. Zen didn't use the PCA pump. He wore a pain patch that contained fentanyl, a narcotic to control severe pain; the patch had to be changed every three days.

"He's been amazingly stoic," said Popp. "He has a huge pelvic mass that's invading the nerve supply to his left leg. He doesn't have enough strength to walk. He won't be able to have surgery. He's had a variety of chemotherapy and been schlepped back and forth for radiation. Gregory Todd, his physician, said the patient is in terrible pain."

When we gathered around Mr. Zen's bed, he blinked his eyes in greeting.

Popp had asked the speech pathologist to interpret, but she hadn't arrived yet. In English, the physician asked Mr. Zen, "What is your pain?" A sign with cartoon faces calibrated a pain scale of one to ten. Smiling faces at the low end, sad ones in the eight, nine, ten area.

"Between eight and nine," said Mr. Zen in a weak voice, in English.

What was it before?

He barely opened his mouth. "Over ten," he whispered.

The sun poured in through the window.

He pointed to his hip. "It hurts here, a little," he said.

Popp nodded and asked if he pushed the button when he had pain.

"No pain," he said.

"When you lie in bed and aren't moved, do you have pain?"

Yes.

"Do you push the button when you have pain?"

No.

"If you have pain and push the button, you get medicine."

No.

"It doesn't help?"

No.

"So you don't push the button."

Yes.

The nurse-practitioner went to the computer in the hallway to make an entry, and the speech therapist arrived, a young Asian woman who had a long discussion with the patient in Cantonese.

"His leg really hurts him," she told Popp.

"Did the medicine we give him help?"

The interpreter nodded and turned back to Mr. Zen. After more discussion, she said, "He would like more medicine."

Popp said, "From yesterday to today, he pushed his button very few times. Why?"

The question was conveyed. "He says he did press it," the interpreter said. "I asked him if he knows what it is for. He said yes. He knows to press it when he is in pain."

The discussion continued for half an hour, and then the pain group stopped at the nurses' station, where Popp made an entry in the chart in neat left-handed script. She was wearing a new wig. Mr. Zen's chart was in a binder several inches thick. Eileen Keilitz, the floor nurse who had taken care of Mr. Zen since he arrived in the hospital the previous summer, came to talk to the doctors.

"Until very recently he wanted to do everything himself," she said. "For us, because we've been with him all the time, we've seen him through a long process. I can't imagine he would want to be in tremendous pain. Usually Chinese people are very stoic, but maybe it's the human being who doesn't want to leave planet Earth. Most times you say to him, 'How is your pain?' and he says, 'Okay, okay okay.' With someone like that complaining, he must be in excruciating pain."

Keilitz said sometimes she went into Mr. Zen's room and pushed the PCA pump button for him. "I know this defeats the purpose." She sighed. "He's supposed to push it. My concern is for him to be comfortable. We're his family now, in essence. You don't want to see them suffer."

The pain team left for another patient on another floor, a Pakistani woman in her early forties with metastatic breast cancer. She would be followed by a ninety-two-year-old Alzheimer's patient, tended by his son, who wore a yarmulke. Next on the list was a Jehovah's Witness from Jamaica, followed by an elderly Italian woman who didn't explain why she burst into tears when lunch arrived, mashed potatoes and meat.

As we left Mr. Zen's floor, Popp said to me, "I think the nurse was more or less saying, 'Nice for you to pop by for a half hour and have your opinions, but we've really been with this patient for almost eight months, and we know him.'"

The following Friday, Gregory Todd, the Kentucky convert to Buddhism who was Mr. Zen's attending physician, told Keilitz to go say good-bye to Mr. Zen. "I went in and put my hands on his head, and I said a little prayer over him," she said. "I didn't think it mattered what his religious or spiritual beliefs were."

Todd read to his patient from the Heart Sutra, a brief but fundamental text of East Asian Buddhism containing a mantra that addresses the quest for Perfection of Wisdom. Mr. Zen was not a religious man, but he had discussed Buddhism with the doctor. Todd told me he didn't know if Zen heard him as he read, "'Go, go, go beyond, go thoroughly beyond, and establish yourself in enlightenment.'"

"I'm not sure exactly what he knew at that point," he said. "We often believe people hear things when they are dying. That was the least I could do for him."

Eleven

The Big Brass Ring

If you want a happy ending, that depends,
of course, on where you stop your story.
—ORSON WELLES

I n the parallel universe of the hospital, many motives competed and collided. The desire to heal scuffled with ambition and exhaustion; the reality of sickness and death fed vague desires for eternal life through legacy. Buildings and pavilions were named for dead and living relatives, while the people who worked in them carved out little empires, not quite believing that nothing lasts forever. Almost every evening, somewhere in Borough Park, it seemed that someone was being honored for something, a plaque was being inscribed. Abraham Gellman, the young doctor killed in the previous century's World War II, smiled his Mona Lisa smile in perpetuity in the lobby of the wing that carried his name. The bronze bust of Lena Cymbrowitz, death by colorectal cancer, greeted patients at the Maimonides Cancer Center.

Yet the very mechanism of the hospital militated against the wish for permanence. Almost everything was transitory: length of stay, standards of care, payment systems, drug protocols, technology, patients, doctors, nurses, bosses, underlings—even the buildings themselves, as architecture and design tried to keep up with the fast-moving changes in medical theory and practice. In New York, as in other densely populated cities, the process of physical redesign was complicated by the scarcity of affordable real estate. Expansion often required grafting one building onto another, by going up, under, or around existing structures.

Spring came, and the anatomy of the latest addition to the main hospital was taking shape. One way I marked my year at Maimonides was by how high the girders had risen on the sleek, nine-story building that would contain an expanded emergency room, new surgical facilities, and a neonatal unit, plus attractive patient rooms. It was scheduled to open in early 2007 (a date that would be postponed). The construction had to swallow and reconfigure the Hortense and Jacob Aron Pavilion, a living example of visionary miscalculation. Completed in 1964 by a distinguished Manhattan architecture firm, Charles B. Meyers Associates, Aron was round, on the theory that a circular structure would allow nurses sitting at the center a 360-degree view of patient rooms. The design didn't anticipate the storage closets and elevators that obscured the 360-degree sight lines. This lack of foresight gave the building the dubious distinction of almost instant obsolescence. Month by month, bit by bit, the Aron Pavilion disappeared, an evaporating mirage.

Dr. Joseph Cunningham remembered what it was like to be the next new thing. Twenty-three years had passed since he was the prodigy from Manhattan, part of an earlier Maimonides effort to play in the big leagues, to reinvent itself as an academic center, not just a good local hospital. Bypass surgery and stents had revolutionized cardiac care; the hospital's ambitions were focused on heart doctors, the industry's superstars. At the time, 1982, Cunningham was forty-two years old, part of the heart team at New York University's medical center. These self-described "young Turks" trained under Frank Spencer, a legendary heart surgeon whose minions went on to become chiefs in many prominent hospitals.

Cunningham had been wary of me from the beginning. The first time we talked, he explained why he thought I should make the book a work of fiction. "Who wants their dirty laundry hanging out there?" he asked. He told me that after he'd been at Maimonides a few years, *Esquire* magazine had assigned a reporter to do a story about him. They met two or three times, in Cunningham's recollection, and then the conversation got personal. "I'd been married before, and I gave him crap about that stuff," Cunningham said. When the writer refused to agree to let Cunningham preview the article, the surgeon pulled out. "It became important to me that there were certain things about myself I didn't want exposed to the world," he said with a look I took as a warning.

I understood that this was a man who wanted to control his own mythology.

Cunningham told me he got a call from Edward Lichstein, Maimonides' chief of cardiology, who would become the chief of medicine, asking the heart surgeon if he would come to Brooklyn. Lichstein was the same man who, twenty-three years later, would deliver roughly the same message to Alan Astrow, just substituting cancer for heart disease: Too many patients were crossing the bridge toward Manhattan; Maimonides wanted to reverse the traffic flow.

Sitting in his big, masculine office with its sportsman's trappings, including the portrait of Hemingway and the boat, the *Swamp Fox,* Cunningham told me he had been intrigued by Lichstein's invitation for two reasons, one personal and one entrepreneurial. "I had been at NYU almost ten years, and I was forty-two," he said. "I had aspirations to be my own boss, to run my own show, to build something I could call my own. In your early forties, that's your first opportunity. Then, in your mid-fifties, you realize you're either going to stay or make yet another move. Where I am now, I can't go sixteen different places. At forty-two you are fearless because you have many avenues."

Assessing the situation at NYU, he recognized that his boss, Frank Spencer, was at an age where he wasn't going anywhere for a decade or more. Besides, Cunningham wasn't the only hotshot in the pipeline; he knew he wasn't going to jump in front of Wayne Isom, two years ahead of him. (Isom also left NYU. In 1985 he was recruited to become chair of cardiothoracic surgery by the New York–Cornell Medical Center, which would become New York–Presbyterian Hospital after the merger of the New York Hospital and Presbyterian Hospital.)

Cunningham told Lichstein he wanted to be not just chief of cardiothoracic surgery but chief of surgery as well. Lichstein agreed to his terms.

There was ego gratification on the one hand, profit potential on the other: Cunningham saw the chance to earn a good deal of money. "It was the glory days of reimbursement," he recalled. "We were all making nice bucks."

As he saw it, the situation was no-lose. "Maimonides had a failing cardiac program doing a hundred twenty-five cases a year with twenty-percent mortality rate," he said. "What made it easy was that I was already doing a lot of patients from Brooklyn, so I didn't have to come here and develop a new practice. The pie was so big you could slice it fifteen ways and everybody could still have plenty." By 2006, *Crain's Health Pulse,* a newsletter reporting on the health-care business, reported his annual compensation at just over $1 million. The mortality rate for coronary bypass surgery was well below 2 percent, not among the very best in the country but significantly better than the national mortality rate.

The doctor who introduced Lichstein to Cunningham was Israel Jacobowitz, who had trained as a resident at NYU under Cunningham and joined his surgery practice. In Brooklyn they thrived—until, like Sam Kopel and his former partners, they quarreled and disbanded. By the late nineties, Maimonides cardiac surgeons were doing as many as twelve hundred major cases a year, with Jacobowitz as the biggest producer. In the early eighties, Maimonides had also hired Jacob Shani, a former resident who had gone on to train at Beth Israel in Boston, to build cardiology. The hospital's heart program prospered, and eventually Maimonides was designated one of the country's "Top Ten Heart Hospitals" by Solucient, another company whose business was measuring cost, quality, and market performance of hospitals.

Like the Kopel-Bashevkin contretemps, the Cunningham-Jacobowitz split may or may not have been about money but it was certainly about the things that they believed money measures. "It wasn't money, it was principle," Cunningham told me dryly. "Izzy's the Rodney Dangerfield of cardiac surgery. In his mind he don't get no respect. No one can ever stroke him enough."

Yet, as usual, the trigger point had been division of the spoils. Cunningham and Jacobowitz had a third partner. No one disputed that Jacobowitz was the hardest worker; it wasn't unusual to stand outside the hospital at nine-thirty or ten at night and see him walk out and drive away in a pale blue Mercedes convertible. Nor did Jacobowitz resent Cunningham's smaller caseload, understanding that official hospital duties cut into his surgical volume. It was the proportion paid to the other partner, a friend of Cunningham's, that irked Jacobowitz. "It was an ultimatum: 'Either get rid of him or I'm out,'" said Cunningham. "Blood is thicker than water, so I said, 'Well, Izzy, see ya.'"

Jacobowitz left the hospital for a few years and then came back. Bygones were never bygone, however; every slight was recorded and remembered. The lines were drawn through the ranks: doctors, nurses, technicians, and administrators. Some were loyal to Jacobowitz, others to Cunningham. By the time I arrived at Maimonides, the heart doctors were in the midst of their own palpitations. Cardiac surgery, once the fastest-growing procedure, had dropped by 30 to 40 percent, giving way to less invasive remedies like angioplasty. The feud didn't help.

Jacob Shani, the cardiologist, became the heart star (he would be adopted by Brier as a personal friend), designer of the "Shani Right," a specially angled catheter used in angioplasties, the process of clearing clogged arteries. The Shani Right was designed to make a tricky journey, from the groin—where the catheter, a tiny tube, was inserted into an opening of a couple of millimeters or so—through the entrance to the right coronary artery, about a yard away.

Shani, an Israeli who didn't mind feeding gossip about the feuding doctors, cheerfully described the relationship between his group and his surgeon colleagues: "We were eating their lunch."

Cunningham had been replaced by Stephen Lahey as chief of cardiothoracic surgery, but the older doctor remained a power center of the hospital, with a full contingent of friends and enemies eager to adorn or desecrate the legends that grew around him. Remaining head of surgery and the hospital's senior vice president for strategic initiatives, Cunningham commanded respect and fear as he prowled the hospital in his cowboy boots, exuding king-of-the-jungle bravado, even as his allies and antagonists wondered when he would be ready to lay down his scalpel. "One of the most tragic things is to watch a great surgeon at the end of his career become a cranky old man," said Lahey. The new cardiothoracic chief of surgery continued to have a difficult time asserting his authority in Cunningham's old territory, a year after he'd been imported to Brooklyn from Massachusetts for a hefty price tag (*Crain's Health Pulse* reported him in the $1 million–plus category as well).

"Joe is a great figure—a phenomenal figure," Lahey told me. "I'm not saying he's a great man. I don't know about that. He is a tremendous character."

I replied, "But those things are quite different."

Lahey nodded. "They are quite different."

He added carefully, "I told him I respect him tremendously. But now it's my turn to put my imprint on this. He understood that."

That understanding didn't stop the feuding, which remained corrosive,

Lahey said. "I still hear doctors in the community say they won't send patients here because there's feuding, and 'If I send patients to one guy, the other one is going to call me up and say, "Why are you sending patients to him?" ' "

The feuding surgeons were almost perfect archetypes. Cunningham was Alabama molasses; his jabs were coated in sugar. ("It's a shame about Izzy, too, because he's a hardworking guy who's very talented, he just has this problem. . . ."). Jacobowitz was Brooklyn pastrami, salty, spicy, and apt to cause heartburn.

"If he were polished and slick and political, this wouldn't have happened," said Mark McDougle of Jacobowitz, whom the executive admired because he was a good and a fearless surgeon but who also was exasperated with his temper tantrums. "Izzy makes himself an easy target," said McDougle. "He gets angry, loses control, he's emotional."

Like Sam Kopel (and Jacob Shani), Jacobowitz was a product of the Holocaust, born in a refugee camp. He was wired, wounded, defensive. "I don't think I'd be off base saying Marty Payson and Pam Brier feel they owe some debt to Joe Cunningham," he said accurately. "I don't understand it. They weren't here since 1982. I have been. Maybe it's my ego, but I think Jacob Shani and Israel Jacobowitz have had as much to do with the growth of cardiac as Joe Cunningham. I think Joe is a good administrator. He can be charming. I guess along the way he developed the allegiance and support of a number of people from within the institution and the board."

Regarding Cunningham and Jacobowitz, Mark McDougle, the calm man from Ohio, had the diplomat's desire for a dispassionate approach, a rare attitude that made his office an oasis of reason. "There's a lot of bullshit in all the stories," he said. "In my opinion there's enough validity in what Izzy says for me to conclude he was unfairly treated. Whether it was unfairly this much"—he placed his index fingers an inch apart—"or unfairly this much"—hands wide apart—"I'm not going to quibble. These little games of personality are, in my opinion, truly pathetic. I know ultimately we're here to take care of the people who live here. Five years later, maybe ten, pick a number, we're all going to be gone. The idea is to set the place up to make it better than it is now."

No matter what actually transpired, that was almost always the idea, the aspiration, the hope: to make the place better. When Cunningham arrived for work in 1982, the Eisenstadt Pavilion was a construction site; Schreiber Auditorium was being built, and so were the cafeteria and the medical library. The office he'd been assigned was a mess. "Everything was pretty much a shell, plaster hanging off the walls," he told me, leaning back in the chair behind his big wooden desk, drawl caressing every phrase. "I remember the first day I got here, I walked into this office and there was an old desk here, a big cabinet that went ceiling to floor where the prior chief had kept everything from his liquor bottles to his textbooks. He'd been dead five or six years. I open the cabinet, and all this stuff falls out."

Cunningham unspooled his yarn with the patience and timing of the fisherman he was. "There was no welcome reception," he said. "I remember I went to the desk and I wrote in the dust, 'I . . . am . . . here.'"

Jay Cooper, the compulsive, aloof chairman of radiation oncology and director of the Maimonides Cancer Center, was there and not there. The cancer center's location, almost a mile from the hospital, made life difficult for the hematologic oncologists and surgeons who treated cancer patients in both locations. The radiation therapists, tied to their machines, rarely needed to visit the main hospital. Cooper seemed to like the separation, the clean slate, the ability to build an idealized institution removed from the hospital's grit and hurly-burly.

The radiation department in the basement reflected his desire for a calm, orderly process. His six medical physicists sat behind computers measuring the shapes and sizes of tumors and customizing the angles and intensity of radiation beams for each patient. It was like a temple down there: quiet and serene, unlike the bustle upstairs in hematologic oncology, crowded with patients coming for consults and chemotherapy.

Cooper, a thin man who always complained that he was getting fat, could seem uptight and out of touch. He was most at home with theory and analysis. But he did care about patients. I realized that one day when he had paused after an extended dissertation about something; I idly asked him whether it really was that big a deal for patients to go to Manhattan from Brooklyn—lots of people, including him, made the commute in reverse every day.

He cut me off. "You don't understand because you're well," he said impatiently. "If you're well, the trip, whether on the D train or by car, is an annoyance. If you're sick, if you're anorexic, if you have no will to live, if you're dizzy, if you're nauseous, if you're in pain—I could go down a longer list—then that trip is impossible."

At that moment his obsessive meticulousness seemed noble. And I couldn't discount the fact that he surrounded himself with good people. He had won the loyalty of someone like Bernadine Donahue, the radiation therapist whose talents were uniformly praised. It was hard not to like Donahue, who was as warm and natural as Cooper could be cold and awkward. She was that lucky combination of brains, compassion, and common sense, and she had been willing to follow Cooper from NYU to Brooklyn.

The cancer center was approaching its one-year anniversary. Many pieces were in place, many were not. The Breast Cancer Program covered prevention and treatment, from mammography to surgery; the children's oncology service was expected to move in over the summer. The radiation-therapy group was getting more patients but was not busy enough—despite the excellent medical credentials of Cooper and his team. Referrals remained slow, and the intensity modulated radiation therapy function remained on hold, as testing and analysis continued at Cooper's insistence. Despite the setbacks he kept repeating, "The good news is we're a lot further on than we were a month ago, and the bad news is we're not nearly where we want to be."

Lahey had recruited Joseph LoCicero III from the University of South Alabama, where he was chairman of surgery, to be director of surgical oncology. LoCicero came with a weighty résumé, studded with prestigious research and impressive academic credentials, including Harvard Medical School, director of the surgical clerkship program.

Yet almost everyone seemed to agree with Stanley Brezenoff's assessment: The cancer center needed another type of prominent surgeon, the medical equivalent of a movie star, someone who generated the kind of buzz that sold tickets. LoCicero was an academic heavyweight with a national reputation, but what did that mean to patients in Brooklyn? Another problem, in the ephemeral matter of star quality: LoCicero specialized in the depressing area of lung and esophageal cancer, where cure rates remained abysmal, not the happy-ending treatment medical centers liked to feature in their ads. And while LoCicero was indisputably distinguished, it was felt that Maimonides also needed a charmer, preferably in a discipline like breast cancer, with a relatively high rate of success—a surgeon with a golden tongue as well as golden hands, who could capitalize on the gratitude of his or her patients.

While waiting for this surgical pied piper to appear, Cooper had time to dream. One day he told me his hope for the center. "Suppose someone pulls their car into the parking lot and is going to get chemotherapy the next four, five days," he said. "I want a system where we say to them, 'We know you're not feeling well, you're slightly nauseated, and you have two kids who don't understand why mom isn't home making dinner. Tell us what you want tomorrow for dinner, and we'll arrange to have some restaurant to deliver it in take-out containers, and we'll put it in your trunk. Bring in your laundry, and we'll arrange for it to be dry-cleaned, and it will be back in your car when you go home. Need your car inspected by the Department of Motor Vehicles? Leave it with us, and we'll have the local service station inspect it and bring the car back for you.' "

As this inspiring fantasy poured forth, I concentrated on keeping my mouth from dropping open in astonishment. Cooper's relentless pursuit of perfection was admirable, but he sounded like a crackpot. *Have the laundry dry-cleaned? Have the car inspected?*

A mental split screen popped into my head: Cooper's utopian vision appeared on one half like a tidy television commercial; on the other half was Nella Khenkin's real-world existence, a dark, absurdist comedy. I'd spent hours with Khenkin, the cancer center's sole social worker, watching her try to obtain basic services for patients from the surreal tangle of bureaucracies that dictated medical care as it existed that spring—not in the ivory tower of Jay Cooper's imagination, but in the U.S. health-care system as it played out on Eighth Avenue at the tail end of Brooklyn's scrappy Chinatown, in the Maimonides Cancer Center, a converted check-processing plant across the street from an auto-body shop.

Many times I walked into Khenkin's small office to find her with her pale, fleshy hand pressing against her forehead, ear glued to the phone, able to talk to me for a half hour while she waited for an answer almost guaranteed to be unsatisfactory. Here is one example, among dozens, maybe hundreds, Khenkin could describe in her luxurious Russian alto:

"Patient came, and we are talking about bras and prosthesis she needs," said Khenkin. "I was calling HIP, and after forty-five minutes they finally picked up and transferred me to five different people and told me all the DME—'durable medical equipment'—should go through a special partnership organization not with them, with somebody else."

The story unfolded with the excruciating detail familiar to anyone who has suffered on the waiting end of a "Let me put you on hold, please."

"After spending so much time, I was supposed to call this other organization! I call this other organization, which is affiliated with HIP, kind of a management program. They told me they can't tell me anything, they need to get information and get back to me. They called me much later when the patient wasn't here, and told me the patient doesn't belong to the organization and I need to go back to HIP, who sent me there."

Khenkin didn't give up. "I can't even begin to start telling you about the frustrations that go with each patient when you need to get something for them," she said. "So far I didn't get what I'm looking for—simply, the name of the vendor agencies that are dealing with patients from HIP for this particular supply. Finally I got the name and the phone number late in the evening yesterday. I contacted them and"—she took a deep breath, as if girding herself for the finish—"the phone is disconnected and there is no such agency! So. This is the story."

Khenkin's office was a repository of such stories, miserable epics of organizational confusion so rampant it seemed deliberate. The insurance companies had become as insidious and detrimental to the national health as any illness was. The contractual obligation to cover illness and catastrophe had become submerged in a growing mountain of Catch-22's that seemed freshly minted to justify nonpayment.

"These insurances get worse and worse," said Khenkin. "Forget about it! Patient is falling apart, they would not send even a nurse, and forget about the aide. If we present patient is very weak and in pain and end stage of disease, they question to you why the patient is not on hospice. If he is so sick, he needs to be on hospice. If patient is not so sick, why do we need to send him a nurse? He should come to the doctor's office. No matter how hard you try, you can be as a fish on a frying pan. You can't justify unless there is an injection that should be done or he is diabetic, and even with this they want the patient to come to the doctor to save money, they don't want to send the nurse. Very frustrating, dealing with these insurances."

Khenkin found her work dispiriting at times, yet rewarding when she was able to awaken dormant compassion in a bureaucrat, or wheedle drugs from a pharmaceutical company's representative, or provide help in ways she hadn't anticipated.

She told me about a young Chinese mother who needed to come to the center for chemotherapy but was too tired to make the necessary arrangements. She asked Khenkin for help. "She has a job off the books in the nail salon, which she can't keep because she is so frail and weak," said Khenkin. "She can't take care of the child, and the child acts out. The child is constantly not in school. The mother couldn't explain the reasons and now needs to go to court. I believe after I put everything together and talk to the teacher, I will have to involve the lawyer.

"Someone tells me, 'I don't have food,' I arrange food," she said. "Or someone tells me, 'Nella, I forget stuff.' 'Did you have your MRI?' I ask. 'Do you know it's not cancer? If not cancer, let me send you to geriatric doctor to check for Alzheimer's or make a referral to adult health center.' Or sometimes it's just grab somebody I see crying and bring in here, and we cry together."

Khenkin was the heart of the place. She met regularly with a variety of support groups at the center: One for prostate-cancer survivors. Another for people undergoing treatment, or who have recovered. One simply called "the feelings group."

The feelings in all these groups ran the full gamut, pathos and humor, reassurance and resignation, guilt and accusation, fury and acceptance, advice and understanding. Here's an excerpt from one session I sat in on, names changed:

Richard, large man with mustache, new to group—he's here with his wife, Linda, ponytail, in her forties, and a friend in the back of the room, not at the table with everyone else, who forced Richard to come to the meeting. The wife is weeping, he's stoic. "I was diagnosed with colon cancer June twenty-fourth. I went for six weeks of radiation and then removed tumor and colon. I had lung cancer two years ago."

Linda complained about her husband's experience at the hospital. "The day before Thanksgiving, we were set for the operation, and they canceled it because they were busy," she said. "Twice they canceled the appointment on him."

Richard was unemotional. "I considered both cancers my fault. Lung cancer, I smoked all those years. Then with this one, I was supposed to get it checked when I was fifty years old, and I didn't. I didn't want anyone to poke around down there, and now I'm sixty-three years old and everyone and their mother are poking around down there."

Linda was more specific. "He was bleeding for four years. I'd find blood in the laundry, and I'd say, 'Ricky, what is it?' and he'd say, 'Piles.'"

Nella looked around the table in the conference room; eighteen people of various ages and backgrounds, common and uncommon feelings of submission, defiance, hopefulness, and despair.

"So anyone at this table feel like it was your fault?" she asked.

Richard replied in a brisk and businesslike way. "I did it. I had it. They got it. They took it out, and it's over with. I can't say, 'Why me?'"

Nella nodded. "You dealing with colostomy bag," she said. "How do you do it?"

Linda answered. "He can't do it. I do it."

She was talking about changing the colostomy bag, but she was also emoting for both of them. Richard could have been sitting at a card game.

"He says he's weak, but I think he's depressed," Linda continued.

"I have a nurse coming tomorrow, and she will show you how to play with this toy," Nella said. "People are afraid if someone bumps, it will spill, the smell."

Richard acknowledged, "I'm having trouble sleeping at night. I sleep all day. I'll get my energy back when I can sleep. I hate nighttime now. I look at that clock all night long, and they won't give me stronger medication."

Nella gently injected some analysis, which Richard batted aside.

"I think you're afraid of sleep, you're afraid of the disease," she offered.

"No," he said tersely. "I'm not afraid of sleep. I can't sleep."

From the back, his friend spoke. "I see Richard sleeping all day. I know he's depressed. He can't stand the bag. But he's a lucky man. He had lung cancer and survived, and now he had colon cancer and they got it out."

Richard's voice didn't change. "I know I'm lucky."

A large-boned woman with an angular, lined face looked at him. She, too, was a no-nonsense type who had earlier described her reaction to a breast-cancer diagnosis. "This happens to other people." She had advice. "My brother had a colostomy," she said. "Carry a match. It gets rid of the smell."

Another woman, sixtyish, small, chimed in, looking disapprovingly at Richard's friend sitting next to the wall. "When this man tells him to be grateful, I feel like when someone tells me, 'Look at the person with two amputated legs.' It doesn't make you feel better."

She had said she was treated for melanoma seven years earlier and was scheduled for a breast biopsy the next day. "I was a nurse, and I dealt with colostomy bags," she said. "It isn't the nicest thing. But please God give you the strength you need to change your own bag."

Nella took the cue. "We need to give you some help," she said to Richard, and then glanced at the woman who had just spoken. "But in the end you are saying it's his problem and he's the one who needs to deal with it. We need to deal with concrete situations. We will send a nurse and social worker to help you."

The small woman spoke again, offering one of those unexpected moments of grace with a tender ferocity. "I had keloid scars from when I was a kid and my mother was so judgmental," she said. "I was ashamed. Then, when I was married, my husband said that scar is a sign of life. Maybe one day instead of seeing that colostomy bag as an ugly, foul, and smelly thing, you'll see it as life."

Khenkin sensed that Jay Cooper found her methods too homespun. When she asked to take one of her groups to the family room, designed for private conversations, she was told no, because they were not allowed to eat there. "We are not animals," she said. "I tell myself I should not be upset by little things, but it hurts."

Another cultural divide loomed before her. Could she cross it, and did she want to?

Khenkin, who had been in charge of office celebrations, had planned an elaborate presentation for the staff holiday party, built around the idea of the birth of the cancer center. She bought a large stuffed cow, representing the milk supply for the new baby, and a Spider-Man doll to present to Jay Cooper, as protector of the baby, and other gifts for the "uncles"—Astrow and Huang. She bought a chess set for Kopel, the mastermind. When she presented her ideas for the center's staff holiday party to the planning committee, the group told Nella they worried that Cooper would think the gifts were too corny. Khenkin understood. She left the gifts under her desk and canceled the entertainment she had planned, a man who dressed as a big Gypsy doll and made people dance.

Several months later she still felt unsure about the direction the center was taking. They were preparing for National Cancer Survivors Day in June. The year before, Khenkin had planned the party, with an Elvis impersonator and music. Cooper had met with the center's directors and told them the program should be educational, that Elvis didn't set the right tone. Khenkin worried: Had they become so intent on luring more affluent patients, or those with better insurance, that they would forget their mission to serve the community? Their patients had enjoyed the Elvis party.

"Maybe we will need to wear a tie now," Khenkin told me. "I felt in the past my role was to get to every patient, but especially to those who are more in need, who are indigent, who do not have anything and I need to help them. Now I also learned that now we need to concentrate on people who have good insurances, to serve them better, and by serving them we will get money we can redistribute for other people. I'm learning new attitudes, but some things I can't understand. We need to find the happy middle. Sometimes I would agree we need to wear a tie, and sometimes I would be willing to take off the tie, to be closer to the patients."

Khenkin understood the need for change. She agreed with the decision to restrict the pharmaceutical-company representatives from freely wandering around the center peddling their goods, the way they used to (even though she risked losing a backchannel source for medicine some patients couldn't get any other way). She saw the value of adding a more professional veneer, just as she appreciated the design and comfort of the décor approved by the feng shui consultant.

But she worried about what might be lost. "I just don't want us to be too uptight," she told me. "We've come to another extreme. Now when I start talking to someone, they say, 'Write me a memo.' I don't need to write a memo for each little thing. I don't understand it. Maybe it's a new way of how people communicate. However, when you work with people, you can't do it all by e-mail. I believe we should find the middle. We should be with a smile, and we should be buttoned up and zipped up, but in an appropriate way. I'm afraid we might lose our soul."

The changes Khenkin was pondering at Maimonides had been happening everywhere. In the United States, it is the custom to mow down the old to make way for the new, but the pace had accelerated. Deference to the past had historically been left to the rotting empires of Europe and Asia, but now the bulldozers were ubiquitous, from Shanghai to Coney Island. Rents in Brooklyn were climbing, even in once-blighted areas like Bedford-Stuyvesant and Red Hook. Medicine, however, could be gentrified only so much. Yes, the technology was amazing. But the profession remained a peculiarly hands-on trade that required manual dexterity as well as a good mind, apprenticeship as well as academics, affability as well as ability. The skill to acknowledge and detect individual deviations from randomized trials required intuition as well as intelligence, a willingness to receive and pass along wisdom. Despite the push to standardize care, hospitals are very much creatures of their environments, tied to the customs and desires of their locales, the peculiarities and ambitions of the people who keep them running.

I once asked David Kho—the Spanish- and Chinese-speaking resident who was born in Singapore, raised in San Francisco, graduated from Columbia University College of Physicians and Surgeons—what he thought distinguished Maimonides.

"Giving people a second chance," he said, a twenty-seven-year-old doctor-in-training swiveling kidlike on a chair at a nurses' station during a break. "Making gold out of water, or wine out of water."

Could he explain that?

"It's one thing to take a lot of resources and transform it into a great hospital, which is how the Manhattan hospitals run, with a huge endowment, doing this for a couple of hundred years, getting the smartest doctors and best equipment," he said. "This place is the opposite of that. With barely any endowment, they cover really most of specialized care that any community could want; that's amazing to me. And to be profitable! Unfortunately, because of that razor-thin balance, the institution has a lot of insecurity. It is not the Manhattan hospitals. This place day to day has a lot of insecurity about where it's going."

Then he brought up a subject that had been nagging at Alan Astrow for months, as the hematologic-oncology chief tried to recruit full-time doctors for his staff. Who should the next generation be?

"A lot of the doctors here are osteopaths or trained overseas, in the Caribbean or Europe," Kho pointed out. "Most of the other hospitals in Manhattan, the doctors are trained in traditional big medical schools in the States. It is significantly more difficult to get a residency spot if you're from overseas. Here they take people who have a hard time applying for a job in Manhattan—not because they're no good, but there is built in discrimination against foreign schools. My point is, they take people that weren't regarded as being the top and turn them around and build this amazing place with people who wouldn't have been given a chance at many other places. They aren't this flashy, fancy, get-all-these-doctors-from-Harvard place, but they get the job done, and that's amazing to me."

But many of the new chiefs at Maimonides were flashy and fancy, and they wanted to mold the place in their image. Steve Lahey told me, "I trained at Brigham [and Women's Hospital, in Boston]. They take five residents a year, so they'll take one from Stanford, one from Duke, maybe one from MIT, and one other one, maybe the Midwest. My job is to make this place as good as that in attracting residents."

All winter Astrow had agonized over what kind of credentials should weigh most heavily as he picked members of the future team. Should he choose Mohammad Razaq, the Pakistani fellow who would demonstrate to the growing Pakistani and Muslim communities that Maimonides welcomed them? Or was the preferable choice Sam Kopel's man, Mendel Warshawsky, the yeshiva-trained South African cancer survivor? Maybe Warshawsky would lure the Orthodox community—the Bashevkin group's constituency—that had yet to show up at the cancer center in significant numbers? Astrow had also interviewed Yiqing Xu, a gentle, unassuming Chinese doctor he liked very much—a friend of Yiwu Huang's—who had trained at Ohio State and was living in Columbus. Jay Cooper made it clear that his favorite candidate was Petra Rietschel, a product of Harvard's Massachusetts General Hospital, currently at Sloan-Kettering. Rietschel was pedigreed—and intense and attractive and interesting. She was a German who had spent eighteen months after medical school working at Chris Hani Baragwanath Hospital in Soweto, South Africa, the largest hospital in the world, where more than half the patients were HIV-positive. She was in the middle of a messy divorce and custody fight and with visa issues that made living and working in Brooklyn appealing—but only on her terms. She was a tough negotiator.

Astrow finally decided on the two women, Rietschel and Xu. Then Kopel made an end run on behalf of Warshawsky, getting McDougle to agree to pay his salary separately from the hematologic-oncology budget, so the department got an extra oncologist.

Razaq accepted defeat graciously. "I didn't blame Dr. Astrow," he told me. "I know it wasn't his decision alone. I think he likes me, but there are other factors, people who think it's better to take people from the outside. I got a little upset, but I don't blame him."

Warshawsky, too, said he had no hard feelings. "I think Astrow's a nice guy. A very nice guy. He's just weak. I think he's worried that people don't take him seriously. He's always saying, 'I'm the boss here,' and trying to put his foot down to show he has the authority, and I think that comes because he really doesn't have it yet. I like him, I think he's a good guy, a good doctor, but I don't know if he's ready to take on this place. This is a very tough place. This is a really tough place. This is not a simple walk in the park here. This takes a Kopel."

But when I asked him if he saw a difference in Astrow from when they first met, almost a year earlier, Warshawsky nodded and blithely contradicted himself. "Oh, yeah!" he said. "He's much more authoritative, less meek. If you come through this place, you've got survival skills."

• • •

The cancer center continued to be a financial drain. Bill Camilleri, the administrator hired by Brezenoff and ignored by Brier, felt a noose tightening around his neck, squeezing forth the anger and helplessness of the unjustly condemned. "I defy anyone else to build this place the way I built it," he told me. "When I arrived here three years ago, we did not have drawings, a plan. We did not even have the property. We had a verbal agreement between upper management of HIP and upper management of Maimonides on a price of what the building would be. The people who worked in the building for HIP were not aware they were going to move, so the lease itself was a six-month process. HIP had nowhere to go, so they vacated only forty percent of the building at first; the rest didn't leave until March of last year, two months before the opening! We were still able to finish the construction in an occupied building. In less than two full years, we went from nothing to an operational building."

He was breathing hard. He had a reputation as a fighter but he looked like a weary munchkin, a short, stocky man with a thick beard and a tired heart. He was fifty-two years old, yet appeared to be a decade older. Just a few months earlier, he'd had what he called "a major cardiac event" but returned to work two weeks later. The heart defect that had dogged him since birth— tetralogy of Fallot, the "blue baby" disease—never let him rest. He'd changed his pacemaker sixteen times since the first one was installed when he was fifteen years old. He knew he needed a heart transplant; it was a struggle to walk back from lunch on Sixty-third Street, a block away. But he didn't have time.

Camilleri took stock of what had happened in the past year, positive and negative, in the building he'd brought into being. He ticked off a long list of accomplishments and frustrations: systems that had had to be installed, transferred, coordinated, or repaired—the electronic medical records, the lab, reimbursement coding for drugs and chemotherapy infusion, security, marketing, staffing, billing, food. The damn food. A year later, and they still hadn't found a kosher caterer who would come to Chinatown. So the elaborate plans for a comforting dining area had been downgraded to snacks out of vending machines.

He'd had to bat a few heads, and he would bat a few more if that's what it took to get the job done. He got things done. He finished the cancer center on schedule. When Astrow had his spirituality conference in the fall, Camilleri had turned unfinished space into a beautiful meeting room in record time.

It was all coming together, he told me. "The cancer center isn't a building but a program, and it's jelling. Hematologic oncology has recruited a couple of new physicians. Dr. LoCicero is coming on board. Volumewise, things are good; patient-mix-wise, in terms of insurances, not as strong as we'd like it to be. We still have our political issues with the Bashevkin group. We have lots of instances when patients don't follow instructions. We had a Chinese-speaking patient who spoke English and Chinese. He was told in English and in Chinese by a doctor not to eat when he came in for a PET/CT scan and he walked in eating a candy bar. He did it twice."

That kind of mistake would happen less often when they began the patient-navigator program, he believed. One of Douglas Jablon's patient representatives would soon take the job, to guide patients through the system from the minute they walked in the door.

A couple of years earlier, Camilleri told Sondra Olendorf, who had been a friend to him, "The writing is on the wall. Pam hates me." With everything he had done for the hospital, Camilleri had begun to hope the president would relent. Maybe she would recognize his merit, and he would be able to stay at Maimonides until he retired. There was so much he wanted to do! But events and signals over the last few months had led him to believe he should rethink his plans again. Pam Brier had never warmed to him. He had never been invited to her monthly meetings with Cooper, and she never picked him for a single committee he volunteered to be on. Now the cancer center was the albatross dragging down the hospital's bottom line, and he was the administrator.

Olendorf worried about Camilleri. "He did get the cancer center built, and that should be celebrated," she said. "But it's a slow start-up and an expensive one, and he's in this position where every budget meeting we're talking about the loss from the cancer center, the loss from the cancer center. I feel bad about that."

The single-minded doggedness and self-reliance that were virtues during the building phase had sometimes made him seem truculent when he had to deal with daily administration. "He has irritated people," Olendorf told me. "There have been too many fights. Fight with information services, fight with some of the doctors, fight with some of the construction people. He is so proud he didn't reach out often and early enough to other people for advice. He is strong-willed. In nursing he wanted to fire everyone in hematologic oncology, and I said, 'Get them some specialty training, give them a chance.'"

She wondered if the organization hadn't set him up for failure. "We didn't welcome him here with open arms," she said. "Not anyone. Stan met him and hired him on the spot and just sort of let us know he'd hired an administrator for the cancer center, and then Stan left. Bill, poor guy, innocently enough kept bumping up against people's ideas of how things should go."

Mark McDougle had supported him and protected him, but not long after Camilleri returned from work following the heart incident, McDougle took him out for dinner and told him they were bringing in another administrator. Just to help, McDougle assured him. Camilleri chose to believe McDougle when he said that the new person—Jill Patel—was to be his partner, his helper, not his replacement. After all, Camilleri said to me, would Pam Brier want to take a fifty-two-year-old person who did an excellent job, who had a serious heart condition and needed a heart transplant, and tell him to go out and die? If that is what she wanted, she would have to make it happen, because he had no intention of leaving.

Brier had only recently turned serious attention to the cancer center. Brezenoff had hired Camilleri just before Brier was scheduled to become chief executive. Then the accident. By the time she was beginning to feel back in control at the hospital, McDougle had been hired. He was interested in the cancer center, so Brier let him be the point man. But her pet project, the free colonoscopies, had gone nowhere for almost nine months after she'd made the big announcement at the cancer center's opening. So she added that program to David Cohen's responsibilities, and things started to happen.

In February the hospital held a press conference, and Brier was asked to go on early-morning television to talk about the program. She bought a new scarf. The phones started ringing. Within a month several hundred people had signed up for the rectal screenings. "It was amazing," Cohen told me. "We've had a lot of younger people calling and saying they want the test, and we say, 'No, unless you're in a high-risk group.' As soon as people hear there's something you can get for free, they want it. Even if it is a colonoscopy."

I asked Brier how she felt about the largesse now, in a tough budget season. She said she chose not to worry about the financial ramifications. "Most people, I suspect, will have insurance, or we will make them eligible," she said. "It's the undocumented who will have a tough time. But I can't believe you couldn't call discovering colon cancer an emergency, and you could certainly get the surgery covered. But we'll treat those people. You know what? It's going to be fine. I'm sanguine about it. I don't think Bob Naldi loves it. But it's already generated so much positive goodwill, and it's a good thing to do. I think it's good for us to be known as the hospital that walks the extra mile and really cares about patients in the community. I love to be able to say that and not have it be words. You know me. I'm into that. I love this! I love this!"

David Gregorius had made his peace with Brooklyn, he told himself that spring, and with the cockroaches, with living three thousand miles away from Jenn, with shifts that were routinely so busy he might go fourteen hours without eating or drinking anything. He had come to appreciate the local community doctors who insisted on being called when one of their patients was admitted, even if they complained about it at 4:00 A.M., a phenomenon he had not experienced at other hospitals. He told me, "After I've dealt with Maimonides for a year, if you cut me loose in a little ER in western Nebraska by myself, I'd be competent, actually. A year ago I was a med student, and the first day of internship it's eyes wide open, especially in this ER. Now I feel comfortable."

Then John Marshall, his program director, forwarded all the residents an e-mail he'd received from the medical center at Loma Linda University in Southern California. There was an opening for a second-year resident.

Davey clicked onto the Loma Linda Web site and saw a picture of a curved white building set against a blue sky, palm trees, flowers, in a place romantically called "the Inland Empire."

> Loma Linda University and Medical Center are located in a vast metropolitan area east of Los Angeles known as the Inland Empire. It is considered to be the crossroads of Southern California. The beaches of Newport, Laguna, and Malibu are only 60 to 90 minutes to the west, with superb swimming, sun-bathing, surfing, and sailing. Also 60 minutes to the west is downtown Los Angeles, with its top-quality restaurants, world-renowned museums, opera, theater, and other cultural opportunities. . . .

Gregorius was the only resident from Maimonides who applied for the spot. Still, he didn't know if he would be accepted; he had heard that more than thirty people from around the country were competing. He told me he didn't have his hopes up, but he felt he had to try. He said he could never feel truly happy in New York. He and Jenn were game, but it was hard to have a bicoastal relationship. And sometimes he thought Maimo might just kill him.

That spring came, another e-mail brought another promise of change—this one from a headhunter hired by Maimonides, looking for oncology surgeons. One reply looked like it could be the answer to management's prayers for the cancer center. Patrick Borgen, a forty-eight-year-old surgeon, chief of the breast service at Memorial Sloan-Kettering, said he—he himself, not one of his underlings—was interested in coming to Maimonides. Borgen was said to have star quality plus: the résumé, the charm, the experience, the patina of Sloan-Kettering, and a large Brooklyn clientele who now traveled to Manhattan to see him.

Jay Cooper was so excited he forgot science and fell back on ancient superstitions, refusing to mention Borgen's name. "I don't say the person until I see a signed contract," he told me. "Someone said, 'You mean that person is not coming?' That person told Pam he's coming. That person told Marty Payson he's coming. That person told me he's coming. However, I haven't seen a signed contract, so I don't believe it yet. When I have a signed contract, until he shows up the first morning, I won't believe it. And if you show up the first morning, I still won't believe it, but if you show up after lunch, I'll begin to accept you are really here."

I admit it. I was elated at the prospect of Dr. Borgen swooping in to save the day, just as I was approaching the end of my year at Maimonides, even though I knew that happy endings were as fleeting as everything else. As Orson Welles put it, in a parenthetical note at the very end of the screenplay for *The Big Brass Ring,* a labyrinthine thriller that was never made into a movie: "If you want a happy ending, that depends, of course, on where you stop your story."

In Jewish tradition, endings were never really endings. Stories in religious texts never stopped but became fodder for endless commentary and analysis, which were often relayed in the form of additional stories. At Maimonides, as in any community, the past, present, and future were linked by these individual narratives that connected in obvious and mysterious ways, one ending beginning yet another story.

Later, after I'd stopped going to the hospital almost every day, Lili Fraidkin offered a commentary on the events that were unfolding at the cancer center. It was her cancer story.

In the summer of 2001, on the eve of September 11, in retrospect a time of innocence, Fraidkin was diagnosed with adenocarcinoma, a form of cancer that can be found in many organs. Fraidkin's was in her uterus. The cancer was slow-growing but had advanced to the lining of the uterus, raising the fear of metastasis to a serious pitch, because Fraidkin had been too busy to take time out for her annual visit to the gynecologist.

Fraidkin knew she wanted the surgery done laparoscopically, a capability Maimonides didn't have at the time. She didn't plan to tell anyone at the hospital, but before she could make arrangements, Pam Brier walked into her office and gave her the name of a doctor to call at Mount Sinai. "She eavesdropped," Fraidkin told me. "Then she personally paid for my daughter to fly in from Vegas, first class, the first time my daughter ever flew first class."

The day Fraidkin returned from the hospital Brier appeared with her driver and four big trays of food. During the week people from the hospital started dropping in. One morning Fraidkin got a call from Joyce Leahy, the hospital's lawyer, saying she couldn't come to see her that day—could she come tomorrow? "Joyce Leahy?" Fraidkin remembered thinking. "We say good morning every day, that's it, and now, 'I was going to come to see you—is it okay if I come tomorrow?'"

Then it hit her. Brier had assigned everyone on the executive floor to visit Fraidkin.

Fraidkin told me the arrangement wasn't Brier's only response to Fraidkin's illness. "That week she announced at the staff meeting, 'I want every one of you females to see your gynecologist this month. No delays,' and on and on with the smears and the breasts," Fraidkin told me. "'This happened to Lili, it can happen to you,' were the words she used. And then she tells the men, 'You men might as well have your prostates checked.' She even had a town-hall meeting about two or three months after that. I was sitting there, mortified. She just went on this preventative-medicine campaign that boggles the mind."

Fraidkin would never stop missing Stanley Brezenoff, and sometimes she felt shut out by McDougle and Brier. But for a slender woman, Brier exerted a mighty grip. "That's my cancer story," Fraidkin told me. "And my Pam story."

It was also a warning story.

Fraidkin had had an incredible experience with the surgeon from Mount Sinai recommended by Brier. Fraidkin was so impressed that when he came in to check on her the morning after the procedure, she asked him, "Would you consider going to Maimonides?"

Her daughter protested. "Mom!" she wailed.

Fraidkin smiled sweetly at the doctor. "This is what I do, honey," she snapped at her daughter. "Back off."

She learned that half the surgeon's patients were from Brooklyn and that he was interested in splitting his practice between Maimonides and Mount Sinai. He and his partner met with Brier and Howard Minkoff, chair of obstetrics, and with Cunningham, she said. They made a deal, did a blitz in the Jewish papers.

And then? "We waited and waited, and waited and the patients never materialized," said Fraidkin. "This was a major cancer surgeon, and they didn't want people to know they had cancer. Those same patients who lived in Brooklyn, they all chose to see him in Manhattan."

He stayed a year, and then he left.

"They don't want the world to know," said Fraidkin, referring to the Borough Park patients, the Orthodox specifically. "When you come to Maimonides, the world knows. Their world knows."

What if Patrick Borgen, chief of the breast service, Memorial Sloan-Kettering, signed the contract and came to Brooklyn? Would he prove to be the keystone for Sam Kopel's ambition, the big brass ring, the happy ending, or a disappointing indication that all their assumptions about the cancer center had been wrong?

"If you want a happy ending, that depends, of course, on where you stop your story."

Twelve

Medical Advances and Retreats

. . . it struck Oleg that Shulubin was not delirious, that he'd recognized him and was reminding him of their last conversation before the operation. He had said, "Sometimes I feel quite distinctly that what is inside me is not all of me. There's something else, sublime, quite indestructible, some tiny fragment of the universal spirit. Don't you feel that?"

—From *Cancer Ward* by aleksandr solzhenitsyn

Evening approached. From the boardroom's fifth-story view, Brooklyn appeared to be a sea of green, shimmering in the heat of a summery Monday; the temperature had climbed to near ninety degrees that afternoon. The hospital brass and directors were arriving for the June board meeting, which Marty Payson and Pam Brier had agreed would be an upbeat gathering.

As Payson headed toward the podium set up at the front of the room, I overheard Brier tell someone that Marty Markowitz, the Brooklyn borough president, was in the hospital. Heart trouble; he needed a stent.

Mark McDougle was standing outside the door, talking urgently on his cell phone. When he walked in, Brier glanced at him and raised her eyebrows. He gave a brief shake of his head, indicating no.

The meeting began after the board members had a chance to seat themselves at the large conference table that almost filled the room, set for dinner with flower arrangements. Payson said the construction was going well, that the sleek, glassy building was a symbol of the new Maimonides. He discussed the cancer center in glowing terms, glossing over the $8 million operating loss. "We've been seeing red ink for a year and a half, and one of our challenges will be to see red go to black," he said. "But I believe that five, ten years from now the cancer center will parallel the main institution."

Next a cheerful physician gave a frightening report about dangerous infectious diseases. Then Brier spoke. "News bulletin," she said. "The borough president is a patient here. It's all over the Internet. He chose to come here Saturday afternoon and is doing extraordinarily well, treated by Dr. Shani. Who knows, that may be another advertisement."

She pointed out that Maimonides had just been featured prominently in the *New York Times;* the previous week the Metro section had displayed a front-page article under the headline SPOONFULS OF CULTURE HELP MEDICINE GO DOWN, about Bing Lu's Chinatown clinic. Then board members watched an *NBC Nightly News* report about overcrowding in emergency rooms, with the Maimonides ER front and center. Carl Ramsay, the ER medical director, offered the national television audience a perfect doomsday quote.

Marty Payson leaned over and whispered to Brier, mischief on his round face, "Couldn't they have done the birthing center?"

After the video clip, Brier reported that *New York* magazine had just published its annual list of "Best Doctors," and Maimonides had the biggest representation of any hospital in Brooklyn. Then, irrepressibly, she deflated the moment. "Ask me what goes into the Best Doctors list, and I haven't the vaguest idea," she said to the board, as though talking to herself. "Many great doctors aren't on it, and I know at least one who is on the list who is deceased."

She announced that Joe LoCicero was just about to sign his contract and dropped a big hint about Patrick Borgen ("a top breast surgeon from a leading cancer hospital in New York" may be arriving).

"Why would he want to come to Maimonides?" a board member asked.

Without pause Payson answered, "He's in his forties, he can build his program; it's a career change to get out of a corporate culture to a culture where he can treat patients the way he wants."

Brier gave a brief report on Victory, acknowledging that Maimonides' investment had not produced the hoped-for results. The turnaround plan hadn't worked; the failing hospital's discharges were lower in May than in the previous year.

Payson chimed in, "We went there as a defensive move, and that has worked," he said. "Some goodwill came out of it, but not a heck of a lot. Our future is in modernization and recruitment of world-class doctors. Regarding Victory, I have zero regret. We were right to do it, but there is a limit to what we want to do, and we have reached that limit."

A board member complained about the lack of coordination that kept patients languishing in the emergency room. Sondra Olendorf knew that the man's elderly mother-in-law was a patient in the intensive-care unit, languishing even as her son-in-law spoke. The patient's doctor had ordered a CAT scan at nine that morning and now it was 7:00 P.M. and the CAT scan still hadn't been done. Olendorf said that she wanted the problem fixed before the meeting was over.

Her beeper alerted her as excuses poured in. The ER was exceptionally busy that night, and once again they were short of beds, so everything was backed up, they said. Olendorf wasn't interested. Out of earshot, the hospital's top nurse got someone on the phone and said quietly but with unmistakable intent, "I want to be able to take this board member to see his mother-in-law after this meeting is over and she will have had her CAT scan and be back in bed!"

As the discussion of the emergency-room situation wound down, Sam Kopel announced that the intensity modulated radiation therapy function was up and running at the cancer center.

Mark McDougle spoke after that. "The bad news is that Bill Camilleri has decided to resign," he said. "Now that the cancer center is built, it's time for him to take care of his own health issues."

Brier stared across the large conference table at McDougle, a strange expression on her face. "Bill almost always comes to board meetings," she added in an odd, wandering voice. "He's very quiet. He was the brains behind the brick and mortar. He was hired because he was an expert in building cancer centers, and he didn't disappoint us—in that respect."

"In that respect."

Brier was annoyed with Camilleri. She had planned a proper, official farewell, and he chose not to show up—even after she sent Mark McDougle out of the room to call Camilleri and tell him to get over there.

Camilleri had no intention of accepting public praise from Brier, not after she had pushed him out. Earlier that month McDougle had given him the news, though Camilleri wasn't fooled. He had every intention of wrapping things up at the cancer center before he left, but he would not be part of a show for the board of directors—not even to help McDougle, whom he felt had tried to be fair to him.

"Mark called and tried to talk me into going, and I said, 'Pam doesn't want me there,'" Camilleri told me later. "Mark said, 'Everyone wants you there to say good-bye,' and I said no. No! That was a political decision on my part. Pam, for the first time in a year, would have put her arm around me and said, 'We'll really miss you,' and I didn't want to give her that photo op."

The board meeting was only the first stop in the busy evening Brier had planned for herself. She invited me to come along. As we left the boardroom around 8:00 P.M., the hot, bright sky softened into pink dusk. We headed over to Gellman, to the windowless intensive-care unit, where day and night were indistinguishable, so Brier could say hello to Marty Markowitz. We were joined there by Marty Payson.

Markowitz was wan and scared-looking, his usual bounce flattened. But he mustered strength to make a joke about needing a glass of wine. His wife tried to smile. She was pretty, despite tired lines, her graying hair pulled back into a ponytail. Payson told the politician that he, the hospital chairman, had been in this same ICU twice after having heart stents put in, and now he was fine. Brier said she would try to do something about the heat; the air-conditioning was on the fritz.

After a few minutes, Brier and I left. As we walked out of the ICU, past the elevators, Brier glanced at the door of the room reserved for the Orthodox volunteers, the Bikur Cholim, Guardians of the Sick. The door was covered as usual by scuff marks. She pulled out her cell phone and called Derek Goins, the senior vice president for facilities and building operations.

"I am standing by the Bikur Cholim room, and I am indignant," she said. "This door is filthy. I want it painted, and in high gloss, because it cleans better." She closed the phone and forced a pleasant look. "Not to micromanage," she said lightly.

Our next destination was a high-school gymnasium for a meet-the-doctor evening sponsored by Maimonides and Kingsbrook Jewish Medical Center and the Crown Heights Hatzolah. Steve Lahey would be speaking about heart disease and its prevention. Sitting in the back of her black town car, Brier said to me, "Rarely does Douglas not do things perfectly, but we should have advertised this as a partnership with Kingsbrook," she said. "When I mentioned this to Douglas, he was scrambling to get a banner with both our names on it. Hah!"

She leaned forward to give instructions in halting Spanish to Freddy, the driver substituting for Leon, the Russian who was usually at the wheel. As we drove through quiet residential streets lined with two- and three-story brick houses, Brier mentioned that Rebbetzen F. had given her a cheesecake to celebrate Shavuot, the Jewish holiday commemorating the giving of the Ten Commandments to Moses at Mount Sinai. It was the custom among observant Jews to eat a dairy meal.

How was the cheesecake? I asked.

"Delicious," Brier replied.

Not a moment later, unprompted, she confessed.

"I gave away Rebbetzen F.'s cheesecake," she said. "The last thing Peter and I need is another cheesecake in the house." Then she told me she had mentioned the rebbetzen not because of the cheesecake but because when Brier had seen her on the street the other day, the lady asked, matter-of-factly, "How is the recruitment of Dr. Borgen going?"

There were no secrets in Borough Park, Brier said.

How *is* the recruitment going? I asked.

Brier said she thought it was going well. After her last meeting with the breast surgeon from Sloan-Kettering, he sent her a bouquet of flowers. But they were still negotiating.

The car pulled up next to the curb at our destination. As we got out, a man with a beard and yarmulke snapped photographs of Brier. Her maroon silk jacket became incandescent in the flashes of light.

A crowd was waiting in the school's gym, which had been divided by an accordion gate into a men's section and a women's section. There was a banner, containing the names of both Maimonides and Kingsbrook.

Folding chairs faced a large picture of the late Rabbi Menachem Mendel Schneerson, beloved descendant of the Chabad-Lubavitch dynasty. A heretical thought: This crinkly-eyed, white-bearded man, in another setting and another season, wearing red and white instead of all black, would have made a convincing Santa Claus. Here, though, Schneerson's legacy was serious business: He was believed by many of his followers to be the Messiah; the Lubavitchers had yet to choose a successor.

Jablon, who was pacing in the back of the room waiting for Brier, whispered to me. "Did Pam see the banner?" he asked. He glanced at his watch. "Oy, I have four weddings tonight after this," he said.

Brier stared at the thicket of black hats between her and the podium. At 9:05 she shuffled through the crowd of Orthodox Jews and one black man, Mathieu Eugene, a Haitian-born physician who was running for city councilman. As she stood at the podium, in front of Rabbi Schneerson's portrait, the angle between them made it appear as though the rabbi's uplifted hand was just above the hospital president's head, giving her a benediction as she gave one of her convincing stump speeches. "I have this goal of stamping out colon cancer in Brooklyn. . . ."

The applause continued as she concluded and walked halfway down the men's side of the gym, taking a seat next to an Orthodox man in a black hat. No one revealed displeasure, if any was felt.

Jablon, watching with me from the back, saw the faux pas and whispered. "She's the only woman in the world who can do whatever she wants here," he said.

As Lahey began his presentation on early detection and prevention of cardiac disease, Brier looked around and abruptly rose and made her way to the other side of the partition, where she took a seat and whispered with some of the women. After a few minutes, she glanced back at the always-waiting Jablon, who immediately came to her side to pull her away, as she apologized for having to leave.

Next stop: Flatbush. The son of a Hatzolah boss was engaged to marry, and there was a party at Hatzolah headquarters, a building with five large doors to accommodate ambulances and a sign: DEDICATED BY MAIMONIDES HOSPITAL. Another sign said ME'HITZAH, meaning "the women's entrance." Brier and I entered there.

Upstairs we found a large room packed with tables laden with dried and fresh fruit, pastries, and large bouquets of flowers. On one side of a partition, men danced in a circle to klezmer music played on a keyboard, while on the other side, women in festive shirts and jackets and long dark skirts, verging on fashionable, ate and talked. The groom's mother, a small woman wearing a honey-colored wig, greeted Brier, who asked her hostess how many children she had. "Nine," she said with a laugh. "I iron fifty-five shirts a week—six boys."

Brier bit into a piece of dried fruit and ate half a cookie, wrapping the remains in a napkin, which she deposited on a table. After a bit more chat, she said it was time to leave. On the way to the car, we saw Elliot "Lazer" Rosman, of the Borough Park Hatzolah, standing in the mist. A light, warm rain had begun to fall.

Brier told him that Marty Markowitz had been admitted to the hospital for a couple of stents.

"He could lose a couple of pounds," Rosman said.

On the way back to the hospital, in the intimacy of the dark, I asked Brier why she never talked about her father. I had heard about her eccentric mother and her crazy aunts, about her past and present husbands and their other wives, about her daughter and her daughter's girlfriend. I knew that Brier was an only child. She'd told me her parents were first cousins, who had met during World War II.

"My father?"

She sounded surprised but answered.

"I was thirteen when he left, and before that I didn't see him much, because he lived in other places," she said without inflection. "He was an entrepreneur, and we didn't know what he was doing. I'd get little postcards from him from Russia saying he was selling Sony transistor televisions. He lived in Uganda for a long time and convinced the government he should set up a television station that would broadcast in four different dialects. Ultimately they kicked him out of the country for being Jewish. He lost everything, but that's the way life is. He was a very interesting man, very driven, but I didn't see that much of him."

Her face faded and reappeared as we drove past lights on dark, quiet streets. "He moved to western Australia, lost a lot of money on the Australian stock market, and ultimately moved to Maui," she said. "He had just set up another TV station, sort of was getting back on his feet, when he died. He must have been in his seventies."

She fell silent, and I asked her what it was like after her parents split up. Did she see him then?

"Not much," she said, her voice revealing nothing. "He married right away, a younger woman, a physical therapist from Iceland. The only person I ever knew from Iceland. There isn't that much to tell about him. I remember one night when he was in town, we had dinner at the Beverly Hilton with the education minister from Uganda, who was assassinated about six months later. There were always weird things circulating around my father. There was an air of excitement with him I would sometimes catch when I spent time with him. But if I saw him twice a year, it was a lot."

The approaching bright lights of the hospital put an end to her dutiful recollection. The woman who seemed unable to keep secrets had the politician's gift: She could at once be transparent and elusive.

It was ten-fifteen. She had more than an hour to kill before the eleven-thirty meeting she'd scheduled with the night-shift environmental workers and their bosses to discuss cleaning procedures and why they weren't working.

"Let's go visit Marty Markowitz again," she said. On the way back to the ICU, she leaned over and picked up a soiled towel that was on the floor next to a leaky pipe. She handed it to a nurse, who told the hospital president to go wash her hands. Another nurse complained that she was sweating; could Brier do anything about the air-conditioning?

We found Markowitz alone, slack-jawed in his hospital bed. Brier apologized again about the heat and then assured him that he would go home the next day.

His laugh was hollow. "I'll go home and face my future."

Brier understood. "To tell you not to have stress is like telling you to fly to the moon," she said. "I love my stress."

He sighed. "When I think of what you and Peter went through . . ." The recognition of mortality lay in the unfinished sentence.

Brier changed the subject and asked him to tell us how he'd met his wife. He obliged. Neither of them had been married before, he said, when they met seven years earlier. He was fifty-four, and she was forty-two. "Three dates later we were engaged," he said, smiling.

He looked at me apologetically. "I'm sorry," he said. "I didn't catch what you do at the hospital."

Brier introduced me again, this time more formally.

For Markowitz the presence of a writer taking notes had an adrenaline effect. He immediately sat up in his bed and began a politician's spiel.

"The hospital is a microcosm of Brooklyn," he said enthusiastically. "All the languages, the religious and ethnic backgrounds! Before the new cancer center opened—state-of-the-art, by the way—this borough, a city of two point four million—no, two point six million—people didn't have a cancer center."

Even his color seemed to improve.

"This hospital is an independent entity," he said. "The last of the Mohicans! Not a Manhattan-channeled health institution, an outpost of the mother ship! This is the mother ship and the satellite all wrapped up in one!"

Laughing, Brier patted Markowitz on the arm. "You can stop, Marty," she said, and told me we should go.

As we left, she offered him a final reassurance. "Once you get past this, you'll feel better."

On the way to the conference room on the executive floor, she stopped to scold a technician for not wearing her identification badge. She approached three nurses, talking in the hallway, wearing the standard baggy slacks and shapeless patterned blouses. They looked startled at the unexpected apparition, a blond woman in an elegant silk jacket, who planted herself in front of them and said, "Hi there. I'm Pam Brier, president of the hospital."

When we arrived at the conference room, fourteen workers were waiting for her, along with the men they reported to, including Derek Goins, senior vice president of operations; he told Brier someone would paint the Bikur Cholim door first thing in the morning.

The night cleaning staff was mostly black and Hispanic, but there were a couple of older white men and one woman. They sat quietly at the table, eyes on the president.

"I know how hard it is to keep this place clean," Brier began. "First, I wanted to say thank you and to tell you we are going to invest five hundred thousand dollars on environmental staff, to make sure every shift gets help. The hospital isn't clean enough, and one of the reasons is that we've greatly increased the number of patients and not the number of you."

Almost everyone nodded.

"If any of you have ideas on how to improve things, share them with a supervisor," Brier said.

One or two people spoke up, mainly to confirm the need for more staff. None of the workers seemed to know what they were expected to do in this circumstance, but a few of them approached Brier afterward with suggestions.

The next morning Brier called me to let me know a painter had begun to clean the Bikur Cholim door. She said he told her he had painted the door three weeks earlier. "It had gotten dirty again so fast," she mused. Then, as she was about to hang up, she said, "I must apologize to Derek."

Five days earlier I had spent the morning on Gellman East with Margie Morales, a member of the environmental "study-action" team, a subgroup of a DLMC (departmental labor management committee), the labor-management experiment of consultant Peter Lazes. The team was charged with finding better ways to keep the place clean.

Morales, a substantial woman with a shy, eager manner who wore her hair pulled back, had offered to let me follow her around as she cleaned rooms. She was using the Seven-Step Cleaning Procedure the team had developed after interviewing fellow workers and visiting other hospitals.

She told me the hospital's unchecked stream of visitors was the biggest impediment to cleanliness. The other major problem was staff resistance. "Before, the men mopped and the women picked up the garbage," she said. "Now we're all doing the same jobs, forming a concept of teamwork so it's not a man's job and not a women's job. A lot of people don't want to make the change."

We entered an empty room, and she began to go down the Seven Steps checklist. "First thing you do is ask, 'What's here that doesn't belong here?'" she explained. "Remove it if there's a newspaper on the floor or old flowers on the sill, remove it before you do the shine. That's our first S. Sorting the unwanted from the wanted."

Morales, who told me she had three children between the ages of seventeen and eleven, had worked as a secretary and a bookkeeper before she took the cleaning job at Maimonides two years earlier.

Her reasons were personal. "My husband passed away six years ago, and he was here three months," she said. "He had cancer. So it means a lot to me to have the rooms clean. I like doing this type of work, making sure the patients have rooms that are clean. What if it's my family member? I treat every patient like it's my family. I want to make sure the IV poles are where they are supposed to be and the garbage pails aren't in the middle of the room where people can slip on them."

Every day at Maimonides, I was reminded that the "health-care system" wasn't anonymous or abstract; it was the sum of individual human successes and failures, each of which could build or destroy. Most people didn't set out to screw things up; they just didn't take time to remember (or to learn) the legacy of the man whose name the hospital carried. Maimonides the philosopher/physician valued daily self-scrutiny. In his commentaries he wrote that "the perfect man needs to inspect his moral habits continually, weigh his actions, and reflect upon the state of his soul every single day."

The hospital, however, was populated by humans, imperfect men and women, existing in an imperfect world. Politicians started out believing in the social contract and then forgot their duty to fight for the people they represented. Drug and insurance executives said that their desire was to improve and protect health care, but their jobs and fortunes depended on profitability, not making medicine available to everyone. Technocrats worshipped faster and more efficient machines that helped prolong health and life, but they neglected empathy, understanding, and the probing that requires genuine conversation and time. Doctors planned to devote their lives to healing and then spent too much time analyzing their bank accounts or nursing bruised egos instead of making sure the system provided for their patients. Patients agreed with all of the above but failed to accept responsibility for the abuses they inflicted on themselves by working too hard, exercising too little, and smoking, drinking, and eating too much.

Depending on the day or night, life in the hospital could seem full of exquisite promise or pointless despair. The system was tainted by callous disregard for decent and equitable care, by money lust, by corporate influence, and by lack of political will. But a great many people who were part of the system wanted something better. Yes, individual doctors and nurses behaved badly, sometimes inexcusably so. Clerks were rude to patients and to each other. People made mistakes. Yet I was constantly struck by the sense of urgency that accompanied desires for fairness, for compassionate medicine, for efficiency, for meaning—and yes, for cleaner rooms. Both Pam Brier and Margie Morales struggled to sort the unwanted from the wanted, to make the hospital what it should be. They needed their lives to matter.

Toward the end of my year at the hospital, Alan Astrow asked me, "Did you know what you were getting into?"

His question had been prompted by a visit with one of his patients, Marie, a forty-five-year-old woman with metastatic gastric cancer. The first time I met her, she was sitting up in bed hunched over a plastic bin, retching, while her sister, Tina, watched, her face contorted in sympathetic pain. Tina had more or less moved into her sister's hospital room. She had done all she could to maintain the illusion that they remained the same people in the picture frame on the room's windowsill—the young girls, now middle-aged, mothers but still sexy, buff, glowing size-two blond women with large dark eyes. Marie and Tina were only thirteen months apart, so similar (when Marie was healthy) that people mistook them for twins.

Tina often had circles under her eyes, but her own weariness didn't prevent her from making sure her sister's hair was combed and her makeup was right. The patient's bed was covered by a faux-leopardskin blanket from home; she had a matching headband. She wore pretty shorty pajamas. She intended to defy this sickness and go home.

This remained Marie's professed intention, even during the weeks she lay dying in a comfortable room on Kronish 5, the refurbished wing, which had broad hallways, shiny wood floors, sage green walls.

I told Astrow that I admired how sensitively he talked to Marie and her family, the way he laid hands on his patients during physical exams. For a sometimes-awkward man, he had a remarkably natural touch.

He dismissed the compliment. "I've been doing this a long time," he said.

Yet there was nothing rote or complacent about his manner or his concern. He had been preoccupied with this patient since the first time they met, and she looked at him and said, "You're going to cure me."

She was divorced, the mother of two young children, daughter of Italian immigrants, sister of a policeman, a friend of Douglas Jablon's. Astrow was a doctor who believed in telling the truth, yet he was leery of those who believed there was a moral imperative to give people information they didn't want to hear. He turned to Jewish theology for help on the question of truth versus *chesed*, Hebrew for "kindness." He concluded that neither is privileged, that there was a tension between truth and kindness that could not be resolved.

"There is such a thing as a white lie," he told me one day. "Telling someone they are going to live when they are going to die is too serious a white lie." Yet when Marie told him in winter to cure her by June, he did not tell her that it was almost impossible to cure stage-four gastric cancer. He told himself he had some doubts. There were false-positive CAT scans and false-positive PET scans sometimes. He, like almost every doctor, had had patients who'd been written off and then, after treatment, lived for years.

So he offered Marie a partial truth. He said, "I'll try."

The chemotherapy didn't work, and neither did the pain medication, as the mass in her stomach created unbearable nausea every time she tried to eat. When he visited her room, he always pulled a chair next to her bed so they could talk face-to-face. He would begin, "Let me tell you how I see things, and you tell me how you see things."

She told him that she was in terrible pain, but the pain medication made her so nauseated that even water made her vomit. She said she hadn't eaten for a week, but she didn't care about food. "I just want a glass of cold water," she said. He told her he would try to find a different kind of nourishment, through a tiny tube inserted directly into her stomach, that wouldn't cause vomiting.

By June 1, Marie had become skeletal. The leopard blanket was rolled up on a chair, and she was wearing a standard-issue hospital gown. She was being fed and medicated through intravenous tubes. Her stomach was swollen with fluid.

When Beth Popp and Anita Kaminer dropped by that day, Tina said she wanted to stop all the IVs in her sister and that she would ask Astrow about draining the fluid. Out in the hallway, Tina told me she didn't want people to think her sister was pregnant when she died. She told me Astrow called every night.

Back in the room, we could see that Marie was already somewhere else. Her large eyes looked enormous now, only half open. She didn't respond when Tina leaned over and yelled, "Marie! Mommy's here." Their mother, a small Italian woman with carefully teased hair, wept in the corner of the room.

Tina told us that the previous weekend some cousins had brought her sister a pair of Manolo Blahnik shoes. By then Marie was rarely conscious, but she rallied when her sister showed her the shoes. "She insisted on trying them on in bed even though her feet are so small now," Tina said. "She didn't like the color, but she wore them."

Tina walked to the closet and pulled out a box that had a $628 price tag on the outside. "They are handmade," she acknowledged, as she removed one of the shoes and examined it. "We like a higher heel and more strappy."

Their mother spoke. "She go crazy to buy those shoes."

Kaminer, the nurse-practitioner, offered, "My niece bought a pair like that for her wedding."

All of us stared at the Manolo Blahniks, with their totemic power. Tina said, "She said to me, 'I like them a little strappy,' and I said, 'I'm sorry, I didn't pick them out.'"

Tina had many hours at her sister's bedside to think about what Marie would like to wear at her funeral. There was a beautiful new $200 skirt to consider, and a lovely wig. There was the leopard headband.

I remembered standing with Tina and Astrow by the elevator bank, after a conversation about whether Marie should go into a hospice program.

"So long as she doesn't know," Tina said. "She doesn't want to hear it. She associates hospice with terminal."

Astrow told Tina, "If there's anything she wants to let her children know, now is the time."

She shook her head. "The children were here, but she couldn't communicate, she was so drugged." She said a priest had come to visit.

Haggard from lack of sleep, wearing jeans and a long-sleeved T-shirt, she glanced down at her feet. She apologized for wearing flip-flops and then looked up at Astrow, in his white doctor's coat.

"Marie likes your beard," Tina told him.

Astrow's mother had died that spring, and he decided to follow the dictates of *shloshim*, a thirty-day mourning period during which men don't shave or get haircuts.

He smiled through his stubble. "Dr. Kopel told me to shave."

Then Tina asked him to respect her sister's wishes, to avoid telling her that she was dying. "Out of respect for her, you can't tell her."

Astrow said, "She knows what's going on." Then he said, "You've been doing beyond what any person can do. It's been inspiring to see what you're doing."

Tina said, "My brother won't like you right now, because you can't tell him what he wants to hear. I had to tell my parents, my sister upstate. She lost her husband to cancer a couple of years ago."

Astrow reassured her, "We gave her aggressive treatment."

Tina's face was pierced with grief. "She looked good until the last time you saw her in the office, before the hospital," she said. Her assertion sounded like a question.

Astrow paused, as though making sure he got the answer right. "Your sister looked beautiful," he agreed.

Tina nodded and turned back toward her sister's room.

It was then that Astrow asked me, "Did you know what you were getting into when you decided to write this book?"

Short internal answer: *Of course not, how could I? Who ever knows?*

I must have known that it was likely I would encounter death. I must have known that the likelihood increased exponentially the minute I decided that Alan Astrow, an oncologist, would be a significant figure. As he said to me, "There are plenty of happy cases, but in the hospital you see the worst cases. At the cancer center, you see a range. Most patients are fine, they go to work—they are fine. But for solid tumors—usually lung, stomach, even colon—despite all the hype and hoopla about the progress we've made, the number of people who benefit is a minority."

Did I know what I was getting into?

I responded with the journalist's trick: Answer a question with a question. "Did you know what you were getting into when you decided to be a doctor?"

He conceded the point with good humor. "I guess not," he said.

Months later his son Raphael Astrow, then thirteen, told me he had gone to work with his father three times. The last visit, he said, made an enduring impression.

"It wasn't my favorite," he said. "My dad had to tell someone she was about to die. It was really sad, terrible."

He also said, "I didn't expect anything like that on his job, really. I didn't expect that."

Did it change the way he looked at his father?

Raphael was dark-haired and slender, a smart and earnest boy with pale skin and braces, a boy who appreciated good books and the New York Jets. He took his time to answer.

"No, not really," he said. "It changed the way I look at his job."

How?

"It was tough," he said. "Tougher than I thought. I knew it was very difficult, but I didn't know emotionally it was so tough."

Did he tell you that?

Raphael shook his head. "Not really," he said. "Not so clearly. You can't really know what's going on until you see it."

On National Cancer Survivors Day, Jay Cooper and Nella Khenkin found common ground in a conference room decorated with a large rainbow. Khenkin chose the entertainment, which included a Russian woman playing the keyboard, Chinese fan dancers, and a junior-high student with a thick Brooklyn accent who belted out a Mariah Carey song. The fan dancers were late, so the program was rearranged; next came the long lecture on nutrition and the role of herbs in a healthy diet, to please Cooper. Still waiting for the fan dancers, the patients and former patients joined in a spontaneous sing-along, gaining momentum with "You Are My Sunshine."

Cooper acknowledged the rainbow. "For those of you who like symbols, this year's symbol is a rainbow of hope," he said. "To some degree you can pick how you want to interpret that rainbow. One interpretation is that the rainbow has many colors. There are many kinds of tumors, many kinds of treatment, many ways we make progress day by day. . . ."

Alan Astrow thanked the patients and their families and friends for coming to the celebration and singled out Khenkin for making it happen. Then he introduced Bill Camilleri, who a few days earlier had been told by McDougle that the hospital wanted someone else to take the cancer center to the next stage. "He built this place from the ground up," said Astrow. "It is a beautiful facility, and a lot of that is really thanks to you."

Camilleri was gracious. "I'm happy to see everybody here," he said before reading a canned message from President Bush and introducing Steven Cymbrowitz.

Out in the hallway, a slight elderly man who said he was Marty Payson's cousin complained. "My wife, she has colon cancer, now the lungs, and I'll tell you, she knows more than the oncologist knows," he said. Nodding toward the sounds coming from the celebration, he grumbled, "My approach would be different. No speeches! No songs! You've got to make them laugh, laugh is the thing."

Over at the hospital, a banner had gone up:

Maimonides Congratulates Its Graduates and Welcomes New Interns and Residents

I sat on a bench outside Gellman on a warm, windy afternoon with David Gregorius, about to celebrate his one-year anniversary. I hadn't recognized him when he first walked up; he'd grown a mustache and beard.

"Are you going Hasidic?" I asked.

He laughed and shook his head. "No, I'm not! I'm not!"

"No *payot*?" I teased, twisting my finger next to my ear, referring to the side curls common among the Hasids in Borough Park.

"Is that what they're called?" Gregorius replied. "My attendings are doing that, too. 'Hey, dude, what's up with the beard?'"

He explained he was preparing for his tenth high-school reunion in Nebraska. "Some of my friends are having a mustache-growing contest."

"How are you?" I asked.

"I'm enjoying the warm weather," he said. "Oh. You mean, how do I feel about New York? Maimonides?"

"Yeah."

"New York is growing on me a little bit, but still not somewhere I want to be forever," he said.

That's when he told me about Loma Linda.

"Actually, I attempted to transfer to a program in Los Angeles, where my girlfriend is, but I didn't get in. The whole process made me appreciate here, because I had to tell all my program directors and everybody, and they were so upset. They understood completely. They had met Jenn. They said, 'We don't want to lose you, and we hope it all works out for you, but we also hope it doesn't.' I had to ask five or six attendings for letters, and they were reluctantly happy to help. I never felt so appreciated."

I said, "Like going to your own funeral."

"Exactly!" said Gregorius. "Like the living funeral. So that California thing didn't work out. Which is fine. I took a shot. If it was meant to be, it was meant to be."

As we sat there, some young African-American women in scrubs stood on the curb smoking cigarettes and talking. A group of black hats, Orthodox men in long black coats with beards and *payot,* walked by. Gregorius grinned and tugged at his beard.

Across the street a group of about thirty significantly pregnant Chinese women waddled through the doors of Eisenstadt, following a woman holding a clipboard talking to them in Chinese. Every month the hospital had a special Chinese-language orientation for pregnant women. They met for a couple of hours in the boardroom and then were taken across the street to visit the Stella & Joseph Payson Birthing Center, named for Marty Payson's parents.

Gregorius looked at them. "I did a month in labor and delivery," he said. "It was funny, 'cause a young girl, normal—I shouldn't say 'normal'—a young girl would come in and say, 'I'm having a baby, I'm having a baby.' You say, 'Yeah, yeah, sit down. I'll take a look.' Then you examine them. They're having a baby? They're not having a baby. They'll have a baby in about twelve hours. But when an Orthodox Jewish woman comes in and says, 'I'm having a baby,' the red flag goes up. You say, 'What number is this?' They say, 'Eleven.' You say, 'Let's go!' I'm not kidding. We have so many on more than number ten. Most women are freaking out because they think they're having a baby, but they have plenty of time. When the Orthodox women say they're having a baby, the baby is right there ready to drop out."

John Marshall, Gregorius's program director, had told me that the young doctor from Nebraska had been chosen as Intern of the Year. "He's a good clinician, very much a team player, hard worker, people really like him, people hated the thought of him going." He told me that Gregorius was a leader—"despite his humor and sort of lackadaisical personality"—pretty much a shoo-in for the position of chief resident the following year.

I asked Gregorius, "If you look back on this year—this is a huge question, but how do you think you've changed, if you have?"

Gregorius gave me what I deserved. "Have I changed?" he said slyly. "I have more facial hair."

I persisted. "What do you think the imprint of this experience will be?"

He turned serious. "It's definitely made me a stronger and better doctor, but that's gong to happen anywhere," he said. "Kind of like you, I've learned a lot of stuff about different cultures, that's for sure. I can say a lot of things in Russian and stuff like that now. I don't think it's changed my view of other cultures, but sometimes I am very flabbergasted at the way immigrants who were kids when they moved here now have kids who were born in Brooklyn, and they can be ten or eleven years old and they don't speak English. Usually the child speaks English and the parent doesn't, and sometimes it's even the other way around, where the parent spoke English and the child didn't. I tell that parent every time, 'This kid should learn English. This is America, and eventually they're going to want to leave Brooklyn, I hope. There's so much beautiful stuff to see. Check out Montana. It's great!' "

I asked him if he regretted the mistake he made, pushing the *M* for Maimonides?

"I'm more into living by the mountains, by streams," he began.

By then, weirdly, the wind had kicked up; on my tape recorder, Gregorius sounded like he could be standing on top of a mountain.

"But I don't think of this as a hell nightmare or anything," he said in his laid-back voice. "I've been really lucky my whole life. Things seem to fall into place. I've gotten my second choice in about everything. After high school I wanted to go to the Air Force Academy and didn't get in but got accepted to the Naval Academy, and that was one of the best experiences of my life."

He continued. "I saw *Top Gun* and wanted to be a fighter pilot and then found out I couldn't because my vision wasn't twenty-twenty. I wanted to transfer to Notre Dame, and I had like a three point four average, but that wasn't high enough. So I went to Colorado at Boulder, which was one of the best things that ever happened to me. Then for medical school I wanted to go to Colorado or Nebraska and didn't get in, so I went to Arizona, and that was one of the best things that ever happened to me."

And Maimonides?

He stretched out his legs and crossed his arms, thinking.

"New York is a big city that is not my final destination and a really busy hospital that I appreciate working in, though it's really grueling," he said. "I'm learning from really brilliant guys, like Dr. Marshall. I think, 'Man, that guy could go anywhere he wants, and he stays in Brooklyn! In the long run, I think it's going to be good for me."

A few months later, I received this:

FROM: "DAVID GREGORIUS"

TO: < residents@mmc >; "CARL RAMSAY"

CC: "JULIE SALAMON"

SENT: TUESDAY, SEPTEMBER 26, 2:25 AM

SUBJECT: PLEASE PAY ATTENTION TO THIS ONE . . .

Comrades—

I have something important to say. And it's not-my-usual stupid and aimless email, so please pay attention . . .

It is with heavy (but excited) heart that I must tell you all that I will be leaving Maimo and Brooklyn and taking a residency spot in California. It is a long story, starting last spring with my applying for a position at Loma Linda University, it not working out, then I was contacted about a month ago by their Program Director that they still had an opening, and with Dr. Marshall's blessing I applied for it. And much to my surprise, they chose me for the spot. The timeline for this transition is still up in the air, but I will certainly be moving within a month, probably sooner.

One day I asked Marty Payson what lessons he thought Maimonides could teach people in the hospital business, or was it just doomed to a state of perpetual crisis? Health-care reform was a major platform of Bill Clinton's 1992 presidential campaign. Fifteen years later health-care reform would be a major platform of every presidential candidate, including Hillary Clinton, the former first lady.

The Maimonides chairman had just gone onto the board of the Nassau Health Corporation, responsible for the public health-care system in Nassau County, Long Island. He had been chairman of Tulane University's health-sciences committee, with oversight of the university medical center, and he was chair of Howard University's medical-affairs committee.

Payson's small office in a law firm on Manhattan's East Side was decorated with breathtaking photographs of vistas he had climbed to on his mountaineering and long-distance-biking expeditions. He was a roly-poly daredevil, who insisted that he was careful. He had done plenty of time at black-tie dinners, but he liked to order in lunch from the deli downstairs, using the paper bag as a place mat.

Payson had just turned seventy years old. He had been on numerous boards and a top executive at a huge entertainment company. "The company I helped build, today it's just another big company with all its problems," he said. "The fun has gone out of it. With the hospital, you hope you leave something. You never know, but that's the goal."

What about the big-picture, national health-care policy?

"I believe eventually we'll have a single-payer system, because this system is insane," he said. "And it will be driven not by liberals or people like myself but by people like General Motors. The country can't afford this system. But I don't get involved in any way, shape, or form, because I can't affect it. Life is short. I do what I can affect. Seriously. I'm not an academic, and it's too big. No individual hospital can change it. There are associations and groups that do that, so I hope for the best and focus on what I can do. At Maimonides an opportunity came where I can make a difference at a particular institution that affects people's lives."

Payson took a spoonful of soup from a cardboard cup.

Because of his association with Tulane, he had visited New Orleans often since Hurricane Katrina. He'd seen the disastrous effect on that city's health-care system, not just for the obvious reason of taking care of sick people but because medical jobs were a big part of the local economy. A pillar of the community, to put it in old-fashioned terms.

"The most important thing I've learned and believe is that many of the issues relating to success or failure of hospitals are national in common," he said. "In other words, declining revenues, increasing expenses. But the solutions are not national. You can't wait and hope that model will change. The solutions are local. You have to look at your own hospital. What is its mission, what is its community, who does it serve—and scale it for that mission. Get it well managed and you can survive."

Throughout the year I took time at my computer, transcribing interviews and notes, making to-do schedules that seemed to get longer instead of shorter. At the beginning of June, I checked one of several "people to talk to" lists, which included the following:

—*Sirisha Perumandla, oncology fellow*
—*Chinese healers on Eighth Avenue*
—*Robin Guenther, architect*
—*Rebbes who recommend docs*
—*Clarence Davis about evacuation plan*

I learned that Clarence Davis, the director of safety and security, was scheduled to go on vacation June 7. I moved his name to the July list.

On June 4, Davis went to Macy's to buy a suitcase for the trip he was taking to the Dominican Republic, where he'd met his wife four years earlier. She was Polish, living in Germany, a classic blond beauty. He was African-American, chiseled, movie-star handsome. Rollerblading and racquetball kept him young; he was fifty when they met. She was thirty-four, but she thought they were about the same age. They danced the salsa. They watched basketball games. *Coup de foudre.* Love at first sight. She moved to Brooklyn from Berlin. They married.

On the way to Macy's, he collapsed and went into a coma. On June 15 he died, at age fifty-five. From cancer, diagnosed three months earlier at Mount Sinai; he didn't want anyone at Maimonides to know. His family wanted to bury him in New Jersey with his mother and siblings, but his wife, Magdalena Davis, decided no, he belonged to Brooklyn. She wanted him in

Green-Wood Cemetery, close to where they lived, close to the hospital. Beyond that, she couldn't think.

Clarence's boss, Derek Goins, called Douglas Jablon. Magdalena was relieved to have someone take charge. "First of all, I never did this before, and I wouldn't even know where to start," she said. "I just lost my husband, the love of my life. I couldn't even speak." She was thirty-eight years old, a new arrival, alone.

"They gave us a price, seven thousand dollars, and I said, 'That's too much,'" Jablon told me later, conjuring the vision of him, the giant Orthodox Jew, accompanying two attractive women, the blond Pole and her African-American stepdaughter, to the funeral home. "The undertaker went down to about thirty-eight hundred dollars, A to Z. Do you know how cheap that is? Jewish funerals [with their plain wooden caskets] cost more than that, and this was a beautiful casket. He said to me, 'Thank God I don't deal with Jews all day.' To make a long story short, I said, 'They don't have the money even to pay the thirty-eight hundred,' and he said, 'Don't worry, we'll wait for the insurance.'"

Next stop, picturesque Green-Wood Cemetery, the 478-acre parkland burial place designed as a rural retreat, filled with rolling hills and mansion-worthy crypts; burial place of Henry Ward Beecher, Leonard Bernstein, and the gangster Joey Gallo; a tourist attraction that would be designated a national landmark later that year.

"Soon as I walked in, I didn't even know this guy, the manager, and he said, 'Mr. Jablon, I know who you are. It's ninety-five hundred dollars, not a penny off,'" Jablon told me. "I was greeted like that! We started going around looking for a grave. Twelve thousand dollars for this one, more for that one. Did you ever go in there? Ahhhh. They should sell condos. It's gorgeous."

On the morning of June 21, Jablon went to early-morning services at his shul, satisfied that everything was arranged for Clarence Davis. The Baptist minister was booked for services at the funeral home. A hearse would take Davis and his family to the cemetery. Pam Brier would speak the next day at Schreiber Auditorium; the event was being publicized by flyers all over the hospital.

Instead of settling back to enjoy morning prayers, Jablon was stabbed with a familiar feeling of incompletion. What about all the people who loved

Clarence at the hospital who might want to say good-bye to him today and couldn't get to the service?

From this miasma of nervous energy came a vision. Jablon was a kid again, and an Italian person on his block had died. The hearse containing the body drove slowly up the street, like at a state funeral, so everyone in the neighborhood could say good-bye. At least that was Jablon's interpretation of his memory. He decided that Maimonides should do the same for Clarence.

He called Derek Goins and told him he wanted the hearse to pass by the hospital, to pause beneath the underpass between Eisenstadt and Gellman so people could pay their respects. When Goins asked Jablon how people would be notified—they couldn't put it over the loudspeaker that a hearse would be driving by; it would freak out the patients—Jablon said, "Don't worry, I'll call six, seven people inside of the hospital who are real yentas [gossips] and tell them this is happening."

After the funeral the hearse drove to Forty-eighth Street and turned onto Tenth Avenue toward the hospital entrance. The yentas had done their job. Several hundred people were lined up on the sidewalks. Jablon climbed out of the hearse and had to steady himself; his knees were shaking. As he walked around to the back and opened the door, Davis's men, the hospital security guards, lifted their arms in salute.

"If someone needed root-canal work or some kind of surgery, they could have done it right there without any anesthetic," Jablon said. "The morale in the hospital went straight up to the sky. I said, 'This is what Clarence wants. Everybody should be together.' He touched everybody. He touched everybody. He touched everybody. It was a very rough situation."

As Jablon told the story, his voice shook with holy fervor, like he said his knees did that day, and I wondered how much of his excellent story was true.

All of it was true, Sondra Olendorf assured me. Calm, steady, perceptive Olendorf seemed incapable of exaggeration. She had gone to the service at the funeral home that morning and walked back to the hospital not knowing Jablon's last-minute plan. She wondered why the street was blocked and then noticed crowds of people standing in front of the hospital. She watched as Jablon got out and opened the door, and as the security guards saluted. She found herself clapping and crying and saluting along with everyone else.

When Olendorf told me this story, it was dusk and she was sitting in her office, as usual without the lights on. "Hospital morale goes in peaks and val-leys," she said. "Everyone has been concerned about the budget, about what the state's doing to reimbursements, about all our plans. Things have been at a lower ebb; all you see is the dysfunctional element. And then there are things like this, people are going, 'Yeah, what a place to work, to recog-nize that guy who worked here, that we can be true to ourselves, that family thing, in honoring each other, that you can rely on one another no matter what, and this is one of those times.'"

The morning of the funeral, Magdalena Davis, the widow, had been star-ing out the window of the hearse in a shell of numbness. She had been talk-ing silently to her dead husband, in her newly acquired English, saying, "I wish Clarence Davis would have been a little bit asshole so I wouldn't miss you so much right now."

She didn't know a lot about his work. He would come home and tell her about the big fight he'd had with his boss, and when she visited him the first time, she was shocked to see how frumpy his office was. But she also saw how attached he was to the place, and that the attachment was mutual. When he emerged from the coma at Mount Sinai, his room was packed every day with visitors from Maimonides. She was talking to one of these visitors, a nurse, who was just leaving the room, giving Magdalena her telephone number, telling her to call if she needed anything, at the moment Clarence died.

In the hearse Magdalena realized she wouldn't see Clarence again, but she couldn't cry. She was a quiet person, not the type to scream or wail. She felt she had become a ghost, the fairy-tale romance turned to ashes in three months. But when she saw the people standing at the curb at Maimonides, she began to cry after all, because she saw she wasn't alone.

Acknowledgments

On my first "official" day at Maimonides, Jo Ann Baldwin took me to the security office for a badge. I didn't fit into any of the usual job categories at the hospital so I was simply designated *writer*. At first people were wary, then curious, then more helpful than I could have dared hope. I can't acknowledge everyone who became involved, because some people preferred to talk to me privately and because I would inevitably omit someone who wouldn't mind public thanks. My gratitude, however, extends to everyone I encountered at Maimonides (and in the worlds touched by the hospital) whether they appear in the book or not.

Still, I must single out a few people who were crucial to this enterprise, beginning with Pam Brier and Marty Payson, who opened the door and then let me roam free, and were unstinting with their time and trust. For their amazing candor and generosity, I give deepest thanks to Alan Astrow, Jo Ann Baldwin, Steven Davidson, David Feldman, Lillian Fraidkin, David Gregorius, Douglas Jablon, Lisa Keen, Nella Khenkin, Samuel Kopel, Mark McDougle, Pamela Mestel, and Sondra Olendorf.

Many other people at Maimonides gave me guidance, but the following group provided especially important assistance in a variety of ways: Connie Barone, George Blaine, Annette Cruz, Terri Gagliardi, Derek Goins, Holly Hartstone, Joyce Leahy, Jill Markowitz, Ellie Silver, Kathy Thompson, Dawn Volpe, Velta Willis, and Andrew Yacht.

While writing the book in 2006 and 2007, I had the privilege of being a Kaiser Media Fellow. The programs arranged by Penny Duckham and her staff at the Kaiser Family Foundation provided an enlightening series of field trips and meetings on health policy and medical issues. I greatly appreciate the insights of my colleagues in the fellowship program as well.

Writing the first draft of a book can be lonely and scary. I was lucky to have a cherished band of advisers who were willing to read early versions. Many times I would have been lost without the encouragement and advice—and occasional douses of unfiltered franknesss and tough love—of Megan Barnett, Brian De Palma, Patti Lynn Gregory, Noelle Hannon, Roxie Salamon-Abrams, and Lilly Salcman. I also was sustained by the constant reassurances, patience, and wisdom of my very favorite men: Bill Abrams, Eli Salamon-Abrams, and Arthur Salcman.

For their invaluable legal and medical expertise, I thank Alan Einhorn, Bobby Cohen, and Suzanne Salamon.

A longer list of friends and family deserves gratitude for all kinds of reasons—Rick and Carol Abrams, John and Debbie Abrams, Raquel Cano-Schneiderman, Madeline DeLone, Danny Gregory, Trish Hall, Bill Klein, Barry Kramer, Sara Krulwich, Lila Deis Lauby, Wendy Miller, Lynn Paltrow, Muzzy Rosenblatt, the Saddleback Lake "August Outlaws," Michael and Ilene Salcman, Rob Schneiderman, Pam Schwartz, Andrew Tatarsky, Jane Tylus, the WAT yoga and kick-boxing group, and Veronica Windholz. Endless appreciation to Suzie Bolotin and Peter Workman, who changed much in my life a few years ago, when they asked me to think about Rambam.

Everyone at Penguin Press and the Robbins Office has been gracious and helpful, especially Liza Darnton and Lindsay Whalen at Penguin, and David Halpern, Coralie Hunter, and Ian King at the Robbins Office. Special thanks to Maureen Sugden and her magic red pencil, and to Liz Calamari.

Finally, two incomparable women have had immeasurable influence on me—Ann Godoff, my editor, and Kathy Robbins, my agent. With their clarity, wit, intelligence, and vision they have deepened my outlook on everything that matters.

Annotated Book List

The hospital is only eight miles from my apartment in SoHo. But the trip to Brooklyn could take as long as an hour, depending on time of day and how the subways were running. I always carried a book. Their first lines alone convey the range of subject and style. Here is what I came to think of as my Maimonides reading list, with special thanks to New York City Transit for getting me there on time most days, and for the delays on the D and N lines that gave me extra time to read.

Bartlett, Donald L., and Steele, James B., *Critical Condition: How Health Care in America Became Big Business—and Bad Medicine* (New York: Broadway Books, 2006). One terrible thing after another.

    First sentence: *"You are standing in line at a supermarket to buy a box of Cheerios."*

Belkin, Lisa, *First, Do No Harm* (New York: Random House, 1993). Heartbreaking case studies about the hard ethical questions, beautifully described.

    First sentence: *"It was standing room only in Room 3485 the day the committee voted to let Patrick die."*

Bruck, Connie, *Master of the Game* (New York: Simon & Schuster, 1994). I picked up this biography of Steve Ross, the man who built Time Warner, to learn more about Marty Payson. After checking out the thirteen pages given to Payson in the index, I couldn't resist the rest of this fine saga about Ross's life, accurately described by the *Wall Street Journal* as "a remarkable rag-trade to riches story."

    First sentence: *"Steve Ross would have loved his funeral, his friends and family later agreed."*

Cohen, Rich, *Sweet and Low* (New York: Farrar, Straus and Giroux, 2006). Families, like hospitals, are complex. One of the main buildings at Maimonides is named after Rich Cohen's grandfather, Benjamin Eisenstadt, who invented individual sugar packets and then Sweet'N Low, the artificial sweetener. He made a fortune and became a major benefactor of the hospital. This wonderful, funny, sad, unresolved book combines the history of sugar manufacture with Cohen's family story, both unexpected tales of desire and corruption.

First sentence: *"Everyone in my family tells this story, but everyone starts it in a different way."*

Cohn, Jonathan, *Sick* (New York: HarperCollins, 2007). Not to be confused with *Sicko,* the Michael Moore documentary—much calmer, but just as scary.

First sentence: *"It was 4:43 on a clear November afternoon when the paramedics found Cynthia Kline, pale and short of breath, slumped against a bedpost in her double-decker Cambridge home."*

Committee on Quality of Health Care in America, *Crossing the Quality Chasm* (Washington, D.C.: National Academy Press, 2001). For my purposes, fascinating.

First sentence: *"The American health care delivery system is in need of fundamental change."*

Didion, Joan, *The Year of Magical Thinking* (New York: Alfred A. Knopf, 2005). When a hospital doctor hesitates before telling Didion that her husband is dead, the social worker says, "It's okay. She's a pretty cool cucumber." The coolness of her deliberate, distilled prose becomes a weapon against devastation. I couldn't stop reading.

First sentence: *"Life changes fast."*

Estrin, Joseph, with Barry P. Moskowitz, *An Uncommon Commitment* (Brooklyn: Maimonides Research and Development Foundation, 2003). A helpful and enthusiastic history of the hospital, written by one of its physicians and published on his ninetieth birthday, with a foreword by Dr. Joseph Cunningham.

First sentence: *"From the busy sidewalks of Borough Park, Maimonides Medical Center rises like a jumble of geometric shapes amid the tidy shops and row houses."*

Fadiman, Anne, *The Spirit Catches You and You Fall Down* (New York: Farrar, Straus and Giroux, 1997). This book has become a medical anthropological classic since I first read it almost a decade ago. When I reopened it during my hospital year, I found the story of clashing cultures and the limits of modern medicine hadn't lost its power to haunt and amaze.

First sentence: *"If Lia Lee had been born in the highlands of northwest Laos, where her parents and twelve of her brothers and sisters were born, her mother would have squatted on the floor of the house that her father had built from ax-hewn planks thatched with bamboo and grass."*

Frazier, Ian, *Gone to New York* (New York: Farrar, Straus and Giroux, 2005). Like Frazier, I'm from Ohio, so I read his marvelous adventures in the big city with a particular appreciation, especially his take on Brooklyn.

First sentence: *"If you drilled a hole straight through the earth, starting at the corner of Seventh Avenue and Forty-second Street, you would pass through ten inches of pavement, four feet of pipes, thirty-five feet of Seventh Avenue subway, about twenty-two hundred miles of rock, about thirty-six hundred miles of nickel-iron core, and then another twenty-two hundred miles of rock."*

Gawande, Atul, *Complications* (New York: Henry Holt, 2002). The surgeon gives the inside scoop without cant. He lays out the big picture with crisp authority and handles the intimate details with tender care. Enjoyable and educational.

First sentence: *"I was once on trauma duty when a young man about twenty years old was rolled in, shot in the buttock."*

Ginsberg, Allen, *Kaddish and Other Poems* (San Francisco: City Lights Books, 1961). After Sharon Kopel died, I revisited this brilliant, anguished poem, which I hadn't read since college. Ginsberg's immersion in loss is almost unbearably beautiful in this ode to his mother, who died in an asylum after a life plagued by mental illness ("over and over—refrain—of the Hospitals").

First sentence: *"Strange now to think of you, gone without corsets and eyes, while I walk on the sunny pavement of Greenwich Village."*

Gladwell, Malcolm, *Blink* (New York: Little, Brown, 2005). Medical people constantly have to fight the feeling that they are cogs in a machine. Yet they also acknowledge that changes in systems can radically improve their practice. Gladwell brilliantly gives one such example, the Goldman algorithm for chest pain, that changed the way things are done in emergency rooms and saved lives.

First sentence: *"In September of 1983, an art dealer by the name of Gianfranco Becchina approached the J. Paul Getty Museum in California."*

Goldwasser, Rabbi Dovid, *It Happened in Heaven* (Jerusalem/New York: Feldheim Publishers, 1995). One of the dozens of VIPs Douglas Jablon introduced me to was Rabbi Goldwasser, a kind man with a long beard. His walls were lined with scholarly works, including an entire tome on the rules regulating beards. While many local rabbis were of the fire-and-brimstone school, Rabbi Goldwasser definitely belonged to the good-deeds-and-parables camp. During my visit he gave me this conversational collection of gentle stories aimed at encouraging kindness.

First sentence: *"Traveling down an unfamiliar road, a man notices a magnificent palace in flames."*

Greene, Graham, *The Heart of the Matter* (London: William Henemann, 1948). Confession: I woke up in the middle of the night thinking I knew what my book should be called—*The Heart of the Matter!* In the calm of morning, I remembered the great book that already carried the name. Though I had little spare time during the reporting period, I felt the need to luxuriate in some perfect prose.

First sentence: *"Wilson sat on the balcony of the Bedford Hotel with his bald pink knees thrust against the ironwork."*

Groopman, Jerome, *The Anatomy of Hope* (New York: Random House, 2004). The book strikes deep, especially when the oncologist writer writes about his own nineteen-year battle with unrelenting back pain. Makes his empathy for his patients—and for their incompatible desires for transparency and magic—more understandable and all the more admirable.

First sentence: *"Why do some people find hope despite facing severe illness, while others do not?"*

Gyatso, Tenzin, the Fourteenth Dalai Lama, *Essence of the Heart Sutra,* translated by Geshe Thupten Jinpa (Boston: Wisdom Publications, 2005). When Dr. Gregory Todd told me about reading the Heart Sutra to Mr. Zen, I decided I should learn something about it. This book was instructive and scholarly, yet quite easy to navigate and thought-provoking in ways I didn't expect. The Dalai Lama has a nice sense of humor as well as spiritual depth.

 First sentence: *"Time is always moving forward."*

Havel, Václav, *Disturbing the Peace,* translated from the Czech by Paul Wilson (New York: Vintage Books, 1990). I bought this book after Alan Astrow's spirituality conference, where a psychiatrist discussed Havel's interpretation of hope. This book-length interview with a journalist, Karel Huizdala, records conversations that took place in 1985 and 1986, three years before the playwright Havel became his country's president. Makes you long for serious political discourse. "Life does not take place outside history, and history is not outside of life," said Havel.

 First sentence: *"Yes, I do come from a bourgeois family, you might even say from a grand-bourgeois family."*

Heschel, Abraham Joshua, *Maimonides,* translated from the German by Joachim Neugroschel (New York: Farrar, Straus and Giroux, 1982). [Originally published in 1935 as *Maimonides, Eine Biographie,* by Erich Reiss Verlag in the series "Judentum in Geschichte und Gegenwart."] Excellent, essential biography of Maimonides, who may be associated in Borough Park mainly with the hospital named after him but is more widely known as one of the great Jewish philosophers as well as a physician.

 First sentence: *"Between the Sahara and the much traveled Mediterranean Sea, between the monumental civilization of ancient Egypt and the emptiness of the Atlantic Ocean, lies a land the Arabs fancifully call Maghreb, the Occident, or Barbary, and which geographers simply refer to as North Africa, the northern appendage of a larger continent."*

————, *The Sabbath* (New York: Farrar, Straus and Giroux, 1951). From time to time, I would walk through the streets of Borough Park in the hours before sunset on Fridays, before the Sabbath, and try to absorb the shift in mood I could feel as it occurred. Written with poetic elegance and depth, Heschel's meditation addresses a longing for a time and place apart.

 First sentence: *"Technical civilization is man's conquest of space."*

Kessler, Andy, *The End of Medicine* (New York: HarperCollins, 2006). Too cutesy. Didn't make it past chapter 1.

 First sentence: *"We were on our third pitcher when the conversation started getting interesting."*

Kidder, Tracy, *Mountains Beyond Mountains* (New York: Random House, 2003). This book is very alive. It's about the saintly-annoying-righteous-humbling-doctor-crusader-anthropologist Paul Farmer and contains exotic locations, real global-health issues, and the truthful feel of a good novel.

 First sentence: *"Six years after the fact, Dr. Paul Edward Farmer reminded me, 'We met because of a beheading, of all things.'"*

Kübler-Ross, Elisabeth, *On Death and Dying* (New York: Touchstone, 1997). Kübler-Ross, a psychiatrist, first published this classic work in 1969, and it remains the crucial text for anyone thinking about how people contend with the final stages of death.
First sentence: *"When I was asked if I would be willing to write a book on death and dying, I enthusiastically accepted the challenge."*

Lesser, May H., *An Artist in the University Medical Center* (New Orleans: Tulane University Press, 1989). My friend Danny Gregory, who thinks in pictures as well as words, gave me this lovely book of drawings, paintings, and text that helped me organize my own thoughts about this arcane world.
First sentence (and drawing): *"This is the large weekly teaching conference for doctors-in-training and faculty—called grand rounds."*

Maimonides, Moses ben Maimon, *Ethical Writings of Maimonides,* edited by Raymond L. Weiss with Charles E. Butterworth (New York: Dover Publications, 1975). I bought this book specifically to read the Maimonides treatise "On the Management of Health" but was just as intrigued by the sage's thoughts on character traits and the art of logic. Always good to go back to the source.
First sentence: *"Laws concerning character traits: They include altogether eleven commandments, five positive commandments and six negative commandments."*

Maugham, W. Somerset, *Of Human Bondage* (New York: Doubleday, 1915). I hadn't read this since I was a kid, when I was mesmerized by Philip's infatuation with Mildred the waitress. Still mesmerized, but now with medicine on my mind, I was stuck on a phrase Maugham uses to describe the young doctor's (narcissistic) attitude toward his patients: "There was humanity there in the rough, the materials the artist worked on; and Philip felt a curious thrill when it occurred to him that he was in the position of the artist and the patients were like clay in his hands."
First sentence: *"The day broke gray and dull."*

Millman, Marcia, *The Unkindest Cut: Life in the Backrooms of Medicine* (New York: William Morrow, 1976). This sociological report was deliberately unbalanced. "I did not write extensively about the many 'good' things that I observed doctors do, for I was interested in calling attention to the problems I saw," Millman writes in the introduction. Written in a just-the-facts-ma'am style, the book is more alarming than enlightening.
First sentence: *"Mr. Bernstein was lying on a stretcher, still awake but heavily tranquilized in preparation for open heart surgery."*

Nuland, Sherwin B., *Maimonides* (New York: Schocken, 2005). A good primer on the life of Maimonides, though the best chapter is the first, called "My Son, the Doctor: Jews and Medicine."
First sentence: *"Why is it, in fact, that so many Jews have become doctors?"*

Patterson, Kerry; Grenny, Joseph; McMillan, Ron; and Switzler, Al, *Crucial Conversations* (New York: McGraw-Hill, 2002). This was the "textbook" for Dr. Feldman's Code of

Mutual Respect classes. I was ready to dismiss it as psychobabble but came to respect the authors' plain-spoken commonsense advice, which evidently is not so common.

First sentence: *"When people first hear the term 'crucial conversation,' many conjure up images of presidents, emperors, and prime ministers seated around a massive table while they debate the future of the world."*

Potok, Chaim, *The Chosen* (New York: Ballantine, 1967). One day after watching the little boys from Yeshiva Kehilah Yakov Pupa, the Orthodox school next door to Maimonides, play ball, I decided to look again at this book that I remembered fondly from childhood. Much as I, as a girl in Ohio, had enjoyed the story about the struggle to claim tradition, I appreciated it more deeply as I walked the streets the characters walked.

First sentence: *"For the first fifteen years of our lives, Danny and I lived within five blocks of each other and neither of us knew of the other's existence."*

Rosner, David, *A Once Charitable Enterprise* (Cambridge: Cambridge University Press, 1982). What changes, what remains the same. Excellent academic history of hospitals in Brooklyn and New York City a century ago.

First sentence: *"Nineteenth-century American life revolved around small communities and narrow personal contacts."*

Shem, Samuel, *The House of God* (New York: Bantam Dell, 1978). When I told an orderly (now called "patient transporter") I was writing a book about his hospital, he broke out laughing. "You better read *The House of God*," he said with a sly look. I understood his reaction immediately on reading the first sentence of this book, inspired by the author's internship at Beth Israel Hospital in Boston in the 1970s (Samuel Shem is the nom de plume of Stephen Joseph Bergman, who teaches psychiatry at Harvard Medical School). As David Gregorius might say, "Woo-hoo!"

First sentence: *"Except for her sunglasses, Berry is naked."*

Sontag, Susan, *Illness as Metaphor and AIDS and Its Metaphors* (New York: Farrar, Straus and Giroux, 1977, 1978 and 1988, 1989). Sontag's son wrote a chilling article in the *New York Times Magazine* about his mother's horrible death from cancer. Her insistence on treatment against the advice of most doctors was the subject of biopsychosocial rounds and led me to read this fascinating, provocative book, whose defiant stance weighs heavy in light of Sontag's own final chapter.

First sentence: *"Illness is the night-side of life, a more onerous citizenship."*

Solzhenitzyn, Aleksandr, *Cancer Ward,* translated from the Russian by Nicholas Bethel and David Burg (New York: Farrar, Straus and Giroux, 1968). By the time I finished this book, it was festooned with pink, yellow, and blue Post-it notes scribbled with true but unhelpful exclamations: "Brilliant!" "No wonder he won the Nobel Prize!" That sort of thing. It is a truly great book.

First sentence: *"On top of everything, the cancer wing was Number 13."*

Starr, Paul, *The Social Transformation of American Medicine* (New York: Basic Books, 1982). My health-policy pals told me I had to read this book, which won the Pulitzer Prize in 1984, if I was going to write about an American hospital. They were right, though I soon realized at five hundred–plus pages that it was too heavy to lug around. I bought another copy and chopped it up into chunks that fit nicely into my bag. Worth the trouble.

First sentence: *"The dream of reason did not take power into account."*

Toynbee, Polly, *Hospital* (London: Hutchinson, 1977). Alan Astrow recommended this book by a British journalist. I like Toynbee's intelligent, deadpan realism. Her book is written in the spirit of Frederick Wiseman's fine documentary film (another) *Hospital.*

First sentence: *"It was eight o'clock in the morning and the ward Sister was coming on duty."*

Welles, Orson, with Oja Kodar, *The Big Brass Ring* (London: Black Spring Press, 1987). Convoluted and overwrought, or adventuresome and expansive, but very large either way, like Welles himself—and required reading for anyone interested in his life and work.

First sentence: *"FADE IN: A montage—or maybe a filmed collage is more accurate."*

Author's Note

Throughout my research, I always identified myself as a writer working on a book. The Maimonides administration placed one limit, asking me to protect the confidentiality of patients. While all the patients discussed in the book gave me permission to speak to them and tell their stories, I have altered patient names and identities to protect privacy.

Index

About the Author

Julie Salamon, a bestselling author, was a reporter and critic for the *New York Times* and the *Wall Street Journal*. Her six previous books include *The Devil's Candy*, considered a Hollywood classic; *Facing the Wind*, a true crime account; and *Rambam's Ladder*, a prize-winning book about modern philanthropy and charity. In 2006 she was selected as a Kaiser Media Fellow. Her journalism and essays have been published in several anthologies and have appeared in the *New Yorker, Vanity Fair, Vogue, Bazaar*, and *The New Republic*. A native of Seaman, Ohio, she lives in New York City with her husband, Bill Abrams, and their two children.